Medical Terminology

Workbook
Advanced Course

Fifth Edition

Edited By

Dr. Seigfred W. Fagerberg B.S., M.Ed., D.Ed., C.H.E., C.C.E.
Professor Emeritus of Health Education and Behavior

Dr. Christine B. Stopka, Ph.D., ATC, LAT, CSCS, CAPE, MTAA
Professor, Adapted Physical Activity & Medical Terminology
Department of Health Education & Behavior

Caduceus International Publishing Inc.
100 SW 75th Street, Suite 206
Gainesville, FL 32607
www.cipcourses.com
Author: Seigfred W. Fagerberg
ISBN#: 978-0-9819910-7-8

TABLE OF CONTENTS

MEDICAL AND SCIENTIFIC TERMINOLOGY

With
Dr. Seigfred W. Fagerberg
B.S.; M.Ed.; D.Ed.; C.H.E.; C.C.E.
Professor Emeritus of Health Science Education
Interactive Audio-Visual E-Textbook

FORMAL NOTIFICATION

This learning program is for educational purposes and contains graphic pictures intended to aid in the understanding of word parts. These detailed slides are not intended to be offensive to any individual and should be viewed from the standpoint of a medical professional.

These visual (pictorial) slides are accompanied by detailed lectures to help you build your comprehensive understanding of this unique language of medicine. This method of learning medical terminology by combining word parts and compound terms with medical pictures gives you the insight to understand both the literal and actual meanings of thousands of compound words in medicine, English and many other Indo-European languages.

This program teaches you the literal word part meaning primarily from the Greek, Latin, English, middle English, French, Dutch and German languages. These meanings will help you understand health and medical school lecture content taught during the first four years of medical school. This includes content in the medical sciences of anatomy (the study of body structure), physiology (the study of bodily functions) and human pathology (the study of human diseases). It also provides you with actual descriptive meanings, content information and other language skills that can be useful in most academic disciplines.

Once you complete this learning program, your vocabulary skills will be greatly improved. Your new word power skills will enhance your capabilities of learning and make future educational experiences more complete and enjoyable.

INTELLECTUAL PROPERTY COPYRIGHT

This interactive Medical Terminology Audio-Visual educational program is copyrighted
by
Dr. Seigfred W. Fagerberg
B.S.; M.Ed.; D.Ed.; C.H.E.; C.C.E.
Professor Emeritus of Health Science Education
Interactive Audio-Visual E-Textbook

MEDICAL AND SCIENTIFIC TERMINOLOGY

This course is available through your institution as a
- Campus Course
- Distance Education Course
- Non-Credit Certification Course
- Web-based Non-Credit
- Certificate Course

IMPORTANT COMPUTER INTERACTIVE LEARNING INSIGHTS

ᵀ Lectures: In order to obtain the best results from this program scan the lecture index to determine your weakness in medical terminology. Select the slides that contain pictures and/or terms that you feel you need to emphasize. If you have had a course in anatomy, physiology, Latin, and/or Greek, the number of slides that need special attention may decrease significantly. This is especially true if you can pronounce the terms and give the literal and/or actual meanings.

ᵀ If you understand the literal meaning, the actual meaning and specific word part meanings of the compound terms, you may want to reduce or mute the volume of the audio lectures. In doing so, you can simply read the terms' definitions and reinforce your understanding of terms in that slide. Be sure you can fracture each compound term visually and pronounce the term before you progress.

ᵀ The terms you will be tested on are the key compound terms in each slide, especially the terms at the top. Somewhere in each slide or as part of the audio lecture, both the literal and actual meanings of the word parts and the compound terms are provided to the learner.

ᵀ You should listen to the lectures as often as necessary in order to reinforce both the literal and actual meanings of the specific terms. Most slides contain additional word parts that reinforce the actual definition of the major term at the top of each slide.

ᵀ Each specialized lecture typically lasts less than five minutes, although some last for ten minutes or more. These audio lectures help to clarify more complicated concepts, content and terms taught in anatomy, physiology, pathology and other medical science courses. This knowledge will help you in the future to understand an enormous amount of content and compound terms used in your future profession.

ᵀ Remember, each of us learn best by using educational methodology that incorporates interactive audio, visual and psychomotor learning experiences. This program incorporates all three types of learning.

IMPORTANT DISCLAIMER

† The contents displayed or taught in this program are designed to be educational.

† Under no circumstances should the educational material replace the expert advice or care of a qualified physician or medical professional.

† Several steps were taken to ensure the accuracy of the information presented in this program. However, because of rapid advances in the medical field, some of the information contained in this program may be a variation of current medical information and may result in debate. For this reason, accuracy cannot be guaranteed in each slide. We assume no responsibility for how the information presented in this program is used by the public.

† The author, and others who may distribute this interactive educational distant education program, cannot accept any responsibility for errors, omissions or the consequences that may result from the application of their information.

APPRECIATION

Special appreciation is extended to the late Dr. William David Mowat, a family doctor and friend of Dr. Fagerberg, for permission to use the extensive pictorial library he developed over years of medical practice. A significant number of pictures and graphics used in this presentation are from his personal files.

The author obtained exclusive copyright permission from him before undertaking this project. His unique collection of anatomy, physiology and disease pictures, representing most of the health problems that affect the human body, were important to the completion of this audio-visual program.

Sincere appreciation is also extended to doctors throughout the southern United States and North America for sharing their medical pictures for use in this educational program.

AUDIO-VISUAL LECTURES

This information may reinforce or review information you learned in courses of anatomy, physiology, pathology, Latin, Greek or health. You need to decide in each slide if you need to listen closely to the lecture accompanying that specific audio-visual slide or turn down the sound and read the script to enhance your knowledge base. You need to listen to the specific slides that will prepare you for the examinations as well as for future courses in health medicine. If you need to skip over materials that you feel you already understand, simply click ahead to advance slides or files. You may do this at your own discretion.

Remember, the formal lectures and visuals are to develop both literal and actual word part and compound medical and scientific word or term meanings on which you will be evaluated during the course examinations.

These materials also take you beyond the minimum cognitive knowledge for the course and prepare you for advanced health and medical courses.

IMPORTANT INSIGHT

- This is a comprehensive Medical Terminology program that presents information in a sequential format.

- It is very important to view and listen to each lecture slide in the proper sequence before progressing to more advanced lecture slides.

- You must learn the key medical terms and the content information in each slide in order to be prepared for the next lecture.

- Review and reinforcement activities (viewing, listening to the lectures and writing (typing) activities) are extremely important in your successful acquisition of this unique language of medicine.

HEALTH INFORMATION WEBSITES

Click the 'Search Reference' link to view these resources.

1. http://www.cdc.gov/DiseasesConditions/
2. http://www.webmd.com/
3. http://www.healthcentral.com/
4. www.allnurses.com (Nursing Topics)
5. http://www.nlm.nih.gov/medlineplus/ (Drug Encyclopedia & Medical Directory)
6. http://www.fda.gov/ (Current Topics and Subjects)
7. http://www.nih.gov/ (Subject Links)
8. http://www.centerwatch.com/ (Clinical Trials and Listings)
9. hardinmd.lib.uiowa.edu (The Hardin Medical Directory)
10. http://www.drweil.com/ (Dr. Andrew Weil Homepage)
11. http://www.answers.com/main/health.jsp
12. http://www.medicinenet.com/script/main/hp.asp
13. http://www.mayoclinic.org/
14. http://www.drugs.com/
15. http://www.everydayhealth.com/
16. http://familydoctor.org/familydoctor/en.html
17. http://www.qualityhealth.com/
18. http://floridarecoverycenter.ufhealth.org/
19. http://www.who.int/en/
20. http://www.biomedcentral.com/

THE BASIS OF MEDICAL TERMINOLOGY

Intrapneumonultramicroscoposilicovolcanoconiosis
INTRA/PNEUMONO/ULTRA/MICRO/SCOPIC/SILICO/VOLCANO/CONI/OSIS
within/lung/beyond/small/view/silicon carbon/vent/dust/condition (literal meaning)
AKA: Mount St. Helen Disease (Volcano erupted May 18, 1980)

Pneumono/coni/osis (AKA: Black Lung Disease)
Lung/dust/medical condition or disease (literal meaning)
Lung inflammation caused by the inhalation of small dust particles
resulting in scarring of the air sacs (actual meaning)

Coal miner's black lung   Arc welder's black lung

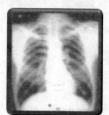 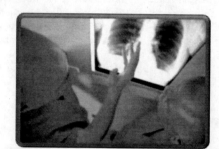 

INTRODUCTION

Medical Terminology is a specialized language developed mainly from Greek and Latin word parts.

The majority of the two hundred thousand (200,000) plus scientific and medical terms and words are derived from the following languages and cultures:
Anglo-French (A.F.); Arabic (Ar.); Anglo-Saxon (A.S.); Chinese (Ch.); Dutch (D.); English (E; middle ME); French (F.); Greek (Gk.); Gaelic (Gael.); German (Ger.); Hebrew (Heb.); Hungarian (Hung.); Icelandic (Ice.); Italian (It.); Japanese (J.); Latin (Lt.; late LL.; middle ML.; new NL.; vulgar VL.); Old Norse (ON.); Persian (Per.); Portuguese (Pg.); Scandinavian (Scand.); Sanskrit (Skr.); Spanish (SP.); Swedish (Swed.); and Teutonic (Tent.).

The key vocabulary terms and words studied in this comprehensive language program usually relate to anatomical structures, physiological processes, illnesses and diseases of the human body. Additionally, they often describe diagnoses, prognoses, procedures, processes, equipment and treatment.

Note: This unique language of medicine was created for health professionals so they could communicate as briefly and concisely as possible.

THE ANCIENT MEDICAL WRITERS
HIPPOCRATES (c.550 to 450 B.C.)

Hippocrates, of the Greek island of Cos, was a contemporary of Socrates. He is referred to as "The Father of Medicine." Although Hippocrates is the most famous of the ancient physicians, very little personal information is known about him. The only statement that can be issued with any certainty is that Hippocrates was a physician and that a large number of works have come down to us under his name. Modern scholars reject the authenticity of most of these works on various grounds. However, his importance and influence cannot be denied. He is the first figure in history who can be credited with freeing medicine from the bonds of superstition and basing its practice and theory upon scientific observation and reporting. Hippocrates' works demonstrate that he understood the workings of the human body quite well. He kept exact records of his observations and concluded that certain morbid signs indicate what we would call dis/ease (O.Fr.). He realized that these morbid signs ran their course, and led to either death or recovery. He also realized that the patient could aid in their own recovery by altering their lifestyle.

Hippocrates' greatest influence upon the history and development of medicine may be his influence upon the later writer Galen.

HIPPOCRATIC OATH

I swear by Apollo Physician and Asclepius and Hygeia and Panacea and all the gods and goddesses, making them my witnesses, that I will fulfill according to my ability and judgment this oath and this covenant:

To hold him who has taught me this art as equal to my parents and to live my life in partnership with him, and if he is in need of money to give him a share of mine, and to regard his offspring as equal to my brothers in male lineage and to teach them this art - if they desire to learn it - without fee and covenant; to give a share of precepts and oral instruction and all the other learning to my sons and to the sons of him who has instructed me and to pupils who have signed the covenant and have taken an oath according to the medical law, but no one else.

I will apply dietetic measures for the benefit of the sick according to my ability and judgment; I will keep them from harm and injustice.

I will neither give a deadly drug to anybody who asked for it, nor will I make a suggestion to this effect. Similarly I will not give to a woman an abortive remedy. In purity and holiness I will guard my life and my art.

I will not use the knife, not even on sufferers from stone, but will withdraw in favor of such men as are engaged in this work.

Whatever houses I may visit, I will come for the benefit of the sick, remaining free of all intentional injustice, of all mischief and in particular of sexual relations with both female and male persons, be they free or slaves.

What I may see or hear in the course of the treatment or even outside of the treatment in regard to the life of men, which on no account one must spread abroad, I will keep to myself, holding such things shameful to be spoken about.

If I fulfill this oath and do not violate it, may it be granted to me to enjoy life and art, being honored with fame among all men for all time to come; if I transgress it and swear falsely, may the opposite of all this be my lot.

THE ANCIENT MEDICAL WRITERS
GALEN (c. 131 to 201 A.D.)

Galen was born in Pergamum in Asia Minor. He studied medicine at the Asclepium, the famed medical school in his native town, and in Alexandria, Egypt. In 162 he traveled to Rome and authored medical books. He remained there until his death. His fame and reputation were such that he became court physician to the emperor Marcus Aurelius. Galen wrote extensively on anatomy, physiology and general medicine. He relied upon his training (the best available in his time), the dissection of human corpses and experiments upon living animals to provide information for his writings. It was the work of Galen above all other medical writers that profoundly influenced the physicians of the early Renaissance (14th to 17th centuries). His theories on the flow of blood in the human body were not challenged until the discovery of the circulation of blood by William Harvey in the 17th century (thus, modern medicine).

THE ANCIENT MEDICAL WRITERS
CELSUS (c.1 to 55 A.D.)

Aulus Cornelius Celsus was a Roman encyclopediast who, under the reign of the emperor Tiberius (14-37 CE), wrote a lengthy volume on the current state of knowledge of many fields, including medicine. Only the portions detailing medical knowledge remain. In the introduction, he deals with the history of medicine up to his own time. It is thought that Celsus was layman writing for other laymen who practiced as physicians. Evidence for the theory that Celsus was not a professional physician is especially clear in his discourses on surgery. Nonetheless, his anatomical observations are acute, though marred by many inaccuracies. His anatomical observations along with other medical practitioners and anatomists gave this unique language its basis for existence today.

Note: Medic/al in Latin means "remedy, drug or therapy/refers to"

KEY PRIMARY OBJECTIVES

1. To define prefixes, suffixes, stem or root words and compound medical term meanings, both literal and actual.
2. To describe how medical terms are derived.
3. To identify and explain the function and meaning of specific compound term words parts.
4. To build and define compound medical terms related to anatomy, physiology, pathology, diagnosis, equipment, instruments, treatment and related processes or procedures in health and medicine.
5. To identify the specific disease states and relate description and/or definitions with the correct term.

YOUR SUCCESS

The most difficult part of this course is the first few days. You will settle into a sequence for success after you have completed chapters one to four and the related flashcard writing activities.

Many students have passed this course with an A or B by putting in the appropriate study time and motivation.

Learning the language of medicine will create a foundation for future medical courses and careers.

Remember: Some word parts have multiple meanings (literal and actual), spellings, and pronunciations. Body parts have multiple word parts that identify them (os-, oro- and stomo- all mean mouth).

PARTS OF SPEECH
Word Classification

Words are grouped into eight parts of speech: Nouns, Verbs, Adjectives, Pronouns, Adverbs, Prepositions, Conjunctions, and Interjections.

Nouns name something, **verbs** describe an action or condition, and **adjectives** modify nouns to show or describe a quality. Ninety-nine percent of words listed in medical dictionaries are comprised of nouns, verbs, and adjectives (medical vocabulary).

1. **Nouns** function as subjects, objects, complements, and modifiers. They name persons, places, things, ideas, animals, body parts, and medical objects.
2. **Verbs** function as sentence predicates or as part of a predicate. The endings -algia or -dynia (meaning pain) are examples of verb suffixes.
3. **Adjectives** modify or qualify nouns and pronouns. Suffixes such as -al, -ic, -ous may be added to certain nouns or verbs to form adjectives. Numerous adjectives simply modify terms by adding a suffix that means pertaining to or referring to something.

ROOT WORDS, PREFIXES, AND SUFFIXES
NOUNS, VERBS, AND ADJECTIVES
SPELLING AND PRONUNCIATION

1. In order to master this unique language, it is important to spend time memorizing word roots (stems), prefixes, and suffixes. It is also important to learn the word parts taken from Greek or Latin that form verbs and adjectives.
2. By memorizing the root words that identify or describe specific medical items or problems like diseases, instruments, equipment, treatments, disorders, medical procedures, and body parts and functions (anatomy and physiology), it will be easier for you to analyze and comprehend terms not covered in this course.
3. By breaking the terms down into separate component parts (fracturing) and then analyzing each part separately, you will be defining the compound terms literally (which is the word part meanings from the original language). You can also combine these same word parts and actually redefine the term. You do this by starting from the suffix and moving backward to the prefix, giving an actual descriptive term meaning (detailed description is usually longer).
4. To build an extensive and impressive vocabulary, always fracture new terms that you encounter and practice giving both the word or term's literal and/or actual meanings.
5. Remember, it is impossible to learn and recall the meaning of the thousands of medical terms found in a large medical dictionary. If needed, use a good medical dictionary to assist you in clarifying how a term is fractured, analyzed, spelled, and pronounced. It can also help you to identify a literal or actual meaning for the term.

COMPOUND TERMS, SYN/O/NYMS, ANT/O/NYMS, AND HOM/ONYMS

A compound word is a word formed from two or more word roots that are frequently used together in spoken language.

A compound word in its closed form has a meaning that is derived from the fracturing and analyzing of each of the smaller words.

An example of a compound word with two root words and a suffix is: **Arterio/scler/o/sis** (arterio- = artery; sclero- = hardening; -osis = suffix meaning condition)

Word parts that comprise medical terms also have:

Syn/o/nyms (same/word): words with similar meanings.
Pectero-, thoraco- and stetho- for chest; or utero-, hystero-, and metro- for uterus

Ant/o/nyms (against/word): words with opposite meanings.
Homeo- or homo- for same; hetero- for other or opposite

Hom/o/nyms (same/word): words that sound like another but differ in spelling and meaning.
Ilium: flank (largest bone of the pelvis)
Ileum: twisted (twisted structure that is the 3rd part of the small intestine)

44 KEY MEDICAL AND ENGLISH PREFIXES

Prefixes are one or more letters (often syllables "a or e") attached to the beginning of a word stem (root). The word "pre/fix" is an example of a term with a literal Latin meaning: "pre- (before) and -fix (to fasten)." The actual word meaning is "to fasten in front of a word." Prefixes expand or modify stem word meaning and usage. These 44 examples are used in thousands of medical and English terms or words.

Basic Prefix	Meaning (Gk. or Lt.)	Key Examples
1. a-, an	without, lack of,	a/febrile (without/fever); an/emia (lack of/blood)
ir-, ar-	no-, not	ir/regular (not/normal); ar/rhythmia (no/rhythm)
2. ab-, ef-	away from	ab/norm/al (away/normal/refers to)
		ef/ferent "nerve" (away/carry)
3. ad-, af-	to, toward	ad/hes/ion (to/stick/process of)
		af/ferent "nerve" (toward/carry)
4. ambi-	both, double, two	ambi/dextr/ous (both/right/refers to)
5. ana-	apart, up, back, again	ana/tom/y (cutting/apart/procedure of)
6. ante-	before, in front of	ante/cubit/al (in front of/elbow/refers)
7. anti-	against, reversed	anti/sepsis (against/infection or poison)
8. bi-, bin-, di-,	two, twice, double	bi/foc/al (two/foci/refers; bin/ocul/ar (two/eyes/refers);
diplo-, co-		diplo/coccus (double/berry); co/lateral (two/sides)
9. cata-	down, under, against	cata/bol/ism (down/lump/state of)
10. circum-	around, about, circle	circum/duct/ion (around/draw/process of)

Basic Prefix	Meaning (Gk. or Lt.)	Key Examples
11. com-, con- co-	together, with, both (two)	com/minuted (together/small); co/lateral (both/sides); co/herent (together/stick); con/junctiva (together/join)
12. contra-	against, opposite	contra/cept/ion (against/conception/refers)
13. de-	away from, remove	de/hydr/ate (remove/water/refers to)
14. dia-	across, complete, between, total, apart, through	dia/phragm (across/wall) dia/gnosis (complete/knowledge)
15. dis-	apart or away from, reverse	dis/infect (away from/poison or infection)
16. e-	out, to remove, protrude	e/viscer/ate (take out/organ/refers to)
17. ec-	out from, out	ec/topic (out/of place/refers to)
18. ecto-	on outer side, situated on	ecto/derm (outer/skin)
19. em-, en-	in, within	en/cephal/on (in/head/refers to "brain")
20. endo-	within	endo/metri/um (within/uterus/refers to)
21. epi-	upon, on	epi/derm/is (upon/skin/refers to)
22. ex-, exo-	upon, on, outside, on outer side, outer layer, protrude	exo/gen/ous (outside/originating/refers) ex/ophthalm/ic (protrude/eye/refers)
23. extra-	outside	extra/cellul/ar (outside/cell/refers to)
24. hyper-	excessive, over, above, more	hyper/troph/y (over/growth/process of)
25. hypo-	under, below, deficient, low, less, lesser	hypo/tens/ion (low/contract or stress/process of)

Basic Prefix	Meaning (Gk. or Lt.)	Key Examples
26. im-, in-	in, into, or not	im/mature (not/mature) in/cis/ion (in/cut/process of)
27. infra-	below, under	infra/clavicul/ar (below/collar bone/refers)
28. inter-	between	inter/cost/al (between/ribs/refers to)
29. intra-	within	intra/cerebr/al (within/cerebrum/refers to)
30. intro-	into, within, in, into	intro/vers/ion (inward/turning/process of)
31. meta-	beyond, after, change	meta/carp/al (beyond/wrist/ refers to)
32. para-	beside, near, beyond	para/cardi/ac (beside/heart/refers to)
33. per-	through, excessive, in	per/meate (through/opening)
34. peri-	around	peri/oste/um (around/bone/refers to)
35. post-	after, behind	post/part/um (after/childbirth/refers to)
36. pre-, pro-	before, in front of	pre/maxillary (front of/jaw/refers to) pro/gnosis (before/knowledge)
37. re-	back, again, contrary	re/flex (again/bend)
38. retro-	backward, behind	retro/grade (backward/going)
39. sub-	under, low, beneath	sub/cutane/ous (under/skin/refers to)
40. super-	above, upper, upon, excessive	super/i/or (above/one who)
41. supra-	above, upper, upon, excessive	supra/stern/al (above/sternum/refers to)
42. sym-, syn-	together, with	sym/phy/sis (together/growing/state of) syn/drome (together/run)
43. trans-	across, through, beyond	tran/sect/ion (cut/across/process of)
44. ultra-	beyond, in excess	ultra/violet (beyond/spectrum color)

COMBINING FORMS

When you see a word part in its combing form it makes that word part **easier to pronounce** when used in a compound term.

This combining form of a root word may be made by adding or leaving a vowel at the end of the word. The vowel "o" is most frequently used. The other vowels often seen are "**a, e, i, o, u,** and **y,** or **io, eo,** and **ie.**" The vowels make the compound medical term easier to pronounce.

Examples:

1. Quadr(i)/pleg/ic (four/paralyzed/refers to)
2. Oste(o)/arthr/itis (bone/joint/inflammation)
3. If a stem word ends in a vowel, usually another vowel is not added.
4. One vowel is usually dropped when two or more vowels are together (especially if the word part meaning isn't affected):
   Ost/ectomy derived from ost(e)/(ec)tomy or ost(eo)/(ec)tomy.
   Ost-, osteo-, oste-, and osteon- are examples of acceptable forms of Greek and Latin words or word parts that mean bone.
5. The suffix -ec/tom/y can be fractured into 3 word parts:
   ec- = out from; tom- = to cut; -y = procedure of or process of
6. The key is to make sure you fracture each compound term correctly. This sometimes means breaking suffixes and stem words into smaller parts.

FRACTURING COMPOUND TERMS

a/men/orrhea (prefix: a-; without / stem word: menos; monthly / suffix: -orrhea; flow)

Some vowels have a specific meaning and cannot be dropped or added without changing the meaning of the word or medical term (see examples in chapters). An example would be the letters a/- in arthros. If you fracture off the a/- in "a/rthron" in the Greek noun for joint, then the remaining letters (rthron) don't make sense, or an inappropriate or confused meaning is used with the remaining letters or new word part.

Examples of Incorrect Fracturing:

1. Ankylos: "an" isn't a prefix (incorrect fracture: an/kylos)
   Ankylos/ing Gk. (correct fracture: fused/process of)
2. -ectomy "e/, ect/, or ecto/-" (these word parts within this surgical suffix: -e/ctom/y, -ect/omy, -ecto/my)
   Usually the suffix is used as one (surgical) suffix without fracturing off the incorporated word parts within the suffix. Correct fracturing within this word part would be -ec/tom/y. It literally means: out/to cut/process; actual meaning: to excise, or the procedure of cutting something out or away from the body. Tonsill/ectomy (almond swelling/excised)
3. Note: myos/itis; my/o/ma (muscle); colon/oscopy; colo/scope (large intestine) are examples of writing the entire Greek term within a compound term, removing (typically) the term's last consonant (s and n, respectively) to form a compound term.

COMPOUND TERM BUILDING AND FRACTURING

1. The principle method of identifying the meaning of a compound medical term or building a medical term consists of fracturing a word into its identifying root or stem word part(s), suffix, and prefix.
2. Except for those terms used in anatomy (nouns that name body parts), medical terms are not usually derived from a single term, but rather a combination of two or more word elements.
3. This identification of a word through structural analysis involves a search for the meaning of each of its components. When identified separately, the components give the work its essential literal meaning and/or actual meaning in medicine (which is often the same as the literal meaning).
4. Most terms are compound words consisting of: prefixes + word root(s) in the combining form + suffix (suffixes with or without combining form vowels at their beginnings).
5. Prefixes and suffixes usually describe changes in our body systems.
6. It is crucial in medicine to describe accurately the smallest change that occurs in the body. That is why we need to combine word parts that refer to specific anatomical structures and physiological functions with prefixes and suffixes that correctly modify these word parts.

BUILDING COMPOUND MEDICAL TERMS

Word parts examples

1. PREFIX + WORD ROOT anti/febrile
   Literal definition: against/fever;
   Actual definition: this is an agent suppressing fever.
2. WORD ROOT + SUFFIX gastr/ic
   Literal and **actual** definition: stomach/refers to or pertains to.
3. PREFIX + SUFFIX an/emia
   Literal definition: without, lack of, or no/blood
   Actual usage: a decrease in the number of red blood cells (RBC's), iron, hemoglobin, or healthy cell shapes.
4. STEM WORDS (3) + SUFFIX oto/rhino/laryng/olog/y
   Literal definition: ear, nose and throat/science of or study of
   ot/o = root for ear; + rhin/o = root for nose; + laryng/o = root for voice box (throat) + -olog/y = suffix for science of or study of/process
   Actual descriptive meaning (usage): The process of or procedure of the science or study of diseases of the ear, nose, voice box and throat

7 KEY STEPS TO BUILDING COMPOUND TERMS

1. Define the term you want to build. Actual and literal meanings are often the same. An example would be: "the inflammation of an area before the mouth, tongue, and throat."
2. Choose a suffix that will modify the stem (root) word or words. -itis = inflammation of.
3. Choose a prefix, which is one or more letters placed before a stem word or another prefix, that will modify the next word part.
4. Arrange the prefixes and root word parts in order of increasing importance or anatomical body sequence (occasionally they are arranged in the order of anatomical site progression). Be sure to have each prefix and root word end with a vowel so that it can be combined with the next word part beginning with a consonant (non-vowel). The combining form vowel of the suffix takes priority over the combining form vowel of the word part that is being attached to the suffix.
    Example of the term created: pre/stomato/glosso/pharyng/itis
    {Before = pre/; mouth = stomat/o-; tongue = gloss/o-; throat = pharyng/o; and inflammation = -itis} [1 prefix / 3 stem words / 1 suffix]
5. Place this suffix after the last word root (often a body part) and remove the vowel of the last stem word (o-) if the suffix begins with a vowel.
    {-pharyng/o- = -itis : the o is removed and the -itis retained = -pharyng/itis}
6. Combine all word parts into one compound term and check your spelling.
7. Finally, pronounce term and repeat its meaning: pre/stomato/glosso/pharyng/itis (actual/literal meaning: an inflammation before the mouth, tongue, and throat)

SOME PRACTICE DEVELOPING A COMPOUND TERM

Example: **Osteoporosis**
The definitions of specific word parts enable the student to interpret most medical words, both literally and actually. The word osteo/por/o/sis can be interpreted literally as follows:

1. oste/o-, pertaining to bone (osteon = Greek term)
2. -por/o-, pertaining to porous or small orifice "mouth-like openings" (Poros = Greek)
3. -o/sis, a suffix meaning a medical condition, disease, or state of (Greek)
4. The combining form vowel from #2 above is dropped and the vowel at the beginning of the suffix (combining form suffix vowel) is retained without affecting the meaning of the term.
5. Thus we have the term: osteo/por/o/sis
6. The actual meaning is the thinning or condition of an increase in the porosity of bones. The bone becomes brittle and is subject to fracture (Fx: fracture).
7. Practice developing or building combining forms of word parts regularly.

Note – Some important keys to this unique language of medicine are:
A. There are multiple word parts that mean the same thing;
B. There are multiple meanings for many word parts;
C. There are multiple pronunciations for some terms;
D. There are multiple spellings for some terms;
E. There are multiple actual definitions for many compound terms.

28 COMMON SUFFIXES OR SUFFIX GROUPS

Common Suffixes	Suffix Meaning and Examples
1. -a, -ia, -on, -os, -is, -us, -um, -ium	(names a thing when attached to root word) (means: refers to; pertains to) derm/a (skin); nephr/on (kidney); cement/um (thin layer of tooth – to harden in French); glott/is (voice box); gastr/os (stomach); ren/os (kidney); and card/is (heart)
2. -al, -tic, -ic, -iac, -oius, -ous, -ent	(add to nouns – makes adjectives, express relationships) (means: pertains to, refers to; concerning) neur/al (nerve refers to); neoplas/tic (new/form/refers to); recipi/ent (one who receives/refers)
3. -an, -ion, -ian	(means: pertains to, process of, procedure of) sect/ion (cutting up/process of); physic/ian (treat or cure/procedure of)
4. -ance, -ancy	(means: state of; condition of) pregn/ancy (conceive/condition of)
5. -er, -or	(added to verbs to make adjectives or nouns) (means: one who; process of) doct/or (teaches/one who); practition/er (practices or performs/one who)
6. -form	(means shape; resembles) denti/form (tooth/shaped)
7. -gen-; -troph-; plas-	(means: beginning; produce; development; cause) carcino/gen/esis (cancer/producing/condition); hyper/troph/y (excess/development/process); neo/plasm (new/formation or development)
8. -gram	(means: to record; write) cardio/gram (heart beat/recording)
9. -graph	(means: an instrument) cardio/graph (instrument that records heart beats)
10. -graphy	(means: procedure of; process of using an instrument to make a recording) cardio/graph/y (procedure of using an instrument to record electrical heart beats)

Common Suffixes	Suffix Meaning and Examples
11. -ia, -ity	(add to adjective or nouns to express: quality; condition; state of) chlamyd/ia (cloak/state of); acid/ity (excess acid/pH below 7/condition of)
12. -ible, -ile	(add to verbs to make adjectives) (means: ability to; capacity of; refers to) flex/ible (bend/ability); con/tract/ile (together/draw/able to)
13. -ician	(means: person – belonging to; associated with; one who) Ped/iatr/ician (children/treat or care/doctor associated with)
14. -ics, -tics	(means: art of; science of) aqua/t/ics (water "exercise"/art of)
15. -id	(add to verbs or nouns to make adjectives) (means: state of; condition of; refer to; pertains to) flacc/id (weakness/state of)
16. -ist	(add to verbs to make nouns) (means: a specialist one who practices "something") an/esthet/ist (without/feeling "physical"/specialist or one who practices)
17. -ite	(means: nature of) cellul/ite (cells/chambers, or cellulose/nature of)
18. -ion, -tion, -ition, -ation, -iation, -ing, -y	(means: procedure of; process of; action of; condition of) hyster/ectom/y (uterus/cut out/procedure of); prohib/ition (prohibiting/process of)
19. -itis, -isy or -icy	(add to nouns) (means: to express condition of inflammation; infection) sinus/itis (cavity/infection); pleur/isy (lung covering/inflamed)

Common Suffixes	Suffix Meaning and Examples
20. -ium, -olus, -iole, -cule, -culus, -cle, -culum, -ellum	(add to nouns) (means: small; smaller; lesser) alve/olus (cavity/small) bronch/iole (bronchi-like/small) cereb/ellum (brain/small or lesser) cut/icle (skin/small or lesser)
21. -ize, -ate	(add to nouns or adjectives to make verbs) (means: act like; use; subject to; make into; refer to) hypnot/ize (sleep/acts like); im/person/ate (not/human/acts like)
22. -ma (-mata), -men (-mina), -ment, -ure	(add to verbs to make nouns) (means: many; multiple "results from health condition"; act of) liga/ment (binding/act of); carcino/mata (crab-like/many "tumors")
23. -oid, -form	(add to nouns to form adjectives) (means: likeness; resembles) epiderm/oid (upper skin/likeness); vermi/form (worm/shape resembles)
24. -o/log/y	(means: process of the study of, science of, or knowledge of) dermat/ology (process of the science or study of the/skin) bio/log/y (life/science of/process) (-y denotes process of, procedure of)
25. -oma	(add to nouns to make verb) (means: tumor; swelling) lip/oma (fat/tumor) glauc/oma (cloudy/swelling)
26. -osis, -esis, -asis, -iasis, -sis	(add to nouns to make verbs) (means: condition; medical condition; disease; state of) scoli/osis (crooked/conditions); kyph/osis (humpback/condition); lord/osis (swayback/condition)
27. -ous	(add to nouns to make adjectives) (means: material; refers to; state of) ser/ous (composed of serum/state of)
28. -tic	(add to a verb to make an adjective) (means: relates to, pertains to; refers to) caus/tic (burning/relates to or refers to)

19 SURGICAL (PROCEDURES) SUFFIXES

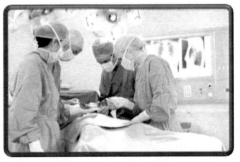

Here are some surgical procedural suffixes. Many of the root words that you already know can be used with these endings.

Suffix	Meaning
1. -centesis	surgical puncture – to remove fluid abdomino/centesis (belly/fluid removed by surgical puncture)
2. -ec/tom/y	out/cut/procedure or removal ex/cis/ion (to cut out); hyster/ectomy (uterus/removal or excision or womb/out/cut /procedure of or process of)
3. -o/pex/y	to fixate, position or to attach salpingo/pex/y (tube/repositioned or attached/procedure of)
4. -oplast/y	plastic surgery (to improve function, looks, or relieve pain) rhino/plast/y (nose repair) (cosmetic, reconstructive, or plastic surgery/procedure of)

Suffix	Meaning	Examples
5. -o/rrhaph/y	Surgically to suture or repair	Nephro/rrhaphy (kidney/suture/procedure of)
6. -o/tom/y	Cutting into, to open, make incision	Tracheo/tom/y (windpipe/cut into/procedure of)
7. -os/tom/y	New permanent opening or mouth	Col/ostom/y (colon/opening/procedure of)
8. -o/tripsy	Crushing or destroying	Litho/tripsy (stone/crushing); Neuro/trips/y (nerve/crushing/procedure)
9. -o/desis	Binding or stabilization	Arthro/desis (joint/binding)
10. -clasis	To break down	Osteo/clasis (bone/refactoring)
11. -lysis	To loosen (free from adhesion) or destroy	Entero/lysis (intestine/destroyed)
12. -cis	To cut	Circum/cis/ion (around/cut/procedure)
13. -cid	To kill	Germi/cid/al (bacteria/kill/pertains to)
14. -stasis	To stop or control	Hemo/stasis (blood/ controlling or stoppage)
15. -sis	Medical condition or disease	Necro/sis (death or dying/condition or state)
16. -age	Something is related to	Mass/age (kneading/relates to): tri/age (sorting or separating/relates to)
17. -iatr/y	To treat, to heal or cure	Psych/iatr/y (mind/treat or cure/procedure)
18. -therap/y	To treat or cure	Chemo/therap/y (chemical/treatment/process)
19. -sect/ion	To cut or make several slices of a body part (to cut a part)	Hepato/sect/ion (liver/several cuts/procedure – including removal or excision)

(Note: A medical procedure involves a specific method or exact steps performed to complete a set task)

47 KEY VERBS
VERBAL VARIATIONS OF STEM WORD
Verbs Specifically Describe the Action or Condition Taken

They may be attached to stem word parts to form additional words. Prefixes may also be added to form new variations of the words.

The following 5 slides give 47 key verbs (often in their combining forms):

Verb or Combining Verb Form	Meaning	Examples
1. -algia	pain	neur/algia (nerve/pain)
2. -audi, -audio	hear; hearing	audio/meter (hearing/measure)
3. bio-	to live	bio/logy (study of living)
4. cau-, caus-	to burn	caus/algia (burning/pain)
5. -centesis	puncture; perforate	pneumono/centesis (lung/puncture)
6. -clas-;-clast;-clasis	to smash; breakdown	cyto/clasis (cell/breakdown)
7. -duct-;-doch-	canal or to draw	ab/duct/ion (away/draw or lead/process); chole/doch/itis (bile/duct/inflamed); duct/al (canal/refers to – makes adjective)

Verb or Combining Verb Form	Meaning	Examples
8. -dynia	pain	thoraco/dynia (chest/pain)
9. -ecta, ectasis	to dilate	vas/ectasis (vessel/dilated)
10. -edem-	to swell	lymph/edema (watery/swelling)
11. -ethes/ia	to feel (physical)	an/esthesia (without/body feeling)
-phoro-	to sense (mental)	eu/phoria (good mental feeling)
12. -fiss-, -schiz-	to split	fiss/ion (splitting/process of)
13. -flec, -flex-	to bend	re/flex (again/bend)
14. flu-, flux-	to flow	af/flu/ent (toward/flow/refers to) re/flux (again/flow); flux/ion (to become fluid/process)
15. -gen	to produce, form, develop, or begin	carcino/gen/esis (crab-leg like/development/condition)

Note: Cancer (crab, Lt.) is the growth or development of tissue projecting outward from the original site into surrounding areas, like crab legs. This projection is referred to as metastasis (or spreading). This spreading occurs regionally or to other body regions by means of the blood and lymph vessels.

Remember: aesthesia means awareness, feeling or sensation.

Verb or Combining Verb Form	Meaning	Examples
16. -iatr-, -iatr/o-, -therap/y	to treat; cure	ger/iatr/ics (old age/cure/procedure of); ped/iatr/ics (children/cure/procedure of)
17. -kine-, -kino-, kinesio-	to move	kinesi/ol/og/y (study of motion/procedure of)
-praxia		pharmaco/prax/ia (drug/movement/refers to)
18. -liga-, -desis	to bind	liga/ment (to bind/smallness)
19. -o/log/y	to study	cardi/o/log/y (heart/science and/or study of/process of)
20. -ly-, -lysis	to break up; to dissolve	auto/lysis (cell self-destruction)
21. -morph-, -morpho	form; shape	a/morph/ous (no definite form or shape/refers to)
22. olfact-, -osmia	to smell	olfacto/phobia (fear of smells); an/osmia (without/smell/refers to)
23. -op-, opt-, -opto, -opsy	vision; sight; or to see	my/opia (near-sighted); hyper/opia (far-sighted); opto/metr/ist (vision/measure/specialist); bi/o/psy (live/viewing)

Verb or Combining Verb Form	Meaning	Examples
24. palpit-	to flutter	palpit/ation (flutter/refers to)
25. -par-, -part, -partus- -toci-	to labor	partur/ition (giving birth/process of) dys/toc/ia (act of difficult/birth/refers to)
26. -pep-	to digest	dys/pep/sia (faulty/digestion/refers to)
27. -pexy	to fix	nephr/o/pex/y (kidney/surgical fixation/procedure of)
28. -phag-, -phago-	to eat	phago/cytosis (eating/cells increase)
29. -phas-	to speak; utter	dys/pha/ia (difficulty/speaking/refers to)
30. -phil-	to like; love; affinity for	hemo/phil/iac (blood/love/refers to) acido/phili/a (acid stain-liking or staining with acid stains/refers to)
31. -phob-	to fear	hydro/phob/ia (water/fear/refers to)
32. -phrag-	fence off; to wall off	dia/phragm (across/partition or wall "separates thorax from abdomen")
33. -plas-, -plasm, -plast/y	repair; to form; grow	neo/plasm (new/growth); rhino/plasty (nose/repairing)
34. -pleg-	to be paralyzed	quadri/pleg/ia (four/paralysis of limbs/refers to)
35. -pnea	to breathe	a/pnea (lack of/breathing)
36. -phono-	voice or sound	a/phon/ia (lack of/voice or sound/refers to)

Verb or Combining Verb Form	Meaning	Examples
37. -poie-	to make	hemat/o/poie/sis (blood/making/condition)
38. -ptosis	to fall; to droop	splanchn/o/ptosis (viscera/dropping)
39. -o/rrhagia	to burst forth; pour	men/o/rrhagia (monthly "abnormal bleeding" menstruation/refers to)
40. -o/rrhaphy	to suture	nephr/o/rrhaph/y (kidney/structure or sewing/procedure of)
41. -o/rrhea	to flow; discharge	leuk/o/rrhea (white/discharge or flow)
42. -o/rrhexis	to rupture	enter/o/rrhexis (intestines/rupture)
43. -therap/y	heal; treat; cure	chem/o/therap/y (chemical/cure/procedure of)
44. -tomy	to cut; in/cise	append/ec/tom/y (appendage/out/cut/refers to)
45. -troph-, -troph/y	to nourish; to develop; formation process	hyper/troph/y (increase/in size or over-nourishment/process of)
46. -volvo-	to turn; twist	volv/ulus (twisting of internal part/refers to)
47. -vulvo-	to cover	vulv/us (female genital covering/refers to)

50 KEY ADJECTIVES MODIFIERS

Adjectives appear in compound terms and are joined to nouns or verbs. Adjectives are modifiers of nouns (something named) and denote quality or extent, or make a distinction. If you add suffixes, you produce nouns.

Stem or Combining Form	Meaning	Example of Adjective Form
1. auto-	self	auto/lysis (self/decline or dissolve)
2. brachy-	short	brachy/dactylia (short/finger)
3. brady-	slow	brady/pnea (slow/breath)
4. brevi-	short	brev/ity (short/state of)
5. cav-	hollow	cav/ity (hollow/state of)
6. cryo-	cold	cryo/therapy (cold/treatment)
7. crypto-	hidden; concealed	crypt/orchidism (hidden/testis)

Several suffixes are adjectives modifiers that are often used to mean pertaining to or referring to: -ac, -al, -ary, -ic, -ual, -us, -tic, (e.g. cardi/ac – heart/pertaining to)

Stem or Combining Form	Meaning	Example of Adjective Form
8. dextro-	right	ambi/dextrous (using both/hands [like dominant hand])
9. diplo-	double; twice	dipl/opia (double/sighted)
10. dys-	difficult; bad; faulty disordered; painful	dys/tocia (different/birth and labor: parturition-birth) dys/cyesis (faulty/pregnancy)
11. eu-	normal; good; well	eu/tocia (normal/birth)
12. glyco-	sugar; sweet	glyco/penia (blood glucose level/low)
13. gravid	heavy; pregnant	gravida (pregnant)
14. haplo-	single; simple	hapl/oid (having a single set of chromosomes)
15. hetero-, heter-	other; a relationship to others	hetero/sexual (other/sex)
16. homo-, homeo-	same	homeo/path (same substances/causing like disease)
17. hydro-	wet; water	hydro/pneumo/thorax (fluid/in lung/chest)
18. iso-	equal	iso/cellar (similar cells); iso/lateral (equal/sides)
19. latus-, lat-	broad; side	lat/issimus dorsi (muscles adducting humerus)
20. longus-	long	long/itude
21. macro	large; abnormal size	macro/cheiria (hands)
22. magni-	large; great	magni/tude
23. malaco-	soft	osteo/malacia (bones)
24. mal-	bad	mal/ignant (bad/growth)
25. medi-	middle	medi/an; medi/um (toward the median plane)
26. mega-	great	mega/colon (great size of/large intestine)
27. megalo-	huge	hepato/megal/y (liver/enlarged/process of)
28. meso-	middle; mid	meso/derm (skin/layer)

Stem or Combining Form	Meaning	Example of Adjective Form
29. micro-	Small	Micro/glossia (small/tongue)
30. minimus-	Smallest	Gluteus minimus (butt/smallest [hip muscle])
31. multi-; -poly	Many; much	Multi/lobar (many/lobes/refers to)
32. necro-	Dead	Necr/o/sis (dead tissue/condition)
33. neo-	New	Neo/plasm (new/formation)
34. oligo-	Few; scanty; little	Olig/ur/ia (little or slight/urine/refers to)
35. ortho-	Straight; normal; correct	Ortho/dont/ics (straight/teeth/refers to)
36. oxy-	Sharp; quick; acute	Oxy/esthes/ia (sharp/feeling/refers to)
37. poly-	Many; much	Poly/dips/ia (many/thirst/refers to)
38. pronus-; prono-	Face down	Prone or pron/ation (turn down/process of)
39. pseudo-	False	Pseud/o/ps/y (false/sight or hallucination/process of)
40. sclero-	Hard	Arteri/o/scler/o/sis (artery/hard/condition)
41. scolio-	Twisted; crooked	Scoli/o/sis (spine-lateral curve/condition)
42. sinistro-	Left	Sinistro/manual (left/handed)
43. stasis-	Stop	Hemo/stasis (blood/stoppage)
44. steno-	Narrow	Mitral sten/o/sis (mitral valve/narrows/condition)
45. stalsis	Contract	Peri/stalsis (around/contract)
46. tachy-	Fast; swift	Tachy/cardia (fast/heart)
47. tele-; tel-; telo-	End; far away	Tele/cardio/gram (end/heart/reading)
48. thermo-	Heat	Thermo/meter (heat or temperature/measure)
49. trachy-	Rough	Trachy/phon/ia (rough/voice/refers to)
50. xero-	Dry	Xero/derma (dry/skin)

SPELLING AND PRONUNCIATION

1. Phonetic spelling rarely occurs with medical terms.
2. Correct spelling and pronunciation is very important.
3. The wrong emphasis on a word's sound or a misspelled word could change the entire meaning or diagnosis of a medical health problem. For example, hypoglycemia means low blood sugar, while hyperglycemia means high blood sugar. This spelling error could cause serious problems or even death for a patient. Another example is macro (large) as opposed to micro (small), which could result in the wrong drug dose or weight of a substance.
4. Some words are pronounced alike but are spelled differently. One pair of homonyms are the terms ilium, which means flank or hip bone, and ileum, which means twisted, or refers to the third part of the small intestine that is very twisted.
5. Medical terms that are difficult to find in a medical dictionary often have unusual spellings, such as the term Chlamydia, which literally means "to cloak or cover/refers to."

23 SPELLING HELPS

Sound	Correct Spelling	Sound	Correct Spelling	Sound	Correct Spelling
1. af	aph (Aphasia)	11. ik	Ic (Hepatic)	17. s, sh, si	c, ps, psy (Psychology) (Cytology)
2. ak, ek	ac, ach, ech (Echogram)	10. J	G (Gestation)	18. si	sci (Scientific)
3. ap	ep (Epiglottis)	11. k, ku, ki	C, ch (Chiropractic)	19. sk	sc (arteriosclerosis)
4. az	as (Aspirin)	12. lay	Lei (Leiomyoma)	20. t	pt, pht (Ptosis)
5. def	deaf (Deaf)	13. mi	My (Myopia)	21. u	eu (Euphoria)
6. dif	diph (Diphtheria)	14. n, nu, na	Pn, pneu, gn (Pneumonia)	22. z	x (Xeroderma)
7. dis	dys (Dyspepsia)	15. of	Ophth (Ophthalmology)	23. i	y (Neurology)
8. a, fle, fe, fiz	ph (Physiology)	16. r, ra, re, ri, ro, ru	Rh (h often follows r) (Rheumatoid)		

DEVELOPING COMBINING FORMS OF WORD PARTS

Word roots are the starting blocks for the anatomical terms, medical processes, procedures, techniques, prefixes and suffixes. Most anatomical terms from the Greek language use the vowels **o** or **i** as their combining vowel. Examples are:

Root (Stem) Word	Actual Greek Nouns	
Cardi-	Cardi/a (heart)	"Cardi/ectomy"
Gastro-	Gastr/os (stomach)	"Gastr/itis"
Osteo-	Osteo/n (bone)	"Osteo/porosis"

Most medical terms have a body part in the compound medical term. These body part names often are derived from the Greek language. In these cases you don't add a vowel to form the combining word part; you simply remove the end letter from the original Greek word for it to be in its combing form (see above). If the term originally comes from Latin it usually ends in an **-a**, **-us**, **-is**, or **-um**, in which case you drop the ending like -us in ocul/us (Lt. for eye) and add the **o** to form the combining form of the term. Sometimes you retain the **-u**, **-e**, **-i** to develop the combining form of the word part or term (genu/flex/ion Lt. or cardi/olog/y Gk).

Compound words must use a **vowel** to connect the first stem word with a second root word of the second stem begins with a consonant (non-vowel).

Remember: The suffix that is added to the last stem word part begins with a vowel. The vowel is dropped from the word part before the suffix.

Leuko/-cyte (2 root word parts with a vowel and consonant)
Leuko/cyt(e)/-osis (suffix added to last stem word – stropping the root (cyt/e) vowel (e)
Leuko/cytosis (white/blood cells increased – condition)

If the second word stem (root word) begins with a vowel, the "o" sometimes must be retained.
Ex.: Gastro/-enter/itis doesn't drop the "o," and so is written as gastro/enter/itis (stomach/intestines/inflamed)

It also may be retained between root word and suffix.
Ex.: Lymph/angi/-oma retains the o," and is written as lymph/angi/oma (watery/vessel/swollen)

PREFIXES

The following additional and unique prefixes are presented for your memorization:

14 Color Prefixes:

1.	Red	erythr/o-;	Erythro/cyte (red/cell)
		ruber/o;	Rubr/o/sis (red/condition)
		rhod/o-;	Rhodo/gen/esis (red/development/condition)
		eosin (rose red)	Eosin/ophil (rose red stain/love of)
2.	White	albus;	Albin/oid (white/resembles) Albumino (white serum)
		leuc/o-; leuk/o	Leuc/emia (white/blood cells)
3.	Brown	fulvus	Fulv/o/sis (brown/condition)
4.	Blue	cyano/o-;	Cyan/o/sis (blue/condition)
		livid/o	Livid/ous (blue/state of)
5.	Black	melan/o-;	Melan/oma (black tumor)
		nigra	Nigra bodies (black particles in a cell)

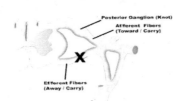
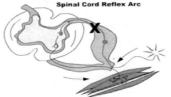
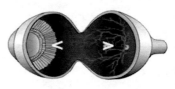

Motor "Efferent-Away" Fiber
Anterior Polio/myel/itis

Sensory "Afferent-Toward"
Fiber Posterior

Glauc/oma
(Cloudy or gray/swelling)

6.	Gray	glauc/o; cinerous; polio	Glauc/oma (gray/swelling) Polio/myel/itis (gray/spinal cord/inflammation)
7.	Purple	purpur/o; porphyr/o	Purpur/ic (pertaining to purple/refers to)
8.	Yellow	cirrh/o-; flavus xanth/o-; luteo-	Cirrho/sis (yellow/condition) Xanth/emia (yellow/blood)
9.	Rose	eosin/o-	Eosino/phil (rose colored blood cell/love for)
10.	Green	chlor/o-; viridis	Chlor/o/phyll (green-plant foliage)
11.	Scarlet	coccideus; crimson	Coccid/ia (berry-color protozoa/refers to) Crimson/ate (scarlet/state of)
12.	Violet	violaceus	Violac/eus (skin violet-purple/state of)
13.	Lemon	citreum	Citr/eum (lemon or citric acid fruits/state of)
14.	Pink	rosaceus	Rosac/ea (red skin/state of)

13 NUMBER PREFIXES

Numbers	Latin	Greek	
1. One	uni-	mon-, mono-	
2. Two	bin-, bi-, duo, di-, diplo-, co-	dy-, dyo-	
3. Three	tri-	tri-	
4. Four	quadr-, quadri-	tetr-, tetra-*	*terat/ology means
5. Five	quinqu-	pent-, penta-	monsters/the study of
6. Six	sex-	hex-, hexa-	(terat- does not mean four)
7. Seven	sept-, septi-	hept-, hepta-	
8. Eight	octo-	octo-, octa-, oct-	
9. Nine	novem-, ninus-	ennea-	
10. Ten	decem-, deca-	dek-, deka-	
11. First	primi-	proto-, prot-	
12. Second	secundi-, secondo-	duet-, deuto-, deutero-	
13. Third	tert-, terti-	trito-, trit-	

Uni/later/al (one/side/refers to)

21 MEASUREMENT PREFIXES

1.	Centi- (also one hundred)	one-hundredth part
2.	Milli- (also one thousand)	one-thousandth part
3.	Centi-, Hecto-, Hect-, Hecato-	one hundred
4.	Kilo-	one thousand or one-thousandth
5.	Semi-, Hemi-	one half
6.	Sesqui-	one and one half
7.	Hyper-	over, above, excess
8.	Hypo-	under, below
9.	Multi-, Poly-	many
10.	Macro-	large
11.	Micro-	small
12.	Deci (1/10)	deciliter (dl) (1/10 of liter)
13.	Deca (10)	(0.1)
14.	Centa (100)	
15.	Kilo (1000)	
16.	Mega (1,000,000 – 1 Million)	
17.	Micro (0.000,001 – 1 Millionth)	
18.	Giga (1,000,000,000 – 1 Billion)	
19.	Nano (0.000,000,001 – 1 Billionth)	
20.	Pico (0.000,000,000,001 – 1 Trillionth)	
21.	Fento (0.000,000,000,000,001 – 1 Quadrillionth)	

20 BODY POSITION PREFIXES

1.	ambi-	both
2.	amphi-	on both sides
3.	ante-	before
4.	anter/o-	before
5.	dextr/o-	right of
6.	dors/o-	back
7.	epi-	upon
8.	hypo-	under
9.	infra	beneath or below
10.	inter-	between
11.	later/o-	side of
12.	mes/o-	middle of
13.	medi-	middle of
14.	post-	behind
15.	postero-	behind
16.	pre-	before
17.	pro-	before
18.	retro-	after
19.	sinistro-	left of
20.	sub-	under

5 Negative Prefixes:

1. a- (before consonant/no vowel) without, not, or lack of: a/febrile (no/fever)
2. an- (before vowel) without, not, or lack of: an/orchidism (No/testes)
3. ar- without, not, or lack of: ar/rhythmia
4. im- not or in: im/permeable (not penetrable)
5. in- not or in: in/continent (not contain)

19 BODY DIRECTIONS

1. ab-   from, away from
2. ad-   to, toward, near
3. circum-   around
4. peri-   around
5. ec-   out from
6. ex-   out from
7. dia-   through, across
8. per-   through, across
9. trans-   through, across
10. ecto-   outside
11. exo-   outside
12. extra-   outside
13. endo-   within, in
14. intra-   within, in
15. par-   beside, near, beyond
16. para-   beside, near, beyond
17. super-   above
18. supra-   above
19. ultra-   beyond, excess

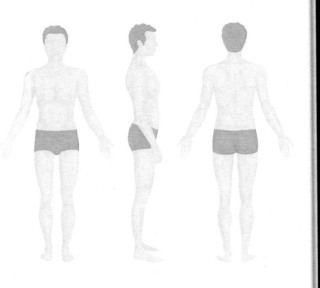

33 DIAGNOSIS AND SYMPTOM SUFFIXES

Suffix	Meaning	Example
1. -algia	pain	Ceph/algia (head/pain)
2. -cele	hernia, swelling tumor, protrusion	Hepat/o/cele (liver/protrusion)
3. -dynia	pain	Cephal/o/dynia (head/pain)
4. -ectasis	dilation	Bronchi/ectasis (bronchus/dilation)
5. -emia	blood	Poly/cyth/emia (many/cells/blood)
6. -gen	producing, beginning	Carcin/o/gen (cancer/producing)
7. -gram	record	Encephal/o/gram (brain/recording)
8. -graph	instrument	Cardi/o/graph (heart/instrument)
9. -graphy	process of recording	En/cephal/o/graphy (in head/recording/process of)
10. -iasis	condition or disease	Cholelith/iasis (gall (bile) stones/abnormal condition)

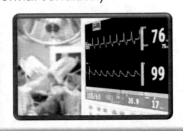

Suffix	Meaning	Example
11. -itis	inflammation	Gastr/itis (stomach/inflammation)
12. -logy	study of/science of	Bio/log/y (life/study/process of)
13. -malacia	softening	Osteo/malac/ia (bone/softening/refers to)
14. -megaly	enlargement	Hepato/megal/y (liver/enlargement/process of)
15. -meter	instrument for measuring	Cranio/meter(cranium/measuring/procedure of)
16. -metry	process of measuring	Pelvi/metr/y (pelvis/measuring/procedure of)
17. -oid	resemble	Lip/oid (fat/resembling)
18. -oma	tumor or swelling	Aden/oma (gland/swelling)
19. -osis	abnormal condition	Dermat/osis (skin/abnormal condition)
20. -pathy	disease	Nephro/path/y (kidney/disease/process of)
21. -penia	disease, deficiency	Leukocyto/pen/ia (white/cell decrease)
22. -phagia	eating, swallowing	Dys/phag/ia (difficult/swallowing/refers to)
23. -phasia	speech	A/phas/ia (without/speech/refers to)

Suffix	Meaning	Example
24. -plegia	paralysis	Hemi/plegia (half/paralysis)
25. -phobia	fear	Acro/phobia (top or extremities/fear)
26. -ptosis	prolapse, falling, dropping	Hystero/ptosis (uterus/prolapse)
27. -rrhage	burst forth, hemorrhage	Hemo/rrhage (blood/burst forth)
28. -rrhea	discharge, flow	Meno/rrhea (monthly/flow)
29. -rrhexis	rupture	Angio/rrhexis (vessel/rupture)
30. -sclerosis	hardening	Arterio/scler/o/sis (artery/hard/condition)
31. -scopy	examination, view	Oto/scop/y (ear/exam/procedure of)
32. -spasm	involuntary, contraction, twitching of a muscle	Blepharo/spasm (eyelid/contraction)
33. -desis	bind, fixate	Teno/desis (fix tendon to bone)

RULE FOR MAKING PLURAL FROM SINGULAR WORDS

10 Rules

1. Keep a and add e
2. Keep ma and add ta
3. Drop en and add ina
4. Drop ix, ex, add ices
5. Drop is and add es
6. Drop on and add a
7. Drop um and add a
8. Drop us and add i
9. Drop y and add ies
10. Drop ax and add aces

Singular	Plural	Singular	Plural
-a	-ae	pleura	pleurae
-ma	-mata	carcinoma	carcinomata
-en	-ina	lumen	lumina
-ix, -ex	-ices	appendix	appendices
-sis	-ses	diagnosis	diagnoses
-on	-a	ganglion	ganglia
-um	-a	bacterium	bacteria
-us	-i	digitus	digiti
-y	-ies	deformity	deformities
-ax	-aces	thorax	thoraces

62 BODY PARTS
Stem or Root Forms

Stem Combining Forms	Literal Meaning
1. abdomin/o- (celio, laparo, ventro)	belly
2. aden/o-	gland
3. andr/o- (gynec/o-)	man (woman)
4. angi/o- vaso-	vessel (lymph; blood)
5. append/o-	appendage
6. arteri/o-	artery
7. arthr/o-	joint
8. bronch/o-	trachea-like (rough)
9. cardi/o-	heart
10. cephal/o-	head
11. cerebr/o-	brain
12. cheil/o- (labi/o)	lip
13. cholecys/o-	gallbladder

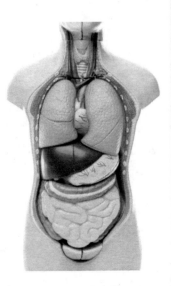

Stem Combining Forms	Literal Meaning
14. choledoch/o-	common bile duct
15. chondr/o-	cartilage
16. col/o-	big intestine
17. cost/o-, pleur/o-	rib
18. crani/o-	skull
19. cyst/o-, vesico-	bladder
20. dent/o-, dont/o-	tooth
21. derm/o-, cuti-	skin
22. duoden/o-	twelve (fingers)
23. en/cephal/o-	in head (brain)
24. eso/phag/o-	toward eater (mouth)
25. gastr/o-	stomach
26. gloss/o-, linguo-	tongue
27. hepato-, hepa-	liver
28. hyster/o-, metr/o-, uter/o-	uterus

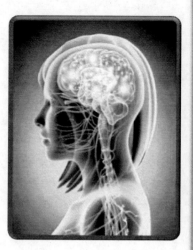

Stem Combining Forms	Literal Meaning
29. ile/o-	twisted (3rd part of small intestine)
30. irid/o-, iro-	rainbow (eye)
31. kerat/o-	cornea (eye); horny (substance)
32. lamin/o-	thin flat part (vertebra)
33. lob/o-	lobe (lung)
34. mast/o-, mamm/o-	breast
35. my/o-, myos-	muscle
36. myel/o-	bone marrow, spinal cord
37. myring/o-, tympan/o-	eardrum
38. neuro-	nerve
39. nephr/o-, ren/o-	kidney
40. oophor/o-	ovary
41. ophthalm/o-, ocul/o-	eye
42. orchid/o-, testo-	testicle
43. oste/o-	bone

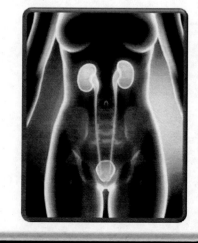

Stem Combining Forms	Literal Meaning
44. ot/o-, aur/i-	ear
45. pan/creat/o-	all/fleshy
46. pharyng/o-	throat
47. phleb/o-, ven/o-	vein
48. pneum/o-, pulmon/o-	lungs
49. proct/o-	rectum, anus
50. prostat/o-	lying before (male gland)
51. pyel/o-	pelvis (kidney pelvis)
52. rect/o-	straight (rectum)
53. rhin/o-, nas/o-	nose
54. sacr/o-	sacrum
55. salping/o-, doch/o-, duct/o-	tube (fallopian and Eustachian)
56. splen/o, leino-	spleen
57. spondyl/o-	vertebra (joined)
58. steth/o-, pect/o-, thoraco-	chest
59. stomat/o-, or/o-, os-	mouth
60. ten/o-, tend/o-, tendin/o-	stretcher (tendon)
61. thyr/o-	shield-like (shape)
62. trache/o-, trach/y-	rough (windpipe)

INTERNAL ANATOMY BY BODY SYSTEM

17 Skeletal System
Some Key Combining Forms and Meanings

1. arthro-   joint
2. articulo-   joint
3. chondro-   cartilage
4. cleido-   clavicle
5. condylo-   knuckle bone
6. costo-, pleuro-   rib
7. ilio-, ilium   flank
8. myelo-   marrow (bone); spinal cord
9. oro-   mouth
10. os-   bone orifice, opening or mouth
11. osteo, oste-   bone
12. phalango-, digito- fingers and toes
13. rachio-   spine
14. sacro-   saucer; sacred
15. spondylo-   vertebra
16. stomato-   mouth
17. tendino-   tendon

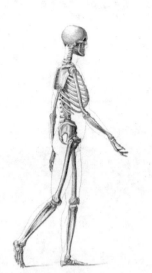

Muscular
6 Combining Forms

1. fibro-   fiber;
2. myo-, myos muscle;
3. fascio-   band;
4. leio-   smooth;
5. rhabdo-   striated;
6. tendo-   sinew or tendon

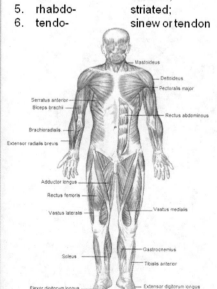

Nervous
13 Combining Forms

1. cereb/ello-   brain/little
2. cerebro-   brain
3. duro-   hard
4. en/cephalo-   brain (in/head)
5. glio-   glue
6. hystero-   neurotic reaction
7. mater-   mother
8. meningo-   membrane (CNS covering)
9. myelo-   spinal cord
10. neuro-   nerve
11. phreno-, psycho-, mind
    -noia
12. pia-   gentle
13. schizo-, fiss-   divide/split

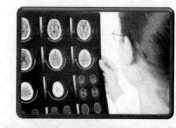

Circulatory
12 Combining Forms

1.	angio-	vessel
2.	arterio-	artery
3.	arteriolo-, arteriole-	small
4.	atrio-, atrium	chamber (upper heart)
5.	auriculo-	ear-shaped
6.	cardio-, card-, car-	heart
7.	cyto-	cell
8.	lympho-	watery
9.	phlebo-	vein
10.	vaso-	vessel
11.	veno-	vein
12.	ventriculo-	little belly

Respiratory
9 Combining Forms

1.	bronchio-	trachea-like
2.	laryngo-	voice box
3.	pharyngo-	throat
4.	phreno-	diaphragm, mind
5.	pleuro-	rib, side
6.	pneumo-	air, lung, respiration
7.	pulmo-, pulmono-	lung
8.	tracheo-	rough or windpipe
9.	chordo-	vocal cord

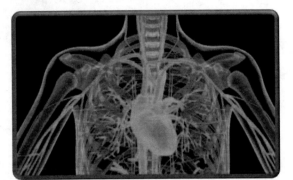
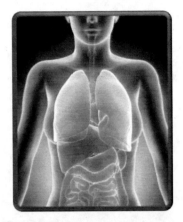

Skin or Integumentary
13 Combining Forms

1.	kerato-	horny tissue (skin or corneas)
2.	sarco-	fleshy
3.	vesico-, cysto-	blister, sac
4.	curio-	little skin
	corio-	true skin
5.	dermo-, dermato- derm-	skin
6.	erythemo-	flush, red
7.	maculo-	large spot
8.	papulo-	pimple
9.	pilo-	hair
10.	tricho-	hair
11.	pruritus-, psoriasis	to itch
12.	rhytido-	wrinkle
13.	steato-, adipo-, lipo-	fat

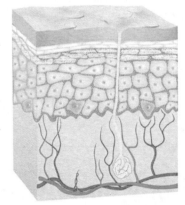

Common Skin Lesions:
maculo – large spot
papulo – pimple
vesico – blister

Di/gestive (two/separations)
17 Combining Forms

1. cholangio-   bile duct
2. chole-   bile or gall
3. chole/cysto-   gallbladder
4. chole/docho-   bile duct
5. colo-, colono-   large intestine
6. cysto-   bladder or sac
7. duodeno-   12 (fingers) = 10" duodenum
                     1st part small intestine
8. entero-   intestine
                     small intestines
9. gastro-   stomach
10. hepato-   liver
11. ileo-   twisted/3rd part of small intestine
12. jejuno-   empty/2nd part
                     small intestine
13. palato-   palate/roof of mouth
14. pharyngo-   throat (eso/phagus means
                     toward/eater)
15. procto-   anus/rectum
16. splanchno-, viscero-   organ
17. spleno-, lieno- spleen

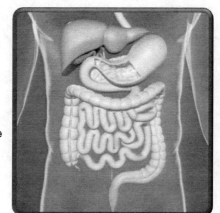

Urinary
7 Combining Forms

1. cysto-   bladder
2. nephro-   kidney
3. pyelo-   kidney pelvis
4. reno-   kidney
5. uretero-   small canal
6. urethro-   canal
7. vesico-   bladder

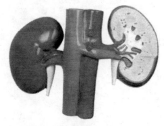

Early anatomists:
Bartolomeo Eustachi: Italian anatomist
1524 – 1574
Gabriele Falloppio: Italian anatomist
1523-1562

Reproductive
9 Combining Forms

1. balano-   glans penis; clitoris
2. chordo-, cordo-   spermatic cord
3. colpo-, vagino-   vagina
4. hystero-, utero- uterus
5. metro-   uterus
6. oophoro-   ovary
7. orchido-, orchio- testes
8. salpingo-   tube (fallopian), canal
9. vaso-   vessel (vas de/ferens)

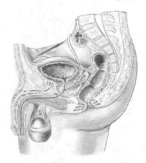

Note: Salpingo- can refer to any body tube
including the Eustachian tubes in the ear or the
Fallopian tubes of the uterus.

Endocrine
8 Combining Forms

1. adeno-   gland
2. ad/reno-   near/kidney
3. thymo-   soul/flowery
4. thyro-   shield-shaped
5. pine/al-   pine cone
6. pituitary-   phlegm
7. para/thyr/oid   near/shield/form
8. gonado-, gono   seed producer

Special Sense
6 Combining Forms

1. auriculo-   ear flap
2. chordo-, cordo-   cord, vocal
3. kerato-   cornea (horny)
4. myringo-, tympano-   eardrum
5. oculo-, ophthalmo-   eye
6. salpingo-   tube (Eustachian)

EXTERNAL ANATOMY
Regional

Head and Neck
29 Combing Forms

1. blephar/o-   eyelid
2. brachio-   upper arm
3. bucco-   cheek
4. capillio-   hair
5. caputo-   head
6. cephalo-   head
7. cervico-   neck
8. cheil/o-, labio- lip
9. cilio-   eyelash
10. core-, coro-   eye pupil
11. dento-, donto-   tooth
12. facio-, facet   face
13. frons-, fronto- forehead
14. gingivo-   gum
15. glosso-, linguo- tongue
16. gnatho-   jaw

17. irido-, iro-   rainbow
18. linguo-, glosso   tongue
19. mento-, genio-   chin
20. nario-, nares   opening to nose
21. naso-, rhino-   nose
22. nucho-   back of neck
23. occiputo-   back of head
24. oculo-, ophthalmo-   eye
25. odonto-   tooth
26. oro-, os-, stomato-   mouth
27. orbit-   socket
28. oto-, auri-   ear
29. palpebro-   eyelid

Note: opto-, op-, and -opsy mean sight or to view.
On rare occasions it refers to the eye.
Cranio- means skull; cephalo- means head.

17 Body Trunk

1. coxa-, ischio-   hip or hip joint
   (isch/emia means hold back blood)
2. dorso-   back
3. inguino-   groin
4. abdomino-; laparo-   abdomen; flank; abdomen wall
5. latero-   side
6. lumbo-   loin
7. mammo-   breast
8. mastro-   breast
9. omo-   shoulder
   scapulo-   shoulder blade
10. omphalo-   navel
11. papillo-   nipple
12. pectero-; pecto-   chest
13. sterno-   sternum
14. stetho-   chest
15. theleo-   nipple; nipple-like
16. thoraco-   chest
17. ventr/icle   little belly
    vestero-   belly

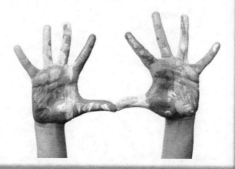

19 Body Extremities

1. axillo-   armpit
2. calx-   heel
3. carpo-   wrist (8 bones)
4. chiro-, mano-   hand
5. cubito-   elbow/forearm
6. dactylo-   finger and toe
7. digito-, phalange-   finger/toe
8. genu-   knee
9. hallux-   great toe
10. mano-, chiro-   hand
11. melio-   limbs
12. onycho-, unguno-   nail
13. pedo-, podo-, pes   foot
    (ped- and pede- mean child
    and -pedia means educate)
14. plantar-   foot sole
15. pollex-   thumb
16. poples-   back of knee
17. talus-   ankle
18. tarso-   foot instep
19. thenar-   base of thumb

20 BODY FLUIDS

1. aqua-, lympho-   water
2. chole-   bile or gall
3. chyle-   lymph and fat
4. dacryo-, lacrimo-   tears
5. emia-   blood
6. lacto-, galacto-   milk
7. hemo-, hema-, hemato-, -emia, blood
   -ema
8. hidro-   sweat
9. hydro-   water
10. gluco-, saccharo-   sugar
11. muco-, myxo-, blenno- mucus
12. plas/mo-   fluid
13. pyo-   pus
14. ptyalo-, sailo-   saliva
15. sanguio-   blood
16. sero-   blood serum
17. sialo-, salivo-   saliva
18. sudoro-   sweat
19. uro-   urine
20. halo-, salo-   salt

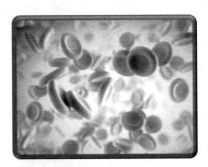

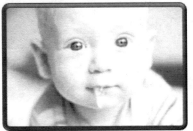

18 BODY SUBSTANCES

1. adipo-, lipo-, steato-   fat
2. amylo-   starch
3. cerumeno-, ceru-   wax (ear)
4. collageno-   albumin substance in connective tissue
5. ferro-, sidero-   iron
6. glyco-, gluco-   sugar
7. halo-, salo-   salt
8. heme-, sidero-   iron; red blood cell iron
9. hormono-   to urge on (chemicals' cell regulators)
10. hyalo-   glassy
11. lapio-   stone
12. natrio-   sodium
    (kali means potassium)
    (calculi means calcium)
13. oleo-, sebo-   oil
14. saccharo-, glyco-   sugar
15. sialo-, ptylo-   saliva
16. sebo-   oil
17. spermato-   sperm
18. uro-   urine

Fat Cells

27 MISCELLANEOUS TERMS

1.	a/telo-	without end (incomplete)	16. scoto-	darkness
2.	conio-	dust	17. sapro-	rotten
3.	cryo-	cold	18. theleo-, papillo-	nipple
4.	crypto-	hidden	19. gamo-	marriage
5.	cyesis-, gravido-	pregnancy	zygoto-	marriage; union
6.	ectesis	dilation	20. gero-, presbyo-	old
7.	eu-	good; new	21. gyro-	circle
8.	feto-	fetus	22. genio-	chin
9.	pachy-	thick	23. genu-	knee
10.	parto-, tocio-	birth	24. celio-, laparo-	belly
11.	physis-	growth	25. anthropo-	human
12.	rhytido-	wrinkles	26. aniso-	uneven
13.	-o/rrhexis	ruptured	27. hamarto-	defect
14.	clysis-	wash; irrigate		
15.	holo-	whole		

(allo- means against, as used in "allopathic medicine")

40 HEALTH PROFESSIONS

1. **Audi/olog/y:** This is the science concerned with the sense of hearing, especially in the evaluation, study, and measurement of impaired hearing, and the rehabilitation of those with impaired hearing.
2. **Bacteri/olog/ist:** a specialist in the scientific study of bacteria such as bacilli, cocci, and spirochetes.
3. **Bi/o/log/ist:** a specialist in the scientific study of living cells.
4. **Cardi/olog/y:** the study of the heart and its functions.
5. **Dermat/olog/y:** medical specialty concerned with the diagnosis and treatment of skin diseases.
6. **Endocrin/olog/y:** the study and science of the endocrine system.
7. **Gastro/enter/olog/y:** the study of the stomach, intestines, and their diseases.
8. **Gynec/olog/y:** a specialty dealing with diseases of the reproductive and genital tract in women.
9. **Hemat/olog/y:** the science of dealing with the morphology of blood, blood cells, and blood-forming tissues, and with their physiology and pathology.
10. **Neur/olog/y:** a branch of medical science dealing with diseases and conditions of the nervous system

11. **Onc/olog/y:** the study of tumors – both benign and malignant.
12. **Ophthalm/olog/y:** branch of medicine dealing with the eye.
13. **Path/olog/y:** the branch of medicine concerning the treatment of disease.
14. **Physi/olog/y:** a science that treats the functions of the living organism and its parts, chemical factors, and processes.
15. **Proct/olog/y:** the specialty concerned with disorders of the rectum (straight tube) and anus (ring).
16. **Psych/olog/y** (M.S. or Ph.D.): science of the mind and mental processes; disturbed mental processes; and abnormal behavior. A psychologist doesn't prescribe drugs.

17. **Radi/olog/y:** the branch of medical science dealing with X-ray substances or radioactive energy to diagnose and treat disease.
18. **Ur/olog/y:** the branch of medicine dealing with the urinary system in the female and the urogenital system in the male.
19. **Psych/iatry:** the branch of medicine that deals with the study, treatment and prevention of mental illness.
20. **Physician:** an authorized practitioner of medicine.
21. **An/esthesi/olog/ist:** a physician who specializes in administrating anesthetics.

22. **Oto/rhino/laryng/olog/ist:** a physician who specializes in the diseases of the ear, nose and throat/voice box.
23. **Ger/iatr/ician:** a physician who diagnoses, treats, and cures diseases and conditions of the aging and elderly.
24. **Obstetric/ian (midwife Gk.):** a physician who specializes in pregnancy, labor, and delivery.
25. **Ped/i/atric/ian:** a physician who diagnoses and treats children's diseases.
26. **General Practitioner (G.P. M.D.):** a physician who is schooled in six basic areas: internal medicine, function, and diseases of internal organs; obstetrics and gynecology; surgery; psychiatry; pediatrics; and community medicine. This doctor treats the whole family and is often referred to as a Family Practitioner or Family Physician.
27. **Preventive Medicine M.D.:** a specialty that includes occupational medicine, public health, and general preventive medicine.
28. **Emergency Medicine:** emergency room care that treats acute illness and crisis situations.
29. **Osteopathy D.O.:** these physicians have the skills of both Medical doctors and Chiropractors.

30. **Nurse R.N.:**
    A. Registered Nurse (R.N.): a specialist licensed to work directly with patients.
    B. Midwife (R.N.): a professional nurse with additional training with women throughout pregnancy, delivery, and the postpartum period.
    C. Nurse Practitioner (N.P.): a registered nurse who has completed advanced nursing education, masters or doctorate. Range of health services varies from state to state.
    D. Public Health Nurse (P.H.N.): a registered nurse concerned with the prevention of illness and care for the sick in a community setting rather than a health-care facility. A P.H.N. is usually employed by public health departments.

31. **Physician Assistant P.A.:** a person trained in some medical procedures who can perform limited duties under the guidance of a physician.
32. **Occupational Therapist O.T.R.:** professional person schooled in the rehabilitation of fine motor skills and coordination of patients' activities.
33. **Optometrist O.D. (vision/measure/specialist):** a professional person trained to examine eyes and prescribe corrective lenses.
34. **Pharmacist R. Ph. or F. PH. (Registration in or Doctorate Degree):** one who is licensed to prepare, sell, or dispense drugs, compounds, and prescriptions.
35. **Physical Therapist R.P.T. or P.T.:** a person skilled in the techniques of physical therapy who is qualified to administer physician-prescribed drugs (Rx) and give treatment (Tx).
36. **Athletic Training Certification A.T.C.:** a person who uses sports medicine techniques, physical therapy, massage, and numerous other modalities.

37. **Radiology Technician R.T.:** one who specializes in the use of X-ray and radioactive isotopes in the diagnoses and treatment of disease and who works under the supervision of a radiologist (M.D.)
38. **Respiratory Therapist A.R.R.T.:** a person who has a degree in respiratory therapy and who assists patients in improving impaired respiratory functions under a physician's direction, usually a pulmonologist (M.D.) – lung specialist.
39. **Veterinarian D.V.M.:** a doctor trained to practice veterinary medicine, perform animal surgery, and carry out animal research.
40. **Chiro/pract/or or D.C.:** a doctor trained in a manner similar to M.D.s and D.O.s but who doesn't use medications or surgery. D.C.s analyze the skeletal system and use holistic approached to treat patients with bone adjustment manipulation, physical therapy, nutrition, acupuncture, massage, and other non-intrusive therapies.

DISEASE DIAGNOSIS

Note: Abbreviation D.D. stands for disease diagnosis and differential diagnosis
Signs = you see – Objective; Symptoms = you're told – Subjective

The following are used for human disease diagnosis:

1. Physical Examinations (PE) (to find signs of disease):
   A. **Inspection**: looking at the patient either directly or indirectly through various instruments, like the ophthalmo/scope for viewing inside of the eye.
   B. **Palpation**: touching or feeling specific areas of patient's body to identify firmness, lumps, irregularities, or other physical findings evaluated by touch.
   C. **Auscultation** (little ear): listening for organ physiology (function). Sounds are diagnosed with special electronic devices such as stetho/scopes, which are instruments used in listening to sounds of the body made by the lungs, blood vessels and heart.
   D. **Percussion**: striking various parts of the body to determine the quality of sounds produced, reflexes of muscles and nerves (knee jerk), or body tenderness. Vital Life Signs (VS): T/P/R and BP or BT/PR/RR/BP (temperature, pulse, respiration, and blood pressure)
2. Medical History (MH):
   A. Family History
   B. History of Present Illness (HPI)
   C. Symptoms of the Chief Complaint or Complaints of (C.C or C/o)
   D. Past History (including diseases) (PH)
   E. Social History (including STIs) (SH)

IMPORTANT REFERENCE TERMS

1. **Acute (quick):** condition that is brief and severe
2. **Ambul/atory (walking):** capable of walking; not confined to bed
3. **A/nomaly (lack of/normal):** irregularity; deviation from normal
4. **A/trophy (wasting):** this is the process of wasting away of the body or its parts. It also can mean without nutrition
5. **Benign (kind):** a disease that isn't malignant
6. **Chronic (long lasting):** condition that lasts a long time; re/occuring
7. **Clinical (bedside):** this is direct beside treatment; observation of signs and symptoms; and observation of the disease course
8. **Dia/gnosis (across or total/knowledge):** identification of a disease; having total (dia-) knowledge (-gnosis) of the disease
9. **Malignant (bad):** a condition that becomes progressively worse and may result in death

10. **Meta/stat/ic (beyond/immediate or standing/refers to):** this is the spreading from one body location to another location. Abbreviation Stat. means immediate or –stat means to keep stationary
11. **Prognosis (before/knowledge):** a prediction based on knowledge (-gnosis) before it happens (before: -pro, pre-, ante)
12. **Sign (objective/seeing):** observable occurrence that indicates a disease (i.e. fever is sign of infection)
13. **Symptom (subjective/telling):** patient describes to physician what he or she is experiencing
14. **Syndrome (together/run):** a group of sign and symptoms that run together
15. **Systemic:** involving systems; affects total body

8 IMPORTANT CLINICAL MEDICINE TERMS

1. Drug, pharmo, or pharmaco: chemical substance administered to treat diseases.
2. Internist (within/specialist): doctor who treats internal diseases
3. Internal (within medicine drug/or remedy): branch of medicine dealing with the treatment of disease with drugs or medication
4. Operation: act of performing treatment using instruments
5. Surge/on (working by hand/one who): this is a physician who treats with surgical procedures
6. Surgery: branch of medicine dealing with treatment of disease through surgical procedures operation or application of devices
7. Therapeutics (to treat): using the medical arts to treat diseases
8. Therap/y (treating/process): treating a patient with different methods used in medicine such as: hydrotherapy, chemotherapy, radiotherapy, recreational therapy, occupational therapy, physical therapy or psychotherapy

22 IMPORTANT DISEASE TERMS

1. **A/genesis (without/beginning):** a condition in which a natural body structure was not (a-) produced (genesis).
2. **Bacteria (rod):** means rod-shaped. Rod-, coccus-, or spirochete- shaped bacteria are three of many types of etiologic agents that affect man. Other diseases or etiologic agents in man and animals include viruses, fungi, worms and parasites.
3. **Cancer (crab-like):** a cancer is a malignant, invasive growth spreading out like crab legs (karinos: crab, Gk. Compare to cancer, Lt.)
4. **Con/genital (together/at beginning):** a condition or defect with which a person is born.
5. **De/generative (away from/develop):** a disease characterized by the breakdown in body structures.
6. **En/dem/ic (within/people/refers to):** a disease that is occurring within (en-) a small group of people or community (demos: people, Gk.): A pan/dem/ic affects all people.
7. **Epi/demic (upon/people):** a disease that is spread among numerous people (demos) in a particular area.
8. **Ex/acerbation (outer/harsh):** a condition in which the disease or condition becomes increasingly severe.

9. **Fung/al tinea or myco:** a disease caused by a fungus
10. **Helminthic worm:** a disease that is caused by a worm
11. **Iatro/genic (treatment or cure/beginning):** disease that is a side-effect of treatment
    (-iatro-) prescribed by a physician
10. **Idio/pathic (self/disease):** disease (pathic) that is specific to one-self (idio) or only to that person. It is usually a disease with an unknown cause.
11. **In/fectious (inner/invasion):** disease that is spread from one person to another
12. **Neoplasm or Neoplastic (new/form):** growth or a disease in which new (neo) cells are formed (plastic = referred to as cancer)
13. **Palliation (to cover or feel):** treatment directed at curing the symptoms of a disease rather than curing the disease
14. **Pandemic (total/people):** disease that is spread over all (pan) people (demic)
15. **Prognosis (before/knowledge):** knowledge (gnosis) of the progress of a disease beforehand (before: -pro, pre-, ante). Prediction of course of disease progress

16. **Sign (objective/seeing):** observable occurrence that indicated a disease state (i.e. fever is a sign of infection)
17. **Symptom (subject/telling):** patient describes to physician what s/he is experiencing (i.e. chest pain is a symptom of heart disease)
18. **Syn/drome (together/run):** group of sign and symptoms that run together
19. **Systemic:** involving systems. Systemic diseases affect the body as a whole
20. **Parasitic (beside/live):** disease caused by parasitic plant or animal
21. **Sepsis (poison):** this is the presence of organisms or their poisons in human blood that produces a breakdown in tissue or tissue function
22. **Trauma (wound):** this is a wound or injury to the body or mind

9 ADDITIONAL TERMS

1. **Bi/o/ps/y (life/view/procedure of)** is the excision of living tissue for examination.
2. **Cauter/y (burning/process)** is the use of a machine or a method used to destroy tissue by electricity, freezing, or chemicals (cauterization).
3. **De/bride/ment (Fr. away/debris/small)** is the removal of dead or foreign tissue from a wound.
4. **Derm/ab/ras/ion (skin/away/scrape/process)** is the scraping of surface layers of skin to remove scars or wrinkles.
5. **Derma/tom/e (skin/cut/instrument)** is an instrument used for cutting thin sections of skin for grafts.
6. **Electro/dessic/ation (electric/dry up Lt./process)** is the destruction and drying out of cells and tissues with short, high-frequency sparks of electricity. Vessels severed during surgery undergo electrodessication, referred to as the process of hemo/stasis (blood/stoppage).
7. **Eschar/otom/y (scab/removal/process)** is the removal of tissue and underlying tissue caused by burns. These scabs restrict blood flow, especially in tight, swollen limb bands of scabs and scar tissue.
8. **Fulgur/ation (to lighten/process Lt.)** this is a type of electro/desiccation that destroys tissue with long, high-frequency electric sparks.
9. **Grafts** occur when tissue is taken from one place on the body to replace skin or defects elsewhere; auto/graft from self, hetero/graft from another person. Pig skin and synthetic forms are also used as skin replacements.

5 INSTRUMENT OR PROCEDURAL TERM SUFFIXES

-SCOP/E: instrument used to examine or view

Micro/scop/e: instrument used to visually examine small cells or organisms;

Fluoro/scop/e: instrument used to view body parts injected with contrast dye;

Cysto/scop/e: instrument used to examine the bladder;

Cardio/scop/e: instrument used to examine the interior of the heart;

Procto/scop/e: instrument used to view the anus and rectum;

Sigm/scop/e: instrument used to instrument used to view the sigm/oid colon

Stetho/scop/y: chest/examining/procedure of

Oto/scop/e: ear/examine/instrument

-SCOP/Y the process or procedure of visual inspection

Colono/scop/y: examination of the upper part of the colon

Cardio/scop/y: examination of the interior of the heart

Procto/scop/y: examination of the anus and rectum

Cysto/scop/y: examination of the bladder

-GRAPH instrument or machine that records or writes

Radio/graph: a picture produced by a machine on a film by X-rays or gamma rays

Electro/myo/graph: instrument used to record skeletal muscle contraction

Electro/en/cephalo/graph: instrument used to record electrical activity of the brain

Thermo/graph: device or machine that records heat patterns on the skin

Sono/graph: machine that emits ultrasonic waves to measure tissue density

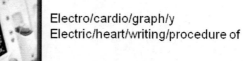

Electro/cardio/graph/y
Electric/heart/writing/procedure of

-GRAPH/Y: Procedure of using machine, instrument, or device to record

Myelo/graphy/y: recording of skeletal muscle contractions
Electro/myo/graph/y: recording of skeletal muscle contractions
Ultra/sono/graph/y: this is the process of using ultra/sound for diagnosis by producing echoes as the strike tissues of different density
Tomo/graph/y: process cutting across and producing single layer tissue images
Thermo/graph/y: this is the process of recording surface heat patterns
Mammo/graph/y: surface X-ray picture of the breast

-GRAM: This is the record, recording, or writing

Sono/gram: record produced from results of ultra/sono/graph/y
Photo/fluoro/gram: X-ray image record from a fluoro/scopic exam
Myelogram: X-ray record of spinal cord using radiopaque contrast dye
Angiogram: X-ray record of blood vessels using radiopaque contrast dye

Cardio/gram
(heart/recording)

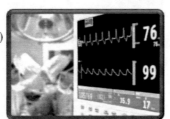

Radio/graph/y
X-ray

PICTURES AND MEDICAL TERMS FOR BODY ORGANIZATIONS; DIAGNOSIS; EQUIPMENT; INSTRUMENTS; AND TREATMENT

Dr. Seigfred W. Fagerberg

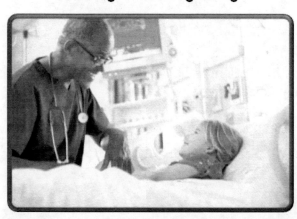

Human Ana/tom/ical Positions and Planes (Body or Part)

1. Sagittal plane (like-arrow)
2. Coronal or frontal plane (crowning skull structure/front plane)
3. Transverse or horizontal plane (across)
4. Medial or median plane (middle)

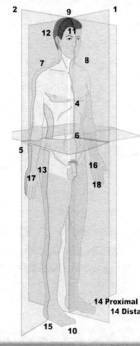
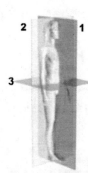

5. Lateral (side)
6. Central (center)
7. Posterior (dorsal)
8. Anterior (ventral)
9. Superior (above)
10. Inferior (below)
11. Cranial (skull)
12. Cephalic (head)
13. Caudal (tail)
14. Pro/ximal/Distal (first and last parts of fingers & toes)
15. Plantar (sole)
16. Palmar (palm)
17. Flex/ion (bend/process of) Ex/tens/ion (out/stretch/process of)
18. Pronation (turn down) Supination (turn up)

BODY POSITIONS

Recovery Position

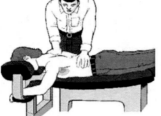
Prone Position

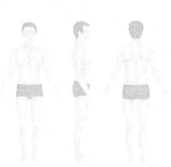
Human Anatomical Position

1. **Recovery Position**: Patient is placed in this position to minimize movement until normal body functions can be restored.
2. **Prone Position**: Patient is placed face-down in anatomical position or face-down with arms at angles to body.
3. **Human Anatomical Position**: Position in which the body is erect with the arms and hands turned forward.

Supine (up) Position

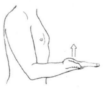
Supinated Hand

Dorso/sacral Position
(Lithotomy Position)

Dorso/recumbent Position

4. **Supine position**: The body or any part of the body in an upward position.
5. **Dorsal recumbent (lithotomy) position**: Used during various gynecological and urinary (female and male) exams and procedures, including vasectomies. The surgical excision of a calculus from the urinary tract is called a lithotomy.

6. **Knee Chest (Genu/pectoral) Position**: Patient on knees, chest face-down.
7. **Sims' Position**: Marion Sims (1813 – 1883), U.S. Gynecologist. Patient is on left side, right knee drawn up, left arm along back, chest inclined forward to rest on. Used for many exams including rectal exams and enemas.
8. **Fowler's Position**: Head is raised up about 18" with knees elevated.
9. **Trendelenburg Position**: Patient is on his/her back with head lowered (abdominal surgery and C.V. Shock).
10. **Dorso/sacr/al (Litho/tom/y) Position**: Similar to Dorsal Recumbent Position, but legs are raised closer to chest area (female and urinary operations)
11. **Opisthotonos Position** (backward bending): Assumed with nervous system complications (Meningitis; Encephalitis; Cerebral Palsy).

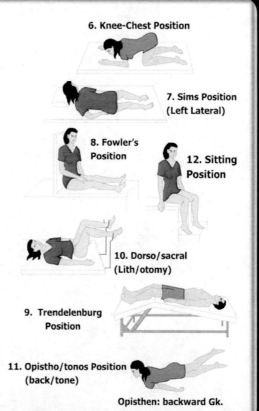

6. Knee-Chest Position

7. Sims Position (Left Lateral)

8. Fowler's Position

12. Sitting Position

10. Dorso/sacral (Lith/otomy)

9. Trendelenburg Position

11. Opistho/tonos Position (back/tone)

Opisthen: backward Gk.

CELL (Chamber Lt.)
Enclosed or Partly Enclosed Cavity

1. This is the basic unit of structure of plants and animals. It is composed of protoplasm.
2. Contains a nucleus (nut Gk.) of nuclear material. Cells and their products make up all tissues in the body. All body functional activities are carried on by cells. Cell structure (anatomy or form) is closely correlated to its physiology or function.
3. The duplication of the cell's chromo/somes (colored bodies) is called mito/sis (thread/condition).
4. The reduction of chromosomes to 23 (in sperm and egg) instead of 23 pairs (normal cell) is called meiosis (lesser/process).
5. There are more than 100 distinct types of cells in the body – from three types of muscle cells, to organ cells, to covering cells, to the many types of blood cells.
6. Most body cells contain the following:

A. **Nucleus (nut in Greek)**: contains the four proteins in the coiled DNA structures of the chromosomes;
B. **Protoplasm (first/form Gk.)**: contains the many cell bodies and structures;
C. **Cell Membrane**: surrounds the cell's contents, and provides for cell exchanges; composed of lipids, proteins, and carbohydrates;
D. **Mitochondria (thread/cartilage-like)**: the powerhouses of the cell involved with protein synthesis and lipid metabolism;
E. **Lyso/somes (breakdown/bodies)**: part of the digestive system containing enzymes that break down proteins and carbohydrates

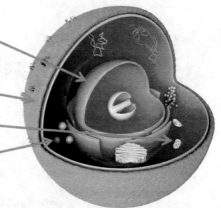

TISSUE (to weave – Old Fr. and Lt.)
Tissue: A woven net-like web made of cells

1. A group of similar cells and their intra/cellular substances that perform a specific function together (histo/log/y: tissue/study/process).
2. Primary tissue forms include: fibrous, epithelial, connective, skeletal, muscular, glandular, nervous, bone, adipose, cartilage, blood and organs.
3. **Cells** form > **tissues** form > **organs** form > **systems** > and **body**.

 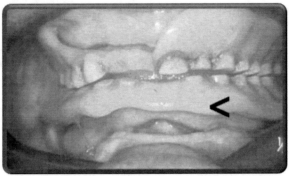

Denture-induced (palatal "roof of mouth" fibrous tissue) hyper/plas/ia (increased/development)

4. **Tissue hyper/plasia or hypo/plasia (an increase or decrease in tissue):** This is the increase or decrease in cells and tissues.
   Ex.: Retinal, blood cells, sperm, bone, cartilage, elastic, erectile, nervous, adipose, fibrous, glandular, lymphoid, mucous, and organ tissues.

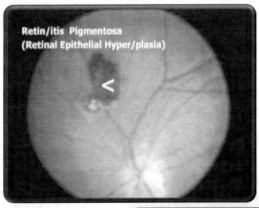

Retin/itis Pigmentosa
(Retinal Epithelial Hyper/plasia)

< WBC

Erythro/leuk/emia Hyper/plasia
(RBC and WBC Increases)
(Malignant Tissue Growth)

< RBC

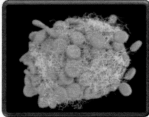

Clot: fibrin, platelets and blood cells

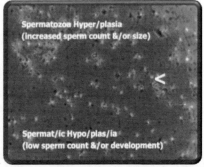

Spermatozoa Hyper/plasia
(increased sperm count &/or size)

Spermat/ic Hypo/plas/ia
(low sperm count &/or development)

ORGAN (Viscero – Lt.; Splanchno – Gk.)

A group of cells and tissues that perform a specialized function.

1. This body part has a specialized function.
2. In general, 30-40% of an organ may be removed without loss of life.
3. Splanchno/tom/y (organ/cut/into/process): the dissection of an organ.
4. Viscera (splanchno-): liver, pancreas, kidneys, lungs, spleen, and heart.

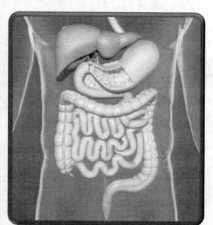

Endo/scop/y:
Viewing of organs

Endo/scop/y equipment
Viewing of organs and
internal surfaces

BODY SYSTEMS

An organized group of structures, parts, or organs related to each other in function and performance.

Ten Body Systems (to classify):
1. Skeletal
2. Muscular
3. Nervous
   (includes special senses)
4. Cardio/vascular
5. Respiratory
6. Integu/mentary
7. Digestive
8. Urinary
9. Reproductive
10. Endocrine

Uro/genital   Integumentary   Endocrine

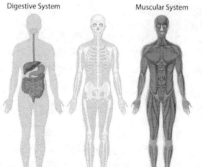

Nervous System   Digestive System   Muscular System

Circulatory System   Respiratory System   Skeletal System

Dis/ease (lack of/ease)
Des- (from or lack of – Fr.) -aise (ease – Fr.)

1. Any abnormal condition, affecting either the body or its parts.
2. It must result in impairment of normal body function or physiology.
3. It is usually accompanied by a recognized cause, identifiable signs and symptoms, and/or altered anatomical condition.

Chicken/pox (chicken/pitted scars)

1. Skin markings resemble chicken feather pits.
2. Dew-drop or rose petal crops of macules with papules and vesicles that become pustules that scale and/or scab.
3. A.K.A.: Varicella

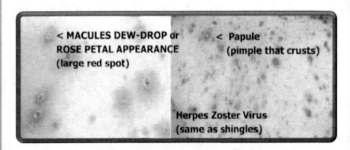

< MACULES DEW-DROP or ROSE PETAL APPEARANCE (large red spot)

< Papule (pimple that crusts)

Herpes Zoster Virus (same as shingles)

Pox (pokkes M.E. pits)

Vesicle > (blister; sac-like)

BODY DEFENSES
(Against Diseases and Infection)

An infection is an invasion and multiplication of micro/organisms in the body's cells and tissues that causes injury to the body's cells and tissues. Some body defenses include physical and chemical barriers:

1. **Mucus** in the respiratory system traps organisms, and the **cilia** that line this system sweep them up and out;
2. **Stomach acid (hydrogen chloride)** is toxic to organisms;
3. **Tears** wash organisms away;
4. **Sweat and saliva** have enzymes that kill organisms;
5. **Nose hairs** trap organisms and the sneeze reflex expels them. **Nose secretion** has enzymes that destroy organisms;
6. **Skin** is a barrier, and **oil** from the sebaceous glands (sebum) is an acidic lubricant that is toxic to many organisms;
7. **Protective bacteria** help the body function and are found in out urethra, vagina, and intestines;
8. **Blood vessels** carry WBCs and antibodies;
9. **Thymus** (endocrine gland) is located behind the sternum and is the location where some WBC grow and mature;
10. **T-Lymphocytes** fight viruses and invade and kill cells;
11. **Bone marrow** produces WBCs which perform immunity functions;
12. **Lymphatic vessels** also carry our WBCs and pathogenic organisms and/or their particles from infected sites to the lymph nodes where they are tapped and destroyed;
13. **Lymph nodes** harbor several types of WBCs. One type (B Lymphocytes) change and produce proteins called antibodies that help identify invaders and lead WBCs to them for destruction;
14. **Non-encapsulated lymphatic tissues** are the tonsils, adenoids, appendix, and small intestines.

SPECIFIC BODY CELL RESPONSE

1. **White blood cells**: These are natural killer cells that target and destroy pathogens and cancer cells by releasing poisonous chemicals and with the process of phagocytosis.
2. **Lymphocytes**:
    A. **T Cells** invade cells or produce chemicals that assist B lymphocytes in destroying foreign protein or pathogenic organisms. **The killer T cell** recognizes antibodies and organism proteins, and destroys the cells with protein chemicals (like B cells) and with the process of phagocytosis. They multiply rapidly. Killer T cells seek out infected body cells or organisms and use proteins like lymphokines to destroy the invaders (AIDS viruses, cancer cells, and/or bacteria). In the process, infected cells and killer T cells are killed.
    B. **B Lymphocytes** recognize organisms and multiply rapidly, turning into plasma cells and memory B cells. Plasma cells produce proteins called antibodies that attach to surface membranes, which identify the organisms for destruction. Memory B cells develop into new plasma cells when needed by recognizing the specific disease agent or organism.
3. **Interferon**: These are proteins that are produced b our cells when exposed to foreign cells and particles with nucleic acid. This protein blocks viral RNA and protects us from specific viral species.

Other Factors that Help the Body to Maintain Health

1. Have regular physical exams that look for signs and symptoms of illnesses that should be treated.
2. Follow good public health practices that include immunizations with virus vaccines including: MMR measles (rubeola 9 day measles); mumps (parotitis), and rubella (German 3 day measles); and DPT: Diphtheria, pertussis (whooping cough), and tetanus; Haemophilus influenzae (B); polio (influenza); yellow fever, cholera, typhoid fever; rabies, and hepatitis A (infectious hepatitis) are other types.
3. Have good sanitary hygiene programs for the use of food and water;
4. Have good education programs for the public about diseases like AIDS, flu, hepatitis; and
5. Use current technology to diagnose diseases by using: MRI, antibody tests, blood and urine cultures, and run various tests for URI, UTI, STIs, or pathogenic organisms. Also, review the body systems (ROS).

BODY INFECTION

1. Infection is an invasion and multiplication of micro/organisms. In body cells and tissues they cause various degrees and types of injuries. Inflammation is cell or tissue reaction to any type of injury, including infections.
2. The localized cellular or tissues injury is due to toxins, competitive metabolism, intracellular replication, and/or antigen-antibody response.
3. The etiologic agents or organisms are viruses, rickettsial bacteria, fungus, worms, and animal parasites.
4. Spread: The organism is food-borne, water-borne, or soil-borne; is transmitted by insect carriers (vectors); is spread by animals, or humans, that carry the organisms; and/or is prenatal.
5. 5 classic symptoms: dolor (pain), calor (heat), rubor (tissue redness), tumor (swelling) and disorders of body function. Inflammation and rubor may occur independently.
6. Infection classification:

   Acute (sudden); chronic (protracted or lengthy); subacute (intermediate between acute and chronic); airborne; apical (tooth tip); concurrent (2 or more infections at once); contagious (spread by contact with people); cross contact (kissing, utensils, people); droplet; dust-borne; endogenous (bacteria living in system – digestive tract); fungal; local (one area, like a boil); low-grade (mild inflammation and no pus); metastatic (moves from infection focus); mixed (2 or more organisms); opportunistic (AIDS); protozoal; pyogenic (caused by pus-producing organism); secondary (an organism different from the primary organism causes the infection); simple (one cause); subclinical (infection immunologically confirmed, but with no clinical symptom); systemic (it is seen throughout the body and not localized like an abscess); terminal (seen in the late stages of a disease – usually acute, septic, and causing death); waterborne (organism present in water).

ACUTE INFECTION

1. Our lymph nodes battle invaders arriving by way of the lymph vessels.
2. Macrophages engulf the bacteria, digest them, and display a chemical identifying marker on its own surface. These macrophages now present this chemical marker to the helper T-white blood cells, which respond by multiplying rapidly.
3. The T-cell offspring produces lymphokines which call more defenders known as B-cells. Only the ones that can recognize the bacteria or markers respond, link up with the bacteria, and keep multiplying.
4. Some of these B-cells become memory cells and store information to help the body fight the germ another day.
5. Other B-cells become plasma cells and join the battle by spewing out thousands of antibodies every second. These antibodies attach to the bacteria and force them to clump together. Now the macrophages swallow the bacterial clump or kill the bacteria or invader by puncturing the organism's cell wall.
6. Scavenging macrophages clean the lymph nodes (debris), engulfing antibodies, and bacteria until the infection subsides.

Acute (sudden, severe, sharp Lt.); Chronic (long, drawn out Gk.)

Bacteria

Macrophages

. Antibodies

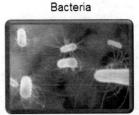 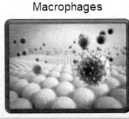 

INFLAMMATION (characteristics)
Rubor (red); Calor (heat); Tumor (swelling); Dolor (pain)

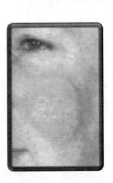

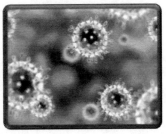

1. Inflammation: This is the body's response to local infection. Its primary function is to contain infections, toxins, or other substances. It is a response within body blood vessels.
2. Histamine and prostaglandins are released into the vessels against the inflammatory substance. Vessels leak, widen, and increase their blood flow. Rubor (redness), calor (heat), and tumor (swelling) result, and eventually these cause dolor (pain).
3. Toxin and chemical messengers released from the damage tissue attract white blood cells (phagocytes). They clump together and squeeze out through the vessel walls to destroy the invaders that have migrated into the tissues.
4. Pus is produced if bacteria, WBCs, and damaged body cells are present.
5. An abscess is a protective membrane around the site.

Remember: An infectious disease is caused by the growth of organisms in the body that may or may not be contagious.

FEVER OR PYREXIA
(to be feverish Gk.)

1. Fever slows or stops the growth of invading organisms. It begins when organisms invade the tissues and the macrophages (WBCs) engulf them, releasing the chemical messenger Interleukin – 1.
2. Interleukin – 1 travels to the brain by the blood and causes the part of the hypothalamus that regulates body temperature to be stimulated, thereby raising body temperature.
3. To assist in this process, the body's muscles contract slightly because of the brain's nerve stimulation; we shiver, which causes heat; our surface blood vessels contract, limiting surface heat loss; and fat is broken down, releasing calories, which causes heat or body warmth (fever).

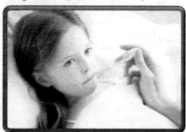

Normal (98.6° (degrees) F. or 37° C.)
Low fever (99° to 101° F.)
Moderate fever (101° to 103° F.)
High fever (103° to 105° F.)

PICTURES OF ETIO/LOG/IC (cause/study of/refers to) DISEASE AGENTS

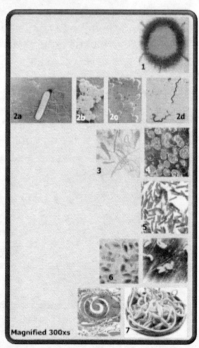

1. **Viruses**: Colds, flu, M.M.R., and polio;
2. **Bacteria**: (Bacillus): T. B. mycobacterium tuberculosis; (coccus): rheumatic fever, pneumonia, and meningitis; Staphylococcus, Streptococcus, Pneumococcus, Meningococcus (Spirochetes) syphilis and yaws;
3. **Fungus**: Athletes foot, jock itch, and dermatitis epidermophyton floccosum;
4. **Chlamydia**: LGV and urethritis (smallest bacteria-like organisms attacking the eyes, genitals, and lungs);
5. **Rickettsiae**: Q-fever and RMSF (Rickettsia coxiella burnetii);
6. **Protozoa**: Diarrhea, trichomoniasis, Giardiasis, toxoplasmosis (single celled animals- Toxoplasma gondii from uncooked meats or feces of infected birds and cats);
7. **Helminths (worms or larva)**: roundworms, pinworms, flatworms, tapeworms, flukes, hookworms (Trichinella spiralis: trichinosis)

Magnified 300xs

SIGN
(Something you SEE: Observation that is Objective)

1. Any objective evidence or manifestation of an illness.
2. Signs are usually definitive and obvious, in contrast with symptoms, which are subjective.
3. Signs might include a rash, bruise, melanoma, or bleeding.
4. Symptoms are subjective.
5. A Syn/drome is a combination of Signs and Symptoms that represent a Specific Disease Process.
6. These are conditions perceived by the examiner – such as a fever, rash, sounds, redness, and itching. They often accompany subjective symptom patient responses.

Penicillin Rash
(Inflammation Diagnostic Sign)

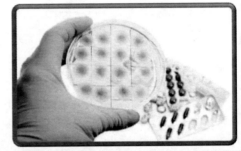

SYMPTOM
(Something described to you: occurrences that are subjective)

1. Symptoma in Greek means an occurrence.
2. Any change in the body or its function that indicates a disease process.
3. Symptoms are usually subjective and include things such as pain, numbness, sounds, nausea, and emesis (vomit).
4. General aspects include:
   A. Onset – date, manner;
   B. Characteristics – location, severity, timing, relieving factors;
   C. Course – progress and effects of therapy.
5. Some symptoms, like numbness, can be clinically confirmed (e.g. by a needle prick).

Example pain: tooth/ache (donto/dynia);
stomach/ache (gastro/dynia);
muscle/ache (my/algia)

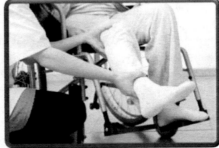

Joint pain associated with osteo/arthr/itis
and osteo/por/osis

SYN/DROME (together/running Gk.)
A running together of signs and symptoms

1. A group of signs and symptoms that together indicate a particular disease or condition.
2. Examples are: toxic shock syndrome (TSS), Marfan syndrome (MS), and acquired immune deficiency syndrome (AIDS).

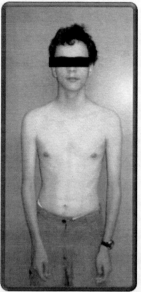

Marfan syndrome in a 17-year-old boy. He had a height of 184 cm, weight of 60.4 kg and head circumference of 57 cm.

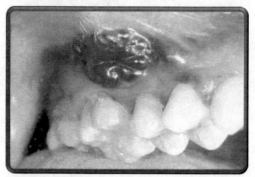

Patient with AIDS (signs and symptoms) The doctor sees the signs and the patient describes the symptoms.

Roberts JL, Gandomi SK, Parra M, Lu I, Gau CL, Dasouki M, Butler MG. Case Reports in Genetics (2014)

PROCEDURE (to proceed Lt.)
Exact steps to follow

1. An established way of accomplishing a desired result in medicine. Exact steps are usually followed by the doctor.
2. Examples are:
   A. Cardiac surgery;
   B. Radiation therapy; or any type of
   C. Dia/gnostic procedure.

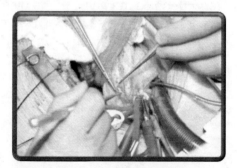

Surgical or diagnostic procedure: Lapar/o/tom/y – abdomen/incision and a Cystectomy – bladder excision

Procedure: specific established steps

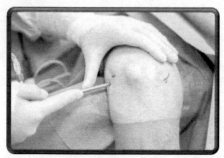

Endo/scop/ic procedure

TREATMENT (therapy/process of Gk.)

1. Medical, surgical, or psychiatric management of a patient.
2. Any specific procedure used to treat, cure, or relieve a health problem associated with a disease (drug treatment or therapy is often used to prevent or cure a disease).

Drug treatment or therapy

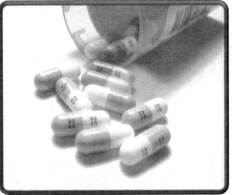

Fluoxetine (Prozac) 20 mg capsules
Varco, T. Wikimedia Commons (2006)

St. John's wort
Seaton, L. Wikimedia Commons (2011)

St. John's Wort herbal medicine or pharmacopoeia prescriptions (for depression)

DIA/GNOSIS (total/knowledge – Gk.)
Dia- complete, across, or total (Gk.); -gno/se knowledge (Gk.); -osis condition (Gk.)

1. Determination of cause or nature of disease.
2. Term denotes the name of the disease or the syndrome. Examples are AIDS and Parkinson's (British physician) disease.
3. Diagnosis is made by evaluating the history, conducting a thorough physical examination, noting signs and symptoms, and reviewing laboratory data and special tests.

Kaposi's (Austrian) sarcoma lesions

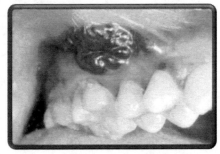

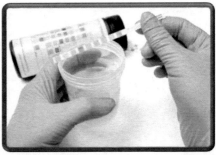

Chemical strips: Testing for glucose, blood, and protein chemistry.

Glucose in urine causes litmus strip color change

CLINIC/AL DIA/GNOSIS
(bedside/refers: complete/knowledge)

1. A clinical diagnosis is when the anatomy and/or physiology of the patient changes sufficiently to show signs and symptoms in the patient without the benefit of a laboratory test or X-ray.
2. Clinical means a place of medical treatment and is formally called a dispensary. A clinical meeting is usually a seminar or a place for bedside instruction for medical personnel.

3. Clinical laboratory tests are tests carried out related to the care of the patient. Materials that are obtained from the patient – not research – are used for diagnosis.
4. Clinical disease is a stage in the history of a disease that begins with a change in structure (anatomy) and function (physiology) that is sufficient to produce signs and symptoms that are recognizable in the patient.

PRO/GNOSIS (before/knowledge – Gk.)
pro- (before Gk.); -gnose (knowledge or forecast Gk.)

1. Prediction of a course or end of a disease. It is an estimation of chance for recovery.
2. Examples would be favorable, unfavorable, doubtful, or poor.
3. Pro/gnosis (before/knowledge): After studying examinations, tests, histories, signs, and symptoms (etc.) you forecast the patient's future (disease or condition expectations).

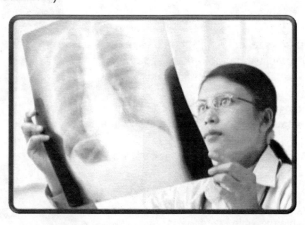

EXAMIN/ATION (inspection/procedure of – Gk.)

In/spect/ion Lt.: A procedure or the inward and outward viewing process.

1. The act or process of inspecting the body and its systems to determine disease (or absences).
2. The term used denotes the type of exam such as oral, physical, rectal, X-ray, or cardiovascular exam.
3. Process includes palpation, percussion, auscultation, and inspection.

Thyroid exam

Electro/photo/micro/scop/e
(tissue exams)

Stress test
(cardio/vascular exam
with EKG)

KNEE EXAMINATIONS (inspection Lt.) AND SURGERY (working by hand – Gk.)

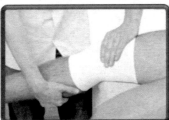

Anterior cruciate ligament exam (Tear: excessive forward movement)

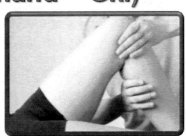

Collateral ligaments (2/sides)
medial aspect exam

1. One of the more common sites of athletic injuries.
2. This exam evaluates the kneecap, tibia, and femoral bones and the ligaments that hold them together (attach bone to bone). These bones are separated by cartilaginous cushions.
3. The two most common ligament tears are the anterior cruciate (cross-shaped) ligament and collateral ligament tear.
4. Anterior cruciate cross laxity (excess backward or downward movements).
5. This picture illustrates arthro/scop/ic knee surgery.

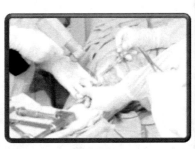

Ligament: shiny flexible band of connective tissue

ARTHRO/SCOP/IC (joint/viewing/refers to) KNEE SURGERY

Katzenberger, M. S.
for Army Medicine.
Flickr (2012)

This individual is performing an exam of the knee. This type of exam tests for pain or tearing in the lateral and medial collateral ligaments.

Endo/scopic surgery: (scope; suction; cutter)

Before meniscus surgery

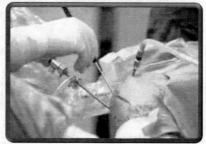

Medial meniscus surgery (Crescent Gk.) torn cartilage

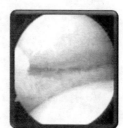

After meniscus surgery

SELF BREAST EXAMINATION
(in/spection/process of – Lt.)

1. A technique that enables women to find changes in their breasts.
2. Should be performed monthly, after menstrual periods.
3. Especially useful for early detection of breast cancer.
4. Forty percent of breast cancers are found as a result of self breast examinations.
5. Skin and breast cancers are the most commonly diagnosed cancers for American women. About 1 in 8 U.S. women will develop invasive breast cancer.
6. Examination includes standing in front of a mirror and inspecting the breasts for changes in the nipple, dimpling (pucker) of the skin, as well as palpating for lumps.
7. Exam should be done in standing and reclining position with chest muscles being contracted and relaxed.
8. Lumps or thickening in breast tissue should be reported to a physician.

Inspection

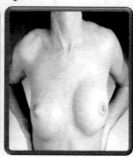

Normal

Palpation: pie shaped slices

Palpation: clockwise and counter clockwise (reclining and sitting positions)

National Cancer Institute. Wikimedia Commons (1985)

MAMMO/GRAM (breast/recording)

Roent/geno/graph/ic or low-dose X-ray recordings of breasts:
Plastic plates compress breast tissue for X-ray

THERMO/GRAM (heat or temperature/recording)

Heat or temperature/recordings: Used to diagnose cancer

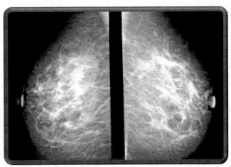

Normal

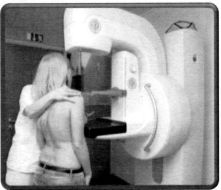

Mammo/graph/y
(breast/X-ray recoding with an
instrument/procedure of)

URIN/ALYSIS
(urine/analysis)

1. Array of tests performed on urine – one the most common methods of medical diagnosis.
2. Urine is examined with test strips or under a light microscope.
3. Used for detecting ions, trace minerals, proteins, enzymes, blood cells, glucose, ketone bodies and other molecules.
4. Pregnancy, drug use and infections (sexually or non-sexually transmitted) along with a number of diseases can be diagnosed with urine tests.

THERMO/GRAM
(heat or temperature/recording)

1. Device used for detecting heat variations. It is used to study blood flow in tissues, to detect pain, tissue changes, and/or cancer.
2. Arterio/scler/o/sis and tumors slows blood flow to tissues.
3. The computer generates colors representing heat in the tissues. Asymmetries in temperature mapping indicate physiological abnormalities.

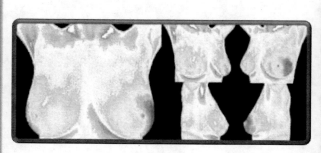 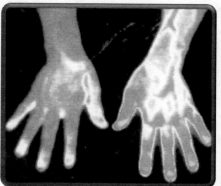

Arterio/scler/o/sis
(Poor Circulation Left Arm)

TEST (exam in vessel – Lt.)

1. Testum in Latin means earthen vessel.
2. It refers to the original tests in a test tube or test vessel.
3. This method is used to determine the presence or nature of a disease or substance.
4. Hundreds of physical tests:
   - **A. Patch skin test**
   - **B. Glucose tolerance test** determines body's ability to metabolize glucose;
   - **C. Blood tests**

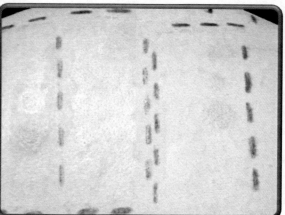

Eczema
(boil out Lt.)
reaction

TEST CONTINUED

D. **Finger to Nose Test**: Used to determine neural function and balance;
E. **Scratch Allergy Test**: Antigens are applied to the skin surface;
F. **Serologic Test**: Performed on blood serum;
G. **Mantoux Test**: Used to detect tuberculosis (TB);
H. **Schick Test**: Used to detect diphtheria.

Mantoux test
(positive-raised response or reaction)

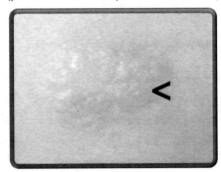

Indicated TB antibodies are present in body
(required X-ray if positive)

CULTURE PLATE TEST

1. Propagation of live microscopic tissue cells or biological organisms in special growth media (agar).
2. Diagnoses specific infectious diseases.
3. Body cells and patho/gen/ic cells are used in culture media.

Staphylo/coccus   **Aureus**

grapes/spheres or berry   gold or gold-like

Many forms are penicillin-resistant.

TUNING FORK EAR EXAM (hearing test)

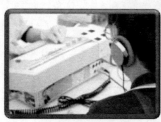

1. When the tuning fork or Instrument is struck at the end, the vibrations are 256 cycles or more per second (this can be heard and felt by the patient). The Heinrich Rinne test (German otologist 1819-1869) distinguishes conductive (air conduction sounds 2X longer) from sensori/neural hearing loss. It uses fork cycles of 256, 512, and 1024.

2. This is a sensori/neural test for loss of hearing (bone conduction and vibrations).

3. Word recognition and impedance tests or measurements and tone and air pressure tests are used to detect middle ear damage. The sound reflects back as pressure changes from the eardrum. This produces a tympano/gram that shows middle ear bone movement.

4. Mechanical deafness is where there is a problem in the middle ear (drum or bones) going to inner ear.

5. Conductive deafness is a problem in the inner ear (auditory nerve – ETC.) going to the brain.

6. Audio/metr/y test (audiometrics) examines loudness of decibels marked on an audio/gram.

7. Weber's test examines bone vibration conduction to the bones of the middle ear and into the inner ear.

8. Tuning fork test on the mastoid process of the skull

9. Ear wax buildup removal with cerumeno/lyt/ic (earwax/breaking/pertaining to) drops.

INTRA/VEN/OUS (IV) IN/JECTION
(within/vein/refers to: within/to throw/refers to)

Phleb/o/tom/ist (vein/cut/specialist)
1. A tourniquet is used to stop the venous return, not the arterial flow, into the arm.
2. Needle insertion is required several inches beyond tourniquet.
3. If no arterial pulse, loosen band.
4. Area heat helps insertion by distension of vessels.

Superficial vein: 3 tunics (layers)

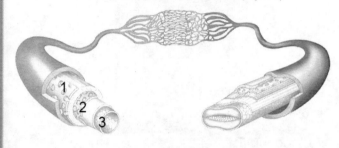 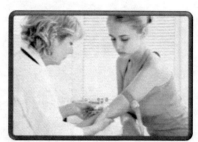

1 T.A. (Tunica Adventitia)
2 T.M. (Tunica Media)
3 T.I. (Tunica Intima)

INTRA/MUSCULAR (IM) INJECTION
(within/muscle/refers to: within/to throw/refers to)

Blood Centrifuging (center/flee Lt.). Blood is spun at high speeds. Plasma rises to the top, WBCs in the middle, and heavier RBCs to the bottom.

5. 5-10 ml syringe helps control the needle.
6. Beveled side of the needle faces up and is rotated away after insertion.
7. The vein gives resistance as the needle enters it.
8. A narrow angle is used so the needle enters the long axis of the vein without pushing through.
9. Used for taking blood samples or injecting fluids and medication.

PHLEB/O/TOM/Y (vein/cut/procedure of – Gk.)

1. AKA: Vene/sect/ion or vene/puncture.
2. Opening or piercing vein (to draw blood for analysis or inject medications).
3. Procedure used for diagnostic purposes.
4. Used in emergencies to access weak or small veins.

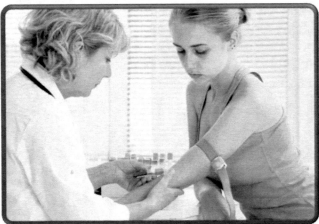

Phlebo/tom/ist

AN/ESTHES/IA (without/feeling (physical) / refers to)

1. Partial or complete loss of sensation with or without loss of consciousness. This is a result of disease, injury or administration of an anesthetic agent by inhalation or injection.
2. There are three main categories of an/esthesia: local, regional, and general.
3. A/phor/ia: Without/feeling (mental)/refers to.
4. Patient-controlled an/algesic device: Self-administered set dose of a drug to prevent pain. A lockout device is used to prevent early or additional administration of analgesic.

Local anesthesia for mole excision 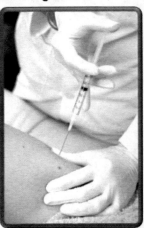 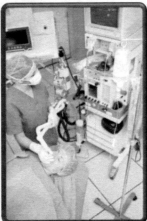 General anesthesia

RADIO/GRAM (X-ray/recording – Lt.)
RADIO/GRAPH (X-ray/process of using instrument/procedure of Lt.)

1. Creating an image of a body part by transmitting radioactive energy (X or gamma rays) through that part and onto a sensitized plate, film, or paper.
2. The image is caused by the action of roentgen rays or radium.
3. X-ray (AKA: radiogram): A picture of internal organs or structures.

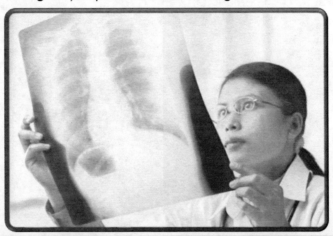

RADIO/GRAMS (spoke-like ray/recording – Lt.)
AKA: X-RAYS

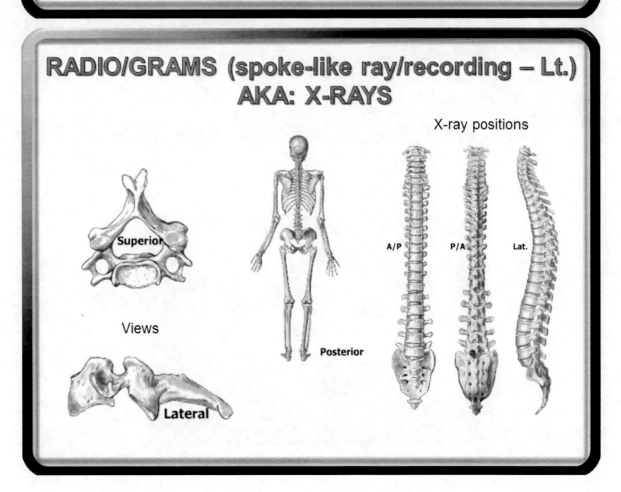

X-ray positions

Superior

Views

Lateral

Posterior

A/P   P/A   Lat.

FLUORO/SCOP/Y (AKA: PHOTO/SCOP/Y)
(discharge "serial motion X-rays"/viewing/procedure of – Lt.)

1. X-ray Fluoro/scop/y: The use of a Fluoroscope for diagnosis or for testing in motion various materials by X-ray.
2. Fluoro/scop/e: A device consisting of a fluorescent screen suitable to monitor either separately or in conjunction with a roentgen tube. The image of an object is seen as shadows.

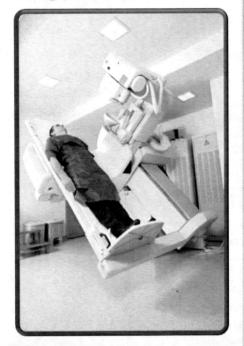

RADIO/THERAP/Y
(radiation/treatment or cure/procedure of – Lt.)

1. Treatment of a disease through the application of roentgen rays, radium, ultraviolet rays and other forms of radiation.
2. Radio/therap/y is shown here being applied to a malignant schwann/oma, also known as a neur/oma (nerve/tumor.)

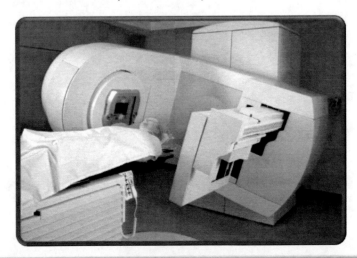

ANGIO/GRAM (vessel/recording – Lt.)

1. Serial X-rays of blood vessels taken in rapid sequence following the injection of radi/opaque dye into blood vessels.
2. Used to determine size and shape of arteries and veins or organs and tissues.

Digital subtraction angio/gram: This is an X-ray that is taken before the injection of dye. X-ray after the dye is injected is subtracted electronically from the picture of the vessels of the same area. The new image is clearly outlined as an abdominal aneurysm. Emergency surgery is required.

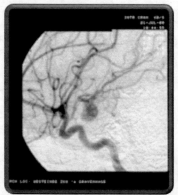

Angiogram of an aneurysm in an cerebral artery
Monfils, L. Wikimedia Commons (2000)

ANGIO/CARDIO/GRAPH/Y

(vessel/heart/procedure of using an instrument to record – Lt.)

1. Serial X-rays of the heart taken immediately after an intravenous injection of a Radi/opaque medium or dye.
2. This special type of roentgeno/graph/y (X-ray procedure) is called: angio/cardio/graph/y.
3. It is the process of taking of a series of pictures of the heart and great blood vessels.

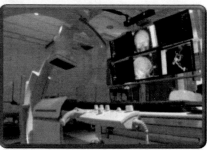

Angio/cardio/graph/ic theater
X-ray machine; monitor; dye catheter (to let down into Gk.)

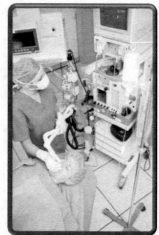

Anesthetic cart
The cart is moveable. It holds gas, oxygen flow rate meter, pump, spare gas cylinder, and various drugs.

KUB EXAMINATION
(kidney, ureter, and/or urinary bladder: inspection Gk.)

1. The KUB examination takes place when a diagnostic radiographic instrument is used to determine the kidney, ureter and/or urinary bladder structure (size, shape, location and malformations).
2. This is usually used to detect urinary system stones and calcified areas.

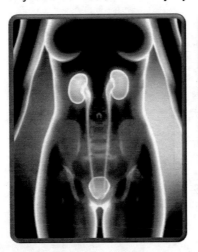
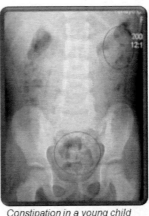

Constipation in a young child
Heilman, J. Wikimedia Commons (2009)

PYELO/GRAM (pelvis (kidney) / recording – Lt.)

1. This is a diagnostic exam of the urinary system by X-ray. Specifically, the kidney and the kidney pelvis where the urine accumulates in the kidney. Remember: A pyelogram is an X-ray recording resulting from the diagnostic exam (pyelography); and this test is done by an instrument called a pyelograph.
2. A radi/opaque material is given intravenously and an X-ray is taken while this material is being excreted.
3. It gives information as to the structure and function of this urine-producing body system.

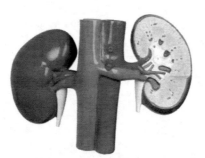

Abnormal urinary dilation caused by ureter stone or steno/tic infection

Kidney

Urinary Bladder

MYELO/GRAM
(spinal cord or bone marrow – Gk./recording – Lt.)

1. Myelo/gram (spinal cord/recording): This is an X-ray film taken after a radio/paque medium (dye) is injected into the meninges sub/arachn/oid space.
2. It is used to demonstrate any distortions of the spinal cord, spinal nerve roots, and sub/arachn/oid space.

MYELO/GRAM
(bone marrow – Gk./recording – Lt.)

1. The term also represents the graphic count of the different types of cells in a stained bone marrow preparation.
2. The differential count of bone marrow cells.

Myelo/graph/y intra/thecal space
recording within spinal cord canal

PHAKIC INTRA/OCULAR LENSES

1. Phakic intra/ocular lenses are an alternative to LASIK and other eye surgeries for correcting moderate to severe myopia (nearsightedness).
2. Phakic IOLs are clear, implantable lenses that are surgically placed between the cornea and the iris, or just behind the iris, without removing the natural lens.
3. It enables light to focus properly on the retina, thus clearer vision. It works like a contact lens, but inside the eye.
4. The implants cannot be felt and typically do not require any maintenance.

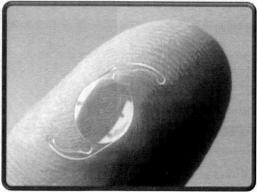

Muller, F. Wikimedia Commons. (2012)

LASIK

(Laser In-Situ Kerato/milieusis)
(laser/into site/cornea middle Fr.)

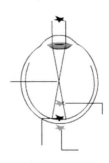

1. As of 2011, more than 11 million Lasik procedures have been performed in the U.S.
2. It involves cutting a flap in the cornea and reshaping the middle of the cornea with a sharp laser beam. 1-5% have side-effects (blurred vision, spots, night glare). The long term effects are still unknown.
3. Athletes and other groups have had great success for several years.
4. Non-candidates include youth under 20 and people with thick or curved corneas.

Cornea too thick

Cornea too thin

ELECTRO/CARDIO/GRAM

(electrical/heart/record or writing – Lt.)

1. Record of electrical activity of the heart showing P, Q, R, S, T and sometimes U waves.
2. The P wave is the depolarization of the atrial muscle tissues, which in turn causes an atrial contraction.
3. The Q, R, S and T waves are related to ventricle contraction.
4. Electro/cardio/graph EKG or ECG machine (instrument).

 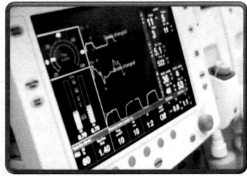

ELECTRO/CARDIO/GRAM
(electrical/heart/record or writing)

1. This records important information on the spread of excitement to different parts of the heart.
2. It is especially important in the diagnosis of irregular heart rhythms and/or heart muscle damage.

Tachy/cardia: HR 120+
EKG stress test

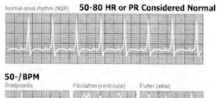

Normal sinus rhythm (NSR) **50-80 HR or PR Considered Normal**

50-/BPM

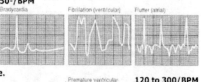

Bradycardia Fibrillation (ventricular) Flutter (atrial)

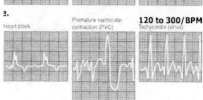

Heart block Premature ventricular contraction (PVC) **120 to 300/BPM** Tachycardia (sinus)

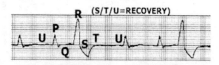

(S/T/U=RECOVERY)

R (QRS ventricular contraction = .12 sec.)
P (U/P/Q atrial contraction = .18 sec.)
T (recovery)

DE/FIBRILLAT/OR IM/PLANT/ATION
(away/small contraction/one who) (in/plant/process)

1. Implantation is the artificial placement of a material or substance into the body.
2. The cardiac defibrillator is a device that automatically terminates lethal ventricular arrhythmias by delivering low-energy shocks to the heart, restoring rhythm. This happens only when beats are rapid or erratic.
3. SA node or pacemaker is located at the junction of superior vena cava and right atrium. It starts atrium contraction that forwards waves to the AV node. Used with bradycardia (slow/heart).

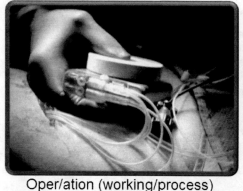

Oper/ation (working/process)

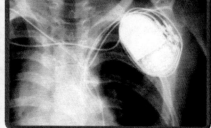

Pacemaker

ELECTRO/EN/CEPHALO/GRAPH/Y
(EEG) (electric/in/head/recording process)

1. The amplification, recording, and analysis of brain electrical activity similar to electro/cardio/graph/y.
2. Electro/en/cephalo/gram (EEG) is the record produced.
3. Diagnostic tool useful in determining epilepsy and brain lesions.
4. The predominant brain waves are beta (alert); alpha (sleepy); theta (light sleep); and delta (deep sleep).

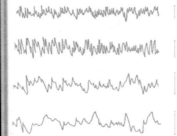

BETA:
Alert, Working

ALPHA:
Relaxed, Reflective

THETA:
Drowsy, Meditative

DELTA:
Sleepy, Dreaming

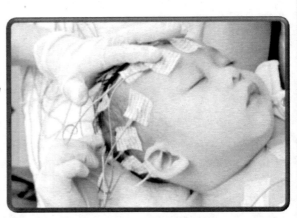

ELECTRO/MYO/GRAPH/Y
(electric/muscle/recording with instrument/procedure of)

1. This is the process of preparing, studying, and interpreting the recordings (-grams).
2. This is the graphic record of the contractions of a muscle as a result of electrical stimulation.
3. It is used to diagnose diseases such as muscular dystrophy, myasthenia gravis, ALS and polio.

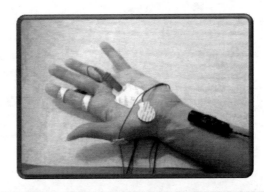

MAGNETIC RESONANCE IMAGING (MRI)

1. Series of cross-sectional images of body parts by means of nuclear magnetic resonance technology.
2. Radio frequency pulses are applied to displace the nuclei of the body's hydrogen atoms.
3. Imaging scanner records radio signals given off by the tissue while lying in a magnetic field bombarded by the radio waves. The computer converts the signals to images.

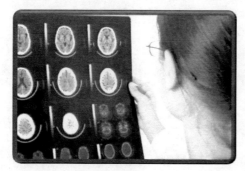 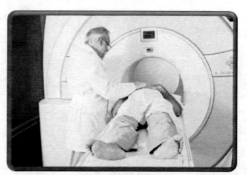

Radio/graph/er
(X-ray/instrument/one who uses)

1. Laboratory examinations include urinalysis, blood tests, cultures, and techniques of viewing body spaces and organs such as the M.R.I.
2. Below is a computer axial tomography, which takes transverse plane tissue Slices with X-ray beam (brain usually) by blurring other plane structures.

3D PRINTING

1. 3D printing technology has opened up numerous avenues for medical treatments for conditions that previously required transplants from living tissue or more expensive prosthetic devices.
2. 3D printing has been used to produce low-cost prosthetic limbs for children and people in developing nations.
3. 3D printed synthetic skull segments have been implanted in the skulls of several individuals internationally to repair damage from traumatic accidents.
4. Experiments are underway in the production of synthetic skin, anatomical features like ears, full bones, and organs like livers and kidneys.
5. Spritam was the first 3D-printed drug to be approved by the FDA. More drugs are expected to be offered in 3D print form over time.

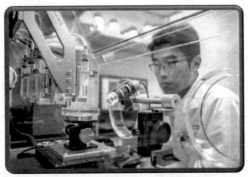

Bioprinting tissue at the Young-Joon Seol Wake Forest Institute for Regenerative Medicine
Dean, R. for U.S. Army Material Command. Flickr. (2013)

GAMMA KNIFE SURGERY

1. The gamma knife is one type of stereo/tactic radio/surgery. The procedure utilizes a linear-accelerator (LINAC) or a cyclotron.
2. Diagnostic images are taken of the patient's brain, then used by the neurosurgeon and radiologist to define the exact margins of tumor that will receive gamma ray energy beams.
3. The patient is then fitted with one of many large metal helmets that have holes through which the beams of energy are transmitted to the exact section of the brain requiring treatment.

4. This special type of head equipment uses approximately 100 head rings that have been fitted into the very heavy head helmet seen below.
5. These openings in the various helmets allow radiation to pass through in a three-dimensional fashion to the precise deep-seated brain tumor or tissue that must be destroyed or treated. These areas can vary in size from 3 to 24 mm.

STETHO/SCOP/E
(chest/examine/instrument)

1. This instrument is used to examine, amplify, and clarify sounds produced in the body, especially respiratory and cardiovascular sounds.
   stethos – chest Gk.; pectoralis – chest or breast Lt.; thorakos – thorax or chest Gk.;
   skopein – scope or examine or view Gk.; -e – means instrument or device Gk.

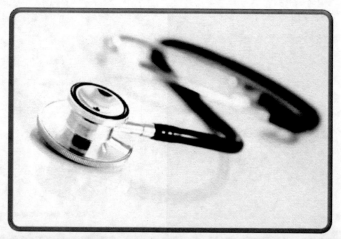

AUSCULT/ATION
(to listen Lt./procedure or process of)

1. Process of listening for sounds in the chest or abdominal areas to detect abnormal conditions.
2. The stethoscope is placed against the skin to examine specific areas in the body according to their anatomical position.
3. Usually the heart and lungs are primary sites of examination.

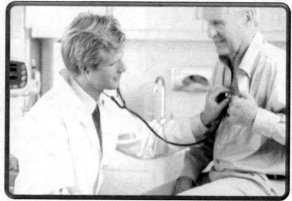

Stetho/scop/ic examin/ation
(chest/exam/refers to : inspection/procedure of)

PERCUSS/ION
(striking Lt./procedure or process)

1. The clinician uses his/her fingertips to tap the body lightly but sharply to determine the position, size, and consistency of underlying structures or the presence of fluid or pus in a cavity.
2. Sound pitch, vibration, and the resistance encountered indicated what is below the skin.

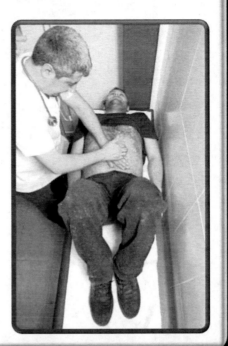

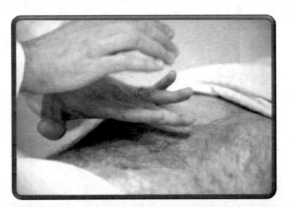

SPHYGMO/MANO/METER
(pulse/hand/measure Gk.)

1. Instrument used to determine arterial blood pressure above atmospheric pressure.
2. There are two types: mercury and aneroid instruments.
3. Normal blood pressure is: less than 120/over 80-mm/Hg. 120 sy/stolic (to draw together) – left ventricle contraction force or to empty.
4. Less than 80 dia/stolic (setting totally empty or relaxation pressure) – chambers filling.
5. (Left ventricle relaxing with the second sound – pressure continues in system because it's a closed system)
6. Hypertension – high blood pressure (HBP): 120/80 + (borderline) requires behavioral changes; 160/100 requires medication.
7. Hypotension – low blood pressure (LBP): 90/60 or lower reading.

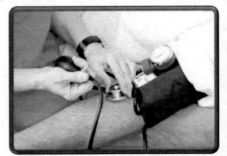
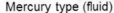

Mercury type (fluid)　　　　Aner/oid type (without/fluid/resembles)

ULTRA/SONO/GRAPH/Y
(beyond normal ranges/sound/process of recording)

1. AKA: Sono/graph/y and echo/graph/y (sono- and echo- mean sound)
2. This is the process of using ultrasound to produce an image or photograph of an organ or tissue.
3. The echoes show density of structure.
4. Inaudible sound frequencies range from 20,000 to 10 billion cycles per second.

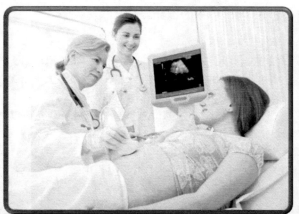

ULTRA/SONO/GRAPH/Y
(beyond normal ranges/sound/process of recording)

1. There are different velocities in tissues that differ with density and elasticity (lower ranges used for images and diagnosis)
2. Used to outline shapes of various tissues and organs during diagnostic procedures.
3. Therapeutic ultra/sound requires special equipment.
4. Higher sound ranges are used for treatment; heat is produced that aids healing.

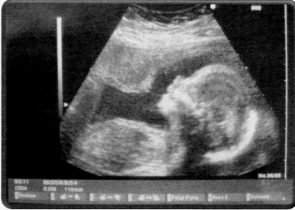

ULTRA/SONO/GRAPH/Y

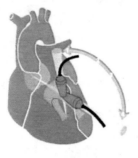

Echo/cardi/o/log/y planes

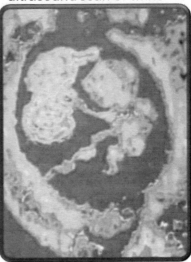

Color-enhanced
ultrasound scan of twins

1. Inaudible sound frequencies from 20,000 to 10 million per second that are used for therapy (heat) or diagnosis (imaging);
2. These echoes are recorded to diagnose tissue or organ changes.
   Types: **echo/cardio/gram**;
   echo/encephalo/gram.

PET SCAN (Positron-Emission Tom/ography)

Brains (below) as diagnosed by PET Scan: (1) normal; (2) schizophrenic; (3) dementia. Scanner is sensitive to radioactive tracer material given with glucose. This nutrient, passing through the brain, indicated whether cells metabolize the glucose nutrients and produce tissue energy. The chemical activity energy bursts are observed below.

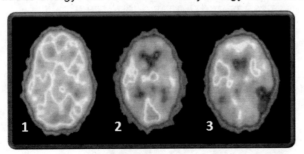
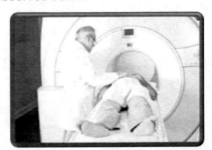

CAT OR CT SCAN
(Computerized Axial Tomography)

The scanner X-rays the brain in rotating beams (360 degrees), slices, or cross sections around the periphery and is 100 times more sensitive than X-rays (17 frames/second shows heart function and blood flow). The computer then screens and displays detailed cuts viewed from any angle (like egg cut crosswise). It shows tissue density of tumor masses, bones and fluid build-up.

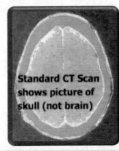

Standard CT Scan
shows picture of
skull (not brain)

PET BRAIN SCANS
(Glucose Mapping)

1. Tissue energy produced by glucose meta/bol/ization by local cells in the brain. This can be carried in other body tissues, including the heart, liver, and kidneys.

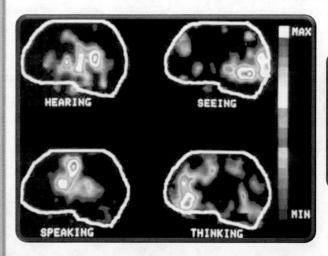 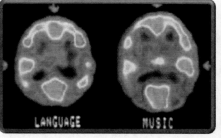

THALLIUM 201 SCAN

1. AKA: Nuclear scan, cold spot myocardial imaging. This is a nuclear or radio/iso/top/ic scan used to evaluate the heart.
2. This non-invasive test is used to evaluate coronary artery disease and the severity of heart attacks.
3. You inject a small amount of radioactive thallium Isotopes intravenously (poisoning leads to thallo/toxic/osis).
4. It is absorbed mainly in normal tissue. If the thallium is not absorbed, that is a cold spot (no blood flow because of a heart attack or disease).

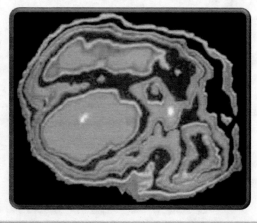

Cardiac thallium scan

BI/O/PS/Y
(bio-: life / ops -: view / -y: procedure of)

1. Ex/cis/ion of a small piece of live tissue for micro/scop/ic exam.
2. Usually performed to establish a dia/gnosis.
3. Trephin/e (to bore Fr.) is a cylindrical saw used for cutting a circular piece of bone.
4. A. **Bone marrow aspiration biopsies** used for leuk/emia; an/emia; infections; various cancers; thrombo/cyto/penia; and a/granulo/cyto/sis;
   B. **Punch tissue biopsy**;
   C. **Needle cyst biopsy**

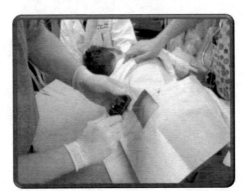

Typical biopsy aspiration sites

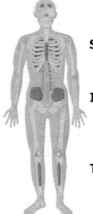

Sternum

Ilium

Tibia

OTHER BIOPSY TYPES

D. **Needle**: Tissue from lumps in breasts, organs and marrow;
E. **Curette**: Fork-like instrument to scrape tissue for biopsy – usually uterus;
F. **Endoscopic**: Flexible lighted tube through nose, mouth, anus to intestines (pincer device removes tissue);
G. **Con/ization**; and
H. **Ex/cis/ion/al biopsy**.

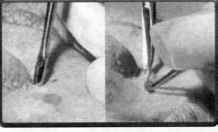

Scalpel conization plug (specialized)

Skin ex/cis/ion/al biopsy (removes entire growth)

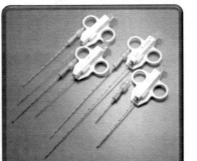

Biopsy aspiration equipment

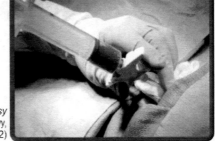

Bone Marrow Biopsy
McNeeley, C. for the U.S. Navy,
Wikimedia Commons (2002)

90

BRONCHO/SCOP/E
(trachea-like/viewing/instrument);
ENDOSCOP/Y
(within/instrument-view: examine/process)

1. Endo/scop/ic exams allow the visual inspection of the trachea and the bronchial tree.
2. Also used to biopsy tissue samples and to remove foreign bodies (lighted and magnified)
3. Hospital endoscopy photoscan.

Bronchoscopy
Barreto, J. Wikimedia Commons (2010)

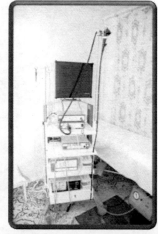

Endoscopic equipment

LARYNGO/SCOP/Y
(voice box/viewing/procedure of)

1. This is a type of endo/scop/y that is used to examine the larynx or voice box aided by a small, long-handled mirror.
2. Also used to visualize the area when placing an endo/tracheal tube.

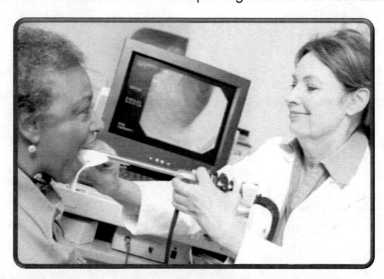

COLPO/SCOP/Y
(vagina/view or examine/procedure)

1. A diagnostic procedure or exam that views the vagina and cervical tissue using a colpo/scope.
2. It is used to select sites of abnormal epithelium for biopsy in patients with suspect Pap smears. It can define tumor extensions and identify benign lesions. It is also used in post/pubertal exams.

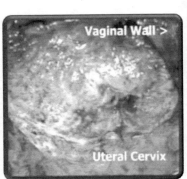

Acute colp/itis

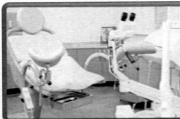

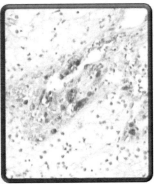

Herpes simplex II virus

SNELLEN EYE CHART

1. This chart is printed with black letters ranging in size (large letters on the top row to small on the bottom row).
2. It is used to test visual acuity (clearness or sharpness).
3. A 20/20 score means that a person standing 20 feet away is able to read the majority of the letters on the 20/20 line.
4. This procedure is named for a Dutch ophthalmologist Herman Snellen (1834 to 1908).
5. The Ishihara test is a red/green colorblindness test. If your color sight is normal you should see the number 57 in the circle.

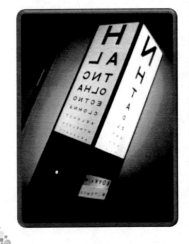

SNELLEN CHARTS
(Letter and E Charts)

6. A 20/40 reading indicates that a person can only read the line 20 feet away that a normal sighted person can read at 40 feet away.
7. A person with an eyesight reading of 20/200 must read the line 20/200 twenty feet away. A person with normal sight could read the same line 200 feet away (legally blind in that eye).

E	1	20/200
F P	2	20/100
T O Z	3	20/70
L P E D	4	20/50
P E C F D	5	20/40
E D F C Z P	6	20/30
F E L O P Z D	7	20/25
D E F P O T E C	8	20/20
L E F O D P C T	9	
F D P L T C E O	10	
P E Z O L C F T D	11	

Novta, D. Flickr (2011)

OPHTHALMO/SCOP/E
(Eye/View or Examine/Instrument)

1. Instrument used to examine eye interior (especially the retina and disc).
2. Important for diagnosing diseases such as diabetes, glaucoma, high blood pressure, and arteriosclerosis.
3. Also measures refractive errors (deflection of straight light path) through the lens of the eye.
4. Opto/metr/ist O.D. (sight/measure/specialist).
5. Fluorescent dye photograph is taken under a blue light as the blood flows through the eye's blood vessels.
6. Slit lamp exam: The inner eye is illuminated by a lamp where intense light is emitted through a slit in the ophthalmoscope.

7. Some diagnosed problems:
   A. **My/opia** (thick cornea);
   B. **Hyper/opia** (thin cornea);
   C. **Presby/opia** (old sight);
   D. **Astigmatism** (oval cornea); and em/metr/opia (normal or good/measured/sight)
   (Note: Emmetros in Greek means proportioned and refers to normal/eye/measurement.)
   This normal sight refers to the light rays focusing correctly on the retina.

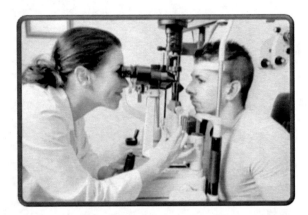

TONO/METER
(tension/measure)

1. Instrument used to measure pressure or tension within eye (on optic nerve and retina).
2. Detects glauc/oma (gray, cataract, or cloudiness – Lt.; opacity – Gk.).
3. Non-contact tono/metr/y uses a puff of air to determine alterations in the cornea that are caused by an increase in intra/ocular pressure.
4. The tono/meter fits a slit lamp with a flat and rounded head – end piece. This is placed against the cornea. The cornea is flattened in a small area and the pressure is increased to determine the intra/ocular eye pressure (normal is 13 to 22; glaucoma is up to 50).
5. Glaucoma exam is carried out to determine the inner eye pressure on the optic disc and retina.

MEDICAL LASER

1. Optic medical laser (light application by stimulated emission of radiation)
2. This is a source of intense monochromatic radiation of visible ultraviolet or the infrared portion of the light spectrum.
3. They are used to divide body tissue, to cause adhesions to form in the body, to destroy tissue, or to fixate tissues in place (-opexy) in the body.
4. Fiber/optic lasers open occluded arteries (like angio/plasty).
5. The CO_2 laser is used in the diagnosis and treatment of diseases of the lungs. In the eye it treats glaucoma (trabeculoplasty or iridotomy).
6. Pain management concentrates the laser beam on acupuncture points. The printers focus the beams on photosensitive areas.
7. Laser eye surgery: porphyrin (purple) dye is injected into tumor cells that retain the dye. Laser stops blood flow to the tumor with a photochemical reaction.
8. Red argon activates laser: Throat laser beams are directed through 4 fiber/optic wave guides or conduits to activate injected drug.

TRANS/CUTAN/EOUS ELECTR/ICAL NERVE STIMUL/ATION (TENS)

1. This is a form of physical therapy that controls pain by applying electrical stimulation to nerve endings.
2. The stimulator is attached to electrodes by flexible wires. The stimulation is similar to the body's own impulses, but different enough to block the transmission of pain signals to the brain.
3. This is non-invasive and non-addictive therapy. It has no side effects.
4. If one has a demand-type pacemaker for the heart, TENS should not be used in treatment.

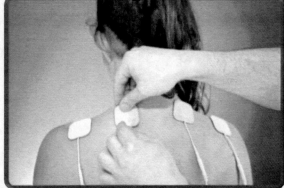

ELECTRO/CAUTERIZ/ATION
Elektron – spark/kauterion – branding iron (Gk.)

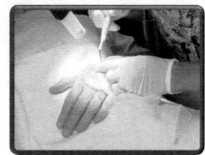

1. This is the use of a needle or snare heated by an electric current to destroy or remove warts or polyps, and to cauterize blood vessels during surgery.
2. AKA: Galvanocautery

DIA/THERM/Y
(through, total, or across/heat/process)

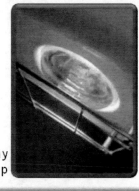

1. This is the use of heat current for therapy. The current is not strong enough to destroy tissues, but increases blood flow to the area for healing.
2. It is used with chronic arthritis, bursitis, fractures, sinusitis, and other conditions.

Diathermy heat lamp

PROSTHESIS
(means an addition Gk.)

1. Any replacement of a missing or damaged part by an artificial substitute.
2. It augments the performance of the body's natural function or structure such as hearing aids, hands, hips, legs, teeth, hair and heart valves.

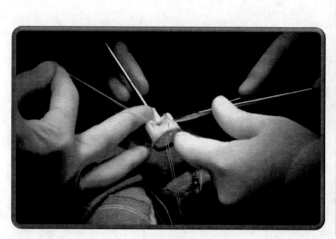
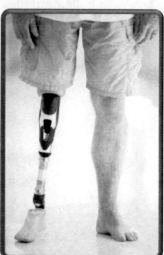

IN/HALER (in/breath)
IN/SPIR/ATION (in/breathing)

1. Inhalare in Latin means "to draw in breath" or in/spir/ation.
2. An inhaler is a device used to administer medicines (especially for asthma and emphysema).

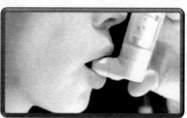

Asthma (panting in Gk.)

Nebulizer or inhaler
(nebula in Latin means mist)

CRYO/SURG/ER/Y
(cold/working by hand/one who/procedure)

1. Technique of exposing tissues to extreme cold to produce a well-defined area of destruction or cell injury.
2. Tissue cooled with liquid nitrogen to less than -20° C.
3. Used on malignant tumors to control pain, to produce lesions in the brain, and to control bleeding.
4. The cold is produced by a probe through which liquid nitrogen circulates.

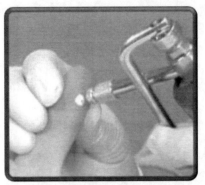

Verrucae (Wart) cryo/surg/ical treatment

OTO/SCOP/E (ear/viewing/instrument)
OTO/SCOP/Y (ear/viewing/procedure of)

1. This instrument is used to examine the outer ear and part of the middle ear.
2. Ear examination (inspection) by lighting and magnification the ear.
3. Negative or inward pneumatic (air) pressure (eardrum is pushed inward).
4. Positive or outward pneumatic (air) pressure (eardrum is pushed outward).
5. Both negative and positive pressures cause discomfort and pain.

TYMPAN/OS/TOM/Y
(eardrum/mouth/cut/process)

1. AKA: Myring/otom/y tympan/ic para/centesis
2. Surgical incision of the tympanic membrane (eardrum) to allow drainage of the middle ear chamber to relieve pressure from ot/itis media (ear/inflamed/middle).
3. This procedure prevents eardrum splitting from pressure.

Tympan/os/tom/y tubes

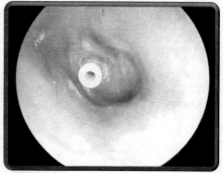

Tube in place: middle ear infection drainage

SPINAL TAP (spine or lumbar: puncture)

1. Puncture is made into the sub/arachn/oid space of the meninges.
2. A needle is placed between vertebra to remove cerebrospinal fluid for diagnostic purposes.
3. This technique is used to administer certain anesthetic agents or to inject a radi/opaque dye before radio/graph/y of the spinal canal.

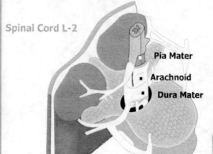

Spinal cord with 3 layered meninges (membrane)
1. Dura mater (hard:mother) - outer layer
2. Arachnoid (resembles a spider's web) - middle
3. Pia mater (gentle:mother) - inner

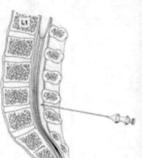

CATHETER
(let down into)
katheter – insert or let down into (Gk.)

1. Tube passed through the body for injecting fluids into or evacuating fluids from body cavity.
2. Made of elastic, rubber, glass, metal or plastic.
   A. **Cardiac catheter**: Designed to pass through blood vessels and into the heart chambers.
   B. **Par/enter/al catheter**: (Near/intestine/refers: insert) For total nutrition that uses route other than digestive canal – mucosal, subcutaneous, intravenous, or intramuscular.

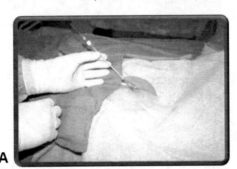

A

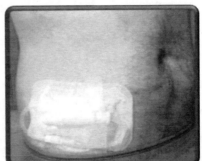

B

C. **Eustachian Catheter**: This passes into the Eustachian tube from the nasal passage.
D. **Urinary Catheter**: Catheter is inserted with care into the female bladder so as not to perforate the posterior wall.
E. **Abdominal Catheter**: This is used to provide nutrition to the body through the abdomen.

C

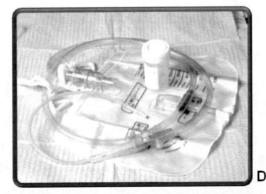

D

E

DE/FIBRILLAT/OR
(away/quiver/one who)

1. Instrument used to stop fibrillation of the heart.
2. Fibrillation is the quivering or spontaneous contraction of individual muscle fibers that causes irregular and uncoordinated heart muscle movement.
3. It is usually caused by mechanical injury, heart blockage, drugs, or electrical stimuli.
4. This defibrillator has 2 metal plates, electric current, and ECG leads to monitor heart rate and the rhythm of the heart (pads).

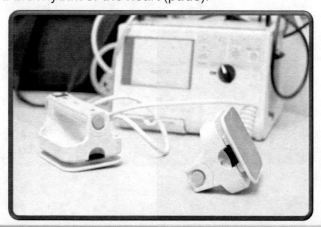

5. The machine sends counter-shocks to the heart through electrodes placed on the chest. This counter-shock will hopefully allow the heart's normal pacemaker to take over.
6. Shock intensity required is calculated by body weight.

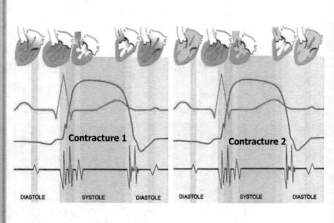

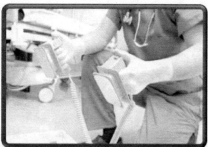

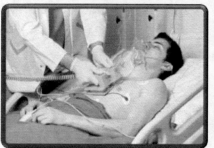

LITHO/TRIPS/Y
(stone/crushing/procedure)

1. Equipment used to crush stones in the urethra or bladder.
2. Many procedures can be used to crush a calculus, including medicine and lasers.
3. This litho/trips/y technique uses high frequency sound waves to crush the calculi.

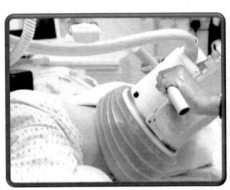 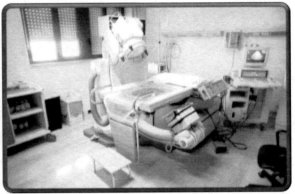

Chole/cysto/litho/trips/y
(gallbladder/stone/crushing/process)

PROTON BEAM THERAPY
(PBT)

1. PBT is used to treat cancer and other tumors in the body.
2. The raw material is hydrogen gas. This gas is separated into hydrogen ions and protons, which are positively charged subatomic particles. These protons are fed into a synchrotron or a circular particle accelerator that whirls the ions, gathering charge until they are rotating at 10 million revolutions per second (nearly light speed).
3. A magnet-lined transport tube redirects the protons to the treatment room, calibrating the speed of the protons to the tumor site. This speed determines the depth at which the protons release their intense high energy.
4. Higher doses of radiation can be delivered to tumors with less risk to healthy tissue.
5. Proton therapy has been shown to be beneficial in the treatment of many kinds of tumors, including brain, breast, esophageal, eye, gastrointestinal, gynecological, head and neck, liver, lung, lymphoma, prostate, soft tissue, spine and many pediatric cancers.

Proton Beam Therapy Center at Hokkaido University
U.S. Embassy Tokyo Press, Flickr. (2015)

ELECTRO/CONVULSIVE THERAP/Y (ECT)
AKA: Electric Shock therapy (EST)

1. ECT or electro/convulsive therapy uses electrical currents to pass through the brain. This shocks the brain and induces a convulsive response. The milliamp dose varies with different psychiatric and/or physical problems.
2. It has been used by psychiatr/ists for treatment of acute depression, schizo/phrenia, and with suicidal patients. It causes immediate confusion.
3. It is usually used as an alternative to traditional drug therapy or with patients that are resistant to normal drug therapy.

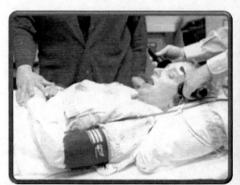 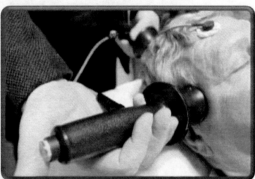

PACEMAKER
(Sino-Atrial or Sino-Auricular Node)

1. It is a group of cells that automatically generate impulses that spread throughout the heart muscle.
2. The normal cardiac pacemaker is the sino-atrial node. This is a group of cells in the upper right atrium where the superior vena cava enters the heart's right atrium.

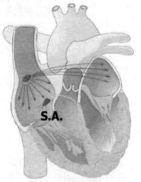 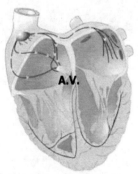 

Atrio/ventricular node and medical pacemaker

HEART PACEMAKER
(chest implant)

3. There are internal and external artificial pacemakers.
   A. **Alternating pacemaker**: Allows heart's own electrical impulses to take precedence over the device.
   B. **External pacemakers**: The electrodes deliver stimulus through the chest wall of intra/venous catheter.
   C. **Fixed rate pacemakers**: Deliver a constant rate of stimulation.

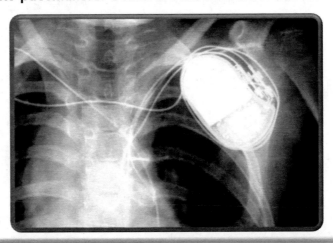

ORIGINAL HEART VALVES

Phulwari28. Wikimedia
Commons (2011)

Junge, M. Wikimedia
Commons (2008)

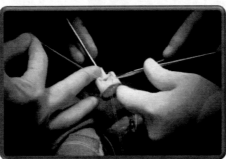

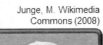

Bjork Shiley

Artificial/synthetic

Starr Edwards

Mitral Valve
Replacement (MVR)

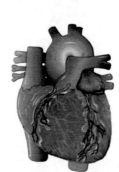

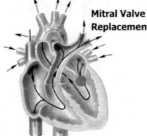

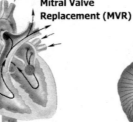

Prosthetic (Additions) Heart Valves

SURG/ER/Y
(works by hand (Gk.)/one who/procedure of)

1. Branch of medicine dealing with manual and operative procedures for correction of defects, injuries, deformities, diagnosis, and cure of certain diseases, such as cancer.
2. The procedure that is carried out is referred to as an operation.

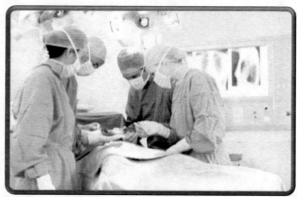

A/sepsis of a/septic environment (AKA: antiseptic)
Free from pathogens and infection;
Free from decay and sterile Lt.

2. A. Conservative surgery: Body parts or structures are retained.
   B. Radical surgery: Structures and adjoining tissues are completely removed.
   C. Minor surgery: Usually not life-threatening.
   D. Major surgery: Life-threatening.

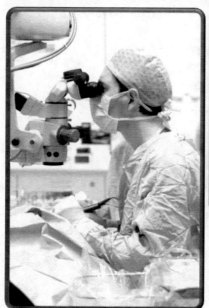
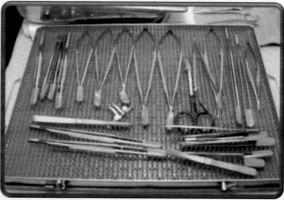

Micro/vascul/ar tools used to suture blood vessels

INTENSIVE CARE UNIT (ICU)

1. Intense care is provided to patients who have experienced trauma, surgery, or serious diseases.
2. 24-hour monitoring is provided to the patient.
3. All vital systems of the body are monitored.

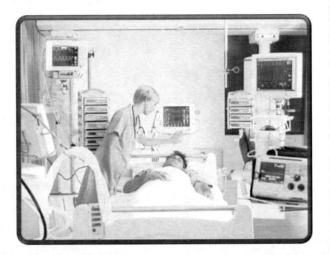

TRIAGE
(to sort or classify Fr.)

1. Triage is a French term that means to sort.
2. It was used during the later part of World War II and extensively during and after the conflict in Korea.
3. It was a method of sorting through the battle injuries to determine who needed care first and what type.
4. Emergency rooms are often called triage centers.

1. **Nuclear medicine**: Branch of medicine that treats, investigates, and diagnoses diseases with radio/nuclides (radioactive, uneven decaying isotopes releasing energy for treatment and diagnostic images).

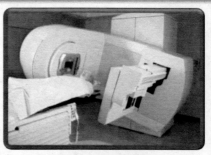

2. **Radiation therapy**

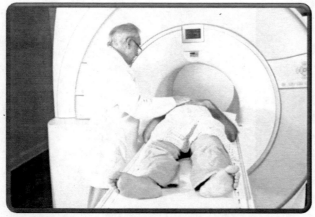

3. **Magnetic resonance imaging** (MRI)

Medical equipment danger or warning signs

TYPES OF MEDICINE
Integrated Medicine AKA: Complementary or Alternative

1. Complementary or alternative medicine: Virtually any form of medicine that remains outside the realm of conventional modern medicine may be labeled alternative. Examples are acupuncture, hypnosis, biofeedback, self-suggestion (AKA: affirmation therapy), massage, aromatherapy, spiritual healing, naturopathy, homeopathy, and therapeutic touch.
2. Folk: Varies from culture to culture. Folk medicine involves a belief in the effectiveness of a chosen cure. Remedies are based on plants, charms, and rituals from various cultures (e.g. Chinese, Seminole, Alaskan, Indian, Hawaiian, and Appalachian).
3. Holistic: Holistic therapies treat the whole person (body and mind) as opposed to focusing only on the part of the body where symptoms occur. The importance of self-care and prevention of illness are stressed.
4. Natural: Any therapy that relies on the body's own healing powers. These include vitamin therapy, herbal remedies, diet and water therapy. (Chiropractic care may be included in vitamin therapy, diet and water therapy.)
5. Orthodox (conventional): This refers to Western or conventional modern medicine (dominant type of healthcare in most developed countries), which uses prescribed drugs and surgery.
6. Traditional: Any medicine system with ancient origins, strong cultural ties, and trained healers. This includes traditional Chinese medicine.

ACU/PUNCTURE
(needle or sharp or clear/puncture or prick)

1. Acus in Latin means needle. Acu/puncture is the insertion of unique long, thin needles at special points in the skin. Acu/pressure is compression of blood vessels and nerves at these same points.
2. Technique for treating nausea and pain (producing a type of regional an/esthesia).
3. The needles' free ends are twisted, heated, or are connected to limited electrical currents.
4. This technique has been used in the United States since the 1970s.
5. This therapy is part of integrated medicine (AKA: Alternative or complementary medicine).

ACU/PUNCTURE NEEDLE SIZES

Larger needles are used for thicker skin. Smaller needles are used for delicate areas like the face and ear.

Uses of Acupuncture
Respiratory problems
Arthritis and rheumatism
Headaches and migraine
Insomnia and back pain
Urinary infections
Menstrual imbalances
Sinusitis
Tinnitus (ringing in the ears)
Eye problems
Allergies
Digestive disturbances
Palpitation and anxiety
Mental and emotional problems
Morning sickness and labor pains
Childhood illnesses

6. Major surgery has been conducted on all body parts with the use of an/esthesia produced by acupuncture.
7. It has been used in Asia for centuries and is currently being researched extensively in the U.S.

MEDICAL HYPNO/SIS (sleep/condition)
SUGGESTIVE THERAPY (Placebo (shall please Lt.) Effect)

1. In this condition of relaxation (state of resembling sleep) positive suggestions or affirmation are presented to the patient in a positive soothing method (movies, tapes, or in person).
2. There are more than 70 different titles for suggestive therapy, including: hypnosis, self-hypnosis, creative visualization, suggestology, alphagenic training, Lamaze method of childbirth, Silva mind control, psycho-cybernetics, progressive relaxation, creative imagery, meditation, believability and affirmation therapy. All of these employ various visual and/or auditory suggestions that are very similar. Belief in the person giving the suggestion and belief in the suggestion or affirmation are extremely important to success.
3. All of these techniques put the individual in a relaxed state of alpha brain wave activity or patterns (active thinking is the beta state, limited or tunneled thought is the alpha state, light sleep or dreaming is the alpha state, and deep sleep is the delta state) and/or spiritual improvements to one's life.
4. In medicine these techniques are used to mask pain, improve the senses, slow bleeding, speed up healing, improve memory, or improve the effects of anesthetics or medications.
5. The placebo effect is well-established in pharmacology and medicine. If you believe the treatment or cure will work, it will.
6. Herbert Spiegel medical hypnotist test for suggestibility: Roll eyes back as far as possible while slowly lowering your lids; When eyes are about half closed note how much white sclera is showing; more white suggests greater ability to be hypnotized.

SELF-SUGGESTION AND/OR BIOFEEDBACK THERAPIES (stress management)

1. **Self-Suggestion**: There are many techniques used to control stress levels and promote homeostasis in the body including biofeedback, medical hypnosis, affirmations, progressive relaxation, exercise, meditation, organization skills, Silva mind control, psycho/cybernetics, progressive relaxation, creative visualization, the Jacksonian technique, suggest/ology, alpha/genic training, and various other titled approaches that promote the same physiological effects in the body. Drugs, the Herbert Benson technique, Fernand Lamaze (Fr.) childbirth technique (1951) and a variety of other marketable techniques are promoted as solutions to mental and physical health problems. All of these methods use the alpha level of brain wave activity or level of relaxation to implement self-suggestion, to aid in relaxation, lower blood pressure, relax muscles, control heart rate and skin temperature, control brain waves, mask pain, and promote homeostasis.

Hypnotherapy

2. **Biofeedback**: This specifically is a training program designed to develop one's ability to control one's automatic (involuntary) physiologic nervous system responses or functions. The patient learns to use monitoring equipment that use lights, gauges, and sound (audio-visual responses) to achieve the desired response. It is used with self-hypnosis therapy, placebo therapy, and/or affirmation therapy to incorporate a positive suggestion in one's psyche ("Day by day, in every way, I am getting better and better." - French psychologist Emile Couié). Through trial and error the patient allegedly learns to consciously control body and mind responses, which were previously regarded as involuntary (to treat HBP, insomnia and body pain).

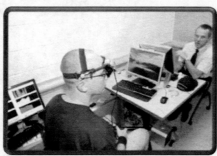

Biofeedback Training Program
Russoniello, C. for Army Medicine. Flickr (2012)

AROMA/THERAP/Y
(Gk. Spice/treat/process of) olfacto- and osmio- mean smell

1. This is the use of agreeable odors or pleasing fragrances to stimulate the central nervous system and eventually body function changes. Ex: Odors start digestive juices flowing and cause hunger.

Lavender is thought to have a calming effect on the mind and body.

2. This type of treatment uses oil fragrances, especially parts of plants, herbs, and/or trees (flowers, roots, bark, wood, leaves, petals, resin, fruit and rinds or oranges and lemons). These relax the body, stimulate body function, or relieve pain. Aromatherapy has been used for centuries in Europe, Asia, and worldwide.

3. Odors strike the nasal nerve cells or olfactory neurons that carry impulses to the limbic system of the brain. This brain part is the seat of memory and emotions. Another example is the memory of perfume smells that stimulates sexual drives.

4. Smell is the most sensitive of the 5 senses (10,000 times more sensitive).

Cassin, C. Flickr (2010)

5. Some research indicates that scents can ease physical maladies like headache, irritability, and nervousness. Other research is studying work productivity, easing violent crimes in society, and treating mental disorders like anxiety and claustrophobia. They use more than 40 highly concentrated oils combined with soy, almond, primrose, or diluted with alcohol.

6. These oils are inhaled, applied during massage, or used with baths.

7. Cinnamon in vapor helps congestion; eucalyptus, thyme, pine, and lavender oils ease bronchitis and sinusitis; juniper oil eases joint pain.

8. A French chemist, Rene Gattefosse, is said to be the founder of aromatherapy (commonly administered in France).

Tara Angkor Hotel. Flickr (2011)

THERAPEUTIC TOUCH
(AKA: Aura/therapy – halo or breath/treatment)

1. Auras are often seen by people who experience epileptic seizures, abnormal PET scans (brain energy levels), and have migraine headaches.
2. Kirlian photographs: This process allegedly shows an energy field that healthy tissues generate. An electric current is applied to a special photographic plate on which the body part rests.
3. These fields are the inner auras. There are various sizes of auras that many feel reflect mental, physical, and emotional conditions.
4. Steps followed by therapeutic touch therapists and other healers in training others to allegedly see these energy fields with the naked eye:
   A. Relax and allow your vision to be slightly blurred or out of focus;
   B. Hold a hand up to a light-colored wall (white or yellow) with the lights put on low (this is very important);
   C. Hold your hand out in front of you with the palm facing your face;
   D. Look about 1/4" under the side of your hand with your relaxed vision;
   E. If at first you don't see a light blue energy field, breathe deeply and continue to look under your hand, moving it to new locations against the wall.

dim the light and allow your eyes to become less focused

"inch inner aura"

5. Many feel that laying on of hands uses this energy field to stimulate the healing process. Allegedly, some can generate stronger energy fields than others.
6. Moods, energy levels, and health can allegedly be determined by viewing auras.
7. Barbara Ann Brennan's book "Hands of Light" indicates the following:
   A. White, light blue, and pink allegedly denote health and happiness;
   B. Red supposedly shows suppressed anger;
   C. Gray and browns allegedly show physical and emotional problems;
   D. Dirty green, according to practitioners, indicates drug and/or alcohol abuse

Barbara Brennan

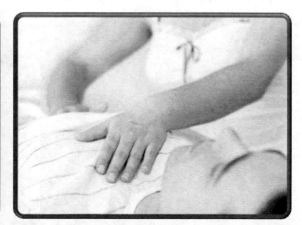

Strebinger, E. Wikimedia Commons (2010)

THERAPEUTIC TOUCH STEPS

1. Dr. Dolores Krieger (R.N. and Ph.D.) has taught thousands of professionals to tap into their own alleged powers of healing energy. She feels that the technique of laying on of hands (spiritual or not), causes these energy fields to increase the levels of blood hemoglobin in the body which transports oxygen to body cells (based on her personal research). It is similar to Chinese traditional medicine energy flow theories. These flows are allegedly produced in massage, spiritual healing, and therapeutic touch (correcting energy flow blocks).

2. Steps: Train the body to become aware of radiant energy of the body. Bring hands as close as possible without touching, with elbows out. Bring your palms apart about 2" and slowly bring them closer like in the starting position. Now slowly pull them apart 4" and slowly return them to stating position. Repeat this at 6 and 8" and then stop for a moment without lowering your hands. Reverse this process from 8", narrowing the distance to 6, 4 and 2". Each time, pause to experience what you feel physically and mentally. Return your hands to the original position and concentrate hard on what you sense (heat, cold, pulsation, tingling, etc.).

3. The healer must be strongly motivated to heal and healthy to generate the field. Hold your hands about 4" from the patient. Sense the patient's energy field (open hands). With sweeping motion follow the body contours. Krieger says you will feel pressure or heat at those spots where the energy field is impaired. The healer tries to "unruffle" this blocked energy and distribute the energy excess to other points in the body.

REI/KI (ray-key)

1. In Japanese it means a universal vital force or a healing energy that transfers. This healing art is based on a universal life energy present everywhere.

2. When channeled properly, it promotes healing. Rediscovered in 1855 by the Japanese theologian Dr. Mikao Usui.

3. Practitioners go through attunements, tracing energy location in the head and then at 12 body locations referred to as chakras.

4. The key to Reiki isn't position, but transfer of energy between healer and patient.

SPIRITUAL HEALING AND DEATH
Divine or Spiritual Healing

1. This relies on summoning a higher power to help treat disease. It is accomplished by prayer, laying on of hands, and/or rituals. Whether it is from a divine source or by triggering an immune response (emotional experience), it is allegedly beneficial in the treatment and cure of disease.
2. Belief in a healing power of prayer is common among Americans.
3. Greeks believed illness was a sign of divine displeasure.
4. In Christian mythology, Jesus cured the blind, the lame and lepers.

Death

Dr. Elisabeth Kubler Ross Stages: Interviews with terminally ill patients indicate that most people go through 5 specific phases:

    A. Denial
    B. Anger
    C. Bargaining
    D. Depression
    E. Final Acceptance

This belief in set stages of grief in response to imminent death has not been supported by subsequent studies. Popular belief in the stages of grief proposed by Ross may be psychologically harmful to grieving people, who may feel there is something wrong with them if their emotional responses don't match up with what's expected.

CHIRO/PRACT/ICS

1. Chiropractors believe in the efficacy of chiropractic spinal adjustment in treating a variety of bodily ailments, including allergies, by promoting nervous system wellness.
2. Spinal adjustments are believed by practitioners and their adherents to regulate histamine release and cortisol production, reducing asthma and allergy symptoms.

Dorausch, M. Flickr (2010)

3. While few relevant studies exist, there is little evidentiary support for the assertion that chiropractic can reduce allergy symptoms or "cure" allergies. Such claims should be regarded with scrutiny, particularly for conditions like severe allergies, as the risks may outweigh any potential benefits, especially for children.

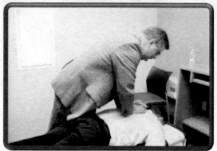

QUACKERY (kwaksalven in Dutch mean salve peddler or quack)
PHREN/OLOG/Y (mind/science/procedure of) and
IRID/OLOG/Y (rainbow/science/procedure of)

1. During the 19th century, many practitioners of medical specialties used these and other methods to diagnose disease.
2. Abnormal bumps on the skull surface and abnormal colored spots in the iris (rainbow) of the eyes corresponded with a body part and disease. Diagnosis was made with these models.
3. A quack or charlatan is one who pretends to have knowledge or skill in medicine (drug or remedy-medicina Lt.)

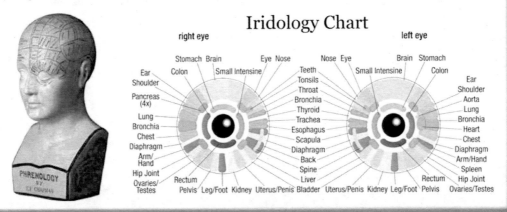

Iridology Chart

MASSAGE (to stroke Fr.)
RE/FLEX/OLOG/Y (again/bends/of/procedure of)

1. Masser in French means to stroke. It is the manipulation of the body's soft tissues by stroking, rubbing, kneading and tapping (by hand or with mechanical device – vibrator). Care is needed with rashes, tumors, sensitive areas and in inflamed tissues (loosen clots).
2. Reflexology: A type of massage of the feet and hands. It treats the body using principles similar to acupuncture and acupressure.

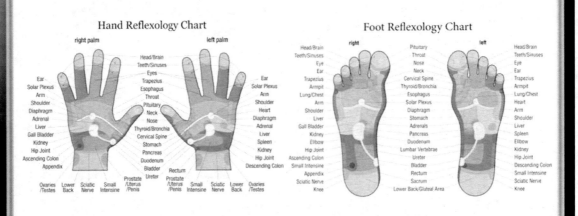

Hand Reflexology Chart

Foot Reflexology Chart

MEDICAL RE/SEARCH
(to heal Lt.: again investigate Fr.)

1. Gene replacement;
2. DNA repair;
3. Stem cell tissue or organ growth.

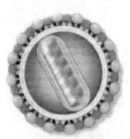

Adeno -Associated Virus
Adeno-associated virus can insert itself into many types of cells without provoking an immune response, but can only carry small genes.

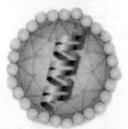

Lentivirus
Lentivirus, a pared-down version of the HIV virus, can carry large genes-such as the one responsible for a blood clotting factor needed by hemophiliacs.

ALLO/PATH/IC MEDICINE (M.D.) (other or opposite of disease/refers) VS. HOMEO/PATH/IC MEDICINE (H.M.D)
(like or same/as disease/refers)

1. Allopathic physicians use antagonistic substances to attach to disease organisms or illness. Quick response in cases of most non-viral infections.
2. Homeopathic physicians administer small doses of similar disease substances to allegedly stimulate the natural body response of immunity. If a large dose of a substance or drug produces symptoms of a disease in healthy people, practitioners believe, then small amounts administered to the patient will cure the same symptoms (allergies).
3. School of medicine founded by Dr. Sam C.F. Hahnemann M.D. (1755-1843) in Philadelphia.

Homeopaths dilute drugs with mild sugar in ratios of 1 to 10 and use one substance at a time.
(Allos = other Gk.)
(Homoios = like or similar Gk.)

TRADITIONAL CHINESE HERBAL MEDICINE AND ANDREW WEIL M.D.

1. Traditional Chinese herbal medicine was founded by Huang-di, the legendary Yellow Emperor, 2,000 years ago. He stressed the balanced yin and yang concept which is the basis of Chinese traditional medicine.

2. This method of healing serves more than 35% of the world's population. Harmony with nature and harmony internally is the basis of health. Emphasis is placed on preventive lifestyles.

3. Dr. Andrew Weil has promoted integrated medicine and is best known for his holistic healing approach to medicine. He is a Harvard graduate who has traveled the world to study what works best for the patient. He incorporated his findings into the specialty medicine degree of integrated medicine, where traditional drugs are used for infections and to mask symptoms, but surgery, herbs, massage, spinal manipulation, biofeedback, vitamins and minerals, deep breathing, exercise, meditation, and various other methods of healing are incorporated into his practice of medicine.

Andrew Weil

4. Below are some of the founders of Dr. Weil's integrated (alternative or complementary) medicine approach to health. Emphasis is placed on preventive behaviors (refer to his best selling books: "Spontaneous Healing," "8 Weeks to Optimum Health," and "Eating Well for Optimal Health.")

Unknown. Wikimedia Commons (1841)

Samuel Hahnemann
1755-1843
Homeopathy founder

Unknown. Wikimedia Commons

Daniel David Palmer
1843-1913
Chiropractic founder

Unknown. Library of Congress (1914)

Andrew Taylor Still
1828–1917
Osteopathic founder

1. The word part that contains the fundamental meaning of a word is the: _____

2. In the medical term 'intra/ven/ous', -ven- is the: _____

3. The word part attached to the beginning of a word root in order to modify its meaning is called a(n): _____

4. In the medical term 'arthr/itis', -itis is the: _____

5. The word part attached to the end of a word root in order to modify its meaning is the: _____

6. The most common combining vowel is: _____

7. In the divided medical term 'arthr/o/pathy', "o" is the: _____

8. In the divided medical term 'sub/hepat/ic', which part is the prefix and which part is the suffix? _____

9. The combining form of a stem word is usually made of two component parts, the _____ _____ and _____ _____:

10. In the divided medial term 'osteo/por/o/sis', the slash lines (/) indicate that the vowel "o" may be used as part of which word parts? _____

11. The phrase "refers to or _____," is a generalized actual meaning (not a literal meaning) used for the suffixes -a, -ia, -iac, -al, -ar, -ic, -is, -on, -os, -us, -ium, and -um. _____

12. Verb variations of a stem word usually describe: _____

13. Adjectives usually modify a noun (thing named) denoting quality, quantity, extent, or _____

14. Breaking a compound term into component word parts (usually with its combining vowel or vowels) is called: _____

15. What cellular organelle contains chromosomes and has the literal meaning "nut"? _____

16. The combining form or term that literally means "internal organs" is: _____

17. The abdominal cavity contains the: _____

18. My/o- is the combining form of a word part that means: _____

19. The combining form hist/o- means: _____

20. A body part which is formed of two or more types of body tissue and performs one or more specific functions is called a(n) :_____

21. The suffix –plas/ia is a compound suffix (2 or more parts) that refers to: _____

22. Bone is described as _____ tissue.

23. The combining form that means "cause of (disease)" is: _____

24. The prefix that means "change or after" is: _____

25. The suffix that means "to control or stop" is: _____

26. The medical term that means "the science of or study of body changes caused by disease" is: _____

27. The combining form onc/o- means: _____

28. If a tumor is found to be benign, it is: _____

29. The medical term for new growth (of abnormal tissue or tumor) is: _____

30. The LITERAL meaning of the medical term carcin/oma is:_____

31. The correct way to fracture or divide the medical term melanocarcinoma is

_____.

32. The directional term 'lateral' describes movement in which direction: _____

33. The directional term that means "toward the lower end of the body" is: _____

34. The term that describes the direction closest to the point of origin is: _____

35. The directional term for movement toward the back of the body is: _____

36. The term that describes movement toward the top of the body is: _____

37. The term that describes movement toward the front of the body is: _____

38. The directional term 'inferior' describes movement: _____

39. The term that divides the body into right and left halves is the: _____

40. The term 'coronal' or 'frontal plane' divides the body into the: _____

41. The regional term that refers to the areas on both the right and left sides of the hypo/gastr/ic body region is the: {NOTE: There are 9 individual abdomino/pelv/ic regions} _____

42. If a wound is considered superficial it is: _____

43. If one is flat on their back and face up, they are in a _____ position.

44. A plantar wart is located on the: _____

45. The term defined as the process of drawing away from the mid-line or middle is: _____

46. The movement in which a limb is placed in a straight position is called: _____

47. The term 'af/ferent' (as in sensory impulses) is defined as: _____

48. If you rotate your shoulder around a central point, it is called: _____

49. "I swear by Apollo the Physician and Asclepius and Hygieia and Panaceia..." is the beginning of what famous oath? _____

50. If an infection is "Chronic" it is characterized by: _____

51. An epithelial or covering cell malignant tumor is referred to as a(n): _____

52. A tumor of the fibrous and cartilaginous tissue is called a(n): _____

53. The study of disease is referred to as: _____

54. Cancers of the circulatory system include: _____

55. A fatty tumor is called a(n) : _____

56. The term "metastasis" means: _____

57. The term "hyperplasia" means: _____

58. The term "diagnosis" means: _____

59. The term "Clinical" means: _____

60. The term "Prognosis" means: _____

61. The term "Mammogram" means: _____

62. The first 3D-printed drug approved by the FDA was: _____

63. The term "Intravenous Injection (IV)" means: _____

64. The term "Phlebotomy" means: _____

65. The term "Radiogram" means: _____

66. "Fluoroscopy" is used to record: _____

67. "Angiograms" are used for: _____

68. "Graphy" literally means: _____

69. The "KUB" examination looks for defects in the: _____

70. A "Pyelogram" records information about the _____:

71. A "Myelogram" is used to record _____ information:

72. Body "X-rays" produce pictures of _____body tissue and bones:

73. A "_____" is a noninvasive roentgenography diagnostic technique.

74. A "_____" produces a radio frequency radiation pulse image of soft and hard tissue in multiple planes. It does not produce ionizing radiation hazards.

75. Laser assisted surgery, "LASIK," is used to correct: _____

76. An "EKG or ECG" is used to record information about _____ electrical activity.

77. An "EEG" is used to record information about _____ electrical activity.

78. An "EMG" is used to record information about _____ electrical activity.

79. A "PET Scan" is used to detect glucose or energy use levels of the: _____

80. A "Thallium Hot Spot Test" is used to detect _____ damage:

81. The term "Stetho/scop/e" literally means: _____

82. The term "Auscult/ation" literally means: _____

83. The term "Percuss/ion" literally means: _____

84. The term "ocular" literally means: _____

85. The term "Sphygmo/mano/meter" literally means: _____

86. The procedure of using an instrument that produces high frequency sound waves to produce an image of the size or shape of a body part is called: _____

87. The term "Biopsy" literally means: _____

88. The term "Laryngo/scop/y" literally and actually means: _____

89. The term "Ophthalmo/scop/e" means: _____

90. A "Tonometer" measures pressure within the: _____

91. The term "Nebul/iz/er" means: _____

92. The term "Cryo/surg/er/y" literally means: _____

93. An "Otoscope" is used to view the: _____

94. The term "Tympanostomy" literally means: _____

95. A "Spinal Tap" is used to: _____

96. The term "Catheter" literally means: _____

97. A "Defibrillator" is used to correct: _____

98. An "Electro Shock Therapy (EST)" is also known as: _____

99. A "Pacemaker" can be external or internal and usually generates electrical stimuli to the heart muscle with _____:

100. The term "Surgery" literally means: _____

101. "Complimentary or Alternative Medicine" is now referred to as _____:

102. "Biofeedback" is a type of _____ therapy:

103. "Aromatherapy" is a type of integrated therapy that some may feel is: _____

104. "Placebo Effect Therapy"(like hypnotherapy) uses the principle of: _____

105. "Therapeutic Touch Therapy" uses the principle that the body produces: _____

106. "Massage and Reflexology" are examples of: _____

107. "Acu/puncture" literally means: _____

108. The term "Bronchoscope" literally means: _____

109. The abbreviation "ICU" refers to a(n): _____

110. The term "Intramuscular Injection (IM)" literally means: _____

111. "Lithotripsy" is a procedure for crushing: _____

112. "Cryosurgery" is used to treat: _____

113. The _____is used to treat brain cancer by directing radiation at precise brain locations.

114. Dr. Elizabeth Kubler-Ross is best known for: _____

1. The word part that contains the fundamental meaning of a word is the: *root word/stem word*

2. In the medical term 'intra/ven/ous', -ven- is the: *word root or stem word*

3. The word part attached to the beginning of a word root in order to modify its meaning is called a(n): *prefix*

4. In the medical term 'arthr/itis', -itis is the: *suffix*

5. The word part attached to the end of a word root in order to modify its meaning is the: *suffix*

6. The most common combining vowel is: *'o'*

7. In the divided medical term 'arthr/o/pathy', "o" is the: *combining vowel "used with both the stem word and suffix"*

8. In the divided medical term 'sub/hepat/ic', which part is the prefix and which part is the suffix? *sub- and -ic*

9. The combining form of a stem word is usually made of two component parts, the _____ _____ and _____ _____: *word root and combining vowel*

10. In the divided medial term 'osteo/por/o/sis', the slash lines (/) indicate that the vowel "o" may be used as part of which word parts? *por- and -osis*

11. The phrase, refers to or _____, is a generalized actual meaning (not a literal meaning) used for the suffixes -a, -ia, -iac, -al, -ar, -ic, -is, -on, -os, -us, -ium, and -um. *pertains to*

12. Verb variations of a stem word usually describe: *action taken, condition, or state*

13. Adjectives usually modify a noun (thing named) denoting quality, quantity, extent, or _____ . *distinction of the object from something else*

14. Breaking a compound term into component word parts (usually with its combining vowel or vowels) is called: *fracturing*

15. What cellular organelle contains chromosomes and has the literal meaning "nut"? *nucleus*

16. The combining form or term that literally means "internal organs" is: *viscer/o-*

17. The abdominal cavity contains the: *liver*

18. My/o- is the combining form of a word part that means: *muscle*

19. The combining form hist/o- means: *tissue or web-like*

20. A body part which is formed of two or more types of body tissue and performs one or more specific functions is called a(n) _____: *organ*

21. The suffix –plas/ia is a compound suffix (2 or more parts) that refers to: *formation, growth or development*

22. Bone is described as _____ tissue. *connective*

23. The combining form that means "cause of (disease)" is: *eti/o*

24. The prefix that means "change or after" is: *meta-*

25. The suffix that means "to control or stop" is: *-stasis*

26. The medical term that means "the science of or study of body changes caused by disease" is: *path/o/logy*

27. The combining form onc/o- means: *tumor*

28. If a tumor is found to be benign, it is: *encapsulated, slow growing, and expansive*

29. The medical term for new growth (of abnormal tissue or tumor) is: *neoplasm*

30. The LITERAL meaning of the medical term carcin/oma is: *crab-like tumor "invades with crab-like leg growths"*

31. The correct way to fracture or divide the medical term melanocarcinoma is: *melano/carcin/oma*

32. The directional term 'lateral' describes movement in which direction: *to the side*

33. The directional term that means "toward the lower end of the body" is: *caudal*

34. The term that describes the direction closest to the point of origin is: *proximal*

35. The directional term for movement toward the back of the body is: *dorsal*

36. The term that describes movement toward the top of the body is: *cephalic*

37. The term that describes movement toward the front of the body is: *ventral*

38. The directional term 'inferior' describes movement: *toward the lower end of the body*

39. The term that divides the body into right and left halves is the: *sagittal plane "like an arrow"*

40. The term 'coronal' or 'frontal plane' divides the body into the: *anterior and posterior portions*

41. The regional term that refers to the areas on both the right and left sides of the hypo/gastr/ic body region is the: {NOTE: There are 9 individual abdomino/pelv/ic regions} *iliac or inguinal*

42. If a wound is considered superficial it is: *situated near the surface*

43. If one is flat on their back and face up, they are in a _____ position. *supine*

44. A plantar wart is located on the: *sole of the foot*

45. The term defined as the process of drawing away from the mid-line or middle is: *abduction*

46. The movement in which a limb is placed in a straight position is called: *extension*

47. The term 'af/ferent' (as in sensory impulses) is defined as: *conveying toward the center*

48. If you rotate your shoulder around a central point, it is called: *circumduction*

49. "I swear by Apollo the Physician and Asclepius and Hygieia and Panaceia..." is the beginning of what famous oath? *Hippocratic*

50. If an infection is "Chronic" it is characterized by: *little change, slow progression, and long duration*

51. An epithelial or covering cell malignant tumor is referred to as a(n): *carcinoma*

52. A tumor of the fibrous and cartilaginous tissue is called a(n): *fibrochondroma*

53. The study of disease is referred to as: *pathology*

54. Cancers of the circulatory system include: *leukemia and lymphomas*

55. A fatty tumor is called a(n) : *lipoma, steatoma, or adipoma*

56. The term "metastasis" means: *to spread*

57. The term "hyperplasia" means: *increase in development*

58. The term "diagnosis" means: *total knowledge*

59. The term "Clinical" means: *at patients' bedside*

60. The term "Prognosis" means: *before knowledge*

61. The term "Mammogram" means: *a recording of the breast*

62. The term "Xerogram" means: *a dry recording*

63. The term "Intravenous Injection (IV)" means: *within a vein*

64. The term "Phlebotomy" means: *to cut into a vein*

65. The term "Radiogram" means: *X-ray recording*

66. "Fluoroscopy" is used to record _____: *moving body parts*

67. "Angiograms" are used for _____: *recording pictures of vessels*

68. "Graphy" literally means _____: *procedure using an instrument to record*

69. The "KUB" examination looks for defects in the: *kidney, ureter, and bladder*

70. The "Pyelogram" records information about the _____: *kidney pelvis*

71. A "Myelogram" is used to record _____ information: *spinal cord/nerve tissue*

72. Body "X-rays" produce pictures of _____body tissue and bones: *dense*

73. A "_____" is a noninvasive roentgenography diagnostic technique. *Computerized Axial Tomography (Scan)-CAT*

74. A "_____" produces a radio frequency radiation pulse image of soft and hard tissue in multiple planes. It does not produce ionizing radiation hazards. *Magnetic Resonance*

Imaging (Scan)-MRI

75. Laser assisted surgery, "LASIK," is used to correct: *myopia (and hyperopia)*

76. An "EKG or ECG" is used to record information about _____ electrical activity. *Heart*

77. An "EEG" is used to record information about _____ electrical activity. *brain*

78. An "EMG" is used to record information about _____ electrical activity. *skeletal muscle*

79. A "PET Scan" is used to detect glucose or energy use levels of the _____: *brain*

80. A "Thallium Hot Spot Test" is used to detect _____ damage: *heart*

81. The term "Stetho/scop/e" literally means: *instrument to examine the chest*

82. The term "Auscult/ation" literally means: *process or procedure for listening*

83. The term "Percuss/ion" literally means: *process or procedure of striking*

84. The term "ocular" literally means: *refers to the eye*

85. The term "Sphygmo/mano/meter" literally means: *to measure the pulse by hand*

86. The procedure of using an instrument that produces high frequency sound waves to produce an image of the size or shape of a body part is called: *Ultra/sono/graph/y*

87. The term "Biopsy" literally means: *the procedure of viewing life*

88. The term "Laryngo/scop/y" literally and actually means: *the procedure of viewing and examining the voice box*

89. The term "Ophthalmo/scop/e" means: *instrument to examine the eye*

90. A "Tonometer" measures pressure within the _____: *eye*

91. The term "Nebul/iz/er" means: *one who causes a mist*

92. The term "Cryo/surg/er/y" literally means: *a procedure of one who works by hand with cold*

93. An "Otoscope" is used to view the: *ear*

94. The term "Tympanostomy" literally means: *procedure of cutting and making a mouth-like opening in the ear drum*

95. A "Spinal Tap" is used to _____: *take fluid samples from the spinal fluid*

96. The term "Catheter" literally means: *to let down, into*

97. A "Defibrillator" is used to correct _____: *abnormal heart beats or rhythms*

98. An "Electro Shock Therapy (EST)" is also known as: *Electric Convulsive Therapy (ECT)*

99. A "Pacemaker" can be external or internal and usually generates electrical stimuli to the heart muscle with _____: *fixed and/or alternate impulses*

100. The term "Surgery" literally means: *procedure of working by hand*

101. "Complimentary or Alternative Medicine" is now referred to as _____: *Integrated Medicine*

102. "Biofeedback" is a type of _____ therapy: *psychosomatic*

103. "Aromatherapy" is a type of integrated therapy that some may feel is _____: *Suggestive, or placebo effect, unsupported by clinical evidence and psychosomatic*

104. "Placebo Effect Therapy"(like hypnotherapy) uses the principle of _____: *suggestion and believability*

105. "Therapeutic Touch Therapy" uses the principle that the body produces: *energy or an aura - "halo"*

106. "Massage and Reflexology" are examples of _____: *integrated medicine*

107. "Acu/puncture" literally means _____: *needle puncture*

108. The term "Bronchoscope" literally means: *instrument to view trachea-like structures*

109. The abbreviation "ICU" refers to a(n): *Intensive Care Unit*

110. The term "Intramuscular Injection-IM" literally means: *within a muscle*

111. "Lithotripsy" is a procedure for crushing _____: *stones or calculi debris*

112. "Cryosurgery" is used to treat _____: *verrucae or warts*

113. The _____ is used to treat brain cancer by directing radiation at precise brain locations. *Gamma Knife*

114. Dr. Elizabeth Kubler-Ross is best known for: *On Death and Dying*

1. A-
without or lack of
a/men/orrhea
without or lack of/monthly/flow

2. AB-
away (away from)
ab/norm/al
away (away from)/normal or regular/refers to
ab/ducens
away/draw or lead

3. ABDOMIN/O-
belly
abdomin/al
belly/refers to

4. -ABLE
capable of or ability to
erg/able
work/capable of
related term(s): -IBLE

5. ABORT/IO-
to miscarry (natural or induced)
abort/ion
to miscarry (natural or induced)/procedure of or process of
(discharge of the embry/o 'early' or fet/us 'young' deliberate or not)

6. ABRUPT/IO-
to tear away from
abruptus placentae
to tear away from (separate quickly) / cake

7. ABSCESS
a going away
abscess
a going away
(tissue disintegration & displacement: 'Staph' infection forming pus)

8. ACANTH/O-
thorny skin growths
acanth/oma
thorny skin growths/swelling (benign) or tumor

9. ACCESS/O-
supplemental
access/ory cranial nerves
supplemental/refers to

10. ACETABUL/O-
vinegar cup or hip joint
acetabul/ectomy
vinegar cup or hip joint/surgical removal or excise

11. ACNE
pointed
Acne/form
pointed/shape
(ACNE is a bacterial inflammation of the hair follicle and sebaceous 'oil' gland. Similar infections may cause acne or form lesions)

12. ACOUST/I-
hearing
acoust/ic
hearing/refers to
related term(s): AUDI-

13. ACR/O-
extremities, height, and pointed
acro/megal/y
extremities/enlarged/refers to
acro/phob/ia
height/fear/refers to
acr/om/ial
extremity/shoulder/refer to
(lateral triangle spine-like projection of shoulder blade forming the point of shoulder & articulating with clav/icle 'key

little' or collarbone)

14. ACTIN/O-
sun, ray, radium
actino/myco/sis
sun, ray, radium/fungus/condition (growth)

15. ACU-
sharp
acu/ity
sharp/process of
(seeing sharply or clearly)
acute
quick, sudden, sharply

16. -AC
refers to, pertains to, or state of
cardi/ac
heart/refers to, pertains to, or state of
related term(s): -AL, -AR, -ARY, -ATE, -EUM, -IAC, -IC, -ICAL, -ILE, -IS, -IUM, -ORY, -OUS, -UM, -US

17. AD-
near or beside
ad/ren/al
near or beside/kidney/refers to
(the ad/ren/al gland is located on top of kidney)

18. ADEN/O-
gland
aden/ectomy
gland/removal
(the following are common glands: lymph nodes, oil, sweat, and endocrine)

19. ADHES/IO-
to stick together
adhes/ion
to stick together/process of

20. ADIP/O-
fat
adip/oma
fat/tumor
(adip/oma is also known as lip/oma)
related term(s): steato-, lipo-

21. AER/O-
air or gas
aero/cele
air or gas/distension of cavity (like a tumor)

22. AF-
toward
af/ferent
toward/to carry
(nerve or blood flow toward a structure)

23. -AGE
relates to or pertains to
tri/age
three/relates to or pertains to
(French term which means to sort or classify into three or more divisions)
mass/age
kneading/procedure of or process of
related term(s): -ATION, -IATION, -ING, -ION, -TION, -Y

24. AGGLUTIN/O-
to clump
Agglutin/ation
to clump/process of or condition of

25. -AGOGUE
inducing or leading
galact/agogue
milk/inducing or leading

26. -AGON
walls
pent/agon
5 sided/walls

27. -AGRA
pain
cardi/agra
heart/pain
related term(s): ALGESIA-, -ALGIA, DOLO-, -DYNIA

28. ALB/O-
white
albin/ism
white/state of
(albo-, leuco-, leuko- all mean white)

29. ALBUMIN/O-
egg white
albumin/ur/ia
egg white/in urine/refers to

30. ALGES/I-
pain
an/alges/ic
without/pain/refers to
related term(s): -AGRA, -ALGIA, DOLO-, -DYNIA

31. -ALGIA
pain
neur/algia
nerve/pain
related term(s): -AGRA, ALGESIA-, DOLO-, -DYNIA

32. ALIMENT/O-
to nourish
aliment/ary
to nourish/refers to

33. ALOPEC/I-
fox mange or baldness
alopec/ia
fox mange or baldness/refers to

34. ALVEOL/I-
cavity
alveol/us
small hollow or cavity (tooth socket and lung air sack)/refers to
related term(s): SIN/O-

35. -AL
refers to
lingu/al
tongue/refers to
related term(s): -AC, -AR, -ARY, -ATE, -EUM, -IAC, -IC, -ICAL, -ILE, -IS, -IUM, -ORY, -OUS, -UM, -US

36. AMBI-
both
ambi/later/al
both/sides/refers to
ambi/dextr/ous
both/right (dominant hand)/refers to or state of
(dextero = right, sinistro = left)

37. AMBLYO-
dull
ambly/opia
dull/refers to vision or sight

38. AMBUL/O-
to walk
ambul/atory
to walk or walking/process of

39. -AMINE
nitrogen compound
anti-hist/amine medic/ation
against-tissue/nitrogen compound cure/process of

40. AMINO-
organic compound
amino/acid/emia
organic compound/PH below 7/refers to

blood
(amino acid compounds containing
Nitrogen (N), Carbon (C), Hydrogen(H), &
Oxygen (O))

41. AMNESI/O-
forgetful
amnes/ia
forgetful/refers to

42. AMNIO-
lamb's caul, small cap
amnio/centesis
lamb's caul, small cap/surgical puncture (to
drain fluid)
(The amniotic sac surrounds the fetus and
contains fluid. This fluid is used in
pregnancy tests for Down syndrome. This is
the birth membrane around the fetus or
lamb and resembles a small cap.)

43. AMPHI-
both
amphi/arthr/osis
both sides/joint/condition of

44. AMYLO-
starch
amyl/uria
starch/in urine
amyl/ase
starch/enzyme

45. AN-
lack of or without
an/orex/ia
lack of or without/appetite/refers to

46. AN/O-
ring
an/al
ring (sphincter of anus)/refer to

47. ANA-
apart or up
ana/tom/y
apart or up/cut/procedure of or process of
ana/phase
up/stage
(mitosis stage when chromosomes move up
or apart)

48. ANCONE-
elbow
ancone/us
elbow (ulna-elbow projection)/refers to

49. ANDR/O-
man or male
andr/olog/y
man or male/study of/process of

50. ANECTO-
without expansion or dilation
anect/asis
without expansion or dilation (no air in
lungs)/condition of
an/ect/asis
not/out/condition

51. ANGI/O-
vessel
angi/oma
vessel/swelling or tumor
related term(s): VAS/O-

52. ANGIN/O-
Vessel
angin/a
(Refers to a vessel condition of choking or
blocking of blood flow to the heart muscle.
which usually results in chest discomfort or
pain.)

53. ANIL/I-
old women

Anil/ism
old women/state of
(anil/ity refers to senile women)

54. ANIS/O-
unequal
aniso/cytosis
unequal/increase in number
(this is an increase in the number of cell that
are unequal in size or shape 'especially
RBC's')

55. ANKYL/O-
fuse or bind
ankylo/spondylo/itis
fuse or bind, stiff,
crooked/spine/inflammation

56. ANOMAL/Y
abnormal
anomal/o/scope
abnormal or not average (not or without
normal development)/viewing or
examining

57. ANTE-
before
ante/nat/al
before/birth/pertain to
ante/pyrect/ic
before/fever/refers to

58. ANTER/O-
before or foremost
anter/ior
before or foremost (in front)/refers to

59. ANTHRAX
coal or carbuncle
anthr/ax
coal or carbuncle/a lesion
(Types of Anthrax: Cerebral, Pulmonary,
Cutaneous, and/or Intestinal)

alternate spelling: ANTHR/O-

60. ANTHROP/O-
human
anthropo/metr/ic
human/measurement/refers to

61. ANTI-
against
anti/sept/ic
against/infection/refers to
anti/bio/tic
against/life/refers to

62. ANTR/O-
cavity
antro/scop/e
cavity/view or examine
(sinuses)/instrument

63. ANEURYSM-
dilation or ballooning
aneurysm/oplasty
dilation or ballooning (usually blood
vessel)/surgical repair

64. ANXIO-
restlessness, uneasy, apprehensive
anxiet/y
restlessness, uneasy, apprehensive/process
of

65. -APHERESIS
to remove or separate (blood into parts)
leuk/aphere/sis
WBC/to remove or separate (blood into
parts)/condition of
(separate blood into component parts or
remove toxins)

66. APO-
above or upon
apo/plex/y

above or upon/paralyzed/process of

67. APONEUR/O-
sheet or sheath around tendon
aponeur/orrhaphy
sheet or sheath around tendon/suturing
(muscle end becoming tendon 'flat sheet or
sheath of muscle')

68. APPEND/O-
appendage
appendic/itis
appendage/inflammation
(projection of cecum, 'blind pouch' first part
of large intestine)

69. AQUA-
water
aqua/therap/y
water/treat/process or procedure
related term(s): HYDRO-

70. AR-
without or lack of
ar/rhythm/ia
without or lack of/rhythm/refer to

71. ARACHINO-
spider
arach/oid
spider/resembles
related term(s): ARACHN/O-

72. ARACHN/O-
spider
arachn/oid
spider/resembles
related term(s): ARACHINO-

73. ARCHE/O-
first
arche/type
first or original/form or shape (it produces

other forms)

74. -ARCHE
first
men/arche
month or monthly/first, original, beginning
(first female cycle)
related term(s): ARCHE/O-

75. -ARIA
air
mal/aria
bad/air
(determined to be caused by protozoa
carried by mosquitos)

76. ARTERI/O-
artery
arterio/gram
artery/recording
arterio/scler/osis
artery/hard/condition
arter/iol/oma
artery/small/swelling

77. ARTHR/O-
joint
arthro/scop/ic
joint/viewing or examining/pertains to

78. ARTICUL/O-
jointed
articula/tion
jointed/process of
(the place of union between two or more
bones)

79. -ARY
refers to
capill/ary
little hair/refers to
related term(s): -AC, -AL, -AR, -ATE, -EUM,
-IAC, -IC, -ICAL, -ILE, -IS, -IUM, -ORY, -

OUS, -UM, -US

80. -AR
refers to or pertains to
patell/ar
little dish (kneecap)/refers to
Related Term(s): -AC, -AL, -ARY, -ATE, -EUM, -IAC, -IC, -ICAL, -ILE, -IS, -IUM, -ORY, -OUS, -UM, -US

81. ASBEST/O-
unquenchable
asbest/osis
unquenchable (magnesium and calcium silicate)/condition of
(lung disease which is a form of pneumono/coni/osis. This is when dust-like particles are inhaled in the lungs)

82. ASCAR/I-
worm
ascari/asis
worm/condition of
(round nematode worm usually infecting intestines)
helminthiasis (worm condition); vermiform (worm/shape)
related term(s): HELMINTH/O-, VERMI-

83. ASCO-
bag
asco/spore
bag/seed
asc/us
bag/refers to

84. -ASE
enzyme
lip/ase
fat/enzyme

85. -ASIS
condition of or disease

psori/asis
itching/condition of or disease
related term(s): -OSIS, -ESIS, -SIS

86. ASPERGILL/O-
to sprinkle
Aspergill/osis
to sprinkle/condition of
mold (fungus) spores scattered over tissue (usually skin or lung)

87. ASTER/O-
star
astro/cyte
star/cell
(large glue (glial) cells of nervous system)

88. -ASTHENIA
weakness
my/asthenia
muscle/without strength; or having weakness
neur/asthenia
nerve/weakness

89. ASTHMA-
panting
asthma/tic
panting/refers to

90. ATELO-
incomplete, without end, imperfect ending
atelo/spir/osis
incomplete, without end, imperfect ending/breathing/condition of

91. -ATE
refers to or action
pall/ate
roof (plate at top of mouth)/refers to or action
satur/ate
penetrating/action or use

related term(s): -AC, -AL, -AR, -ARY, -EUM, -IAC, -IC, -ICAL, -ILE, -IS, -IUM, -ORY, -OUS, -UM, -US

92. ATHERO-
porridge or yellow fat
athero/scler/osis
porridge or yellow fat/harden (in lumen of blood vessels)/condition or disease
(athero/scler/osis kills 45% of U.S. population)

93. -ATION
process of or procedure of
circul/ation
circle/process of
(blood moving from heart and returning)
cardio/graph/y
heart/instrument to record/procedure of
related term(s): -AGE, -IATION, -ING, -ION, -TION, -Y

94. ATM/O-
vapor or steam
atmo/therap/y
vapor or steam/treatment/process of
(aroma/therap/y: vapor/treat/process)

95. -ATRESIA
closure
ven/atresia
vein/closure
(abnormal closure of body opening-occlusion)

96. ATRI/O-
chamber
atri/um
chamber/refers to
(corridors or chambers at top of heart)

97. ATTRIT/I-
wearing out

attrit/ion
wearing out/process of

98. AUDI-
hearing
audi/olog/y
hearing/science of or study of/procedure or process of
audio/meter
hear/measurement
related term(s): ACOUST/I-

99. AUR/I-
ear
aur/al
ear/pertains to
aur/icle
ear/small or little

100. AURICUL/O-
ear
auricul/ar (shape of ear)
ear/pertains to

101. AUSCULT/O-
to listen
auscult/ation
to listen (physical diagnosis)/process of

102. AUT-
self
aut/ism
self/state of
(aut/ism is a mental disorder which causes extreme withdrawal; unable to communicate verbally or relate to others)
related term(s): AUTO-

103. AUTO-
self
auto/hypn/osis
self/sleep/condition of
(simulated sleep in alpha brain state of

consciousness)
aut/ism
self/state of

104. AVULS/I-
to tear
avuls/ion
to tear/process of (ligaments torn from bones)
related term(s): spadi-

105. AXILL/O-
armpit or central
axill/ary
armpit or central/pertain to

106. AXIO-
axle or axis
axio/lysis
axle or axis/destruction
(Destruction of axis cylinder of a nerve 'sinew-like or tendon-like'. Axis is the line through the center of body part where part revolves)
related term(s): AXO-

107. AXO-
axle or axis
axo/lysis
axle or axis/destruction
(Destruction of axis cylinder of a nerve 'sinew-like or tendon-like'. Axis is the line through the center of body part where part revolves) related term(s): AXIO-

108. AZOTO-
urea nitrogen
azot/emia
urea nitrogen/ in blood

109. AZYGO-
single
azyg/ous

single (not paired)/refers to

110. BACILL/O-
rod-like
bacill/us
rod-like (bacteria)/ refers to

111. BACTERI/O-
rod
bacter/ia
rod/refers to
(rod was the first bacteria viewed under microscope)

112. BALAN/O-
penis
balan/itis
penis/inflamed
(also refers to the female clitoris)

113. BARO-
weight
baro/gnosis
weight/prediction (knowledge)

114. BARY-
heavy
bary/phon/ia
heavy/voice(quality)/refers to

115. BAS/O-
basic or at base
bas/al (metabolism)
basic or at base/refers to

116. BENE-
good or normal
bene/fit
good or normal/suited for

117. BENIGN-
kind
benign/iform

kind/shape or appearance
(tumor in capsule: slow growing and
expansive, not invading)

118. BERI-
weakness
beri/beri
weakness/weakness
(vitamin B1 or thiamine deficiency disease)

119. BI-
two
bi/ceps
two/headed (muscle)
related term(s): CO-, BIN-, DI-, DIPLO-,
DUO-, DYO-

120. BIL/I-
bile or gall
bili/ary
bile or gall/refers to or state of
(liver substance stored in gallbladder)

121. BIN-
two
bin/ocul/ar
two/eyes/refers to
related term(s): CO-, BI-, DI-, DIPLO-,
DUO-, DYO-

122. BIO-
life
bio/log/y
life/science of or study of/process of

123. -BLAST
beginning or young
osteo/blast
bone/beginning or young cells
(embryonic primitive cells found in the
body systems)

124. BLEB/O-
blister
bleb/ic
blister or bulla 'bubble'/refers to
(bleb/ic is a bulb or blister that often is filled
with blood)
related term(s): BULLA-, BULBA-

125. BLENNO-
mucus
blen/oma
mucus/tumor or swelling

126. BLEPHARO-
eyelid
blephar/oma
eyelid/swelling or tumor
related term(s): PALPEBRA-

127. BOL/O-
lump or ball
bol/us
lump or ball, choice bit of food (in stomach),
to throw up /refers to

128. BOSS
swelling
boss/ism
swelling/state of

129. BRACH/I-
arm
brachi/al
arm/refers to
(humerus is the bone of upper arm)

130. BRACHY-
short
brachy/dactyl/ia
short/fingers (and toes)/refers to

131. BRADY-
slow

brady/pnea
slow/breathing

132. BREVI-
short
brev/ity
short/state of

133. BRONCH/I-
windpipe or trachea like
bronchi/al
windpipe or trachea like (large lung
tubes)/refers to

134. BRUX-
grinding
brux/ism
grinding (teeth)/state of

135. BUCCA-
cheek
bucc/al
cheek/pertains to

136. BULBA
blister or vesicle
Bulb/us
blister or vesicle (little sac)/refers to
related term(s): BULLA-, BLEB/O-

137. BULIMO-
hunger
bulim/ic
hunger or appetite (excessive)/refers to or
condition of
(eating and purging syndrome)

138. BULLA-
blister
bulla
blister or skin vesicle often filled with fluid
(often blood)
related term(s): BLEB/O, BULBA-

139. BURS/O-
sac, wine sac, pouch
burs/a
sac, wine sac, pouch/refers to
(protective pad-like structure in joints)

140. CAC/O-
diseased or bad
caco/plas/tic
diseased or bad/growth/refers to

141. CAL/O-
heat, heated or hot
cal/or
heat, heated or hot/one who is
(1 of 4 characteristics of inflammation: calor-
heat; rubor-red; tumor-swelling; and dolor-
pain)

142. CALCANE/O-
heel
calcane/al
heel (of foot)/refers to

143. CALCIN/O-
calcium
calcin/osis
calcium/condition of
(excessive calcium buildup on bones)

144. CALCO-
pebbles or granules of calcium mineral
calc/ium
pebbles or granules of calcium
mineral/pertains to
calc/urea
pebbles or granules of calcium mineral in
urine

145. CALIGI/O-
dim vision
calig/osis
dim vision/condition of

146. CALL/O-
hardened skin
call/us
hardened skin
(increase in horny upper layer for
protection)/refers to

147. CALX-
heel or lime
calx/ectom/y
heel (foot bone)/removal/procedure of

148. CALYX-
cups
calyx/itis
cups or cup-like organ or cavity/inflamed
(structures in kidney)
alternate spelling: CALIX-

149. CANDID/I-
glowing white
candidi/asis
glowing white (fungus infection)/condition
of

150. CANTH/O-
corner of eye
cantho/plast/y
corner of eye (eyelid)/cosmetic or plastic
surgery/procedure of

151. CAPILL/O-
hair-like
capill/ary
hair-like/pertains to or refers to
(little blood vessels)

152. CAPIT/O-
head
capit/al
head/refers to
related term(s): CAPUT, CEPHAL/O-

153. CAPN/O-
carbon dioxide
capno/graph
carbon dioxide (or smoke)/instrument
(instrument used in exercise physiology to
measure CO2)

154. CAPSULO-
little box
capsul/itis
little box/inflamed
(capsules types: kidney, bacteria, cartilage,
etc.)

155. CAPUT
head
caput femoris
head or head of (chief part of structure or
organ)/thigh bone
related term(s): CEPHAL/O-, CAPIT/O-

156. CARB/O-
carbon atoms, coal, charcoal
carbon/uria
carbon atoms, coal, charcoal/in urine
carbo/hydrate

157. CARBUN/O-
glowing ember
carbun/cle
glowing ember/small
(numerous boils)
related term(s): CARBUNCUL/O-

158. CARBUNCUL/O-
glowing ember
carbuncul/osis
the appearance of many glowing embers
related term(s): CARBUN/O-

159. CARCIN/O-
crab-like
carcino/gen/ic

crab-like/producing/refer to
(cancer causing)

160. CARDI/O-
heart
peri/card/itis
around/heart/inflammation
(inflamed 2 layered membrane of heart:
causing pain)
(car-; card-; cardi-; cardio- all refer to the
heart)

161. CARP/O-
wrist
meta/carp/al
beyond/wrist/refers to

162. CATA-
breakdown or down
cata/bol/ism
breakdown or down/choice bit of food or
lump/state of

163. CATARACT
waterfall or cloudiness
cataract
waterfall or cloudiness
(eyes lens under the cornea that is
impervious to light)

164. CATARRH-
to flow down
Catarrh/al
to flow down/refers to
(any drainage from mucus membrane:
especially in the nose, sinuses, and throat)

165. CATHETER/O-
to let down into
catheter/iz/ation
to let down into/act of/procedure of

166. CAUD/O-

tail or toward tail
caud/al
tail or toward tail/refer to

167. CAUS-
burn or heat
caus/tic
burn or heat/refers to
related term(s): CAUST/O-, CAUTER/O-

168. CAUST/O-
burn or heat
caus/tic
burn or heat/refers to
related term(s): CAUS-, CAUTER/O-

169. CAUTER/O-
to burn or to heat
cauter/iz/ation
to burn or to heat/act of/procedure of
related term(s): CAUS-, CAUST/O-

170. CAV-
hollow
cav/ity
hollow/state of or refers to

171. CEBO-
meal or food
ceb/um
meal or food/pertain to
(cena- and dino- also means dinner)

172. CEC/O-
blind pouch
Ceco/pexy
blind pouch/surgically attached to
abdominal wall
(dead end pouch or 1st part of colon -right
side)

173. -CECE
navel

omphalo/cele
navel (belly button)/swelling, tumor,
protrusion
(outie)

174. -CELE
swelling or tumor
laparo/cele
abdominal/swelling or tumor

175. CELI/O-
abdomen or belly
celi/oma
abdomen or belly/tumor

176. CELLUL/O-
chambers
cellul/itis
chambers or body cells (tissues are cell
groups)/infection

177. CEMENT/O-
hard
cement/um
hard/refers to
(tooth root covering)

178. CENO-
empty or common
cen/esthes/ia
empty/feeling/refers to
ceno/phob/ia
common/fear/refers to
related term(s): KENO-

179. -CENTESIS
surgical puncture to drain fluid
thoraco/centesis
chest/surgical puncture to drain fluid
(procedure)

180. CENTI-
one-hundredth part (100)

centi/meter
one-hundredth part (100)/of meter
(metre- or -meter means to measure & a
meter is 39.37 inches)

181. CENTR/I-
center
Centri/fug/al
Center (middle of circle)/to flee/refers to
(heavy particles move to bottom or outside
from the center)

182. CEPHAL/O-
head
en/cephal/itis
within/head/inflamed
(refers to brain within the head)
related term(s): CAPIT/O-, CAPUT

183. -CEPT-
receiver
chemo/cept/or
chemical or drug/receiver or to recieve/one
who

184. CEREBR/O-
brain
cerebr/al
brain/refers to or pertains to

185. CERU-
wax
cerumen/ous
wax (in ear)/refer to or state of

186. CERV/I-
neck
cerv/ical
neck (seven upper vertebrae of spine)/refers
to
cerv/ix
neck/pertains to

187. CHALAS/I-
relaxation
pre/chalas/ia
before/relaxation/refers to

188. CHALAZ/IO-
hailstone
Chalaz/ion
hailstone (eyelid sebaceous cyst)/process of
(tumor that is small and hard on the eyelid)

189. CHANCR/O-
ulcer (sore)
chancr/oid
ulcer (sore)/resembles
(this V.D. has granular lesions that form
ulcers or sores like syphilis)

190. CHEIL/O-
lip
cheil/oma
lip/tumor
alternate spelling: CHILO-

191. CHELO-
to claw
chel/ation
to claw/process of
(removal of heavy metals from the blood
and body)

192. CHIASMA
a crossing
chiasma
a crossing
(like an X the optic cranial nerves "Cr. N. 2"
crosses before reaching the eye)

193. CHIRO-
hand
chiro/pract/or
hand/practice/one who
(mano also means hand)

194. CHLAMYD/I-
to cloak or cover
Chlamyd/ia
to cloak or cover/refers to

195. CHLOR/O-
green
chlor/emia
green (chlorides)/in blood

196. CHOLANGIO-
bile duct
cholang/itis
bile duct/inflamed

197. CHOLE-
bile or gall
chole/sterol
bile or gall (ingredient of)/ solid
(Chole 'bile' is used to refer to anything
related to bile: CHOLE/DUCTO- = bile duct,
CHOLE/CYTO- = bile sac)
(Hyper/cholesterol/emia is the increase in
cholesterol levels in the blood. Normal
Levels: 160 to 200 mg/dcl. Blood vessels
become plaqued 'occlusion-closure' and it
can be seen in the skin & eyes. Remember
body hormones & enzymes also need
cholesterol)

198. CHOLECYST/O-
gallbladder
cholecyst/ectomy
gallbladder/removal

199. CHOLEDOCH/O-
gallbladder duct (canal)
choledoch/ectomy
common bile duct/removal or excision
(duct removed from the liver and
gallbladder)
alternate spelling: CHOLEDUCTO-

200. CHOLERA
biliary acute diarrhea
cholera
biliary acute dia/rrhea
(bowel or intestinal diarrhea 'flow'. The
bacteria causes de/hydra/tion and death)

201. CHONDR/O-
cartilage
chondr/oma
cartilage/tumor
dys/chondro/plas/ia
faulty/cartilage/formation or
development/refers to

202. CHORDO-
cord
chord/itis
cord (spermatic or vocal)/inflamed
related term(s): CORDO-

203. CHOREA
dancing or shaking
Huntington's chorea

204. CHROM/O-
colored
chromo/some
colored/body
(23 pair in each body cell - see Watson-Crick
Helix Chromosome Model)

205. CHYME-
juice
a/chym/ia
lack of/juice/condition
(small intestinal juices are lacking: lack of
food, liquids, and juices)
alternate spelling: CHYLE-

206. -CICATRIX
scar
brachio/cicatrix

arm/scar

207. -CID
to kill
sui/cid/al
oneself/to kill/refers to

208. CIL/I-
eyelash-like
cil/ia
eyelash-like (structures lining lungs)/refers
to

209. CILI-
eyelash or eyelash like
cili/um
eyelash or eyelash-like/refers to

210. CIMEX
bug
cimex
bug
(the bed bug saliva irritates the skin)

211. CINE/O-
movement filming
cine/angio/cardio/graph/y
movement/vessel/heart/filming
instrument/procedure

212. CIRCUM-
around
circum/flex
around/bend
circum/cis/ion
around/cut/process of
circum/duct/ion
around/movement/state of

213. CIRRH/O-
yellow-orange
cirrh/o/sis
yellow-orange (jaundiced) or

yellow/condition of
(disease or infection causing liver failure:
bile pigments remain in the body and blood
resulting in color abnormality)

214. CISTERN/O-
cavity
cistern/oma
cavity or reservoir/swelling or tumor
(cavity or space of cranial cavity containing
cerebrospinal fluid 'CSF')

215. -CIS
cut or to cut
in/cis/ion
into/cut/procedure of
related term(s): sect/o-

216. -CHALASIA
relaxation
a/chalasia
not/relaxation
(muscle, sphincter, mind)

217. -CLAST
breakdown
osteo/clast
bone/breakdown of cells
cyto/clas/is
cell/breaking/refers to
related term(s): -CLAS

218. -CLAS
breakdown
cyto/clas/is
cell/breaking/refers to
related term(s): -CLAST

219. CLAVICUL/O-
collarbone
infra/clavicul/ar
beneath/collarbone or clavicle (little key

shape)/refer to

220. CLEIDO-
clavicle or collar bone
sterno/cleido/mast/oid
sternum/clavicle, collar
bone/breast/resemble

221. CLINO-
bent
clino/dactylia
bent/finger or toe

222. CLON/O-
turmoil
clono/spasm
turmoil/contraction
(rapid alteration of muscle spasm and
relaxation: slower progressing to tremors)

223. CLUBB/O-
rounding
clubb/ing
rounding/process of
(enlarged FINGER & TOE ends 'heart &
nutrition problems')

224. -CLYSIS
irrigation or injection
hydro/clysis
water/irrigation or injection

225. CO-
two
co/llater/al liga/ment
two (2 outer knee ligaments)/sides/refers:
binding/act of
co-operat/ive
two/working/state of
related term(s): BI-, BIN-, DI-, DIPLO-,
DUO-, DYO-

226. COAGUL/O-

clotting or to clot
coagul/ation
clotting or to clot/process of

227. -COCCUS
berry
staphylo/coccus
grapelike/ berry (shape of bacteria)

228. COCCYG/O-
tailbone
coccyg/eal
tailbone/refers to or small

229. COCHLE/O-
snail-like
cochle/ar
snail-like/pertain to
(lower part of inner ear: for hearing sound)

230. COEL-
hollow belly or cavity
coel/iac
hollow belly or cavity/pertains to

231. COIT/O-
to come together
coit/us
to come together/refers to

232. COL/O-
colon (big or large intestine)
col/os/tom/y
colon (big or large intestine '5 feet
long')/mouth or opening/cut/procedure of
related term(s): COLON/O-

233. COLLA/O-
glue
colla/gen/ic
glue or albumin substance of connective
tissue/beginning/refer to

234. -COLLIS
neck
torti/collis
twisted/neck
(also known as wryneck or contracted neck)

235. COLOB/O-
to mutilate
colob/oma
to mutilate/swelling
(often seen in the eyes iris 'rainbow' -
opening that appears mutilated)

236. COLON/O-
colon, big or large intestine
colono/scop/y
colon or big intestine/view or
examine/procedure of
related term(s): COL/O-

237. COLPO-
vagina
colp/itis
vagina/inflamed

238. COM-
together
com/press/ion
together/contract/process of
com/minuted fracture
together/small: break
related term(s): CON-, SYM- SYN-

239. COMATO-
deep sleep
comat/ose
deep sleep/condition or state

240. CON-
together
con/duct/ion
together/draw
related term(s): COM-, SYM- SYN-

241. CONCH/A-
shell
conch/itis
shell/inflamed
(shell shaped part of ear or nose)

242. CONCUSS/I-
violent shaking
concuss/ion
violent shaking/process of
(brain injury resulting in bleeding,
headaches, and other symptoms)

243. CONDYLO-
knuckle
condyl/oma
knuckle (nob)/tumor or swellings
(bone and wart points or projection)

244. CONI/O-
dust
pneumo/coni/osis
lung/dust/condition

245. -CONIS
cone-shaped
kerato/conis
cornea/cone-shaped
(outer covering of iris 'cornea' elevated or
protrudes)

246. CONJUNCTIV/O-
joined together
conjunctiv/itis
joined together (united)/inflammation
(inflammation of the membrane that covers
the eye and the eyelid 'they join' or unite at
the back of eyelid and at base of the sclera.)

247. -CONTINENCE
contained
in/continence
not/contained or to hold

(Urinary or fecal incontinence. Involuntary
voiding of urine and/or feces)

248. CONTRA-
against
contra/cept/ion
against/heads (coming together)/process of

249. CONTRECOUP
counter blow
contre/coup
counter blow
occurs on the opposite side of injury,
usually occurring on the opposite side of
the brain impact

250. CONTUS/I-
bruise
contus/ion
bruise/process of
(non-broken skin injury with pain, swelling,
& discolored)

1. CONVOLO-
to roll together
convol/ution
to roll together/pertains to

2. CONVULS/I-
pull violently
convuls/ion
pull violently/state of

3. CORAC/O-
shape of a crows beak
corac/oid
shape of a crows beak/resembles
(the upper anterior part of the scapula
'shoulder/blade' that forms the shoulder
surface joint)

4. CORD-
vocal chords or cord
cord/itis
vocal chords/inflamed
related term(s): CHORDO-

5. CORE/O-
pupil, iris, rainbow
cor/ec/tom/y
pupil, iris, rainbow/out/cut/process

6. CORI/O-
skin
cori/um
skin/refers to
related term(s): CUT-, CUTI/O-,
DERMAT/O-, DERMO-, -PELL

7. CORNE/O-
cornea or horn shape
corne/itis
cornea or horn/inflamed
(horn shape structure 'cornea' that covers
the eyes iris and pupil covering)

8. CORNU-
horn or horny
stratum cornu (corneum)
layer/horn or horny (upper epidermis skin
layer)

9. CORON/O-
crowning
coron/ary
crowning (heart blood vessels)/refer to

10. CORONAL PLANE
crowning or frontal body cut
coron/al
crowning or frontal body cut/refers to
(downward cut through coronal suture
right to left of skull cuts the body into a
front and back part. Also known as
'FRONTAL PLANE')

11. CORP/O-
body
corp/us
body/refers to
(corpus pediculosis means 'body lice')

12. CORTIC/O-
bark, outer bark, rind, cortex
cortico/ster/oid
bark, outer bark, rind, cortex/solid/resemble

13. COST/O-
rib
cost/al
rib/refer to
related term(s): PLEURO-

14. COX/A-
hip or hip joint
cox/al
hip or hip joint/pertains to
cox/algia
hip joint/pain

alternate spelling: COX/O-

15. CRANI/O-
skull
crani/otom/y
skull (cranium)/cut into/procedure of
crani/al
skull/refer to

16. CRAS/O-
mixture
su/crase
sugar/mixture
eu/cras/ia
good/mixture/refers to

17. -CREAS
fleshy or flesh
pan/creas
all/fleshy or flesh
(this is the appearance of a 6″ compound
gland in the abdominal cavity)

18. CRENAT/O-
notched
crenat/ion
notched/process of
(irregular shaped red blood cells)

19. CRIC/O-
ring
cric/oid
ring/resembles
(part of voice box 'larynx')

20. -CRINE
secrete
endo/crine
within/secrete (into blood)
exo/crine
outside/secrete (into duct or canal)

21. -CRIT

separate
hemato/crit
blood/separate

22. CRUC/I-
cross or cross-like
cruci/ate
cross (shape)/state of or condition of
(crossing ligaments in knee: ACL and PCL)

23. CRUR/O-
leg
crur/al
leg (bands resembling legs)/refer to
crus/al
leg /refer to
related term(s): CRUS/O-

24. CRUS/O-
leg
crus/al
leg/refer to
related term(s): CRUR/O-

25. CRUST/-
scab or outer coat
crust/ic
scab or outer coat/refers to

26. CRYO-
cold
cryo/therap/y
cold/treat or cure (killing cells)/procedure of

27. CRYPTO-
hidden
crypt/orchid/ism
hidden/testis/state of or condition of

28. CUB/O-
cube or cube-shaped
cub/oid
cube or cube-shaped/resemble

(an ankle bone shaped like a cube)

29. CUBIT/O-
elbow
cubit/al
elbow, forearm region/refer to
elbow region

30. CULD/O-
blind pouch
culdo/scop/y
blind pouch/viewing/procedure of
(an instrument examines the pelvic
viscera 'organs' with an endo/scop/e after
introducing it through the posterior
fornix 'arch' cul-de-sac 'blind pouch' wall of
the vagina)

31. -CULE
little
mole/cule
mass/little
(small quantity can be divided without loss
of characteristics)
related term(s): -ICLE, -IOLE, -ULE, -ULA

32. CUNE/I-
wedge
cunei/form
wedge/shaped
(bone in foot 'middle and to outside')

33. CURETT/O-
scooping or scraping
curett/age
scooping or scraping/refers to
(carried out inside uterus 'abortion' or to
remove a skin lesions)

34. -CUSIS
hearing
an/cusis
without/hearing

35. CUSP/I-
pointed
cusp/id
pointed (end)/refers to
(pointed flaps of heart valves or teeth)

36. CUSP-
Point
Cusp/id
Pointed/refers to
related term(s): CUSPID (Canine Teeth);
BI/CUSPID and TRI/CUSPID (Major valves
with pointed flaps or parts that separate the
upper and lower parts of the heart.)

37. CUTI/O-, CUT-, CUTI-
skin
cut/icle
skin/little
sub/cut/aneous
under/skin/refers to
(the word part CUTIO- is a suffix, the
words part -CUTIS is a prefix)
related term(s): CORI/O-, CUT-,
DERMAT/O-, DERMO-, -PELL

38. CYAN/O-
blue
cyan/osis
blue/condition of

39. CYCL/O-
circle
cycl/itis
circle/inflamed
(muscles around iris or rainbow of eye are
inflamed)

40. -CYESIS
pregnancy
multi/cyesis
many/pregnancy

41. CYST/O-
bladder or sac
cyst/itis
bladder or sac/inflamed
alternate spelling: CYST
related term(s): CYSTI-

42. CYSTI-
bladder or sac
cyst/itis
bladder or sac/inflamed
related term(s): CYST/O-

43. CYT-
cell or chamber
cyt/olog/y
cell or chamber/study of or science
of/process of
related term(s): CYTE-, CYTH-

44. CYTE-
cell or chamber
cyt/olog/y
cell or chamber/study of or science
of/process of
related term(s): CYT-, CYTH-

45. CYTH-
cell or chamber
erythro/cyth/emia
red/cell/clod
related term(s): CYT-, CYTE-

46. -CYTOSIS
increase in numbers
leuco/cytosis
white (WBC)/ increase in numbers

47. DACRYO-
tear
dacry/doct/itis
tear/duct/inflamed
related term(s): LACRIMO-

48. DACTYLO-
digits (fingers and toes)
lipo/dactyl/ia
fat/digits (finger or toes)/refers to

49. DE-
away
de/gluti/tion
away/swallowing/process of
de/form
away/shape

50. DEBRIDE-
removal
debride/ment
removal/act of or ability to
(the removal of foreign matter, dead,
damaged tissue, 'wounds')

51. DECI-
one-tenth (1/10)
deci/liter
one-tenth(1/10) / liter
(Deca- means 10)

52. DECUB/O-
to lie down
decub/itus
to lie down/refers to
(bed-sores or ulcer of the skin resulting
from patients prolonged bed position)

53. DEEP
most inward
deep
most inward
(structure more internal than another)

54. -DEFERENS
to separate or apart
vas de/ferens (vessel: away carry or to
separte from)
related term(s): DIFFERENT-

55. DEKA-
ten
deka/gram
ten/grams
(15.432 grains = 1 gram; 28.35 grams = 1 ounce)

56. DELTA
fan-shaped or triangular
delt/oid (shoulder muscle)
fan-shaped or triangular/resembles

57. DEM/O-
people
Dem/o/graphy
people/procedure of recording with an instrument

58. DEMI-
half
demi/facet
half/little face
(superior and inferior projections of the vertebral arch)
related term(s): DEMI-, HEMI-, SEMI-

59. DENDR/O-
tree-shaped
dendr/ite
tree-shaped/state of

60. DENT/O-
tooth or teeth
dent/al
tooth or teeth/pertains to
related term(s): DONT/O-

61. DEPRESS/O-
lower
depress/or
lower/one who

62. DERM/O-

skin
pachy/derm/al
thick/skin/pertains to
related term(s): CORI/O-, CUT-, CUTI/O-, DERMAT/O-, DERMO-, -PELL

63. DERMAT/O-
skin
dermato/phyte
skin/plant
(fungus or other plant that causes parasitic skin diseases)
dermat/itis
skin/inflamed
(Remember: -mat, -mata, -matosis mean many, multiple, extensive)
related term(s): CORI/O-, CUT-, CUTI/O-, DERMO-, -PELL

64. -DESIS
binding or to bind
ligo/desis
to bind/binding
(surgical procedure to reattach ligaments to bone)

65. DESMO-
ligament or tendon
desmo/dynia
ligament or tendon/pain
desm/o/log/y
ligament or tendon/science of or study of

66. DEUTER/O-
second or secondary
deutero/plasm
second or secondary/growth, form, development
(reserve food supply in embryo yolk or ovum)
deutero/path/y
secondary/disease/process
(disease secondary to primary disease)

67. DEXTR/O-
right
dextro/card/ia
right/heart/refers to
(tilting of heart to the right)

68. DI-
two
di/gest/ion
two/separate or to separate/process of
related term(s): CO-, BI-, BIN-, DIPLO-,
DUO-, DYO-

69. DIA-
across, through, total, between
dia/phragm
across, through, total, complete,
between/petition or wall
dia/meter
across/measure
dia/gnosis
total/knowledge
dia/stole
'between/contractions'

70. DIAPHOR/O-
excessive sweating
diaphor/esis
excess sweating/condition of

71. -DIDYMUS
testis or teste
epi/didymus
upon/testis or teste
(coiled structure on top of teste 'seed
producer')

72. DIFFERENT-
to separate
different/ial dia/gnosis
to separate or apart/refers to:
total/knowledge
(different/ial dia/gnosis - also known as

D.D. means to identify the differences
between two or more similar conditions)
related term(s): -DEFERENS

73. DIGIT-
finger or toe
Digit/al
finger or toe/refer to
digit/ate
finger or toe/action of or refers to

74. DIPLO-
double or two
dipl/op/ia
double or two/sight or vision/refers to
(person experiencing double vision)
related term(s): CO-, BI-, BIN-, DI-, DUO-,
DYO-

75. DIPS/O-
thirst or thirsty
poly/dips/ia
many/thirst or thirsty/refer to
multi/dips/ia
many/thirst or thirsty/pertain to

76. DIPHTHER/I-
membrane
diphther/ia
membrane/refer to
(Klebs Loeffler Bacteria identified with
the 'Schick Test'. The membrane forms in 2
days on the body. Organism causes toxicity
& breathing problems.)

77. DIS-
away from or reverse
dis/ease
away from or reverse/comfort or ease

78. DIST/O-
farther from
dist/al

farther from/refer to

79. DIVERTICUL/O-
outpouching
diverticul/itis
outpouching/inflamed
(rugae or folds usually of the large intestine
become inflamed)

80. DOCH/O-
duct or canal
chole/doch/itis
bile or gall/duct or canal/inflamed

81. DOCT/O-
to teach or teacher
doct/or (Latin docere)
to teach or teacher/one who

82. DOL/O-
pain
dol/or
pain/one who (causes)
related term(s): -AGRA, ALGESIA-, -
ALGIA, -DYNIA

83. DOLICH/O-
long, separation, dislocation
dolicho/cephaly
long/head
(anterior-posterior diameter)

84. DONT/O-
tooth or teeth
ortho/dont/ist
straightening/teeth/specialist
related term(s): DENT/O-

85. DORS/O-
back
dors/al
back (posterior)/refers to
(e.g. the top or back of a dog, the back of a

standing human)
dorsi/flex/or
the back/to bend/one who

86. DOSE-
a giving or to give
dos/age
a giving/act of or relates to
related term(s): DOSE

87. -DOTE
what is given
anti/dote
against/what is given

88. DRACUNCUL/O-
little dragon
dracuncul/osis
little dragon/condition of
(parasitic nematode guinea worm infection;
Etiology is water; Treatment is slow traction
on the head of the worm located in skin
lesion or ulcer 'sore', clean water, and
drugs)

89. DROMO-
running
dromo/mania
running/madness
pro/drom/al
before/running/pertains to
(this is a specific phase of an infection: after
incubation and before convalescence stages
of the disease)

90. DU/O-
two
du/al
two/refers to
related term(s): CO-, BI-, BIN-, DI-, DIPLO-,
DYO-

91. DUCT/O-

to draw or to lead away
ab/duct/ion
away/to draw or to lead away
(motion)/process of

92. DUODEN/O-
twelve
duoden/itis
twelve/inflamed
(duodenum is the first part of the small
intestine)

93. DURA-
hard
dura mater
hard: mother
(outermost layer of membrane called the
meninges that cover the brain and spinal
cord)

94. DWARF/O-
small
dwarf/ism
small/state of

95. DY/O-
two or a pair
dy/ad
two or a pair/refers to
(pair of chromosomes formed during
meiosis 'reduction division of gametes')
related term(s): CO-, BI-, BIN-, DI-, DIPLO-,
DUO-

96. DYNAM/O-
work or strength
dynam/ics
work or strength/refers to
dynamo/meter
strength/measurement
(measure the strength of muscles)

97. -DYNIA

pain
coccygo/dynia
tailbone (coccyx)/pain
related term(s): -AGRA, ALGESIA-, -
ALGIA, DOLO-

98. DYS-
difficult, faulty, painful
dys/toc/ia
difficult or painful/birth/pertains to
dys/chondro/plas/ia
faulty/cartilage/development/refers to
dys/meno/rrhea
painful/monthly/flow

99. -E (suffix)
instrument
rhino/scop/e
nose/view or examine/instrument
related term(s): -graph

100. E- (prefix)
out or remove
e/viscer/ate
out or remove/organs/act of or state of
related term(s): ec-, ect-, ex-, ext-

101. -EAL
refers to
pharyg/eal
throat/refers to

102. EC-
outside, outward, outer, out
ec/top/ic
outside/location/pertaining to
related term(s): ECT-, ECTO-

103. ECCHYMO/-
juice out
ecchymo/sis
juice out/condition
(A bruise that causes bleeding under the

skin that turns the skin a yellow orange color)

104. ECCRINE-
secreting or to secrete
eccri/tic
secreting or to secrete/state of or quality of
(promoting secreting from body structures)

105. ECHIN/O-
prickly, spiny, notched
echin/osis
prickly, spiny, notched/condition of or state of
(this is the unusual spiny appearance of red blood cells)

106. ECHO-
sound
echo/gram
sound/writing or recording
related term(s): SONO-

107. ECT-
outside, outward, outer, out
ect/asia
outward (dilation)/condition or state
related term(s): EC-, ECTO-

108. -ECTASIS
enlargement or dilation
bronchi/ectasis
windpipe like tube/enlargement, dilation
cardio/ectasis
heart/enlargement condition

109. ECTO-
outside, outward, outer, out
ecto/derm
outer/skin
related term(s): EC-, ECT-

110. -ECTOMY

excision or removal
tonsill/ectomy
almond or small mass/excision or removal

111. ECZEMA
to boil out
eczema
to boil out (skin lesions)

112. EDEMA-
swelling
lymph/edema
lymph/swelling

113. EF-
away or out
ef/ferent
away or out/to carry (nerve or blood flow away from a structure)
ef/ferent means
away or out/to carry
ef/fus/ion
out/attached/process

114. ELECTR/O-
electrical
electro/encephalo/gram
electrical/in head (brain)/recording

115. -ELLUM
lesser or smaller
cereb/ellum
brain/lesser or smaller

116. EM-
in
em/py/ema
in/pus/refers to (collection of pus in body cavity)
em/bol/ism
within/lump/state

117. EMAC/I-

to grow thin
Emac/i/ation
to grow thin (leanness or to waste)/process of

118. EMBRYO-
early
embryon/ic
early (2nd through 8th to 10th week of pregnancy)/refers to

119. -EMESIS
vomit
hem/emesis
blood/vomit

120. -EMIA
blood
leuc/emia (leukemia)
white/blood
(abnormal increase in WBC's)

121. EMMETR/O-
normal or correct
emmet/opia
normal or correct/vision

122. EMPHYSEMA
puffed up
emphysemat/ous
puffed up/state of or refers to
(inner air sacks of lung swollen)

123. EN-
in
en/cephal/itis
in/head (refers to brain)/inflamed

124. ENAMEL
hard
enamel
hard (hard outer covering of upper tooth)

125. EN/CEPHAL/O-
within head (referring to the brain)
encephalo/gram
within head/recording

126. ENDO-
within or inside
endo/derm
within or inside/skin

127. ENEMA
injection
enema
injection (water forced into colon for cleansing)

128. ENTERO-
intestine (usually refers to small intestine)
enter/itis
intestine (usually refers to small intestine)/inflamed

129. ENURESIS
to void or expel urine
enuresis
to void (expel) urine
(involuntary: like bed-wetting)

130. EOSIN/O-
rose red color
eosino/phil
rose red (color)/love of
(staining of WBC's)

131. EPI-
upon
epi/didymis
upon/teste (coil structure upon teste)
epi/gastr/ic
upon/stomach/pertains to
epi/glott/itis
upon/tongue/inflamed

132. EPISI/O-
pubic region or vulva
episi/orrhaphy
pubic region/to stitch
(repair of a lacerated or torn vulva or of a
episiotomy)
episi/o/tom/y
pubic region (vulva)/cut/process of
(upside down 'V' cut from vagina towards
anus: to ease childbirth in some women)

133. ERGO-
work or labor
ergo/meter
work/to measure
ergot
work or labor (birthing drug)

134. ERUCT/O-
belching
eruct/ation
belching/process of

135. ERYTHERMAT/O-
red or flushed
erythermat/ic
red or flushed/refer to

136. ERYTHR/O-
red
erythro/cyte
red/cell (chamber)
(a red blood cell that carries oxygen to the
body's cells)

137. -ER
one who
pract/ition/er
performs/process of/one who
related term(s): -IOR, -OR

138. ESCHAR
scab

eschar
scab
eschar/ification
snail like (scab)/process of (development)

139. -ESIS
condition of or disease
hemato/poi/esis
blood/development/condition of

140. ESO-
toward
eso/phag/us
toward/eater/refers to (tube from stomach
to mouth)

141. ESTHES/I-
physical feeling
an/esthes/ia
without/physical feeling

142. ESTR/O-
female
estro/gen
female/beginning (phase of cycle)

143. ETHM/O-
sieve
ethm/oid
sieve/resemble (base of skull and nose with
many openings)

144. ETI/O-
cause
eti/olog/y
cause/study or science of diseases/process

145. EU-
good or normal
eu/toc/ia
good or normal/birth/pertains to
eu/gene/tics
good, new or normal/ to produce or form/

state of
eu/phor/ia
good or normal/feeling (mental)/pertain to

146. EX-
out, outside, outward
ex/tens/ion
outward/to stretch/process of
related term(s): EXO-, EXTRA-

147. EXO-
out, outside, outward
exo/crine
outside/secrete
gland secreting through duct
related term(s): EX-, EXTRA-, EC-, ECTO-

148. EXTRA-
out, outside, outward
extra/pulmon/ary
outside/lung/refers to
related term(s): EX-, EXO-

149. FACET/O-
face
facet
little face (upper and lower small articular
faces of vertebral plates)
related term(s): FACI/O-

150. FACI/O-
face
faci/al
face/pertains to
related term(s): FACET/O-

151. -FACIENT
making
cale/facient
calcium or stones/making

152. FASC/I-
band

fasc/ia
band (covering around and between
muscles 'membranous')/refers to

153. FEBR/O-
fever
febr/ile
fever/state of or refers to

154. FEC/O-
stool or fecal matter
fec/o/lith
stool (feces waste)/like stone
related term(s): SCATO-, STERCO-

155. FELON
bad or malignant
felon
bad or malignant
(suppurative 'pus forming' at end of finger
or toe - often a nail abscess)
related term(s): WHITLOW

156. FEMOR/O-
thigh
femor/al
thigh/refer to

157. FENESTR/O-
window
fenestr/ial
window (opening in body or
forcepts)/refers to

158. -FERENCE
to carry
vas de/ference
vessel: away/to carry
(duct from teste)

159. FERRO-
iron
ferr/ous

iron/state of
related term(s): sider/o-, heme

160. FET/O-
young
feto/graph/y
young/instrument/procedure of
fet/us
young (last 6 & 1/2 months of development
in uterus)/refer to
(embryo means early)

161. FIBRILL/O-
to quiver
fibrill/ation
to quiver (muscle fiber contraction)/process
of

162. FIBRIN/O-
fiber like
fibron/osis
fiber like/condition
(a whitish filament of protein formed by
thrombin on fibrinogen found within the
blood stream)

163. FIBRO-
fiber
fibr/oma
fiber (thread like structures)/tumor

164. FIBUL/O-
to clasp
fibul/a
to clasp/refers to (noun)
(smaller outer long bone of lower leg)

165. FIL-
thread
fila/ment
thread/state of or refers to
related term(s): FILI-

166. FILI-
thread
fili/form
thread/shaped
related term(s): FIL-

167. FIMBRI/O-
fingers
fimbr/ia
fingers/refers to
(finger-like end projections of fallopian
tubes over the ovaries)

168. FISS-
to split or splitting
fiss/ion
splitting/refers to
fiss/ure
cleft or split/state of

169. FISTUL/O-
pipe or pipe stem
pyo/fistula
pus/pipe or pipe-stem
(pus found within a pipe or tube that opens
to body surface)

170. FLACCI/O-
soft
flacc/id
soft/state of

171. FLAGELL/O-
whip
Flagell/ation
whip/process of
(protozoa tail)

172. FLAT/O-
to blow
flat/us
to blow/refers to
(expelling gas from intestine)

flat/ulence
gas/state of (passing gas)

173. -FLECT
bend
de/flect
away/bend or divert
related term(s): FLEX-

174. FLEX-
to bend
ante/flex/ion
before/to bend or divert/process of
(to decrease angle of joint)
related term(s): -FLECT

175. FLU-
flowing
in/fluenza
inward/condition of flowing
(mucoid material)

176. -FLUX
to flow
re/flux
again/flow
(the movement of a substance backward or
upward)

177. FOC/O-
center or hearth
foc/al
center or hearth/pertains to

178. FONTAN/O-
little fountain
fontan/el
little fountain
(soft spot or non-bone membranous tissue
at the junction of babies' skull bones)

179. FORAMEN/O-
opening

foramen/al
opening/refers to
(also known as meatus or opening)

180. FORE-
before
fore/arm
before/brachium or arm
(between elbow and wrist)

181. -FORM
shaped, shape, form
vermi/form
worm/shaped
(appendix shape)

182. FOSSA-
furrow or shallow depression
foss/al
furrow or shallow depression
(pit like structure on a bone)

183. FRACT/O-
to break
fract/ure
to break/refers to

184. FRONT/O-
forehead or before
front/al
forehead or before (front brow)/pertains to

185. -FUGE
to flee
centri/fuge
center/to flee
(cell separation in tube)

186. FULGUR/O-
to lighten
fulgur/ation
to lighten/procedure of (process of)
(the destruction of tissue with a long, high-

frequency, electrical sparks)

187. FULV/O-
brown
fulv/us
brown

188. FUND/O-
base or large part
fund/us
base or large part/pertains to
(stomach and uterus body)

189. FUNGI-
mushroom
fungi/form
mushroom or plant/shape
related term(s): LICHEN/I-

190. FURC/O-
branch or fork
bi/furc/ation
two/branch or fork/procedure of (making)

191. FURUN/O-
boil
furun/cle
boil/small
(may vary in size and characteristics)

192. GALACT/O-
milk
galacto/poiesis
milk/production

193. GAMET/O-
to marry, unite, sexual union
gameto/cyte
to marry, unite, sexual union/of cells
(spermatozoon or ovum 'sperm and egg'
before conception)
alternate speling: GAM/O-

194. GANGLI/O-
knot, swelling, or collection
ganglion/ectomy
knot, swelling, or collection/excision
(removal of the fibrous swelling 'dorsal
root' formation on post. spinal nerve)

195. GANGREN/O-
eating sore
gangren/ous
eating sore/refers to
(dead tissue caused by isch/emia 'poor
blood flow')

196. GASTR/O-
stomach
gastr/itis
stomach/inflamed
gastrocnemi/us
calf of leg or stomach shaped muscle in
back of lower leg

197. GELATINO-
freeze or congeal
gelatin/ous
freeze or congeal/state of

198. GEN/O-
race
geno/type
race/classification (gene)

199. -GENESIS
origin, develop, to produce, to form, to make
spermato/genesis
sperm/development or formation/condition of
related term(s): -GEN

200. GENI/O-
chin
geni/ec/tom/y

chin/out/cutting/procedure of

201. GENIT/O-
reproductive or birth
genit/al
reproductive or birth/refers to
(reproductive structures)

202. GENU-
knee
genu/clast
knee/breaking
(instrument to break knee joint adhesions)

203. -GEN
origin, develop, to produce, to form, to make
carcino/gen
crab-like/ to produce, to form, to make,
origin, develop
(substance that causes cancer)
carcino/gen/esis
crab-like/origin or beginning/process of
related term(s): -GENESIS

204. GER/O-
old or old age
ger/iatr/ic
old or old age/treat or cure/study of or
science of
(studying all aspects of the aging process)

205. GEST-
to bear or separate
gest/ation
to bear or separate/process of
(time period from conception to birth)

206. GIBB/O-
hunchback
gibb/ous
hunchback (humped or protuberance)/state
of

207. GIG/A-
one billion or one billionth
giga/cytes
one billion or one billionth/cells

208. GINGIV/O-
gum
gingiv/itis
gum/inflamed
related term(s): ULO-

209. GLANDUL/O-
little acorn or gland
glandul/ar
little acorn or gland/refers to

210. GLAUC/O-
waterfall or gray
glauc/oma
waterfall or gray/swelling
(inner eye pressure causing loss of sight)

211. GLI/O-
glue or glue-like
gli/oma
glue or glue-like/tumor
(gliocytes are body cells that hold neurons
or nerves together)
alternate spelling: GLIA-

212. -GLOBIN
protein
hemo/globin
blood/protein
(specific type protein required for oxygen
carrying capacity of red blood cells)

213. GLOMERUL/O-
small round mass or tiny ball
glomerul/itis
small round mass or tiny ball/inflamed
(mass or capillary tuft of nephron "kidney
functional unit or filter")

214. GLOSS/O-
tongue
gloss/itis
tongue/inflamed
glosso/pharyng/eal
tongue/pharynx or throat/refers to

215. GLOTT/O-
back of tongue
epi/glott/itis
upon/back of tongue/inflamed
(structure protecting voice-box: consists of
two vocal cords & glottis rim)

216. GLUT-
buttocks
glut/itis
buttocks (rear-end)/refer to

217. -GLUTITION
to swallow
dys/glutition
painful or faulty/to swallow (down)

218. GLYCO-
sugar
glyco/pen/ia
sugar/decrease or lower/refers to

219. GNATH-
jaw or cheek
gnatho/dynia
jaw or cheek/pain

220. -GNOSIS
knowledge
dia/gnosis
total or complete/knowledge

221. GOITER
swelling (throat)
goiter/ectomy
swelling (throat)/removal of thyroid goiter

222. GON/O-
seed or seed producer
gono/rrhea
seed or seed producer/flowing from
related term(s): orchi/o

223. GONI/O-
angle
goni/meter
angle/measurement
(usually be for surgery)

224. GOUT
a drop
gout
a drop
(uric acid crystals larger than blood cells
which drop to lower joints causing pain.
Type of arthritis - usually found in big toe)

225. GRACIL/O-
slender
gracil/is
slender (muscle shape)

226. -GRADE
a step, stage, or degree in a process
retro/grade
backward or behind/a step, stage, or degree
in a process

227. -GRAFT
to probe or cut with a knife
dermo/graft
skin/to probe with knife (pole; probe; or
steak)
(the removal of skin to be placed on new
body part - like a flap)

228. -GRAM
to record
myo/gram
muscle/to record (write or take down)

229. GRANULO-
little grain
granul/oma
little grain/swelling or tumor

230. -GRAPHY
procedure of using an instrument to do recording
myo/graphy
muscle/procedure of using an instrument to do recording

231. -GRAPH
instrument
myo/graph
muscle/instrument
(used to do recording)
related term(s): -e

232. GRAVID/O-
heavy or pregnant
gravid/ium
heavy or pregnant/refers to
(gravida means pregnant woman)

233. GROIN
inguinal region
groin
inguinal region
(depression between thigh and trunk)

234. GRYPH/O-
crooked or bent
gryph/onych/ia
crooked or bent/nail/refers to

235. GUMM/O-
gum or gum-like
gumma
gum or gum-like
(lesions of 3rd stage of syphilis)

236. GUST/O-

tasting or to taste
gust/ation
tasting or to taste/process of

237. GYNEC/O-
woman
gynec/olog/ist
woman/science and study of/specialist
alternate spelling: GYN/O-

238. HALIT/O-
breath
halit/osis
breath/condition of
(offensive or bad breath)

239. HALLUX
great or big toe
hallux/ectomy
great or big toe/removal

240. HALO-
salt
hyper/hal/osis
excessive/salt/condition

241. HAMAT/O-
hooked shape
Hamat/ectomy
hooked shape/excision
(medial bone in distal row of wrist 'carpal' bones)

242. HAPLO-
half (single)
hapl/oid
half or single/resembling
(set of 23 chromosomes in cell 'not paired')

243. HEALTH
wholeness
health
wholeness

244. HECT/O-
one hundred
hecto/hedron
one hundred/sides

245. HELICO-
spiral
helico/bacter pylori
spiral (shaped)/bacteria: gatekeeper (lower end of stomach)
(digestive system bacteria that causes most digestive ulcers 'sores')

246. HELIO-
sun
helio/pathy
sun/injury (caused by)

247. HELMINTH/O-
worms or worm
helminth/iasis
worms or worm/disease of or condition of
related term(s): ASCAR/IS, VERMI-

248. HEM/O-
blood
hem/o/rrhage
blood/bursting forth
hemo/kinesis means: blood/movement or flow
alternate spelling: HEMATO-

249. HEME-
iron
hem/atin
iron/small part
(non-protein portion of hemoglobin where iron is in ferrous state)
related term(s): sidero-, ferro-

250. HEMI-
half or one half
hemi/plegia

half (right or left side of body)/paralyzed
related term(s): DEMI-, SEMI-

1. HEPAT/O-
liver
hepat/itis
liver (cells)/inflamed

2. HEPT/A-
seven
hepta/dactyl/ia
seven/fingers or toes/refers to

3. HERNI/O-
rupture or protrusion
hern/ia
rupture or protrusion/condition of

4. HERPES
to creep
Herpes (Herpes Simplex Virus)
to creep

5. HETER/O-
other or opposite
hetero/gen/ous
other or opposite/form/state of

6. HEX/A-
six
hexa/dactyl/ia
six/fingers or toes/refers to
hex/agon
six/sided

7. HIAT-
an opening
hiat/al
an opening/refers to
(esophageal hiatus in diaphragm)

8. HIDR/O-
sweat
hidr/osis
sweat (watery)/condition of
(abnormal sweating and usually causes

blisters)
related term(s): sudorifer/o-

9. HIRSUT-
hairy or profound hair
hirsut/ism
hairy or profound hair/state of
(bearded women or extremely hairy people)

10. -HISCENCE
to gape open
de/hiscence
away/to gape (open)
(wound, incision, injury that gapes open)

11. HISTO-
web-like or tissue
hist/olog/y
web-like or tissue/science or study
of/process of
(tissues are composed of similar cells)

12. HOLIST/O-
whole
holist/ic medicine
whole/state of: remedy or drug
(refers to treating the whole individual -
comprehensive total patient care: physical,
mental, social, and economic. New
approach to care by H.M.O.)
alternate spelling: HOLO-

13. HOMEO-
same, constant, or unchanged
homeo/path/y
same, constant, or
unchanged/disease/process of
related term(s): HOMO-

14. HOMO-
same
Homo Sapiens
same: wise man

homo/sex/ual
same/sex/refers to
related term(s): HOMEO-

15. HORDEOL/O-
barley corn
hordeolum
a barley corn or stye
(This is the inflamed sebaceous gland and
hair follicle near an eyelash follicle)
related term(s): STY/E

16. HORMON/O-
to urge on
hormon/al
to urge on/refers to
(chemicals that stimulate specific cell
performance)

17. HUMER/O-
arm (upper)
humer/al
arm (upper)/refers to

18. HYAL/O-
glassy or glass-like
hyal/ase
glassy or glass-like/enzyme
(enzyme found in head of sperm that break
down tissues on contact)

19. HYDRO-
water
hydro/pneumo/thorax
water/lung (within)/chest
hydro/cephalus
water (cerebral spinal fluid)/head (within)
related term(s): AQUA-

20. HYGRO-
moisture
hygro/blephar/ic
moisture/eyelid/refers to

(lacrimal gland or an agent to moisten the
eyelid)

21. HYMEN/O-
membrane
hymen/ectomy
membrane/removal
(usually performed in younger women)

22. HYPER-
increase or above
hyper/tens/ion
above or excess/pressure (above 140
systolic/90 diastolic -BP)/process of
hyper/troph/y
increase/development/process of

23. HYPN/O-
sleep
hypn/osis
sleep/condition
(alpha state of brainwave patterns: this is
not true sleep)
related term(s): somn/o-

24. HYPO-
under or below
hypo/tens/ion
under or below (pressure in
vessels)/contraction/process of
hypo/derm/ic
below/skin/pertaining to

25. HYSTER/O-
uterus
hyster/ectomy
uterus /removal
hyster/ia
nervous reaction/refers to

26. -IAC
pertains to
card/iac

heart/pertains to
related term(s): -AC, -AL, -AR, -ARY, -ATE, -EUM, -IC, -ICAL, -ILE, -IS, -IUM, -ORY, -OUS, -UM, -US

27. -IAL
refers to
card/ial
heart/refers to
related term(s): -AC, -AL, -AR, -ARY, -ATE, -EUM, -IAC, -IC, -ICAL, -ILE, -IS, -IUM, -ORY, -OUS, -UM, -US

28. IATR/O-
treat or cure, procedure of treating
ger/iatr/ic
old age/treat or cure/pertains to
related term(s): -IATR/Y

29. -IATR/Y
treat or cure
psych/iatr/y
mind/treatment or cure/procedure of or process of
related term(s): IATR/O-

30. -IA
refers to, condition, state of
esthes/ia
feeling (physical)/refers to, condition, state of
dys/phag/ia
difficult/eating or swallowing/refers to
related term(s): -A

31. -IBLE
ability to
flex/ible
bend/ability to
related term(s): -ABLE

32. -ICAL
refers to

med/ical
drug, treatment, cure/refers to
related term(s): -AC, -AL, -AR, -ARY, -ATE, -EUM, -IAC, -IC, -ILE, -IS, -IUM, -ORY, -OUS, -UM, -US

33. ICHOR/O-
serum or watery pus
ichor/ous
serum or watery pus/state of

34. ICHTHY-
fish or fish-like
ichthy/osis
fish or fish-like (resembles fish scales)/condition of
(often seen with fungus infections on feet)

35. -ICIAN
one who
diet/ician
food/one who (performs)

36. -ICLE
small or tiny
oss/icle
bone/small or tiny
related term(s): -CULE, -IOLE, -ULA, - ULE

37. ICTER/O-
jaundice
ictero/hepat/itis
jaundice (yellow-orange color)/liver/inflammation

38. -ISY
inflamed
pleur/isy
side or rib/inflamed
(2 layer serous membrane 'like pericardium and peritoneum' covering of lungs inside the ribs) related term(s): -itis

175

39. -IC
refers to
hepat/ic
liver/refers to
related term(s): -AC, -AL, -AR, -ARY, -ATE, -EUM, -IAC, -ICAL, -ILE, -IS, -IUM, -ORY, -OUS, -UM, -US

40. IDE/O-
idea, thoughts, emotions, image
ideo/motor
idea, thoughts, emotions, image/movement
ideo/vascul/ar
emotions/vessels/refers to
(vessels contract because of stress)

41. -IDE
specific quality of
derm/ide
skin/specific quality of

42. IDIO-
unique to or unknown cause
idio/path/ic
unique to or unknown cause/disease/refer to
(distinctive or individualized personal health problem)

43. -ID
state of
morb/id
disease/state of

44. ILE/O-
twisted
ile/um
twisted/pertains to
(3rd part of small intestine - 15 feet long)
ile/itis
twisted/inflamed
related term(s): torsi-, varic/o-

45. -ILE
state of
vir/ile
masculine/state of

46. ILIO-
flank
ili/um
flank (area)/refers to
(ili/acus muscle in outer pelvic flank area)

47. IM-
into or not
im/plant
into/place or locate
im/potent
not/powerful, strong or capable
(not capable of having a firm penile erection)

48. IMMUN/O-
safe, protect, immune
immun/o/log/y
safe, protect, immune/science of/process of

49. IN SITU
in position or location
in situ
in: position or location (original or first)
(early phase or stage of cancer)

50. IN-
into or not
in/di/gest/ion
not/two/separations/process of
in/cis/or
into/cut/pertain to
(4 front teeth top center and 4 bottom center)

51. INCUS
anvil
mallus/incus/stapes

hammer/anvil/stirrup (shapes)
(3 tiny ossicles or middle ear bones)

52. -INE
substance or chemical
holo/crine (gland)
all or whole/secretes substance or chemical
related term(s): -IN

53. INFARCT-
to stuff into
infarct/ion
to stuff into/refers to
(clot blockage that causes diminished blood
flow to heart or other body parts 'muscles or
organs')

54. INFECT/O-
to invade
infect/ion
to invade/process of

55. INFLAMM/O-
flame within
inflamm/ation
flame within/process of

56. INFRA-
under or below
infra/clavicul/ar
under or below/collar bone/refers to
infra/mur/al
below/wall/pertaining to
related term(s): hyp/o-, sub-

57. INFUNDILL/O-
funnel shape
infundill/um
funnel shape/refers to
(choana also means funnel)

58. INGUIN/O-
groin

inguin/al
groin/refers to
(area between belly and thigh)

59. -ING
procedure of or process of
operat/ing
working/procedure of or process of
related term(s): -AGE, -ATION, -IATION, -
ION, -TION, -Y

60. INTEGU-
covering
integu/ment
covering/refers to or state of
(skin of body)/refers to or state of

61. INTER-
between
inter/cellul/ar
between/cell or chamber/refers to

62. INTRA-
within
intra/nuclear
within/refers to nut

63. INTRO-
within
intro/spect
within/to view

64. INTUS-
within
intus/suscept/ion
within/to receive/process of
(invagination or the slipping of a body part
into a lower body part 'like the intestines' -
often seen in children and animals)

65. -IN
substance or chemical
gastr/in

stomach/substance or chemical
holo/crine (gland)
all or whole/secretes substance or chemical
related term(s): -INE

66. -IOLE
smaller, lesser, diminutive
bronch/iole
trachea-like (tubes of lungs)/smaller, lesser,
diminutive
alternate spelling: -OLE
related term(s): -CULE, -ICLE, -ULA, -ULE

67. ION/O-
going, ion movement
iono/therap/y
going (of ions)/treat or cure/procedure of
(treatment by introducing ions into body
related term(s): IONT/O-

68. IONT/O-
going or ion movement
ionto/therap/y
going or ion movement/treat or
cure/procedure of
(treatment by introducing ions into body)
related term(s): ION/O-

69. -ION
procedure of or process of
in/cis/ion
into/cut/procedure of or process of
related term(s): -AGE, -ATION, -IATION, -
ING, -TION, -Y

70. -IOR
one who is
infer/ior
under or below/ one who (is)
related term(s): -ER, -OR

71. -IOUS
state of

delir/ious
mental confusion or excitement/state of
(illusions and hallucinations)

72. IPSI-
equal
ipsi/later/al
equal/side or sides/process of

73. IR-
not or lack of
ir/regul/ar
not or lack of/consistent or regular/refers to

74. IR/O-
rainbow
ir/is (noun)
rainbow/refers to
ir/idescent
rainbow/having or exhibiting
related term(s): IRID/O-

75. IRID/O-
rainbow, eyes, iris
irido/cele
rainbow, eyes, iris/herniated or protruding
related term(s): IR/O

76. ISCH/O-
deficiency, blockage, to hold back
isch/emic
deficiency or blockage/refers to blood
(myocardial ischemia: angina pectoris or
chest pain because of poor blood supply to
the heart muscle)
isch/emia
hold back/pertains to blood

77. ISCHI/O-
hip joint or hip
Ischio/dynia
hip joint or hip/pain

78. -ISH
resembling or related to
lap/ish
stone/resembling or related to

79. -ISM
state of or condition of
giant/ism
large/state of
albin/ism
white/state of or condition of

80. ISO-
equal or same
iso/ton/ic
equal or same/tone/refers to
iso/cell/ar
equal/cells/refers to
(chamber 'inside cell membrane' pressure)

81. -IST
specialist
endo/crin/olog/ist
within/secrete/science or study of/specialist
(glands that secrete directly into or within
the blood)

82. -IS
refers to
rach/is
spine, spinal column, backbone/refers to
related term(s): -AC, -AL, -AR, -ARY, -ATE,
-EUM, -IAC, -IC, -ICAL, -ILE, -IUM, -ORY, -
OUS, -UM, -US

83. -ITES
dropsy or drooping
tympan/ites
drum/dropsy or drooping

84. -ITIS
inflamed or inflammation
gloss/itis

tongue/inflamed or inflammation
related term(s): -icy

85. -ITY
state of
steril/ity
barren (without fertility)/state of
related term(s): -ous

86. -IUM
refers to
card/ium
heart/refers to
related term(s): -AC, -AL, -AR, -ARY, -ATE,
-EUM, -IAC, -IC, -ICAL, -ILE, -IS, -ORY, -
OUS, -UM, -US

87. -IZE
state of or acts like
cauter/ize
burn/state of
hypnot/ize
sleep/state of or acts like

88. JEJUNO-
to empty (2nd part of small intestine)
jejun/um
to empty (the second part of the small
intestine/refers to
(five foot long 2nd part of the small
intestine with rugae 'folds' and villi 'hair-
like projections' for absorption)
related part(s): 1st part duodenum, 3rd part
ileum

89. JUNCTIV/O-
joining or to join
con/junctiv/itis
together/joining or to join/inflamed
(ocular and eyelid parts)

90. JUXTA-
near, close by, adjoining

juxta/position
near, close by, adjoining/place or location

91. KAKO-
bad
kako/smia
bad/smell

92. KALI-
potassium
kali/penia
potassium/decrease of

93. KARY/O-
nucleus
karyo/kinesis
nucleus/movement or motion

94. KEL/O-
scar
kel/oid
scar/resembling
(raised hard reddened scar)

95. KERAT/O-
cornea or horny
kerato/malac/ia
cornea (eye)/softening/refers to
(cornea of children - lack of Vitamin A)

96. KET/O-
sour or acid
keto/sis
sour or acid/condition
(an increase in ketone bodies referred to as
acidosis, associated with starvation)

97. KIL/O-
one thousand
kilo/gram
one thousand/grams
(recording weight of about 2.2 lb.)
note: a milli/gram is one thousandth of a

gram

98. KINE-
movement or motion
kine/tic
movement/state of or condition of
alternate spelling: KINESI/O
related term(s): KYM/O-

99. KRAUR/O-
dryness
Kraur/o/sis
dryness/condition
(associated with mouth and vagina)

100. KYM/O-
movement or motion
kymo/sis
motion/condition of
related term(s): KINE-,

101. KYPH/O-
hunchback
kyph/osis
hunchback/condition

102. LABIO-
lip
labi/oma
lip/tumor
(the term 'cheilo' also means lip)

103. LABYRINTHO-
maze
labyrinth/itis
maze/inflamed
(top portion of inner ear - balance)

104. LACER/O-
to tear
lacer/ate
to tear/refers to

105. LACRIM/O-
tearing or tear
lacrim/al
tearing or tear/refer to
related term(s): dacryo-

106. LACT/O-
milk
lact/ose
milk/sugar

107. -LALIA
talk or talking
neo/lalia
new/talk or talking

108. LAMIN/O-
thin flat plate or layer
lamin/ectomy
thin flat plate or layer/removal
lamin/ent
thin flat plate or layer/having or possessing
(bridge part of vertebrae arch)

109. LAP/I-
stone
lap/is
stone/refers to
related term(s): PETRO-, LITHO-

110. LAPAR/O-
abdominal wall
Lapar/o/tom/y
abdominal wall (belly)/cutting
into/procedure or process

111. -LAPSE
falling or slippage
pro/lapse
before/falling or slippage (means normal
before slippage)
(sinking down of a body part or organ,
usually at a normal or artificial opening)

re/lapse
again/falling or slippage

112. LARVA-
mask
larv/al
mask/refers to (stage of disease)

113. LARYNGO-
voice box
laryng/itis
voice box (larynx)/inflamed
(hoarseness or loss of the voice)

114. LAT-
side
lat/eral
side/refers to
lat/issimus
side (dorsal chest muscle)/refers to
alternate spelling: LATER/O-

115. LAX-
to loosen or loosening
re/lax/ation
again/to loosen/process of
alternate spelling: LAXAT/O-

116. LEI/O-
smooth
leio/my/oma
smooth/muscle/tumor
(smooth muscle tumor usually found in
stomach or uterus)

117. -LEMMA
sheath
neuro/lemma
nerve/sheath
(sheath 'husk or rind' around a body part)

118. LENT/O-
freckle

lent/icle
freckle/small
small skin blemishes

119. LEPR/O-
scaly
lepros/y
scaly/process of
(skin lesion appearance)
related term(s): LEPROS-

120. LEPROS-
scaly
lepros/y
scaly/process of
(skin lesion appearance)
related term(s): LEPR/O-

121. -LEPSY
seizure or convulsion
epi/leps/y
upon/seizure/process of
(short circuiting of brain waves)

122. LEPTO-
thin or slender
lepto/morph/ic
thin or slender/shape or form/refers to

123. LETH/O-
sluggish
leth/argic
sluggish (fall, sag, drowsy)/pertains to
leth/al
drowsy/refers to
(so sluggish or drowsy it leads to death)

124. LEUC/O-
white
leuco/cytosis
white (white blood cells: WBC's)/increase in
number (WBC's)
related term(s): LEUK/O-

125. LEUK/O-
white
leuk/aphere/sis
white (white blood cells:
WBC's)/separation/condition of
related term(s): LEUC/O-

126. LEVAT/O-
lift up
levat/or
lift up (muscle)/one who

127. LEVO-
left
levo/card/ia
left(position)/heart/refers to

128. LEX/I-
diction or word
dys/lex/ia
difficult or faulty/diction or word/refers to
(difficulty in reading words or phrases)

129. LIBID/O-
desire
libid/al
desire/refers to
(conscious or unconscious sex drive)

130. LICHEN/I-
plant
lichen/ific/ation
plant/process of making (plant-like)
(irritations that cause thickening or
hardening of skin surface - it now looks like
lichens growing on rocks)
related term(s): FUNGI-, PHYTO-

131. LIENO-
spleen
lien/itis
spleen/inflamed

132. LIGA-
to bind
liga/ment
to bind/state of
(binding bone to bone)

133. LINGU-
tongue
bi/lingu/al
two/tongue/pertain to
(use of tongue for producing sounds or
speech in two languages)

134. LIP/O-
fat
lip/oma
fat/tumor or swelling

135. -LISTHESIS
slippage
spondylo/listh/esis
vertebrae/slippage/condition of

136. -LITER
liter
milli/liter
one-thousandth/litre of fluid measurement
(liter is an unit of liquid: 1.0567 quarts or
1000 ml or cc.)
alternate spelling: -LITRE (European)

137. LITH/O-
stone, calculus or rock
nephro/lith
kidney/stone calculus or rock
related term(s): LAP/I-, PETRO-

138. LIVID/O-
blue
livid/ity
blue/state of

139. LOB/O-

lobe
lob/ectom/y
lobe/removal or excision 'cut out'/procedure
of
(usually in the lung)

140. LOCO-
place an object
locomotion
place an object/movement

141. -LOG-
science or study of, process or procedure of
hist/o/log/y
web-like (tissue appearance)/science of or
study of/process of
related term(s): -OLOGY

142. LOGO-
speech or words
log/o/rrhea
speech or word/flowing or running
(unusual speech seen in insanity)

143. LOIN
lumbar
loin
lumbar or lumbus
(area around lumbar vertebrae - between
ribs and pelvis)

144. LONG/O-
long
long/us
long (muscle shape)/refers to

145. LORD/O-
swayback (to bend)
lordo/sis
swayback (to bend)/condition of
(lumbar spine is bent anterior: often seen in
horses)

146. -LUCENT
to shine or shining
trans/lucent
through or across/to shine or shining

147. LUMB/O-
loin
lumb/ar
loin
(5 large lower back vertebrae: just above
sacrum or large tail bone)

148. LUMP-
small mass
lump/ectomy
small mass/excised or removed

149. LUNA-
moon or crescent-shaped
lun/ate
moon or crescent-shaped/refers to
(Lunar literally means moon, month, silver.
Moon is usually seen in a 'C' shape like the
2 crescent cartilages of the knee.)
related term(s): MENISC/O-

150. LUPUS
wolf
lupus erythematosus
wolf: red (faced)
(a progressive ulcerating skin condition:
auto-immune disease with skin lesions)

151. LUTE/O-
yellow
lute/al
yellow/refers to
(spot on retina 'macula lutea' or body
structure on ovary 'corpus luteum')
related term(s): XANTH/O-

152. LUX-
to dislocate

sub/lux/ation
under or less/to dislocate/refers to
(osteopaths, chiropractors, and orthopedic
doctors manipulate or adjust these bone
dis/articulations)

153. LYMPH/O-
watery
lymph/oma
watery (clear fluid or serum)/tumor or
swelling
(12 major types of lymphatic cancers:
Hodgkin's, Leukemias, & Reticular Cancers)

154. -LYSIS
destruction, breakdown, declining
auto/lysis
self/destruction, breakdown, declining
hemo/lysis
blood/breakdown

155. LYSSO-
frenzy, hysteria, rabies
lysso/phobia
frenzy, hysteria, rabies/fear
lyss/oid
rabies/resembling
alternate spelling: LYSSA-

156. MACER/O-
to make soft
macer/ation
to make soft/process of

157. MACRO-
large or huge
macro/phage
large or huge/eater(WBC's)
macro/scop/ic
large/viewing or seeing (eyeballing)/refers
to

158. MACUL/O-
large spot or flat skin freckle
macula lutea
large (flat spot on retina, lesions, mole
'nevus'): yellow macule large spot or flat
skin freckle (lenticel)
related term(s): MACULE

159. MAGNI-
large or greater
magni/ficat/ion
larger or greater/to make/process of

160. MAL-
bad, harm, injury
mal/ignant
bad, harm, injury/refers to
(growing worse or resisting treatment)
mal/practice
bad/action

161. MALAC/O-
soft or softening
osteo/malac/ia
bone/soft or softening/pertains to

162. MALL/E/OLUS
little hammer
malle/olus
hammer (little bony protuberance on either
side of ankle joint)/small
related term(s): MALLE/O-

163. MALLE/O-
hammer
malle/us
hammer (middle ear bone)/refers to(noun)
related term(s): MALLEOLUS

164. MAMM/O-
breast
mamm/ary
breast/refers to

related term(s): MAST/O-

165. MAN/O-
hand
manu/al
hand/pertain to
mano/meter
(thin or hand measurement)

166. MAND/I-
chew or chewer
mand/ible
chew or chewer/ability to(lower jaw bone)

167. -MANIA
madness
klepto/mani/ac
theft or steal/madness/pertains to
(obsession or preoccupation with stealing)
alternate spelling: MANI/O-

168. MASSET/O-
chewer or to chew
masset/er
chewer or to chew/one who
(muscle from cheek bone to lower jaw)

169. MASSEUR
male massager
masseur
French term for a male that gives massages
related term(s): MASSEUSE

170. MASSEUSE
female massager
masseuse
French term for a female that gives
massages
related term(s): MASSEUR

171. MAST/O-
breast
mast/ectom/y

breast/removal/procedure of
(partial or complete)
mast/oid
breast/resembling
(large bone projection of temporal bone:
posterior & interior to outer ear)
related term(s): MAMM/O-

172. MASTIC/O-
to chew or chewing
mastic/ation
to chew or chewing/process of
(refers to chewing with the large muscle of
the cheek -the masseter)

173. -MATA
multiple
carcino/mata
crab-like (cancerous growths)/multiple
(many)

174. MAXILL/O-
upper jaw
maxill/ary
jaw/refers to

175. MEASLES
rubella, reddish or red
measles
rubella or reddish or red
(3 Day or German Measles - 'Dutch
Mesalen'. Red spots appear with 'Papules,
Macules, and Vesicles'. Dangerous if
pregnant. Rubeola also means reddish and
this 9 or 10 day measles is more dangerous
because of high fever - 104 to 106 degrees F.
- usually respiratory virus)

176. MEAT/O-
opening
meat/us
opening/refer to

177. MECONI/O-
poppy juice
meconi/um
poppy juice/refers to
(opium poppy juice appearance for first '1st'
stool or feces of newborn)

178. MEDI-
middle
medi/an; medi/um; medi/al
middle/refers to

179. MEGA-
great or big
mega/colon
great (big)/large intestine

180. MEGALO-
huge or large
hepato/megal/y
liver/huge/process of

181. MEI/O- and MIO-
lesser, smaller, fewer, and constrict
mei/osis and Miotic
lesser, smaller, fewer/condition of
(reduction of cells chromosome from 23
pairs to 23 in egg or sperm. Miotic drops
lessen the size of the eyes pupil: mydriatic
drops dilate pupil) related term(s): MI/O-

182. MEL-
sweet, honey, cheek, limb
mel/itis
cheek/inflamed
mel/algia
limb/pain
mel/on
sweet/one who is

183. MELAN/O-
black
melan/oma

black/tumor (skin cancer)

184. MEN/O-
monthly or month
men/arche
monthly or month/start
meno/pause
monthly/stoppage

185. MENING/O-
membrane
mening/itis
membrane/inflamed
(covering of Central Nervous System 'CNS')
meninges
membrane
(3 parts: dura mater layer (hard mother);
arachnoid layer (spider-like web);
and pia mater layer (gentle mother))

186. MENISC/O-
crescent
menisc/ectomy
crescent ('C' shaped)/excision
(knee cartilage that are half moon or 'C'
shaped)
related term(s): LUNA-

187. MENT/O-
mind
ment/al
mind/pertains to

188. -MENTUM
chin
ante/mentum
before/chin

189. MERO-
part, part of, partly, to separate
mero/crine (glands)
part, partly, to separate /secreting
(glands like sebaceous oil glands that gibe

of up part of the secretions)
mero/melia
part of/limb (missing)

190. MES/O-
middle
mes/enter/y
middle/intestines/state of
(connective tissue or blood vessels on the
posterior middle wall of abdomen)
meso/derm
middle/skin
(outer layer is ecto/derm and inner layer is
endo/derm)

191. -MESTER
month
tri/mester
third/month

192. META-
beyond or change
meta/carp/al
beyond/wrist/pertains to
meta/bol/ism
change/lump/state of
meta/stasis
change (from)/standing or stoppage
(spreading of cancer or bacteria)

193. -METER
measurement
spiro/meter
breathe/measurement
opto/metr/ist
eye/measurement/specialist
alternate spelling: -METRE (European)

194. METR/A-
uterus or womb
endo/metr/iosis
within/uterus or womb/condition
endo/metr/itis

within/uterus or womb/inflammation

195. -METRY
measurement procedure
opto/metr/y (O.D.)
sight or vision/measurement/procedure or
process

196. MI/O-
lesser, smaller, fewer
mi/o/sis
fewer or smaller (number)/condition or
(reduction division process of gametes or
reproductive cells 'sperm and egg')
related term(s): MEI/O-

197. MICRO-
small
micro/gloss/ia
small/tongue/refers to
micro/scop/e
small/viewing/instrument

198. MICTUR/O-
to make water or urinate
mictur/ition
to make water or urinate/process of
alternate spelling: MICTURIT/O-

199. MILI/O-
millet seed
mili/um
millet seed/refers to
(pin size papule or pimple on skin surface
that is usually white)

200. MILLI-
one-thousandth
milli/meter
one-thousandth/of meter (39.37 inches)
Note: a kilo/gram is one thousand grams or
a recording weight of about 2.2 lb. A
milli/gram is one-thousandth of a gram

201. MINIMUS-
smallest
minim/um
smallest/refers to
(smallest: gluteus minimus is the smallest of
the 3 groups of buttock muscles)

202. MINUTE
small
com/minute
together/small
(com/minuted fractures are caused by the
bone being forced together causing small
bone parts or chips)

203. -MISS
to send or sending
e/miss/ion
out/to send or sending/process of

204. MIT/O-
thread or thread like
mit/osis
thread or thread-like/condition of
(the division of chromosomal thread-like
materials: it is obvious in meta/phase)

205. -MITR/E
head band or mitre box
mitr/al
head band or mitre box/refers to
alternate spelling: MITR/O- (European)

206. MNEM-
memory
mnem/onic
memory/to improve

207. MOGI-
difficult
mogi/phon/ia
difficult/voice, speaking, sound/refers to

208. MOL/O-
to mill or grind
mol/ar
to mill or grind/refer to
(upper and lower sets of back teeth of
humans)

209. MOLLUSC/O-
soft
mollusc/um contagiosum
soft/refers to: coming together (contagious)
(mild skin lesions or warts)

210. MON/O-
one
mono/nucle/osis
one/nut/condition of
(high number of mono/nuclear 'large' white
blood cells)
related term(s): UNI-

211. MORPHO-
shape
a/morph/ous
without/shape or form/state of or composed
of

212. MORT/O-
death
mort/al
death/refers to

213. MORUL/O-
mulberry
morul/a
mulberry/refers to
(cell mass during first week of pregnancy)

214. -MOTOR
movement or motion
oculo/motor
eye/motion or movement
psycho/motor

mind/movement
related term(s): KINESI/O-

215. MUC/O-
slime
muc/oid
slime/resembles

216. MULTI-
many, multiple, excessive
multiple sclera/osis (MS)
many: hardening/condition of
(hardening of nerves and myelin sheath
around nerves causing paralysis)
related term(s): PLURI-, POLY-

217. MUMPS
swelling
mumps
swelling
(viral infection of parotid saliva gland near
ear: progresses to gonad/itis, pancreat/itis,
nephr/itis, myocard/itis, and arthr/itis. Also
known as par/ot/itis 'near/ear/inflamed')

218. MY/O-
muscle
my/oma
muscle or muscular/tumor
alternate spelling: MY-, MYOS-

219. MYC/O-
fungus
myc/oid
fungus/resembles

220. MYDRI/O-
to widen
mydri/opt/ic
to widen/vision/refers to
(pupil of eye dilates)

221. MYEL/O-

spinal cord or bone marrow
myelo/gram
spinal cord/recording
myel/itis
bone marrow/inflamed

222. MYRIA-
numberless or numerous
myria/pod/iasis
numberless or numerous/footed/condition
or disease
(infestation with multiple arthropods)

223. MYRING/O-
eardrum
myring/itis
eardrum/inflamed (infected)

224. MYX/O-
mucus
myx/oma
mucus/tumor or swelling
myx/oid
mucus/resembles

225. NANO-
1 billionth
nano/meter
1 billionth part
nano/meter - 1 billionth/ of meter
(39.37 inches is a meter)

226. NARC/O-
sleep
narco/lepsy
sleep/seizure
(hypno- also means sleep)

227. NARES
nose opening
nares
nose opening

228. NAS/O-
nose
nas/al
nose/refers to

229. NAT-
birth
nat/al
birth/refers to
related term(s): NAT/O-, PARTO-, TOCI/O-

230. NAT/O-
birth
nat/al
birth/refers to
related term(s): NAT-, PARTO-, TOCI/O-

231. NATRI-
sodium or salt
hyper/natr/emia
increase/sodium or salt/in blood

232. NAVICUL/O-
boat or boat-shaped
navicul/ar
boat-shaped/refer to
(ankle and wrist scaphoid bones)

233. NECR/O-
death, dead, dying
necrot/ic
death, dead, dying/refers to
(mortification or the death process of any
body cells)
necr/osis
death, dead, dying/condition of
related term(s): THANAT/O

234. NEO-
new
neo/plasm
new/growth

235. NEPHELO-
cloudiness or mistiness
Nephel/op/ia
cloudiness or mistiness/sighted or
vision/refers to

236. NEPHR/O-
kidney
nephr/itis
kidney/inflamed

237. NEUR/O-
nerve
neur/algia
nerve/pain

238. NEUTR/O-
neither or neutral
neutro/phil(e)
neither or neutral/love for
(WBC that stains with a neutral PH of 7)

239. NEV/O-
birthmark
nev/us
birthmark/refers to
(moles, stains and other skin discolorations)

240. NIGRA-
black
nigra bodies
black: structures in and around cell nucleus
alternate spelling: NIGRI-, NIGRO-
related term(s): MELAN/O-

241. NIN/O-
nine
nin/us
nine/pertains to
related term(s): NOV-

242. NOCT/I-
night or blind

noct/uria
night/urination (excessive)
related term(s): NYCTO-

243. -NOIA
mind
para/noia
beyond/mind
(psychotic mental condition: loss of reality)

244. NOTO-
back, the back
noto/chord
back, the back/chord
noto/melia
back/limb
(extra body limb attached to the back area)

245. NOV-
nine
novo/caine
nine/drug
(series of numbing chemicals)
alternate spelling: NOVEM -
related term(s): NIN/O-

246. NUCH/A-
back of neck
nuch/al
back of neck/pertains to

247. NUCLE/O-
nut
nucle/us
nut (shaped)/refers to

248. NULL/I-
none or no
nulli/para
none or no (null or voided)/births

249. NUTRI/O-
to nourish

nutri/tion
to nourish/process of

250. NYCTO-
night or blind
nyct/op/ia
blind or night/sight or vision
alternate spelling: NYCT/I
related term(s): NOCT/I-

1. NYSTAGM/O-
to nod
nystagm/us
to nod (involuntary eyeball jiggling)/pertains to

2. -O/PEXY
to fixate, attach, sew
nephr/opex/y
kidney/fixate, attach, sew (suture)/procedure of

3. -O/PLASTY
repair or plastic surgery
rhino/plast/y
nose/repair or plastic surgery/procedure of

4. -O/RRHAGIA
bursting forth or heavy flow
meno/rrhagia
monthly (female cycle)/bursting forth (heavy flow)

5. -O/RRHEA
discharge or flow
men/o/rrhea
monthly/discharge or flow (slow)
gon/o/rrhea
gonad/flow

6. -O/RRHEXIS
rupture or protrusion
enter/o/rrhexis
intestine (small)/rupture or protrusion
related term(s): -O/RRHEXIA

7. OBLIQUE
side-long or slanted
oblique
side-long or slanted (at a 45 '+/-' degree angle)

8. OBSTETR/I-

midwife
obstetr/ics
midwife (childbirth)/pertains to

9. OCCIPIT/O-
back of head
occipit/otomy
back of head/opening (surgical procedure)
occipit/al
back of head/pertains to

10. OCCLUSI/O-
closure or blockage
occlus/ion
closure or blockage/process of

11. OCCULT/O-
hidden
occult/a (spina bi/fida)
hidden (thorn: two/clefts)/refers to

12. OCT/O-
eight
oct/agon
eight/walls
alternate spelling: OCTA-
related term(s): OCTI-

13. OCTI-
eight
octi/para
eight/given birth to
related term(s): OCT/O-

14. OCUL/O-
eye
oculo/motor
eye/movement

15. ODONT/O-
tooth
odont/oid
tooth/resembling

16. -OID
resembling
lip/oid
fat/resembling
epi/derm/oid
upper/skin/resembling

17. OLECRAN/O-
around the point of the elbow
olecran/al
around the point of the elbow/refer to

18. OLEO-
oil
oleo/vitamin
oil (fish oil)/life giving (fat soluble vitamins)

19. -OLEUM
oil
oleo/infusion
oil/injection
(formulation of a drug in oil)
petr/oleum
stone/oil

20. OLFACT/O-
smelling or smell
olfact/ory
smelling or smell/process of
related term(s): OSMO-

21. OLIG/O-
few, scanty, slight, little
oligo/meno/rrhea
few, scanty, slight, little/monthly/flow

22. -OLOG/Y
science or study of, process of
hist/olog/y
web-like or tissue/science of or study
of/process of
related term(s): -LOG-

23. -OMA
tumor or swelling
carcin/oma
crab or crab-like/tumor or swelling

24. OMI-
shoulder
acr/omi/on
end of/shoulder/refers to
related term(s): OMO-

25. OMO-
shoulder
omo/burs/itis
shoulder (near arm)/sack/inflamed
related term(s): OMI-

26. OMPHAL/O-
navel or umbilicus
omphal/ectomy
navel or umbilicus/removal (excision)

27. ONC/O-
tumor
onco/log/y
tumor/science or study of/process of
onco/log/ist
tumor/science of or study of/specialist
(Note - all tumors are not cancer. ex: 'benign
growths')

28. ONYCH/O-
nail
onycho/fidia
nail/split
related term(s): UNGUIN/O-

29. OOPHOR/O-
ovary
oophor/itis
ovary (seed producer)/inflamed

30. OPAQ/U-

obscure, dark, darkness
opaq/ue
obscure or dark/refers to
opac/ity
darkness/state of

31. OPHTHALM/O-
eye or eyeball
ophthalm/olog/ist
eye/science or study of/specialist
ophthalm/ic
eye or eyeball/refer to

32. OPIA-
vision, sight, and eye
my/opia
to shut/view (nearsightedness)
related term(s): OPT-, OPTO-, -OPSY

33. OPISTH/O-
backwards (bending)
opistho/tonus
backward (bending)/tone
(muscle contractions tilting head & spine
backward; seen with tetanus and Central
Nervous System injuries)

34. -OPSY
vision, sight, and eye
aut/opsy
self/process of viewing (after death)
related term(s): -OPT-, OPTO-, OPIA-

35. -OPT-
vision, sight, and eye
opt/ic
sight, vision, and occasionally eye/refers to
related term(s): OPTO-, OPIA-, -OPSY

36. OPTO-
vision, sight, eye
opto/metr/ist
vision or sight/measurement/specialist

related term(s): -OPT-, OPIA-, -OPSY

37. ORA-
mouth
or/al
mouth/pertains to

38. ORB-
circle or dish
orbit/al
circle or dish (eye socket)/pertains to
(orbit is actually a circular track)
related term(s): ORBIT/O-

39. ORCHI/O-
teste or seed producer
orchi/oma
teste or seed producer/tumor or swelling
orch/itis
testicle/inflamed
related term(s): GON/O-, ORCHID/O-

40. -OREXIA
appetite
an/orexia
without/appetite (not hungry)

41. ORGAN/O-
viscera, organ or cell parts
organ/elle
viscera, organ or cell parts (specialized body
part)/small
(cells: mitochondria, lysosomes, etc.)

42. -ORRHAGIA
bursting forth
hem/orrhagia
blood/bursting forth

43. -ORRHAPHY
suturing or repair
neur/orrhaph/y
nerve/suturing or repair/procedure of

44. -ORRHEA
flow or discharge
py/orrhea
pus/flow or discharge
gon/orrhea
seed producer or gonad/flow (from) or
discharge

45. -ORRHEXIA
rupture
lein/orrhexia
spleen/rupture
related term(s): -O/RRHEXIS

46. ORTH/O-
straight, normal, correct
ortho/dont/ic
straight, normal, correct/teeth/refers to

47. -OR
one who
doct/or
teacher/one who
praction/er
performs/one who
related term(s): -ER, -IOR

48. OS-
mouth
trache/os/tom/y
windpipe/mouth/cut/process

49. OSCILL/O-
to swing
oscillo/graph
to swing/instrument (that measure electric
activity of heart and muscles)

50. -OSE
sugar
malt/ose
malt/sugar

51. -OSIS
condition of or disease
scoli/osis
crooked (lateral curve)/condition of or
disease
related term(s): -ASIS, -ESIS, -SIS

52. OSMO-
smell
an/osm/ia
without/smell/refers to
related term(s): OLFACT/O-

53. OSS/EO-
bony or bones
oss/icle
bony or bones/small
(3 small bones of middle ear 'malleus, incus,
and stapes')

54. OSTE/O-
bone
osteo/path
bone/disease
(most diseases caused by bone
misalignment)
osteo/por/osis
bone/cavities (pores)/condition of

55. -OSTOMY
mouth-like opening produced by surgery
col/ostomy
colon/opening (mouth-like formation)
procedure

56. OT/O-
ear
ot/itis
ear/inflamed

57. -OTOMY
cutting, to cut, cut into
tracheo/tom/y

rough (windpipe)/cut into/procedure of
ana/tom/y
apart/cutting/procedure of or process of

58. -OTRIPSY
crushing or to crush
neur/otrips/y
nerve/crushing or to crush/procedure of
(surgical)
litho/tripsy
stone/crushing/procedure of (kidney or gall
stones 'calculi')

59. -OUS
state of or refers to
carcinomatous
cancer or malignancy/state of or refers to
ser/ous
liquid/material state or refers to
related term(s): -AC, -AL, -AR, -ARY, -ATE,
-EUM, -IAC, -IC, -ICAL, -ILE, -IS, -IUM, -
ORY, -UM, -US

60. OV/O-
egg
ov/ary
egg/refer to
ovul/ate
egg/state of or process of (producing)
alternate spelling: O/O-, OVA-, OVI-
related term(s): OV/U-

61. OV/U-
egg
ovul/ate
egg/state of or process of (producing)
related term(s): OV/O

62. OX/Y-
sharp or oxygen molecules
oxy/op/ia
sharp/vision/refers to
oxy/gen

sharp (mentally)/producing, developing,
forming
oxy/gen/ation
oxygen (molecules)/development/process of
alternate spelling: OX/O-

63. PACHY-
thick
pachy/derm/ia
thick/skin/refers to
related term(s): PACHY/DERM (elephant-
like)

64. PALAT/O-
palate, plate or plate of the mouth roof
palato/plasty
palate (roof of mouth)/repair
palat/oplasty
roof of mouth or palate/surgical repair
palat/ine
plate of mouth roof (skull bones)/state of

65. PALL/O-
pale or lack of color
pall/or
pale or lack of color/one who
(characteristic of illness)

66. PALM/A-
palm or palm of hand
palm/ar
palm or palm of hand/refer to
(front of the hand 'palms forward' as seen in
the human anatomical position)

67. PALPAT/O-
touching or to touch
palpat/ion
touching or to touch/process of
(physical diagnosis procedure)

68. PALPEBRA-
eyelid

palpebr/itis
eyelid/inflamed
related term(s): BLEPHARO-

69. PALPIT-
quivering or fluttering
palpit/ation
quivering or fluttering (heart)/process of

70. PALSY
slight or moderate paralysis
Cerebral Palsy (C.P.)
brain: paralysis
(injury to brain that causes temporary or
permanent loss of
sensation, movement, control)

71. PAN-
all, total, complete
pan/dem/ic
all, total, complete/people/pertain to
(spread of disease)
pan/creat/itis
all/flesh/inflamed

72. PAPILLA-
nipple
papill/ary
nipple/state of or refer to

73. PAR-
near, beside, beyond, around, similar, abnormal
par/ot/id
near, beside, beyond, around, similar,
abnormal/ear/refers to
related term(s): PARA-

74. PARA-
near, beside, beyond, around, similar, abnormal
para/thyr/oid
near/shield shaped/resembling

related term(s): PAR-

75. -PARESIS
paralysis
hemi/pare/sis
half/paralysis (slight)/condition of
(this occurs in tertiary syphilis of C.N.S.)
related term(s): -PLEG/IA

76. -PAREUNIA
sexual intercourse
dys/pareunia
painful or difficult/sexual intercourse
a/pareunia
without/sexual intercourse

77. PARIET/O-
wall or partition
pariet/al
wall or partition/refer to (skull bone)
partition/refer to (pertains to walls of a
cavity)
alternate spelling: PARIET-
related term(s): PHRAG-, SEPTA-

78. PART/O-
birth or labor
post/part/um
after/birth or labor/refers to
related term(s): NAT-, NATO, TOCI/O-

79. PATELL/O-
little dish or knee cap
patell/ar
little dish (knee cap)/refer to

80. PATH/O-
disease
path/o/log/y
disease/science of or study of/process of

81. PAUS/O-
stoppage

meno/paus/al
monthly/stoppage/refers to
(female 30 day '+/-' cycle)

82. PECT/O-
chest
pector/al
chest (anterior breast area)/refer to
related term(s): PECTERO-

83. PECTIN/O-
comb
pectin/ate
comb/state of or resembles
(teeth like a comb - muscles)

84. PED-
foot or feet
ped/al
foot or feet/refer to
alternate spelling: PEDO-, PEDI-, related
term(s): PES, POD-, PODO-

85. PEDI-
child
ped/iatrics
child/treat
ped/ia/tric/ian
child/treats or cures/one who
related term(s): PEDIA-

86. PEDIA-
child
ped/ia/tric/ian
child/treats or cures/one who
related term(s): PEDI-

87. PEDICUL/O-
lice
pediculo/sis
lice (head, body or pubic)/condition of

88. PELI-
purple
peli/osis
purple/condition of
(purple spots seen in and on
immuno/compromised patients)

89. PELL-
skin
pell/agra
skin/rough or painful
related term(s): CORI/O-, CUT-, CUTI/O-,
DERMAT/O-, DERMO-

90. PELVI/O-
base, basin, pelvis
pelv/ic
base, basin, pelvis/refers to
(bounded by hip bones and sacrum)
alternate spelling: PELV/O-

91. PEMPHIGO-
blister or blistering
pemphig/us
blister or blistering/pertain to
(pustule bulbus skin lesion crops)

92. PEN/O-
tail, organ of copulation, penis
pen/itis
penis/inflamed

93. -PENIA
decrease in number
leuko/cyto/penia
white (WBC's)/cells/decrease in number

94. PENT/A-
five
pent/agon
five/walls
penta/dactyl five (normal)/fingers and toes
on each limb

95. PEPS/O-
digestion
dys/peps/ia
difficult or painful/digestion/refers to
alternate spelling: PEP-, PEPSI-, PEPT/O-

96. PER-
through
per/cutane/ous
through/skin/state of
per/meate
through/opening

97. PERI-
around
peri/cardi/um
around/heart/refers to
peri/stal/sis
around/to clasp and compress/condition

98. PERINE/O-
base or floor
perin/eal
base or floor/refers to
(area between anus and external genital
organs 'scrotum and vulva')

99. PERITON/E-
that which holds the lower viscera
peritone/um
that which holds the lower organs/refers to
(two layered serous membrane in
abdomino/pelvic cavity that hold organs)
periton/itis
membrane holding lower viscera or organs
and structures/inflammation

100. PERO-
maimed
pero/brachius
maimed/forearm and hand

101. PERONEO-
pin or concerning the lower outside leg
bone
perone/al
pin or concerning the lower outside leg
bone/refers to
perone/us
pin/refers to
(one of several muscles of leg that moves
the foot)

102. PES
foot
tali/pes
ankle/foot
(club foot - ankle and foot turn inward)
related term(s): PED-, POD-, PODO-

103. PETECH/I-
small
petech/ial
small/refers to
(usually refers to small hemorrhages or
spots on skin or brain)

104. PETIT
little illness
petit mal
little illness/bad
(less severe than grand mal epileptic
seizures)

105. PETRO-
rock, stone, hard
petro/derma
rock, stone, hard/skin
osteo/petr/osis
bone/stone-like/condition
related term(s): LAP/I-, LITHO-

106. PHAGO-
eat, eating, perverse appetite
phago/cyto/sis
eat, eating, perverse appetite/cells

(WBC's)/refers to
alternate spelling: -PHAGY

107. PHAK/O-
lens
phak/oma
lens/tumor
phac/itis
lens (eye crystalline)/ inflamed
related term(s): PHAC/O-

108. PHALANG/O-
close-knit row (fingers and toes)
a/phalang/ia
without/close-knit row (fingers and toes)/refers to
related term(s): PHALANX-

109. PHALANX-
close-knit row (fingers and toes)
phalanx
close-knit row (refers to fingers and toes)
related term(s): PHALANG/O-

110. PHARMAC/O-
drug relationship, to drug, medicine
pharmac/o/log/ist
drug or medicine/study of/specialist

111. PHARYNG/O-
throat
pharyng/itis
pharynx or throat/inflamed (sore throat)

112. PHAS-
speech or speaking
dys/phas/ia
difficult or faulty/speech or speaking/refers to
related term(s): PHAS/O-

113. PHAS/O-
speech or speaking

dys/phas/ia
difficult or faulty/speech or speaking/refers to
related term(s): PHAS-

114. -PHASE
stage
meta/phase
change/stage or an appearance
(stage of mit/o/sis-chromosomes visible changing)

115. PHENO-
to appear
Pheno/log/y
to appear (climates effect on health) /study of/process of

116. PHEO-
dusty or dark
pheo/chrome
dusty or dark/color

117. -PHERESIS
withdrawal or to separate
hemato/pheresis
blood/to separate
(separating different types of blood cells: leuco/cytes, erythro/cytes, and thrombo/cytes)

118. -PHILE
love of, to love, love for
eosino/phil/ia
rose red (WBC staining)/love of/refers to
alternate spelling: -PHILIA
related term(s): -PHIL

119. -PHIL
love of, to love, love for
eosino/phil/ia
rose red (WBC staining)/love of/refers to
related term(s): -PHILE

120. PHIM/O-
to muzzle or muzzling
phim/osis
to muzzle or muzzling/condition of

121. PHLEB/O-
vein
phleb/itis
vein/inflamed
phleb/o/tom/ist
vein/cut/specialist (draws blood)
related term(s): VENO-

122. PHOB/O-
fear
hydro/phob/ia
water/fear (rabies)/refers to

123. PHOC/O-
seal
phoco/mel/ia
seal/limbs/refers to
(flipper babies caused by thalidomide and other drugs)

124. PHON/O-
voice or sound
dys/phon/ia
faulty or difficult/voice or sound/refers to

125. PHOR/O-
feeling (mental)
eu/phor/ia
good/feeling (mental)/refers to
(esthesia means a physical feeling)

126. -PHORESIS
migration, transport, move or carry
a/phoresis
no or lack of/migration, transportation, movement
hemo/phoresis
blood/carrying, migration, transmitting
chema/phoresis
chemical/not moving
epi/phoresis
above/to carry or bear
(the term -PHORESIS is a suffix, the term PHORES/I- is a prefix)

127. PHOT/O-
light
photo/graphy
light/process of recording with device
photo/phobia
light/fear of

128. PHRAG/O-
wall or partition
dia/phragm
across or through/wall or partition
related term(s): PARIET/O-, SEPTA-

129. PHRASO-
speech or talk
a/phras/ia
without/speech, talk, unable to understand phrases/refers to

130. -PHRAXIA
stoppage or obstruction
hemo/phrax/ia
blood/stoppage or obstruction/refers to

131. PHREN/O-
mind or diaphragm
phren/ia
mind (mental disorder)/pertains to
phren/ic (nerve)
diaphragm/pertains to

132. -PHTHISIS
wasting
somo/phthisis
body/wasting

133. -PHYLAXIS

protection or guard
pro/phylaxis
before/protection or guard
ana/phylaxis
away from/prevention

134. PHYSI/O-
function of or nature of
physi/o/log/y
function or nature of/science of/process of

135. -PHYSIS
growth or nature of
sym/physis
together/growth or nature of
alternate spelling: -PHYSIC

136. PHYTO-
plant
phyto/toxin
plant/poison
(plant poisons effecting human)
related term(s): -LICHEN

137. PIA-
gentle
pia mater
soft or gentle: mother
(innermost meninges 'membrane' layer
covering the spinal cord)

138. PICA-
magpie eating or perverse appetite
pica magpie eating or perverse appetite
(paint, ice, starch, clay, ashes, plaster: not
typical or nutritive foods)

139. PICR/O-
bitter
picro/toxin
bitter/poison
(powerful CNS stimulant: shrub seed
substance that stimulates respiration)

140. PIL/O-
hair
pil/oma
hair/swelling or tumor-like
(condition in hair follicle)
related term(s): -THRIX, TRICH/O-

141. PIN/O-
to drink
pino/cyte
to drink/cell
(RBC or other body cell - enlarging with
fluid)

142. PINE-
pinecone-like gland
pine/al
pinecone-like gland/refers to
(this tiny gland is found at the base of brain
stem and secretes the hormone melatonin
regulating sleep)

143. PINN/A-
feather or feather-like
pinna/form
feather-like/shape
(the outer ear projection is called the pinna)

144. PIP/O-
pipe or tube-like
pip/ette
pipe or tube-like/little

145. PIS/I-
pea
pisi/form
pea/shaped
(smallest outer wrist bone; used in spinal
adjustments by Chiropractors)

146. PITUIT/O-
phlegm or glue-like mucus
pituit/ary

phlegm or glue-like mucus/refer to
(mucoid fluid discharges when gland is
pinched during dia/section)

147. PITYR/I-
bran (cereal-like scales on skin)
pityri/asis
bran (cereal-like scales on skin)/refers to

148. PLACENT/A-
cake
placent/itis
cake/inflamed
(afterbirth or structure attached to uterine
wall during pregnancy that provides
nutrition to the fetus)

149. -PLAKIA
plate or plate-like
leuko/plakia
white/plate
(pre-cancerous lesions on a membrane or
the skin)

150. PLAN/O-
flat or a plane
plan/us
pes plan/us
foot: flat or a plane (flat footed)

151. PLANT/O-
sole of foot
plant/ar
sole of the foot/refer to
(plantar warts 'verruca' are found on the
bottom of foot)

152. PLAS-
growth, development, formation
hyper/plas/ia
excessive/growth, development,
formation/pertains to
alternate spelling: PLAS/O-, PLAST

related term(s): -PLASM

153. PLASM-
growth, development, formation
neo/plasm
new/growth
related term(s): PLAS-

154. PLATY-
broad or flat
platy/pod/ia
broad or flat/foot/pertain to

155. -PLEG/IA
paralysis
quadri/plegia
four (limbs)/paralysis
(often caused by a stroke 'Apoplexy or
CVA')
para/plegia
beyond (lower two limbs)/paralyzed
related term(s): -PARESIS, -PLEXY

156. PLEUR/O-
side or rib
pleur/itis
side or rib/inflamed
(this is an inflammation of the membrane
that covers the lung just inside the ribcage)
related term(s): COST/O-

157. -PLEXY
paralysis
neuro/plexy
nerve/paralysis
related term(s): -PARESIS, -PLEGIA

158. PLIC/O-
fold, to fold, to tuck
plic/ation
folding or tucking/process of
(to reduce a structure or organ size)

159. PLURI-
many, multiple, several, excessive
pluri/para
three or more/births/refers to
related term(s): MULTI-, POLY-

160. -PNEA
breathe or breathing
a/pnea
without or lack of/breathe or breathing
related term(s): PNEUM/O-, PNEUMON/O-, PNEUMAT/O-, SPIRO-

161. PNEUM/O-
lung, air, respiration
pneumo/thorax
air (within)/chest
alternate spelling: PNEUMA-
related term(s): -PNEA, PNEUMON/O-, PNEUMAT/O-

162. PNEUMAT/O-
lung, air or gas, respiration
pneumat/o/log/y
air or respiration/science or study
of/process of
(this is the science of air and gases -
studying their chemical properties for the
treatment of patients)
related term(s): PNEUM/O-, -PNEA,
PNEUMON/O-

163. PNEUMON/O-
lung, air or gas, respiration
pneumon/ia
lung/refers to
related term(s): PNEUM/O-, -PNEA,
PNEUMAT/O-

164. POD-
foot or feet
pod/iatr/y
foot/treatment or cure/process of or

procedure of
(profession that treats hands and feet)
related term(s): PED-, PES, PODO-

165. PODO-
foot or feet
podo/graph
foot/imprint of foot on paper (used in
podiatry)
related term(s): PED-, PES, POD-

166. -POIE/SIS
to make, form, produce
hemato/poie/sis
blood (large amount)/to make, form,
produce/condition or state of
(usually refers to blood production by bone
marrow: erythro/poiesis 'RBC's)

167. POIKIL/O-
irregular or varied shape
poikilo/cytic
irregular or varied shape/cell

168. POLI/O-
gray
polio/myel/itis
gray/spinal cord/inflamed
(virus attaches anterior gray motor horn
rami of the spinal cord)

169. POLLEX-
thumb
pollex/ectomy
thumb/removal

170. POLY-
many
poly/dipsia
many/thirsts (being thirsty)
related term(s): MULTI-, PLURI-

171. PONS

bridge
pons
bridge
(surrounds the brain stem in front and
connects to the cerebellum: switchboard)
related term(s): PONT/O-

172. PONT/O
bridge
pont/oma
pons or bridge/tumor or swelling
(below brain and in front of stem)
related term(s): PONS-

173. POPLES-
back of knee
poplit/eal
back of knee/refer to
(hamstrings area/posterior knee)

174. POR/O-
cavity or passage (porous)
osteo/por/o/sis
bone/cavity or passage (porous)/condition
of

175. PORPHYR/O-
purple
porphyr/osis
purple/condition
(usually skin discoloration)

176. POST-
after or behind
post/part/um
after/birth/refers to
poster/ior
after or behind/refers to

177. -POX
pits
small pox
tiny/pits

(some remain on skin after primary lesions
disappear)

178. PRAND/I-
meal or breakfast
prandi/al
meal or breakfast/pertain to
a/prand/ial
without/meal/refer to

179. -PRAX/IA
movement or action
pharmaco/prax/ia
drug/movement or action/pertain to
myo/prax/is
muscle/action/refers to
related term(s): KINESIO-

180. PRE-
before
pre/natal
before/birth
related terms: ANTE-, PRO-

181. PREPUCE
foreskin or hood
prepuce
foreskin or hood
(skin covering of penis 'tail' and clitoris
'penis-like')

182. PRESBYO-
old
presby/op/ia
old (weak eyes of elderly)/vision/refers to
(vision defect seen with advancing aging
known as far sightedness - 'Hyper/opia' -
where one can see objects clearly far away,
but not close up)

183. PRIM/I-
first
prim/ary

first/refers to
related term(s): PROT/O-

184. PRO-
before
pro/gnosis
before/knowledge
pro/phylax/is
before/prevention or guard/refers to
related term(s): ANTE-, PRE-

185. PROCT/O-
rectum or anus
proct/o/log/ist
rectum or anus/science or study of/specialist

186. PRONAT/O-
to bend forward
pronat/ion
to bend forward/process of
(to lay face down; to lower; to turn hand
palm downward or backward)
related term(s): PRONE-

187. PRONE-
to bend forward
pronat/ion
to bend forward/process of
(to lay face down; to lower; to turn hand
palm downward or backward)
related term(s): PRONAT/O-

188. PROPRI/O-
property (nerve stimuli or information)
proprio/ceptor
property (nerve stimulation or
information)/ones own receives
(these are nerve receivers in the bodies
joints)

189. PROS/O-
face, facial, early, forward
proso/plas/ia

forward, face, early/development/refers to
(early cell transformation to higher degree
of function, like saliva cells)
related term(s): PROSOP/O-

190. PROSOP/O-
face, facial, early, forward
prosopo/plegia
facial/paralysis
related term(s): PROS/O-

191. PROSTAT/O-
one who lies before
prostat/ectomy
one who lies before/excision (cut out)
(prostate gland lies in front of urinary
bladder)

192. PROT/O-
first
proto/zoon
first/animals
(protozoa - the one cell animal)
related term(s): PRIMI-

193. PROXIM/O-
close or closest
proxim/al
close or closest/refer to

194. PRUR/I-
itch or itching
prur/itis
itch/inflamed
related term(s): PRURIT/O-

195. PRURIT/O-
itch or itching
prurit/ic
itching/refer to
related term(s): PRUR/I-

196. PSEUD/O-

false
pseudo/membranous
false/skin like/state of

197. PSOAS
loin (lumbar)
psoas
loin (lumbar)
(these are muscles above the flank and
beside the lumbar region)

198. PSOR/I-
to itch
psori/asis
to itch/condition of

199. PSYCH/O-
mind
psych/olog/y
mind/science of or study of/process of

200. PTERYG/O-
winged
pteryg/oid
winged/resembles
(membrane growth on medial aspect of
eyeball)

201. -PTOSIS
to drop, fall, displace
splanchno/ptosis
viscera or organ/to drop, fall, displace
nephro/ptosis
kidney/to drop, fall, displace

202. PTYAL/O-
saliva
hyper/ptyal/osis
excessive/saliva/condition

203. -PTYSIS
spitting or spit
hemo/ptysis

blood/spitting or spit

204. PUB/O-
pubis; pubic
pub/ic
pubis, pubic/refers to

205. PUDEND/O-
external genitalia and female vulva
pudend/al
external genitalia esp. female vulva/ pertain
to
pudend/um
external genitalia and female vulva
(posterior to mons)/refer to

206. PUERPER-
after childbirth
puerper/ium
after childbirth/refers to
(expulsion of placenta & female structures
returning to normal 42 days after birth)

207. PULMON/O-
lung
pulmon/ary
lung/pertains to
alternate spelling: PULM/O-
related term(s): PNEUM/O-

208. PULP/O-
solid flesh
pulp/itis
solid flesh/inflamed

209. PUNCT/O-
to pierce or a point
punct/ure
to pierce or a point/refers to
puncto/graph
a point/instrument to write
device using X-ray for locating foreign
bodies

210. PUPILL/O-
pupil
pupilo/meter
pupil/to measure (size of ring shape)

211. PURPUR/O-
purple
purpur/ic
purple/refers to
(small purple hemorrhages appear on the skin, membranes, organs, tissues)

212. PY-
pus
py/emia
pus in blood
(WBC's and fluid from inflammatory infection or septic/emic blood poison)
related term(s): PYO-

213. PYCN/O-
thick, dense, compact
pycno/card/ia
thick, dense, compact/heart (muscle wall)/pertains to
related term(s): PYKN/O-

214. PYEL/O-
pelvis or kidney
pyelo/nephr/itis
pelvis/of kidney /inflammation

215. PYKN/O-
thick, dense, compact
pykn/emia
thick/refers to blood
(often causing heart attacks and stroke)
related term(s): PYCN/O-

216. PYL/O-
gatekeeper
pyl/or/ic
gatekeeper/one who/refer to
(lower sphincter (that which binds together) of stomach)

217. PYO-
pus
pyo/gen/ic
pus/produce/refers to
related term(s): PY-

218. PYRET/O-
fever
pyret/ic
fever 'febrile', heat, fire/refers to
pyreto/gen
fever/producing
related term(s): PYREX-

219. PYREX-
fever
pyrex/ia
feverish/refers to
related term(s): PYRET/O-

220. QUADR/I-
four
quadr/ants
four/refers to
(4 abdominal divisions around navel '+')
alternate spelling: QUAD-

221. QUINT/I-
five
quintu/plet
five/offspring or folds

222. RACHI-
jointed vertebrae, spine, spinal column
rachi/algia
spine/pain
alternate spelling: -RACHIS
related term(s): RHACHI/O-

223. RADI/O-

ray, spoke, X-ray, radio activity
radia/tion
ray, spoke, X-ray, radio-activity/process of
or state of
rad/ius
spoke/refer to
(lateral bone of forearm - to side with palm up)

224. RADIC/O-
nerve root or spinal nerve
radicul/itis
nerve root/inflammation
related term(s): RADICUL/O-

225. RADICUL/O-
nerve root or spinal nerve
radiculo/neur/itis
nerve root or spinal nerve/nerve/inflamed
related term(s): RADIC/O-

226. RALES
to rattle
moist rales
damp or wet/to rattle (inhaling chest
sounds)
(air passing through bronchi containing
fluid: many other types - dry, bubbling,
gurgling, clicking, cavernous,
bronchi/ectatic, atelectatic, & redux 'in &
out')

227. RAY-
spoke or wave length
ray
spoke or wave length
(This is one or more lines from a common
center: energy, X-ray, spectrum, radiant,
fluorescence, and heat. Types vary: X-ray,
alpha, beta, gamma, delta, actinic, cathode,
hard, heat, infrared, luminous, medullary,
positive, primary, secondary, roentgen,
ultraviolet, etc.)

228. RE-
again
re/spir/ation
again/breath/process of

229. RECT/O-
rectum or straight
recto/clysis
rectum or straight/washing out
rectus abdominal muscles
straight/belly/muscle

230. REN/O-
kidney
ren/al
kidney/pertaining to

231. RETICUL/O-
network
reticul/ation
network/process of
(a massive net: composed of the net and
WBC's in bone marrow and in lymph
nodes)

232. RETINA
net or net-like
Retin/itis
net or net-like/inflamed
(the appearance of the blood vessels on the
thin inner eye layer at back of eyeball)

233. RETR/O-
back of, behind, backward, after
retro/cervic/al
behind/neck/refers to
retro/grade
back of, backward, behind, after/movement
retro/col/ic
back of/big intestine/refers to

234. RHABD/O-
rod or rod-shaped

rhabdo/virus
rod-shaped (RNA viruses))/poison
(one pathogen in this group is the rabies virus)
rhabdo/phob/ia
rod or rod-shaped/fear
(fear of being hit by rod or fear of nematode 'rods' worm infection)/pertains to

235. RHACHI/O-
jointed vertebrae, spine, spinal column
rhach/itis
jointed vertebrae, spine, spinal column/inflamed
alternate spelling: RACHIO-
related term(s): RACHI-

236. RHEUMAT/O-
discharge or flow through
rheumat/oid arthr/itis
discharge or flow through/resembles: joint/inflamed

237. RHIN/O-
nose
rhino/plasty
nose/repair or plastic surgery (nose job)
rhin/itis
nose/inflamed
rhin/o/rrhea
nose/running

238. RHIZ/O-
root
rhizo/tomy
root/cut into
(this is the incision into a section of a nerve or tooth root)

239. RHOD/O-
rosy red, purple red
rhod/al
rosy red, purple red/pertains to

(usually refers to colors seen by the retina)
rhod/op/sin
purple red/visual/protein found in the rods of the retina

240. RHOMB/O-
parallelogram or diamond-shaped
rhomb/oid muscles (major and minor)
parallelogram (diamond-shaped)/resembles: muscles
(one of two muscles beneath the large trapezius muscles of the neck and back 'cervical and thoracic vertebra')

241. RHYTID/O-
wrinkles
rhytid/ectomy
wrinkles/plastic surgery to remove wrinkles
rhytido/plasty
wrinkles/plastic surgery or repair

242. RICKETTS/IA
Bacteria discovered by Howard Ricketts/refers to
rickets like symptoms in joints/refers to
Dr. Howard Ricketts was an American pathologist '1871-1910' who identified this type of organism.

243. RIG/O-
stiff or hard
rigor mortis
stiff or hard/one who is: death

244. ROENT/O-
X-ray
roent/gen/ic
x-ray/beginning or caused by/refer to

245. ROSACE/O-
rosy, pink, red
rosace/ous (skin lesions)
rosy, pink, red/pertains to

246. ROTAT/O-
to turn or swing around
rotat/or
to turn or swing around/one who

247. -RRHYTHM
rhythm or contraction
a/rrhythm
lack of or without/rhythm or contraction

248. RUBE/O-
red
rube/osis
red/condition of
alternate spelling: RUBER/O-
related term(s): RUBELLO-, RUBEOL-

249. RUBELLO-
red
rub/ella
red/lesser
(rubella is 3 day measles forming red
lesions
related term(s): RUBE/O-, RUBEOL-

250. RUBEOL-
red small
rube/ola
red/small
(rubeola is 9 day measles, with a high fever
related term(s): RUBE/O-, RUBELLO-

1. RUG/A-
folds
rug/ae
folds/refers to (seen in vagina; stomach; intestines)

2. SACCHAR/O-
sugar
sacchar/ide
sugar/likeness

3. SACR/O-
saucer or sacred bone
sacr/al
saucer or sacred bone/pertaining to

4. SAGITT/O-
arrow or arrow-like
mid/sagitt/al
middle/like and arrow or arrow-like (cut)/refers to
(visual or surgical cut separating body or parts into right and left segments)

5. SALIV/O-
spit
saliv/ation
spit (making)/process of
saliva/process of (making or producing)

6. SALPING/O-
tube, duct, canal
salping/itis
tube, duct, canal/inflamed

7. SANGU/I-
blood or bloody
sanguino/poiet/ic
blood (bloody)/production of/refer to

8. SARC/O-
fleshy
sarc/oma
fleshy/tumor
(these are tumors of the body's hard tissue 'bones, muscle, tendons, ligaments, and
cartilage' that become soft or flesh-like)

9. SARTOR/I-
patcher
sartor/ius
patcher/refers to
(longest body muscle in upper front leg)

10. SCAB/O-
to itch
scab/ies
to itch/condition of
(mite infestation of skin)

11. SCAPH/O-
skiff or boat-shaped
scaph/oid
skiff or boat-shaped/resembles

12. SCAPUL/O-
shoulder blade
scapul/ectomy
shoulder blade/removal (surgical excision)

13. SCATO-
dung or feces
scato/scopy
dung or feces/examination of (for diagnostic purposes)
related term(s): FEC/O-, STERCO-

14. SCHIST/O-
split or splitting
schisto/cyte
to split/cell (RBC fragment)
schisto/som/asis
split/body (of nematode worm)/condition of
(infestation caused by eating raw snails from infected bodies of water)

related term(s): SCHIZ/O-, SCISS/I-

15. SCHIZ/O-
split or splitting
schizo/phren/ia
split/mind/refers to
related term(s): SCHIST/O-, SCISS/I-

16. SCINTILL/O-
spark
scintillo/scop/e
spark/to examine/instrument
(viewing effects of ionizing radiation on
fluorescent screen)

17. SCIRRH/O-
hard
scirrh/oma
hard/tumor

18. SCISS/I-
split or splitting
sciss/ion
to split/process of
related term(s): SCHIST/O-, SCHIZ/O-

19. SCLER/O-
hardening
athero/scler/osis
yellow fat or porridge/hardening/condition
of
(this is the leading killer or cardiovascular
disease in the US)
scler/itis
hard/inflammation
(sclera is the hard outer white membrane
layer of eye)

20. SCOLI/O-
crooked or twisted
scoli/osis
crooked or twisted (spine)/condition of

21. -SCOP/E
an instrument that examines or views
micro/scop/e
small/to view or examine/instrument
(process of)

22. -SCOPY
to examine or view
lapro/scop/y
abdomen wall or abdominal/to examine or
view/procedure of

23. SCOT/O-
darkness
scot/oma
darkness (blind spot)/swelling or tumor
(causing)
(portion of retina of the eye: blind spot)

24. SCROT/O-
sac or pouch
scrot/al
sac or pouch/refers to
related term(s): VESIC/O-

25. SCURVY
to scratch
scurvy
to scratch
(vitamin C deficiency)

26. SEB/O-
oil
seb/aceous gland
oil/pertains to
(sebaceous gland of hair follicle: sebum
means oil like -oleum)

27. SECRETO-
separating or to separate
secreat/or
separating or to separate/one who

28. SECT/O-
to cut
sect/ion
to cut (several times) or to cut
apart/procedure of
(to section an organ)
related term(s): -CIS, -TOM

29. SECUND/I-
second
secundi/gravida
second/pregnancy
alternate spelling: SECOND/O-

30. SEMEN/O-
seed or seed producer
semen
seed (male sperm 'with fluid')
related term(s): SEMIN/O-

31. SEMI-
half
semi/conscious
half/aware
related term(s): DEMI-, HEMI-

32. SEMIN/O-
seed or seed producer
semin/al
seed or seed producer/refers to
semen
seed (male sperm 'with fluid')
related term(s): GONO-, SEMEN/O-

33. SENIL/E-
old
senil/ity
old/state of
(mental and/or physical weakness)
(Presbyt/iatrics and Ger/iatrics treat
diseases of old age)

34. SEPS/O-

poison, infection, decay, putrefy
sep/sis
poison, infection, decay, putrefy/condition
of
related term(s): SEPT/O-

35. SEPT/A-
partition or wall
sept/um
partition or wall/refers to
(wall dividing a space: nose and heart)
related term(s): PARIET/O-, PHARG/O-

36. SEPT/I-
seventh
septi/para
seventh/child births or born infants

37. SEPT/O-
poison, infection, decay, putrefy
sept/ic
poison/refer to
related term(s): SEPS/O-, TOX/O-

38. SER/O-
whey or watery portion of blood
ser/um
whey or watery portion of blood/refers
to/refers to
(also refers to any serous fluid that moistens
a serous membrane like the pleura,
pericardium, peritoneum or a gland like the
parotid. It also can refer to animal serum
that can renders immunity to other animals)

39. SESQU/I-
one and one-half
sesqui/liter
one and one-half/liter

40. SEXT/I-
six
sexti/para

six/child births or born infants

41. SHUNT
to turn away or divert
shunt
to turn away or to divert
(the insertion of a plug-like device into a
canal or organ usually to drain fluid.
example - the insertion of a device into the
kidney pelvis to drain urine from the
kidney)

42. SIAL/O-
saliva or spit
sial/aden/itis
saliva or spit/gland/inflammation
hypo/sialo/gogic
low/saliva/production
related term(s): -PTYSIS, SALVI/O-

43. SIDER/O-
iron
sidero/cyte
iron/cell
(specialized RBC's that contain iron in a
form other than hematin)
related term(s): FERR/O-, HEME-

44. SIGMOID/O-
s-shaped
sigm/oid/oscope
s-shaped/resembles/to view or examine

45. SILIC/O-
silicon carbon particles
silico/sis
silicon carbon particles/refers to
(also known as: arc welders disease -
inhaling iron particles)

46. SIN/O-
cavity
sin/us
cavity/refers to
(air-filled or open space in bone)
related term(s): ALVEOL/I-

47. SINISTR/O-
to the left or left
sinistro/card/ia
to the left or left/heart/refers to

48. -SIS
condition of or disease
psycho/sis
mind/condition of (loss of mental reality)
related term(s): -ASIS, -ESIS, -OSIS

49. SKELET/O-
dried up or to attach
skelet/al
dried up or to attach/refers to

50. SOLE-
the sole of the foot
sole/us
sole of foot/refers to
(muscle running from the back of the lower
leg to the sole of the foot)

51. -SOL
in solution or solution
aero/sol
air/solution

52. SOM/O-
body
psycho/somat/ic
mind/body/refer to
(the term SOM/O is a prefix, the term -
SOME is a suffix)
related term(s): SOMAT/O-

53. SOMAT/O-
body
psycho/somat/ic

mind/body/refer to
related term(s): SOM/O-

54. SOMN/O-
sleep
somni/pathy
sleep/disease
(sleep disorder)
related term(s): HYPN/O-

55. SON/O-
sound
sono/gram
sound/recording or writing (diagnosis)
related term(s): ECHO-

56. SPAD/I-
to tear
epi/spad/ism
upon/to tear/state of
(usually abnormal opening on the upper side of the male penis or shaft)
related term(s): AVULS/I-,
tip: DACRY/O- and LACRIM/O- mean "to tear" as in tearing up or crying

57. -SPASM
involuntary contraction
myo/spasm
muscle/sudden involuntary muscle contraction

58. SPERM/O-
sperm
spermo/cide
sperm/to kill
alternate spelling: SPERMAT/O-

59. SPHEN/O-
wedge-shaped
sphen/oid
wedge-shaped/resembles
(this is a bone in the skull)

60. SPHER/O-
ball, globe, round
spher/o/cyte
ball, globe, round/cells

61. SPHINCT/O-
that which binds together
sphinct/er
that which binds together or tight (ring like)
(The 'pylorus sphincter' is known as the gatekeeper to the small intestines. The 'anal sphincter' is this ring that binds together at the end of the colon)

62. SPHYGM/O-
pulse
sphygmo/mano/meter
pulse/by hand/measurement
(this records the pressure of blood above atmospheric pressure 760 mm/hg as it passes through arteries)

63. SPHYXI/O-
pulse or lack of pulse
a/sphyx/ia
without/pulse/refers to
(this refers to lack of a heart beat 'no pulse' due to lack of breathing)

64. SPIN/O-
thorn or thorny
spin/al
thorn or thorny/refers to
(sharp pointed projection of bone: the spine has multiple thorny projections)
related term(s): CORNU- (means horn or horny)

65. SPIR/O-
breathe or breathing
spir/o/meter
breathe, breathing/measure
spiro/gram

217

breathing/record
spiro/graph
breathing/instrument used to record
related term(s): -PNEA

66. SPLANCHN/O-
organ
splanchn/o/log/y
organ (viscera)/study of/process of

67. SPLEN/O-
spleen
splen/o/tom/y
spleen (organ)/cut into/procedure of
related term(s): LEINO-

68. SPONDYL/O-
vertebra
spondyl/itis
vertebra/inflamed

69. SPRAIN
to wring out or press out
sprain
to wring out or press out
(usually with tears, swelling, and bleeding)

70. SQUAM/O-
scaly
squam/ous
scaly/refers to

71. -STALSIS
to contract
peri/stalsis
around/to contract

72. STAPED/O-
stirrup
staped/ectomy
stirrup (shape)/excision or removal
(One of three tiny bones of the middle ear:
mallus/incus/stapes =

hammer/anvil/stirrup)
related term(s): STAPES

73. STAPES-
stirrup
mallus/incus/stapes
hammer/anvil/stirrup
related term(s): STAPED/O-

74. STAPHYL/O-
grape or grape-like clusters
straphylo/coccus
grape or grape-like clusters/berry
(bacteria appearance)
related term(s): UV-, UVE/A-, UVE/O-,
UVUL/O-

75. -STASIS
stoppage, standing, location
hemo/stasis
blood/stoppage
(arrest of bleeding or circulation; blood
stagnation causing clots)
homeo/stasis
same or equal/standing or location
alternate spelling: -STASIA

76. -STAT
to stop or immediately
hemo/stat
blood/to stop
(device or drug that immediately arrests
blood flow. STAT. or stat means
immediately - stop what you are doing and
help)

77. -STAXIA
dripping or trickling
epi/staxia
upon/dripping or trickling
(epistaxis means nosebleed)

78. STEAT/O-

fat
steato/rrhea
fat/flow
(flow from the sebaceous 'oil' glands of hair
follicle)
related term(s): ADIPO-, LIPO-

79. STEN/O-
narrowing
sten/osis
narrowing/condition of

80. STERCO-
stool, fecal matter or dung
sterc/o/lith
stool (feces waste)/like stone
related term(s): FEC/O-, SCATO-

81. STEREO-
three-dimensional or solid
stereo/cine/fluoro/graphy
three-dimensional (viewing)/motion
picture/fluorescence/recording procedure

82. STERN/O-
chest, sternum, or breastbone
stern/al
chest, sternum, breastbone/pertain to

83. STETH/O-
chest
stetho/scope
chest/to examine
related term(s): PECT/O-, PECTER/O-,
THORAC/O-

84. STIGMAT/O-
a point or spot
a/stigmat/ism
without/a point or spot/state of
(light ray not focusing accurately on retina
do to a football shaped cornea)

85. -STOLE
contract
sy/stole
together/contract
(blood pressure created by heart chamber
contraction)
dia/stole
between/contraction
(lower blood pressure that occurs when
heart chamber is filling with blood between
contractions of the heart muscle)
related term(s): -SPASM, -STALSIS

86. STOMAT/O-
mouth
stomat/itis
mouth/inflamed

87. STRABISM/O-
to squint or squinting
strabism/us
to squint or squinting/refers to
(lazy eye 'one eye deviates' due to loss of
acuity, muscle, nerve damage. Types
include: 'cross-eyed, wall-eyed, intermittent,
vertical, paralytic, and spastic')

88. STRAIN
to draw tight
strain
to draw tight (stretch)
(less severe than a sprain)

89. STRAT/I-
layer
strati/form
layer/shaped
strat/um basal
layer/refers to: base of (skin)

90. STREPT/O-
twisted or twisted chain
strepto/coccus

twisted or twisted chain/spheres
(bacteria appearance)

91. STRI/A-
stripes or threads
stria/tion
stripes or threads/process of
(usually associated with muscle appearance
and skin stretch marks)

92. STRICT/O-
drawing or binding
strict/ure
drawing or binding/state of

93. STY/E
raised
stye
raised
(This is the inflamed sebaceous gland and
hair follicle near an eyelash follicle)
related term(s): HORDEOL/O-

94. STYP/E-
contract
styp/sis
contract/condition
(a styp/tic pencil is used as a astringent to
contact skin and stop bleeding of shaving
cuts)
vaso/step/tic
vessel/contraction/refers to
(contracts vessels to stop bleeding)

95. SUB-
beneath, under, less or lesser
sub/lingu/al
under/tongue/pertains to
sub/dur/al
under/hard (meninges layer)/refers to
sub/lux/ation
lesser/dislocation/process of

96. SUDORIFER/O-
sweat
sudorifer/ous
sweat/pertain to
related term(s): HIDR/O

97. SULC/O-
furrow, fissure, split, depression
sulc/us (brain)
furrow, fissure, split, depression/refers to

98. SULF/O-
sulfur
sulfon/amide
sulfur/in protein
related term(s): THIO-

99. SUPER-
above or upon
super/cil/ia
above/hairs/refers to
(eyelash-like)
super/ficial
on or near/refer to surface

100. SUPINAT/O-
to throw backward
supinat/ion
throwing backward/process of
(to turn the body or part upward)

101. SUPRA-
above or upon
supra/pelvic
upon or above/pelvis or basin
supra/cost/al
above/ribs/pertaining to

102. SUR/A-
on calf of leg
sur/al
on calf of leg/refers to
(muscles: area of leg calf)

103. SURG/I-
working by hand
surg/ical
working by hand/refers to
surgeon
one who works by hand

104. -SUSCEPTION
to receive
intus/susception
inward/to receive (intestinal invagination)

105. SUTURE
sewing together
sutur/ing
sewing together/procedure of

106. SYCO-
fig or fig-like
syco/sis
fig or fig-like/condition of
(hair follicle inflammation that appears like a fig)

107. SYM-
together
sym/physis
together/growth
related term(s): COM-, CON-, SYN-

108. SYN-
together
syn/drome
together/running (signs and symptoms)
syn/apse
together/point of contact
syn/ovi/al
together/like egg/ refer to
related term(s): COM-, CON-, SYM-

109. SYNCOPE
to faint or fainting
syncope

to faint or fainting

110. SYSTEM/O-
to classify or arrange
system/ic
to classify or arrange/refers to

111. SY/STOL/O-
to draw together or contract
systol/ic
to draw together or contract/refer to
related term(s): TRACT/O-

112. TACHY-
fast or swift
tachy/card/ia
fast or swift/heart/refers to

113. TAL/O-
ankle
tal/us
ankle/refers to

114. TARS/O-
broad flat surface
meta/tars/al
beyond/broad flat surface/refer to

115. TART/O-
dregs, sediment or particles
tart/ar
dregs, sediment or particles/pertains to
(minerals and other particles deposited on teeth. Also known as Plaque or Calculus)

116. TAX/O-
arrange, to order, to organize, locate
tax/o/nom/y
arrange, to order, to organize, locate/law/process of
(to classify plants or animals, to organize or put a order to items in biology)

117. -TAXIA
muscle coordination
a/taxia
without/muscle coordination

118. TECT-
shield
pro/tect/ion
before/shield/process of

119. TEL/O-
end or outward
telo/phase
end or outward/stage
(the end stage or phase of mitosis)
related term(s): TELE-

120. TELE-
end or outward
tele/vis/ion
at end/sight or vision/process of
related term(s): TEL/O-

121. TEMPOR/O-
temple
tempor/al
temple/refers to
(bones of both sides of skull at its base)

122. TEN/O-
tendon
teno/desis
tendon/binding
(surgical fixating or reattaching a tendon)
related term(s): TEND/O-, TENDON-

123. TEND/O-
tendon
tendo/lysis
tendon/breakdown
(process of freeing a tendon)
alternate spelling: TENDIN/O
related term(s): TENDON-, TEN/O-

124. TENDON-
tendon
tendon/itis
to stretch/inflamed
related term(s): TEND/O-, TEN/O-

125. TENS/O-
to stretch or stretches
tens/or
to stretch or stretches/one who
alternate spelling: TENT/O-

126. TERAT/O-
monster
terat/o/logy
monster/study of
(medical special that studies deformed
offspring)
alternate spelling: TERA-

127. TERES
round
teres
round
(round and smooth muscles or ligaments
that are cylindrical)

128. TERMIN/O-
end, place at the end, boundary
termin/al
place at the end or boundary/refers to
related term(s): TERM

129. TERM
end, place at the end, boundary
a set period of time, like the end of a
pregnancy. related term(s): TERMIN/O-

130. TERT-
third
tert/iary stage
third/state of or condition: phase
(3rd stage of a disease like syphilis, which

forms gummas or gum-like lesions)
related term(s): TERT/I-

131. TERT/I-
third
terti/para
third/birth
tert/iary stage
third/state of or condition: phase
(3rd stage of a disease like syphilis, which
forms gummas or gum-like lesions)
related term(s): TERT-

132. TEST/E-
witness
test/icle
witness/small

133. TETAN/O-
spasm or spasms
tetan/y
spasm or spasms/process of (contraction of
muscles-like in lockjaw)

134. TETR/A-
four
tetra/olog/y (of Fallot)
four/science of or study of/process of
(combination of four abnormalities seen in a
Fallot's Heart)

135. THANAT/O-
death
thanato/log/y
death/studying or study of/process of
related term(s): NECR/O-

136. THEC/O-
sheath
Thec/itis
sheath/inflamed
(this is the inflammation of the sheath of a
tendon)

thec/oma
sheath/tumor
(this is usually a tumor within the ovarian
sheath seen after menopause)

137. THEL/O-
nipple
thel/ectomy
nipple/removal or excision (surgical
procedure)
(usually associated with breast cancer)

138. THEN/O-
palm of hand or sole of foot
then/ar
palm of hand or sole of foot/pertains to
(palm of hand and the fleshy part at base of
thumb)

139. THEO-
God
theo/mania
god/madness
theo/log/y
god/study of/process of

140. THERAP/O-
treating or curing
therap/y
treating or curing/procedure of
chemo/therap/y
chemical (with)/treatment or
cure/procedure of

141. THERM/O-
heat, hot or warm
therm/ometer
heat, hot or warm)/measurement
therm/al
temperature/pertain to
thermo/gram
heat/recording
(diagnostic graphic record of heat

variations: blood flow or tissue changes)

142. THIO-
sulfur
thio/cyan/ate
sulfur/cell/state of
related term(s): SULF/O-

143. THORAC/O-
chest
thoraco/centesis
chest (thorax)/surgical puncture to drain
fluid
(thorax 'chest' relates to the 12 chest
vertebra with 12 pairs of attached ribs)
related term(s): PECTER/O-, STETH/O-

144. -THRIX
hair
endo/thrix
within/hair
related term(s): PILO-, TRICH/O-

145. THROMB/O-
clot, clump together, curdle
thromb/osis
clot, clump together, curdle/condition of
(this is a blood clot somewhere in the
vascular system or an organ)

146. THYM/O-
soul, emotion, flowery smell
thym/us
soul, emotion, flowery smell/refers to
(endocrine gland that is part of the immune
system '1-13 Y/O blood development')

147. THYR/O-
shield or shield-shaped
thyr/oid
shield or shield-shaped/resembling

148. TIBIA-
shinbone
tibi/al
shinbone/refers to
tibi/algia
shinbone/pain

149. -TIC
capable of or state to
caus/tic
burning or burn/capable of or state of

150. TINEA-
fungus
tine/al
fungus/refers to

151. TINNITUS
jingling, tinkling, ringing
tinnitus
jingling, tinkling, ringing
(inflamed lower part of cochlea 'snail' of
inner ear: causing a ringing sound)

152. -TION
process of or procedure of
nutri/tion
nourishment/process of or procedure of
related term(s): -AGE, -ATION, -IATION, -
ING, -ION, -Y

153. -TIVE
nature of or quality of
in/sensi/tive
not/feeling or to feel/nature of or quality of

154. TOCI/O-
birth, giving birth, birthing
dys/toci/a
difficult, painful, faulty/birth/refers to
alternate spelling: TOC-
related term(s): NAT-, NATO-, PARTO-

155. -TOM/E
cutting instrument
derma/tom/e
skin/cut/instrument
(an instrument used to cut into the skin)

156. TON/O-
tension, tone, pressure
tono/meter
tension, tone, pressure/to measure
(instrument used to measure pressure or
tension within the eye 'intra/ocul/ar')

157. TONSILL/O-
almond shape
tonsill/ectomy
almond shape/removal or excision
(this lymph node gland tissue becomes
overwhelmed and swollen with infections)

158. TOP/O-
location
top/al
location/refers to
ec/top/ic
outside/location/pertains to
(usually a mal-positioned pregnancy in the
wombs tube, cervix, on the ovary)

159. TORSI-
twisted
tors/ion
twisted/refers to
(Torsion means twisting of a body part. This
is usually a twisting of the blood vessels
around the vas de/ference in the male
scrotum, causing a blood flow blockage,
pain, & vessel dilation)
related term(s): ILEO-, VARIC/O-, TORTI-

160. TORTI-
twisted
torti/coll/is

twisted/neck/refers to
(neck is twisted or tilted to the side 'causing
pain')
related term(s): TORSI-

161. TOX/O-
poison
tox/ic
poison/refers to
toxic/olog/y
poison/science of/procedure of
(science that studies how poisons are
chemical composed, action tests, and
antidotes)
related term(s): SEPS/O-, SEPT/O- , VIR/O-

162. TRACHE/O-
rough
trache/o/tom/y
rough/to cut into/refers to
(the cut is between the semi-circular
cartilage rings of the windpipe)
related term(s): TRACHY-

163. TRACHEL/O-
neck or neckline
trachelo/dynia
neck or neckline/pain

164. TRACHY-
rough
trachy/phon/ia
rough/voice or sound/refers to
related term(s): TRACHE/O-

165. TRACT/O-
to draw or pull
tract/ion
to draw or pull/process of
related term(s): SYSTOL/O-

166. TRANS-
across or through

trans/fus/ion
across or through/connect/process of
trans/verse
across/to draw
(horizontal cut creating the top and bottom
parts of the body or a structure)
related term(s): DIA-

167. TRAPEZI/O-
little table
trapez/ius
little table/pertain to
(muscle of neck and upper back that form a
four sided trapiz/oid shape)

168. TRAUMA
wound

169. TREPAN/O-
borer or to bore
trepan/ation
a borer (to perforate)/procedure of
(usually drilling a bone to take biopsy tissue
samples)
related term(s): TRYPAN/O-

170. -TRESIA
perforation or opening
a/tresia
without/perforation or opening

171. TRI-
three
tri/ceps
three/headed
(muscle in back of arm - extends forearm)
tri/gemin/al
three (parts)/form or development of/refer
to

172. TRIAGE
to sort or classify
triage

to sort or classify
(screening: in hospitals, at accidents, in war
to prioritize treatment)

173. TRICH/O-
hair
tricho/crypt/osis
hair/hidden/condition
(any hair follicle disease - hidden below
surface)
tricho/mon/iasis
hair/single or one/condition
(STI parasitic infection: protozoa has one
tail 'single hair-like projection')
related term(s): PILO-, -THRIX

174. -TRIGO-
rubbing
inter/trigo
between/rubbing
(friction causes skin weakness usually
between digits & fungus infection)

175. TROCHLE/O-
pulley or pulley-like
trochle/ar
pulley or pulley-like/refer to
(name of fourth '4th' cranial nerve:
innervates superior oblique eye muscles)

176. TROP/O- (TROP/IN)
stimulate or to turn
gonado/tropin (hormone)
teste or ovary/stimulate
trop/ism
to turn/state of
(reaction to stimuli - turn toward or away
from heat, cold, light, etc.)

177. TROPH/O-
development, nourishment or nutrition
hyper/troph/y
increased/development/process of

tropho/therapy
nourishment or nutrition/treatment

178. -TRIPSY
to crush
litho/tripsy
stone/crushing (gall stones)

179. TRYPAN/O-
borer, to bore, drill
trypano/som/iasis
borer/body/disease or condition
related term(s): TREPAN/O-

180. TUB/O-
canal or tube
tub/al ligation (female sterilization)
canal or tube/refers to: to bind (burning or
cauterizing)/procedure of

181. TUBERCUL/O-
swelling, nodule, tubercle
tuberculo/sis
swelling small/condition
(Bacteria bacillus rods – 'Mycobacterium
tuberculosis' that form nodular colonies
'swelling' within lungs, bones, and in other
body tissues.)

182. TUM/O-
swelling or tumor growth
tum/or
swells, to swell, swelling/one who

183. TURGOR/O-
swelling
turgor
swelling (skin test for hydration)

184. -TUSSIS
cough
per/tussis
through/cough

Pertussis (Whooping cough) is
characterized by fits of coughing followed
by a noisy, "whooping" indrawn breath, and
is caused by the bacteria "Bordetella
pertussis"

185. TYMPAN/O-
eardrum
tympan/itis
eardrum/inflamed
(outer part of middle ear)

186. TYPH/O-
stupor
typh/oid
stupor/resembles(bacterial infection causing
high fever and a stupored state)

187. TYPHL/O-
blind pouch or first part of big colon
Typhl/itis
blind pouch or first part of big
colon/inflamed
typhlo/col/itis
cecum/large intestine/inflamed

188. -ULA
small or lesser
uv/ula
grape/small (back of throat)
related term(s): -CULE, -ICLE,- IOLE, -ULE

189. ULCER-
sore
ulcer/ation
sore/process of
(may develop in many diseases or
conditions)

190. -ULE
small or lesser
tub/ule
canal/small or lesser

related term(s): -CULE, -ICLE,- IOLE, -ULA

191. ULN/A-
elbow
uln/ar
elbow/refers to

192. ULO-
gum
ulo/rrhagia
gingival or gum/flow
related term(s): GINGIV/O-

193. ULTRA-
beyond
ultra/sound (US)
beyond (normal hearing levels)/sound
(waves)
ultra/micro/scop/e
beyond/small/view/instrument
(objects invisible through ordinary
microscope: side illumination 'darkfield')

194. ULUL/O-
to howl or scream
ulul/ation
to howl or scream/process of
(yelling or screaming seen with certain
types of mental illness)

195. UMBILIC/O-
navel
umbilic/al
navel (watery)/refers to

196. -UM
state of or refers to
cerebr/um
brain/refers to or state of
epithel/ium
upper nipple-like appearance of skin
tissue/state of or refers to
related term(s): -AC, -AL, -AR, -ARY, -ATE,

-EUM, -IAC, -IC, -ICAL, -ILE, -IS, -ORY, -
OUS, -US

197. UNGUIN/O-
nail
unguin/al or ungun/al
nail/pertain to
(Note: ung 'unguentum' is the abbreviation
for ointment)
alternate spelling: UNGU/O-
related term(s): ONYCH/O-

198. UNI-
one
uni/form
one/shaped
related term(s): MON/O-

199. UR-
urine
ur/olog/y
urine/study/process or procedure of
alternate spelling: URIN/O-
related term(s): UR/O

200. UR/O-
urine
ur/olog/y
urine/study/process or procedure of
alternate spelling: UR/A-, UR/E-, UR/I-
related term(s): UR-

201. URETER/O-
small canal
ureter/itis
small canal/inflamed

202. URETHERO-
canal
urethr/itis
canal/inflamed
(tube running from urinary bladder to
outside of body)

203. URTICARI/O-
hives or nettles
urticar/ia
hives or nettles (skin condition)/pertain to

204. UTERO-
womb
uter/al
womb/refers to

205. UV-
grape
uv/ula
grape/small (back of throat)
related term(s): STAPHYLO-, UVE/A-,
UVE/O-, UVUL/O-

206. UVE/A-
grape
uve/itis
grape/inflamed
(thin membrane between retina and sclera
of eye - iris, ciliary body and choroid
vascular layer)
related term(s): STAPHYLO-, UV-, UVE/O-,
UVUL/O-

207. UVE/O-
grape
uve/itis
grape/inflamed
(thin membrane between retina and sclera
of eye - iris, ciliary body and choroid
vascular layer)
related term(s): STAPHYLO-, UV-, UVE/A-,
UVUL/O-

208. UVUL/O-
grape
uvul/itis
little grape/inflamed
(the grape like structure hanging from the
mouth's palate - back of throat)

related term(s): STAPHYLO-, UV-, UVE/A-,
UVE/O-

209. VAG/O-
wanderer (the longest cranial nerve)
vag/us
wanderer/pertains to
(tenth cranial nerve that wanders down
through torso body cavities)

210. VAGIN/O-
sheath
vagin/al
sheath/refers to
vagin/itis
sheath/inflamed

211. VALG/U-
inward
valg/us
inward/refers to the condition of
(genu valgum) which means the knees are
in "valgus" (i.e., knock knees) "valgum" is
the adjective, "valgus" is the noun.

212. VALVUL/O-
tiny fold or small valve
valvul/itis
tiny fold or small valve/inflamed

213. VAR/U-
outward
var/us
outward/refers to the condition of
(genu varum) which means the knees are in
"varus" (i.e., bow legged) "varum" is the
adjective, "varus" is the noun.

214. VARIC/O-
twisted
varico/cele
twisted/rupture or protrusion
(veins of spermatic cord)

related term(s): ILEO-, TORSI-

215. VARICELLA
tiny spot
varicella
a tiny spot
(chickenpox lesions - macules 'spots',
papules 'pimples', vesicles 'blisters', and
crusting lesions appear on the skin during
different stages. It lasts 10 days and is
caused by the herpes zoster virus that also
causes shingles later in life)

216. VAS/O-
vessel
vas/ec/tom/y
vessel/out/cut/procedure of
related term(s): ANGI/O-

217. VECT/O-
carries or a carrier
vect/or
carries or a carrier/one who
(insect, arthropod, animal that transmits
organism that causes the disease)

218. VEN/O-
vein
ven/ous
vein/pertain to
related term(s): PHLEB/O-

219. VENTR/O-
belly
ventr/al
belly/refer to
ventr/icle
belly/small

220. VERA-
true
polycythemia: vera
many red blood cells: true

(also known as erythremia)

221. VERMI-
worm
vermi/form
worm/shaped
(shape of appendix projecting from the
cecum)
related term(s): ASCAR/IS, HELMINTH/O-,
VERMI-

222. VERRUCA/E-
wart
plantar verruca(e)
foot/refers to: wart

223. VERS-
turn or to turn
e/vers/ion
outward/turn/one who
(the turning outward of a foot or other body
part)
alternate spelling: -VERT/O
related term(s): -VERSION

224. -VERSION
turn or to turn
in/version
inward/turning (usually foot)
related term(s): VERS-

225. VERTEBR/O-
jointed
vertebr/al
jointed/refers to
(six or more articulations or joints on each
vertebral bone)

226. VERTIGO
whirling
vertigo
whirling (maze part or labyrinth of inner
ear inflamed causing a spinning sensation)

227. VESIC/O-
sac or small blister
vesic/al
sac or small blister/pertains to
related term(s): VESICUL/O-

228. VESICUL/O-
sac or small blister
vesicul/ar
small blister/refer to
seminal vesicles (seed/sac)
related term(s): VESIC/O-

229. VESTIBULO-
belly, small space or cavity
vestebulo/plasty
belly, small space or cavity/repair (of
mouth)
vestibulo/cochlear
balance/hearing (auditory nerve)

230. VILL/I-
shaggy hair
vill/us
shaggy hair (appearance)/refers to
(hair-like structure in small intestine that
absorbs nutrients into the blood)

231. VIR/O-
poison
vir/al
poison/refers to
(smallest of etiologic infectious agents -
thought to cause severe poisoning)
related term(s): SEPS/O-, SEPT/O-, TOX/O-

232. VIRG/O-
uncontaminated or a maiden
virg/al
uncontaminated or a maiden/one who
(not exposed to pathogens or a person who
has never had sexual intercourse)

233. VISCER/A-
organ
e/viscer/ate
out (from)/organ/process of or procedure of

234. VIT/O-
alive, life, living
vit/al
alive, life, living /pertains to
(your resume' is your personal vitae)
related term(s): VIV/I-

235. VITILIG/O-
to corrupt
Vitiligin/ous
to corrupt/state of
(leuko/derma: white patches on skin often
seen in dark skinned people)

236. VITRE/O-
glassy, glass, jelly
vitre/ous
glassy, glass, jelly/pertains to
(vitreum 'vitreous body' of eye - clear jelly
in eyeball)

237. VIV/I-
alive, life, living
vivi/par/ous
alive, life, living/birth/condition of
alternate spelling: VIV/O-
related term(s): VIT/O-

238. VOLV/O-
to twist, twisting, rolling
volv/ulus
twisting or rolling/refers to
(bowel obstruction causes by the bowel
twisting - stops forward food movement)

239. VOMER
plough-shaped
vomer

plough-shaped (internal front nasal septum)

240. VOX
voice
vox rauca and vox cholerica
voice: hoarse and voice: cholera
(lost voice during last stage of this diarrheal disease)

241. VULV/O-
covering
vulv/a
covering/refers to
(the covering tissue of the female external genitalia)

242. WHEAL
round or circle
wheal
round
(A circular elevated skin condition with a pale red periphery that itches and white in center. It is associated with urticaria or hives and insect bites)

243. WHITLOW
white flow
whitlow
white flow
(suppurative 'pus forming' abscess at end of finger or toe - often a nail abscess)
related term(s): FELON

244. XANTH/O-
yellow
xanth/derma
yellow/skin
xanth/oma
yellow/swelling
(flat, soft, nodule usually seen on the eyelid)
related term(s): LUTE/O-

245. XEN/O-

strange or foreign
xen/ophthalm/ia
strange/eye/refers to
xeno/phob/ia
stranger/fear of/pertains to

246. XERO-
dry
xero/derm/a
dry/skin/refers to
(X is pronounced like a z)

247. YAWS
raspberry appearance
yaws
raspberry appearance
(spirochetal bacterial infection of skin in humid environments)

248. -Y
procedure of or process of
therap/y
treating or curing/procedure of or process of
related term(s): -AGE, -ATION, -IATION, -ING, -ION, -TION

249. ZO/A-
animal
proto/zoa
first/animal
alternate spelling: ZOAE-, ZOO-, ZOON-

250. ZYGO-
union
zygot/e
union/instrument

1. <
less than
(4 < 6)

2. >
greater than
(9 > 7)

3. A & A
awake and aware
awake and aware

4. A & B
apnea and bradycardia
(no breathing and slow heart)

5. A & O
alert and oriented

6. A & P
auscultation and percussion
(listening and tapping)

7. A & W
alive and well

8. AAA
abdominal aortic aneurysm

9. AAE
active assisted exercise
(Physical Therapy)

10. AAROM
active assistive range of motion
(degrees of motion)

11. AA
Alcoholics Anonymous, amino acid,
achievement age, authorized absence, auto
accident, active assistive

12. ABS

at bed side or absorption

13. Abx
antibiotics
related term(s): ATB

14. Ab
abortion or antibody

15. ACG
angio cardio graphy

16. ACL
anterior cruciate ligament

17. ACS
acute coronary syndrome

18. AC
before meal, acute, acromio clavicular

19. ad. lib.
as desired or at liberty

20. ADD
attention deficit disorder

21. AD
right ear or Alzheimer's Disease
related term(s): RE

22. AEC
at earliest convenience

23. AE
above elbow
(often mentioned in regards to amputation)

24. Ag
antigen

25. AHA
American Heart Association

26. AIDS
Acquired Immune Deficiency Syndrome

27. AI
artificial insemination, aortic insufficiency

28. AJ
ankle jerk

29. AKA
also known as or all known allergies

30. AK
above knee
(often mentioned in regards to amputation)

31. ALA
American Lung Association

32. ALL
allergy or acute leukocytic leukemia

33. ALS
amyotrophic lateral sclerosis or advanced life support

34. ALT. DIEB.
every other day

35. AMAP
as much as possible

36. AMA
against medical advice, American Medical Association or advanced maternal age

37. AMI
acute myocardial infarction

38. AM
morning

39. AND

anterior nasal discharge

40. ANG
angiogram

41. ANS
autonomic nervous system

42. ante
before

43. AOB
alcohol on breath

44. AOC
area of concern

45. AOM
acute otitis media
(middle ear infection)

46. appr.
approximate

47. APX
anterior posterior X-ray

48. AP
aspirin, anterior posterior
(aspirin is also known as Acetylsalicylic Acid)
related term(s): ASA

49. ARC
AIDS related complex, American Red Cross

50. ARE
active resistive exercises
(physical therapy)

51. ASAP
as soon as possible

52. ASA
aspirin
(also known as Acetylsalicylic Acid)
related term(s): AP

53. ASD
atrial septal defect
(upper heart)

54. ASHD
arteriosclerotic heart disease

55. ASIS
anterior superior iliac spine
(pelvic measurements)

56. ASTOL
as tolerated

57. AS
left ear
related term(s): LE

58. ATB
antibiotics
related term(s): Abx

59. ATC
around the clock

60. AU
both ears or Gold
related term(s): BE

61. AV
atrio ventricular node
(AV Node in the Heart)

62. A
assessment, adjustment, artery,
ambulatory, alive

63. B12
Cyanocobalamin Vitamin

64. B1
Thiamine HCL Vitamin or first degree
(Stage I) burn
(a typical sun burn is a first degree burn)

65. B2
Riboflavin Vitamin or 2nd degree (Stage
II) burn
(blistering is present with a 2nd degree
burn)

66. B3
3rd degree (Stage III) burn
(tissue charring is present with a 3rd degree
burn)

67. B4
4th degree (Stage IV) burn
(most tissue destroyed with a 4th degree
burn)

68. B6
Pyridoxine HCL Vitamin

69. B7
Biotin Vitamin

70. B8
Adenosine Phosphate Vitamin

71. BAC
blood alcohol concentration

72. BaE
barium enema
related term(s): BE

73. baso.
basophil
(Type of White Blood Cells - WBC)

74. BA
backache

75. BBB
bundle branch block

76. BBT
basal body temperature

77. BB
bowel and bladder, bed bath, blood bank

78. BCC
basal cell carcinoma

79. BC
birth control

80. BD
brain dead, birth defect, bronchial drainage

81. BEAM
brain electrical activity mapping

82. BE
barium enema, below elbow, both ears
related term(s): BaE, AU

83. BF
bile flow, bleeding frequency, blood flow, breastfed

84. BIB
to drink, brought in by

85. BID
two times per day

86. BK
below knee
(often mentioned in regards to amputation)

87. BMT
bone marrow transplant

88. BM
bowel movement

89. BNO
bladder neck obstruction

90. BPH
benign prostatic hypertrophy

91. BP
blood pressure
(Average Intra/vascular 'BP' is 120/80 mm/Hg above atmosphere pressure. Low 'BP' is 90/60 or lower; High 'BP' is 140/90 or higher)

92. BRP
bathroom privileges

93. BR
bedrest, bathroom

94. BSA
body surface area

95. BSB
body surface burn

96. BS
blood sugar, bowel sounds, before sleep, breath sounds, Blue Shield

97. BTL
bilateral tubal ligation
(female sterilization)

98. BT
body temperature, bleeding time, brain tumor

99. BUN
blood urea nitrogen

100. BW
body weight

101. BX
biopsy or Blue Cross

102. B
bacillus, bands, bloody, black, both, buccal

103. C-1
1st Cervical

104. C/O
complains of or under care of

105. Cath
catherization

106. CAT
computerized axial tomography, cataract

107. CA
cancer, carcinoma, cardiac arrest, chronological age, coronary or carotid artery

108. CBC
complete blood count

109. CBS
chronic brain syndrome

110. CCI
chronic coronary insufficiency

111. CCU
coronary care unit

112. CC
chief complaint or chief component

113. CF
cystic fibrosis

114. CHD
coronary heart disease

115. CHF
congestive heart failure

116. Chol
cholesterol
(average 160 to 200 mg/dcl or 'per 3 ounces of blood')

117. CH
child, chronic, chest

118. CL
contact lenses

119. CMS
Children's Medical Services

120. cm
centimeter

121. CNA
chart not available, certified nurse's aide

122. CNS
central nervous system

123. CN
cranial nerves
(CN 1 through 12)

124. COD
cause of death

125. COPD
chronic obstructive pulmonary disorder

(asthma, emphysema, bronchitis, bronchiectasis)

126. CO
cardiac output or computer order

127. CPR
cardiopulmonary resuscitation

128. CP
cerebral palsy, chest pain

129. CSF
cerebrospinal fluid

130. CSM
cerebrospinal meningitis

131. CS
cesarean section

132. CVA
cerebrovascular accident

133. CVD
cerebrovascular disease

134. CV
cardiovascular

135. CW
crutch walking

136. CXR
chest x ray

137. Cx
cervix, culture, cancel

138. cysto
cystoscopic examination, urinary bladder

139. C

cyanosis, hundred, carbohydrates, Catholic, centigrade, Celsius

140. D & C
dilation and curettage

141. D & D
diarrhea and dehydration

142. D & E
dilation and evacuation

143. D.C.
Doctor of Chiropractic

144. D.D.S
Doctor of Dental Surgery

145. D.M.D.
Doctor of Dental Medicine

146. D.O.
Doctor of Osteopathy

147. D.P.M.
Doctor of Podiatry

148. D/C
discharge, discontinue
(D.C. stands for Doctor of Chiropractic)

149. DAD
drug administration device

150. DAS
dead air space

151. DAT
diet as tolerated

152. DA
direct admissions, dopamine
(dopamine is a drug used with Parkinson's

disease and other neurological brain diseases)

153. dB
decibel
(70+ dB = noise pollution level)

154. DD
differential diagnosis
(differentiating between diseases 'signs & symptoms' or their etiology 'cause')

155. diag. & prog.
diagnosis and prognosis

156. DIM
diminish, one half
diminish, one half

157. DI
diabetes insipidus

158. DJD
degenerative joint disease

159. DM
diabetes mellitus

160. DNR
do not resuscitate

161. DNS
did not show

162. DOA
dead on arrival

163. DOB
date of birth

164. DPT
diphtheria, pertussis, and tetanus

(pertussis is also known as whooping cough, tetanus is also known as lock jaw)

165. Dr.
doctor, dram
(D.R. means delivery room and diabetic retinopathy)

166. DRE
digital rectal exam

167. DX & PX
diagnosis and prognosis

168. DZ
disease or dozen

169. D
dose, day, diarrhea, distal, dead

170. EAC
external auditory canal

171. ECF
extended care facility or extra cellular fluid

172. ECG
electrocardiogram
related term(s): EKG

173. EEG
electroencephalogram, electroencephalograph(y)

174. EJ
elbow jerk
elbow jerk

175. EKG
electrocardiogram
related term(s): ECG

176. ELOP

estimated length of program

177. EMG
electromyography
(diagnostic procedure of recording muscle electricity - muscle fire power)

178. ENT
ear, nose, and throat

179. ER
expiratory reserves, emergency room, estrogen receptors, and external rotation

180. eso.
eosinophil
(Type of White Blood Cells - WBC)

181. EST
electric shock therapy or estrogen

182. ESWL
extracorporeal shock wave lithotripsy

183. E
edema or enema

184. F/U
follow up

185. FACP
Fellow American College of Physicians

186. FBS
fasting blood sugar

187. FB
fasting blood sugar, foreign body, finger breadth

188. FC
fever and chills, finger counting, Foley catheter, foam and condom

189. FHR
fetal heart rate
(FHS means fetal heart sounds. FHT means fetal heart tone)

190. FH
family history

191. fl oz
fluid ounce

192. FL
fluid

193. FN
finger to nose, false negative

194. FOD
free of disease

195. FROM
full range of motion

196. FSH
follicle stimulating hormone

197. FS
frozen section or flexible sigmoidoscopy

198. FTND
full term normal delivery

199. FT
foot or full term

200. Fx
fracture or fractional urine

201. F
female, formula, Fahrenheit, firm, flow, facial

202. GB

gallbladder

203. GC
gonorrhea

204. GERD
gastroesophageal reflux disease

205. GH
growth hormone

206. GI
gastrointestinal or granuloma inguinal

207. GP
general practitioner, general paresis, paralysis

208. GTT
drop, drops, or glucose tolerance test

209. GU
genitourinary

210. GVF
good visual fields

211. GYN
gynecology or women
(gynecology is the study of women)

212. G
gravida, gallop, gauge, gram

213. H & P
history and physical

214. H1
herpes simplex type 1
herpes simplex type 1 are oral herpes

215. H2
herpes simplex type 2

herpes simplex type 2 are genital herpes

216. HAV
Hepatitis A virus

217. HA
headache

218. HBP
high blood pressure
(starts at 140/90 mm/Hg above atmospheric pressure of 760 or higher)

219. HBV
Hepatitis B virus

220. HCV
Hepatitis C virus

221. HDL
high density lipoprotein

222. HD
hip disarticulation, hearing distance, high dose, Hodgkin's Disease, Huntington's Disease

223. HEP
Hepatic

224. HI, HOH
hearing impaired or hard of hearing

225. HID
headache insomnia depression

226. HIP
history of present illness

227. HIV
human immunodeficiency virus

228. HL

hairline, hearing level

229. HS
at bedtime, heel spur, herpes simplex, heel stick test

230. HT
height, heart, hypertension

231. Hx
history, hospitalization

232. Hyperop
hyperopia
(farsighted)

233. H
host, hour, hypodermic, heroin, hydrogen, husband

234. I & O
intake and output

235. IBS
irritable bowel syndrome

236. ICU
intensive care unit

237. IC
intercostals

238. ID
infectious disease, initial dose, intradermal

239. IM
internal medicine, intramuscular, infectious mononucleosis

240. inj
injection or injury

241. IOP
intraocular pressure

242. IP
in patient, intraperitoneal, interphalangeal joint

243. IQ
intelligence quotient

244. IS
intercostal space

245. IV
intravenous

246. I
impression, independent, one

247. J
joint

248. KD
knee disarticulation

249. KIN
kinesiology
kinesiology is the study of movement

250. KJ
knee jerk

1. KUB
kidney, ureter, bladder

2. K
potassium, constant, Vitamin K

3. LBP
low blood pressure
(starts at 90/60 mm/Hg above atmospheric
pressure of 760: 'or lower')

4. lb
pound or 16 oz
(also known as #)

5. LDL
low density lipoprotein

6. LD
labor and delivery, liver disease, lethal
dose, levodopa

7. LE
lower extremities, lupus erythematosus,
left ear
related term(s): AS

8. LFD
lactose free diet, low fat diet, low forceps
delivery

9. LFT
liver function test; left frontotransverse

10. LH
luteinizing hormone

11. LIQ
liquids only

12. LLQ
lower left quadrant

13. LMP
last menstrual period

14. LN
lymph node

15. LOM
limitation of motion

16. LP
lumbar puncture, light perception

17. LRQ
lower right quadrant

18. LT
lumbar traction, light, left, left thigh

19. L
lumbar, lower, liter, left, lingual
(L-1 = first lumbar, L-5 means 5th lumbar,
etc.)

20. M.D.R.
minimal daily requirement

21. M.D.
Medical Doctor

22. MA
mental age, menstrual age, minimum air

23. MBD
minimal brain dysfunction

24. MD
muscular dystrophy, manic depression,
mental deficiency, Medical Doctor

25. MH
medical history

26. MI
myocardial infarction

27. ml
milliliter

28. MMR
measles, mumps, and rubella

29. mm
millimeter

30. mono.
infectious mononucleosis, monocyte

31. MON
month

32. MO
mouth, mineral oil, medial oblique

33. MR
may repeat, magnetic resonance imaging

34. MS
multiple sclerosis, mitral stenosis

35. MVA
motor vehicle accident

36. MVP
mitral valve prolapse

37. MVR
mitral valve replacement

38. MVS
mitral valve stenosis

39. Myop
myopia
(myopia means nearsighted)

40. M
muscle, mix, meter, murmur, micturition, male, monocyte, molar

41. N & V
nausea and vomiting

42. NB
newborn, needle biopsy, note well

43. NED
no evidence of disease

44. NER
no evidence of recurrence

45. neutro
neutrophil

46. NH
nursing home

47. NI
no improvement

48. NKA
no known disease or allergy, no known allergy

49. NKDA
no known drug allergy

50. NM
neuromuscular, nodular melanoma

51. NPO
nothing by mouth

52. NP
no pain, neuropsychiatric, nasopharyngeal, not pregnant

53. NR

no repeat, non reactive

54. NYD
not yet diagnosed

55. N
normal, no, negative

56. O & A
observation and assessment

57. O.D.
Doctor of Optometry

58. OA
osteoarthritis, old age

59. Ob
obstetrics

60. OH
occupational history

61. OOB
out of bed

62. Orth
Orthopedics

63. OS
mouth, left eye

64. OTC
over the counter
(over the counter items are sold without prescription)

65. OTD
organ tolerance dose, out the door

66. OTO
Otology
(Otology is the medical specialty that treats

the ear, including diseases and disorders)

67. OV
office visit, ovary, ovum

68. O
eye, oxygen, oral, open, often, other

69. P & S
pain and suffering, paracentesis and suction

70. p. o.
by mouth

71. PAX
posterior anterior X ray

72. PA
posterior anterior or posteroanterior

73. PCN
penicillin

74. PE
physical exam, pulmonary embolism, pleural effusion

75. PF
push fluids, power factor

76. PH
past history

77. PID
pelvic inflammatory disease, prolapsed intervertebral disc

78. PI
present illness, pulmonary infarction, peripheral iridectomy

79. PM

afternoon

80. PNS
peripheral nervous system

81. POD
post operative day one

82. PRE
progressive resistive exercises

83. PRN
as needed

84. PROM
partial range of motion

85. PS
pathologic stage, pulmonary stenosis,
plastic surgery, performance status

86. PTA
prior to admission, pretreatment anxiety,
physical therapy assistant

87. PT
Physical Therapy, prothrombin time, pine
tar, patient

88. P
pulse, protein, pint, peripheral
(average pulse is 72 B/M. pulse is also
known as Heart Rate)

89. QA
quality assurance

90. QD
every day or once a day

91. QH
every hour

92. QID
four times per day

93. QN
every night

94. QOD
every other day

95. QOH
every other hour

96. QP
as much as desired

97. Qt
total cardiac output, quart

98. quad
quadriplegic

99. Q
every

100. R/O
rule out

101. RBC
red blood cell
(also refers to a red blood cell count)

102. REM
rapid eye movement

103. REP
repeat, report, repair

104. REV
reverse, review, revolutions

105. RE
right ear
related term(s): AD

106. RhA
rheumatoid arthritis

107. RHD
rheumatic heart disease

108. RoRx
Radiation Therapy
(also known as RTx)

109. ROS
review of systems

110. RR
respiration rate or recovery room

111. RS
systems review

112. RTO
return to office

113. RUA
routine urine analysis

114. RXN
reaction

115. Rx
prescription, drug, medication, reaction

116. R
to take, respiration, right, rectum, regular, rate

117. s gl
without correction, without glasses

118. S.O.S.
if necessary, if urgently required, may be repeated once

119. SAD
seasonal affective disorder, sugar and acetone determination, spinal cord compression

120. SA
sarcoma, sinoatrial, salicylic acid, sustained action
(sarcoma is when hard tissue becomes fleshy tumor)

121. SA
sinoatrial node
(SA Node in the Heart)

122. SCC
squamous cell carcinoma, sickle cell crisis, spinal cord compression

123. SCM
sternocleidomastoid, spondyli/tic caudal myelopathy

124. SDH
subdural hematoma

125. SD
shoulder disarticulation

126. SH
social history

127. sig.
Let It Be Written, label, instructions
(often seen on prescriptions)

128. SLE
systemic lupus erythematosus, slit lamp examination

129. SN
spinal nerve, according to nature, student nurse

130. SOAM
stitches out in morning

131. SOB
shortness of breath

132. SOPM
stitches out in afternoon

133. SQ
subcutaneous

134. SS
saline solution, sickle cell, symmetrical strength, salt substitute

135. STAPH
staphylococcus aureus bacteria

136. stat
immediate

137. STI
sexually transmitted infection

138. STREP
streptococcus bacteria

139. SX
symptom, sign, surgery

140. SZ
seizure, suction, schizophrenic

141. S
stage, syphilis, skin, serum, sister, single, sacral

142. T & A
tonsillectomy & adenoidectomy

143. T-1
1st Thoracic

144. TAA
thoracic aortic aneurysm, tumor associated antigen, transverse aortic arch

145. TAB
tablet, therapeutic abortion

146. TBC
tuberculosis, total blood (cell) count
related term(s): TB

147. tbl.
tablespoon

148. TB
tuberculosis

149. TC
tissue culture, throat culture

150. TENS
transcutaneous electric nerve stimulation

151. TFTs
thyroid function tests

152. TF
tube feeding, tetralogy of Fallot, to follow

153. THR
total hip replacement

154. TIA
transient ischemic attack
(Rapid blockage in carotid artery in the neck, that causes stroke symptoms. Typically, the clot suddenly passes through and the symptoms usually disappear: Sign of pending major stroke or CVA - cerebrovascular accident)

155. TID
three times per day

156. TKO
to keep open

157. TLC
total lung capacity

158. TM
tympanic membrane, trabecular meshwork

159. TO
telephone order

160. TPR
temperature, pulse, respiration

161. Tr
traction, tremor, trace, tincture, treatment

162. TSH
thyroid stimulating hormone

163. TV
tidal volume, trichomonas vaginalis

164. T
temperature, thyroxin, tumor
T-a = axillary temperature (arm pit), T-o = oral temperature, T-r = rectal temperature

165. UA
urinalysis, uncertain about, unauthorized absence, uric acid

166. UC
uterine contractions, ulcerative colitis, urine culture

167. UE
upper extremity

168. UGI
upper gastrointestinal series

169. ULQ
upper left quadrant

170. ung
ointment
(url means unrelated, urol means urology)

171. URI
upper respiratory infection

172. URQ
upper right quadrant

173. US
ultrasound, unit secretary

174. UTD
up to date

175. UTI
urinary tract infection

176. U
unit, urine

177. V.D.M.
Veterinary Doctor

178. V.D.
Veterinary Doctor

179. VA
visual acuity, veterans' administration, vacuum aspiration

180. VC
vital capacity
(maximum inhalation and exhalation: approx. 4 liters +/-)

181. Vdg
voiding

182. VD
venereal disease

183. VF
ventricular fibrillation, visual field

184. VLDL
very low density lipoprotein

185. Vol.
volume

186. VOL
voluntary

187. VO
verbal order

188. VSD
ventricular septal defect

189. VSS
vital signs stable

190. VS
vital signs
(vital signs include: body temperature, heart rate, blood pressure, and respiration rate)

191. V
vein, vomiting, vagina

192. W/U
workup

193. WBC
white blood cells or white blood count

194. WK
week

195. WO

without

196. wt
weight

197. W
white, widowed, with
NOTE: WF = white female,
WM = white male,
BF = black female,
BM = black male,
HF = hispanic female,
HM = hispanic male

198. X & D
examination and diagnosis

199. X
times, start of anesthesia, crossmatch, except, break

1.   A/men/orrhea

_____ / _____ / _____

2.   Acro/megal/y

_____ / _____ / _____

3.   Adip/oma

_____ / _____

4.   Ven/atresia

_____ / _____

5.   Benign/iform

_____ / _____

6.   Brachy/dactyl/ia

_____ / _____ / _____

7.   Bulim/ic

_____ / _____

8.   Cal/or

_____ / _____

9.   Cauter/iz/ation

_____ / _____ / _____

10.   Cerv/ical

_____ / _____

11.   Cholang/itis

_____ / _____

12.   Sterno/cleido/mast/oid

_____ / _____ / _____ / _____

13.   In/cis/ion

_____ / _____ / _____

14.   Concuss/ion

_____ / _____

15.   Crenat/ion

_____ / _____

16.   Cyst/itis

_____ / _____

17.   Demi/facet

_____ / _____

18.   Pachy/derm/al

_____ / _____ / _____

19.   Duoden/itis

_____ / _____

20.   Dy/ad

_____ / _____

21.   Cereb/ellum

_____ / _____

22.   Em/py/ema

_____ / _____ / _____

23.   Hemat/emesis

_____ / _____

24.   Encephalo/gram

_____ / _____

25.   Epi/didymis

_____ / _____

26.   Eu/toc/ia

_____ / _____ / _____

27. Fibul/a

_____ / _____

28. Fiss/ure

_____ / _____

29. Genit/al

_____ / _____

30. Con/junctiv/itis

_____ / _____ / _____

31. Gravid/ium

_____ / _____

32. Gust/ation

_____ / _____

33. Helminth/iasis

_____ / _____

34. Hyal/ase

_____ / _____

35. Ichthy/osis

_____ / _____

36. Oss/icle

_____ / _____

37. Infarct/ion

_____ / _____

38. Kali/penia

_____ / _____

39. Keto/sis

_____ / _____

40. Kine/tic

_____ / _____

41. Kyph/osis

_____ / _____

42. Lacrim/al

_____ / _____

43. Leio/my/oma

_____ / _____ / _____

44. Lap/is

_____ / _____

45. Sub/lux/ation

_____ / _____ / _____

46. Macro/phage

_____ / _____

47. Masset/er

_____ / _____

48. Mening/itis

_____ / _____

49. Com/minute

_____ / _____

50. Muc/oid

_____ / _____

51. Narco/lepsy

_____ / _____

52. Nephr/itis

_____ / _____

53. Nev/us

_____ / _____

54. Para/noia

_____ / _____

55. Nulli/para

_____ / _____

56. Occipit/al

_____ / _____

57. Oculo/motor

_____ / _____

58. Lip/oid

_____ / _____

59. Carcin/oma

_____ / _____

60. Omphal/ectomy

_____ / _____

61. Oophor/itis

_____ / _____

62. Oscillo/graph

_____ / _____

63. Col/ostomy

_____ / _____

64. Pachy/derm/ia

_____ / _____ / _____

65. Pall/or

_____ / _____

66. Papill/ary

_____ / _____

67. Ped/al

_____ / _____

68. Poly/dipsia

_____ / _____

69. Quadr/ants

_____ / _____

70. Radicul/itis

_____ / _____

71. Ren/al

_____ / _____

72. Retro/col/ic

_____ / _____ / _____

73. Rug/ae

_____ / _____

74. Sacchar/ide

_____ / _____

75. Salping/itis

_____ / _____

76. Scler/itis

_____ / _____

77. Lapro/scop/y

_____ / _____ / _____

78. Secreat/or

_____ / _____

79. Aero/sol
_____ / _____

80. Sphygmo/mano/meter
_____ / _____ / _____

81. Spondyl/itis
_____ / _____

82. Squam/ous
_____ / _____

83. Hemo/stasis
_____ / _____

84. Steato/rrhea
_____ / _____

85. Dia/stole
_____ / _____

86. Strabism/us
_____ / _____

87. Sudorifer/ous
_____ / _____

88. Sym/physis
_____ / _____

89. Tal/us
_____ / _____

90. A/taxia
_____ / _____

91. Teno/desis
_____ / _____

92. Therm/al
_____ / _____

93. Tox/ic
_____ / _____

94. Per/tussis
_____ / _____

95. Uln/ar
_____ / _____

96. Unguin/al
_____ / _____

97. Helio/pathy
_____ / _____

98. Varico/cele
_____ / _____

99. Xanth/oma
_____ / _____

100. Zygot/e
_____ / _____

1.   A/men/orrhea
without or lack of / monthly/ flow

2.   Acro/megal/y
extremities / enlarged / refers to

3.   Adip/oma
fat / tumor

4.   Ven/atresia
vein / closure

5.   Benign/iform
kind / shape or appearance

6.   Brachy/dactyl/ia
short / fingers and toes / refers to

7.   Bulim/ic
hunger or appetite / condition of

8.   Cal/or
heated / one who is

9.   Cauter/iz/ation
to burn / act of / procedure of

10.   Cerv/ical
neck / refers to

11.   Cholang/itis
bile duct / inflamed

12.   Sterno/cleido/mast/oid
sternum / collarbone / breast /resemble

13.   In/cis/ion
into / cut / procedure

14.   Concuss/ion
violent shaking / process of

15.   Crenat/ion
notched / process of

16.   Cyst/itis
bladder or sac / inflamed

17.   Demi/facet
half / little face

18.   Pachy/derm/al
thick / skin / pertains to

19.   Duoden/itis
twelve / inflamed

20.   Dy/ad
a pair / refers to

21.   Cereb/ellum
brain / lesser or smaller

22.   Em/py/ema
in / pus / refers to

23.   Hemat/emesis
blood / vomit

24.   Encephalo/gram
within head / recording

25.   Epi/didymis
upon / teste

26.   Eu/toc/ia
normal / birth / pertains to

27. Fibul/a
to clasp / refers to

28. Fiss/ure
cleft / state of

29. Genit/al
reproductive / refers to

30. Con/junctiv/itis
together / join / inflamed

31. Gravid/ium
pregnant / refers to

32. Gust/ation
tasting / process of

33. Helminth/iasis
worms / disease of

34. Hyal/ase
glassy / enzyme

35. Ichthy/osis
fish-like / condition of

36. Oss/icle
bone / small

37. Infarct/ion
to stuff into / refers to

38. Kali/penia
potassium / decrease of

39. Keto/sis
sour or acid / condition

40. Kine/tic
movement / state of

41. Kyph/osis
hunchback / condition

42. Lacrim/al
tearing / refer to

43. Leio/my/oma
smooth / muscle / tumor

44. Lap/is
stone / refers to

45. Sub/lux/ation
under / to dislocate / refers to

46. Macro/phage
large / eater

47. Masset/er
to chew / one who

48. Mening/itis
membrane / inflamed

49. Com/minute
together / small

50. Muc/oid
slime / resembles

51. Narco/lepsy
sleep / seizure

52. Nephr/itis
kidney / inflamed

53. Nev/us
birthmark / refers to

54. Para/noia
beyond / mind

55. Nulli/para
no / births

56. Occipit/al
back of head / pertains to

57. Oculo/motor
eye / movement

58. Lip/oid
fat / resembling

59. Carcin/oma
crab-like / tumor

60. Omphal/ectomy
navel / removal

61. Oophor/itis
ovary / inflamed

62. Oscillo/graph
to swing / instrument

63. Col/ostomy
colon / opening

64. Pachy/derm/ia
thick / skin / refers to

65. Pall/or
pale / one who

66. Papill/ary
nipple / refer to

67. Ped/al
foot / refers to

68. Poly/dipsia
many / thirsts

69. Quadr/ants
four / refers

70. Radicul/itis
nerve root / inflammation

71. Ren/al
kidney / pertaining to

72. Retro/col/ic
back of / big intestine / refers to

73. Rug/ae
folds / refers to

74. Sacchar/ide
sugar / likeness

75. Salping/itis
duct / inflamed

76. Scler/itis
hard / inflammation

77. Lapro/scop/y
abdominal / view / procedure of

78. Secreat/or
separating / one who

79. Aero/sol
air / solution

80. Sphygmo/mano/meter
pulse / by hand / measurement

81. Spondyl/itis
vertebra / inflamed

82. Squam/ous
scaly / refers

83. Hemo/stasis
blood / stoppage

84. Steato/rrhea
fat / flow

85. Dia/stole
between / contraction

86. Strabism/us
squinting / refers to

87. Sudorifer/ous
sweat / pertaining to

88. Sym/physis
together / growth

89. Tal/us
ankle / refers to

90. A/taxia
without / muscle coordination

91. Teno/desis
tendon / binding

92. Therm/al
temperature / pertains to

93. Tox/ic
poison / refers to

94. Per/tussis
through / cough

95. Uln/ar
elbow / refers to

96. Unguin/al
nail / pertain to

97. Helio/pathy
sun / injury

98. Varico/cele
twisted / rupture

99. Xanth/oma
yellow / swelling

100. Zygot/e
union / instrument

1. The outermost layer of bone (bone parts) is called the: _____

2. The dense, hard layer of bone tissue that lies just underneath the periosteum is called: _____

3. Bone tissue that contains little spaces (like a sponge) and is encased in layers of compact bone is called: _____

4. The myeloid tissue in cancellous bone is semi-liquid and produces most RBCs, WBCs, and Platelets is usually referred to as: _____

5. The upper jawbone is called the: _____

6. The first seven bones of the vertebral column (forming the neck) are the: _____

7. The third set of 5 large vertebrae, which form the inward curve of the lower spine and are the spinal column's major weight bearers, are called: _____

8. The medical name for the collarbone is the: _____

9. The medical name for shoulder blade (blade back of the shoulder) is the _____ and the word part omo- refers to the shoulder:

10. The wrist bones composed of 8 small bones in two rows are called the: _____

11. The word part for arm (upper arm bone) is called the: _____

12. The upper wing-shaped portions of the pelvis (each side) are called the: _____

13. The upper leg bone (meaning thigh) is called the: _____

14. The ankle bones are called the _____ bones:

15. A band of tissue that attaches muscle to the bone is called a(n) : _____

16. The combining forms or terms that literally mean "rib" are: _____

17. The combining word form that refers to the "spine, vertebral column, and/or vertebra" is: _____

18. The diagnostic term Spondyl/itis means: _____

19. The term that means cartilage swelling or cartilage tumor is: _____

20. The diagnostic term that literally means inflamed joint is: _____

21. The medical term Burs/itis literally means: _____

22. The term Ankylosis literally means: _____

23. The combining form of a term that means "hump or hunchback" is _____, and the medical condition of _____ is the backward bending of the thoracic (chest vertebrae) spine.

24. The Greek term or word that means bone and is usually seen in medicine in its combining form osteo- is:_____

25. The diagnostic term Genu Varum (knees are in the varus position) means: _____

26. The combining form _____ means bone marrow or spinal cord.

27. The combining forms that mean "movement or motion" are: _____

28. The combining forms that mean "stone" are: _____

29. The combining form scolio- means: _____

30. An ankle sprain is often characterized by: _____

31. The diagnostic term Phoco/melia literally means: _____

32. The suffix -physis literally means: _____

33. The diagnostic term Ankylos/ing Spondyl/itis refers to the auto-immune condition of Rheumatoid Arthritis and actually means: _____

34. The diagnostic term that actually means the inflammation of bone is: _____

35. The diagnostic terms My/asthenia and Neur/asthenia mean: _____

36. The diagnostic term that means pain in the tendon is: _____

37. The diagnostic term Arthrochondritis means: _____

38. The diagnostic term that means abnormal build up of calcium on the kneecap (patella) surface is: _____

39. The diagnostic term that means twisted or wry neck is: _____

40. The diagnostic term Avulsion means: _____

41. The term that usually refers to a malignant tumor in bone marrow is: _____

42. The diagnostic term for a disease that causes excessive amounts of uric acid crystals in the blood to be deposited in joint (elbow or toe) is: _____

43. The diagnostic term Herniated Disc means: _____

44. The diagnostic term that means abnormal loss of bone density or increased bone poros/ity is: _____

45. The surgical terms Lamin/ectomy and Rachi/o/tomy actually mean: _____

46. The surgical term Arthr/o/desis means: _____

47. An instrument used to cut bone is called a(n): _____

48. The surgical term for the repair of cartilage is called: _____

49. The term Chiro/pract/or literally means: _____

50. The surgical term that means fusing together of the spine (vertebrae) is: _____

51. The surgical term Osteo/clas/ia means: _____

52. The surgical term Phalang/ectomy means: _____

53. The surgical term that means "incision into the skull to drain fluid" is: _____

54. The surgical term that actually means "surgically breaking joint apart" is: _____

55. The surgical repair or plastic surgery of a tendon and muscle is called: _____

56. The surgical term Cephal/os/tomy means: _____

57. CTS and TTS are abbreviations for _____ Syn/drome (sign and symptom complex).

58. The term Dys/chrondro/plas/ia literally refers to: _____

59. The term for X-ray film (recording) of a joint is: _____

60. The procedural term that means visual examination inside a joint is: _____

61. The medical term that means pertaining to below the rib is: _____

62. The medical term that actually refers to a young, embryonic, or primitive developing bone cell is: _____

63. The medical term that refers to vertebrae and ribs is: _____

64. The medical term stern/oid literally means: _____

65. The medical term that means pertaining to the arm is: _____

66. The medical term that means abnormal death of bone tissue is: _____

67. The anatomical term Sym/physis Pubis literally means: _____

68. The medical term "Gangli/ec/tom/y" means: _____-

69. A _____ fracture has multiple small bone pieces or chips:

70. The diagnostic reference term "Spina Bifida Occulta" literally means:

_____

71. A physician who uses techniques and treatments common to Medical Doctors and Chiropractic Physicians is a(n): _____

72. The modern medical term for a specialist who treats and diagnoses foot disease and disorders such as corns, bunions, claw foot, ingrown toenails, and par/onych/itis is a Chiro/pod/ist. A more current name would be: _____

73. The healing specialty that emphasizes a system of therapy based on the manipulation of the vertebral column and other bones of the body by hand is: _____

74. The medical term that means an artificial substitute or addition replacing a missing body part (teeth, feet, hearing aid, eye lens) is: _____

75. The diagnostic term Ankylosing Spondylitis means: _____

76. The diagnostic term Mon/arthritis means: _____

77. The diagnostic term Rheumat/oid Arthr/itis means: _____

78. The diagnostic reference Bilateral Hallux Arthritis means:_____

79. The diagnostic term Bunion (turnip sac) actually means:_____

80. The diagnostic term Rotator Cuff Avulsion actually means:_____

81. The diagnostic term Calcin/osis literally means: _____

82. The diagnostic term Omo/burs/itis actually means: _____

83. The diagnostic term Osteosarcoma means: _____

84. The diagnostic term Myelo/carcino/mata literally means: _____

85. The diagnostic term Hip Disarticulation (HD) also means: _____

86. The combining form that means "calcium" means: _____

87. An Osteopathic Physician is represented by the Medical Abbreviation _____ and a Chiropractic Physician is represented by the Medical Abbreviation : _____.

88. The diagnostic term Hammer Toe means: _____

89. The diagnostic term "A/dactyl/ia" means: _____

90. The diagnostic term Pigeon Chest or Chicken Breast means:
_____

91. The term Examination means: _____

92. An Optometric Physician uses the Medical Abbreviation: _____

93. Muscle terms that literally mean chewer are: _____

94. Body location terms used with muscles, bones, chromo/somes, and other body parts that actually refer to the end part of that structure are: _____

95. A bone process or eye membrane disease term that means resembling a wing is: _____

96. A muscle term for greater is: _____

97. A muscle term for large is: _____

98. Muscle terms for belly or abdomen are: _____

99. A term for square is: _____

100. A muscle term for sawtooth is: _____

101. A muscle term for a fatty tumor in a muscle is: _____

102. A muscle directional term for middle or toward the middle is: _____

103. A muscle term for round is: _____

104. A muscle term that literally means resembling a fan or fan-shaped is: _____

105. A term that actually refers to a muscle connecting the breastbone (sternum) and the clav/icle (collar bone) to the breast-like projection from the skulls temporal bone is: _____

106. A muscle term gluteal minimus means: _____

107. The muscle term levat/or means: _____

108. The muscle term rhomb/oid/eus literally means: _____

109. The muscle terms for wall or partition are: _____

110. Musculoskeletal System (Muscle and Bone: Classification) terms for straight include _____ and _____. They are used by certified Orthot/ist and Prosthet/ist members (A.O.P.A.) who design & fit prescribed appliances.

111. A procedure of making a record of muscle activity is called: _____

112. The condition resulting in spasms of the nerves and muscles due to an abnormally low concentration of calcium in the blood is: _____

113. A muscle term for crosswise (slanting) is: _____

114. A muscle term that means little table is: _____

115. The term ortho/ped/ic surgeon (ortho/paed/ic) actually means: _____

116. The muscle term that means cheek is: _____

117. The muscle term that actually means smallest or least is: _____

118. The muscle term peroneus means: _____

119. The diagnostic term Anterior Polio/myel/itis means an: _____

120. The diagnostic term My/asthenia Gravis actually means: _____

121. The muscle term profundus means: _____

122. Epi/leptic Seizures that cause major involuntary muscle contractions are: _____

123. The diagnostic term Ex/ost/osis means: _____

124. The muscle or bone term radialis (radial) refers to the: _____

125. The muscle or bone term olecranon means elbow tip and the term ulnaris (ulna) simply refers to the: _____

126. The muscle or bone term tibial literally means: _____

127. The muscle term soleus means: _____

128. The muscle term psoas means: _____

129. The diagnostic term Syn/dactylia means: _____

130. The diagnostic term Muscular Dys/trophy means: _____

131. The muscle term anterior means: _____

132. The muscle term brevis means: _____

133. The muscle or body term trauma means: _____

134. The term gastrocnemius means: _____

135. The term brachialis actually means: _____

136. The muscle term tri/ceps literally means: _____

137. The muscle term pronat/or literally means: _____

138. The muscle term flexor means: _____

139. The muscle term indicis means: _____

140. The muscle term iliacus (ilium area) means: _____

141. The muscle term tens/or literally means: _____

142. The muscle term femoris literally means: _____

143. The term pollux means: _____

144. The muscle term ad/duct/or literally means: _____

145. The muscle term vastus means: _____

146. The diagnostic term tendon/itis means: _____

147. The diagnostic term Pes Planus means: _____

148. The muscle term supinator means: _____

149. The muscle term sphincter means: _____

150. The muscle term fascia means: _____

151. The muscle flexor hallucis brevis means: _____

152. The machine that records muscle activity is called the: _____

153. The "actual meaning" of the diagnostic term cardio/myo/path/y is:

_____

1. The outermost layer of bone (bone parts) is called the: *periosteum*

2. The dense, hard layer of bone tissue that lies just underneath the periosteum is called: *compact bone*

3. Bone tissue that contains little spaces (like a sponge) and is encased in layers of compact bone is called: *cancellous*

4. The myeloid tissue in cancellous bone is semi-liquid and produces most RBCs, WBCs, and Platelets is usually referred to as: *bone marrow or red marrow*

5. The upper jawbone is called the: *maxilla*

6. The first seven bones of the vertebral column (forming the neck) are the: *cervical*

7. The third set of 5 large vertebrae, which form the inward curve of the lower spine and are the spinal column's major weight bearers, are called: *lumbar vertebrae*

8. The medical name for the collarbone is the: *clavicle - little key*

9. The medical name for shoulder blade (blade back of the shoulder) is the _____ and the word part omo- refers to the shoulder: *scapula*

10. The wrist bones composed of 8 small bones in two rows are called the: *carpus or carpals*

11. The word part for arm (upper arm bone) is called the: *humerus*

12. The upper wing-shaped portions of the pelvis (each side) are called the: *ilium*

13. The upper leg bone (meaning thigh) is called the: *femur*

14. The ankle bones are called the _____ bones: *tarsal "flat surface"*

15. A band of tissue that attaches muscle to the bone is called a(n) _____: *tendon*

16. The combining forms or terms that literally mean "rib" are: *cost/o and pleuro-*

17. The combining word form that refers to the "spine, vertebral column, and/or vertebra" is: *"rachi/o- and "spondyl/o-"*

18. The diagnostic term Spondyl/itis means: *inflamed vertebra*

19. The term that means cartilage swelling or cartilage tumor is: *chondroma*

20. The diagnostic term that literally means inflamed joint is: *arthr/itis*

21. The medical term Burs/itis literally means: *wine sac or sac inflamed*

22. The term Ankylosis literally means: *"crooked, stiff, bent/condition; bones pathologically fused together*

23. The combining form of a term that means "hump or hunchback" is _____, and the medical condition of _____ is the backward bending of the thoracic (chest vertebrae) spine. *kypho- - kyph/o/sis*

24. The Greek term or word that means bone and is usually seen in medicine in its combining form osteo- is: *osteon*

25. The diagnostic term Genu Varum (knees are in the varus position) means: *Knees are bent outward (bow-legged)*

26. The combining form _____ means bone marrow or spinal cord. *myelo- "osteomyelitis or myelogram"*

27. The combining forms that mean "movement or motion" are: *kinesio- and -praxia*

28. The combining forms that mean "stone" are: *petro- and litho-*

29. The combining form scolio- means: *crooked and curved - lateral or side curve (to bend) of vertebrae, along with rotation*

30. An ankle sprain is often characterized by _____: *hematoma formation, with ligaments that are stretched, partially, of fully torn*

31. The diagnostic term Phoco/melia literally means: *seal limb*

32. The suffix -physis literally means: *Growth; as in growth plate*

33. The diagnostic term Ankylos/ing Spondyl/itis refers to the auto-immune condition of Rheumatoid Arthritis and actually means: *the abnormal condition of stiffness and fusion of vertebrae*

34. The diagnostic term that actually means the inflammation of bone is: *osteitis*

35. The diagnostic terms My/asthenia and Neur/asthenia mean: *muscle weakness and nerve weakness*

36. The diagnostic term that means pain in the tendon is: *tenalgia or tenodynia*

37. The diagnostic term Arthrochondritis means: *inflammation of a joint and its cartilage*

38. The diagnostic term that means abnormal build up of calcium on the kneecap (patella) surface is: *calcin/osis*

39. The diagnostic term that means twisted or wry neck is: *torti/collis*

40. The diagnostic term Avulsion means: *tearing lose of a body part like a bone chip or ligament*

41. The term that usually refers to a malignant tumor in bone marrow is: *myelosarcoma*

42. The diagnostic term for a disease that causes excessive amounts of uric acid crystals in the blood to be deposited in joint (elbow or toe) is: *gout*

43. The diagnostic term Herniated Disc means: *ruptured or protruding inter/vertebral disk cartilage*

44. The diagnostic term that means abnormal loss of bone density or increased bone poros/ity is: *osteo/por/o/sis*

45. The surgical terms Lamin/ectomy and Rachi/o/tomy actually mean: *excision of posterior vertebral arch and cutting the vertebral column*

46. The surgical term Arthr/o/desis means: *surgical fixation or binding of a joint*

47. An instrument used to cut bone is called a(n): *osteo/tom/e*

48. The surgical term for the repair of cartilage is called: *chondr/o/plasty*

49. The term Chiro/pract/or literally means: *one who practices by hand*

50. The surgical term that means fusing together of the spine (vertebrae) is: *spondyl/o/syn/desis*

51. The surgical term Osteo/clas/ia means: *refers to surgically breaking bone*

52. The surgical term Phalang/ectomy means: *excision of a finger or toe bone - digit*

53. The surgical term that means "incision into the skull to drain fluid" is: *cranio/centesis*

54. The surgical term that actually means "surgically breaking joint apart" is: *arthroclasia*

55. The surgical repair or plastic surgery of a tendon and muscle is called: *tenomyoplasty*

56. The surgical term Cephal/os/tomy means: *forming a mouth like opening or canal in the head*

57. CTS and TTS are abbreviations for _____ Syn/drome (sign and symptom complex). *Carpal or Tarsal Tunnel*

58. The term Dys/chrondro/plas/ia literally refers to: *faulty cartilage formation*

59. The term for X-ray film (recording) of a joint is: *arthro/gram*

60. The procedural term that means visual examination inside a joint is: *arthroscop/y*

61. The medical term that means pertaining to below the rib is: *sub/costal or infra/costal*

62. The medical term that actually refers to a young, embryonic, or primitive developing bone cell is: *osteo/blast*

63. The medical term that refers to vertebrae and ribs is: *vertebro/cost/al*

64. The medical term stern/oid literally means: *resembling the sternum or breastbone*

65. The medical term that means pertaining to the arm is: *brachi/um*

66. The medical term that means abnormal death of bone tissue is: *osteonecrosis*

67. The anatomical term Sym/physis Pubis literally means: *growing together : at private parts*

68. The medical term "Gangli/ec/tom/y" means: *procedure of cutting out a knot*

69. A _____ fracture has multiple small bone pieces or chips: *com/minuted*

70. The diagnostic reference term "Spina Bifida Occulta" literally means: *a thorn/that is cleaved into 2 parts/and is hidden*

71. A physician who uses techniques and treatments common to Medical Doctors and Chiropractic Physicians is a(n): *Oste/o/path*

72. The modern medical term for a specialist who treats and diagnoses foot disease and disorders such as corns, bunions, claw foot, ingrown toenails, and par/onych/itis is a Chiro/pod/ist. A more current name would be: *Pod/iatr/ist*

73. The healing specialty that emphasizes a system of therapy based on the manipulation of the vertebral column and other bones of the body by hand is: *Chiropractic*

74. The medical term that means an artificial substitute or addition replacing a missing body part (teeth, feet, hearing aid, eye lens) is: *prosth/esis*

75. The diagnostic term Ankylosing Spondylitis means: *fusing/process vertebrae/inflamed*

76. The diagnostic term Mon/arthritis means: *inflammation of one joint*

77. The diagnostic term Rheumat/oid Arthr/itis means: *auto-immune disease often with cartilaginous hyper/troph/y*

78. The diagnostic reference Bilateral Hallux Arthritis means: *inflamed outer joints of both (2) big toes*

79. The diagnostic term Bunion (turnip sac) actually means: *inflamed bursa of the big toe's metatarsophalangeal joint*

80. The diagnostic term Rotator Cuff Avulsion actually means: *tearing of shoulder joint's soft tissues, ligaments, and deep tendons (rotator cuff muscles)*

81. The diagnostic term Calcin/osis literally means: *lime/condition*

82. The diagnostic term Omo/burs/itis actually means: *inflamed bursa of the upper shoulder*

83. The diagnostic term Osteosarcoma means: *bone tumors that causes hard tissue to become soft and fleshy*

84. The diagnostic term Myelo/carcino/mata literally means: *multiple/crab-like tumors/in the bone marrow*

85. The diagnostic term Hip Disarticulation (HD) also means: *A surgical amputation through the joint capsule of the hip joint*

86. The combining form that means "calcium" is: *calc/i-*

87. An Osteopathic Physician is represented by the Medical Abbreviation _____ and a Chiropractic Physician is represented by the Medical Abbreviation _____. *DO and DC*

88. The diagnostic term Hammer Toe means: *the toe or toes of the foot are bent over or down - like a hammer*

89. The diagnostic term "A/dactyl/ia" means: *refers to missing toes, fingers, or digits*

90. The diagnostic term Pigeon Chest or Chicken Breast means: *an abnormal anterior protruding sternum - caused by rickets or asthma*

91. The term Examination means: *the process or procedure of inspection*

92. A Optometric Physician uses the Medical Abbreviation: *OD*

93. Muscle terms that literally mean chewer are: *masseter and mandible*

94. Body location terms used with muscles, bones, chromo/somes, and other body parts that actually refer to the end part of that structure are: *distal and telic*

95. A bone process or eye membrane disease term that means resembling a wing is _____: *pteryg/oid*

96. A muscle term for greater is: *major*

97. A muscle term for large is: *magnus*

98. Muscle terms for belly or abdomen are: *abdominus or laparal*

99. A term for square is: *quadratus*

100. A muscle term for sawtooth is: *serratus*

101. A muscle term for a fatty tumor in a muscle is: *lipo/my/oma "lipo-, pio-, steato-, and adipo- all mean fat"*

102. A muscle directional term for middle or toward the middle is: *medi- or meso- "medium, medial, mesomorph"*

103. A muscle term for round is: *teres*

104. A muscle term that literally means resembling a fan or fan-shaped is: *delt/oid*

105. A term that actually refers to a muscle connecting the breastbone (sternum) and the clav/icle (collar bone) to the breast-like projection from the skulls temporal bone is: *sterno/cleido/mast/oid*

106. A muscle term gluteal minimus means: *buttock : least*

107. The muscle term levat/or means: *to lift up/one who*

108. The muscle term rhomb/oid/eus literally means: *pertains to shape resembling an oblique parallelogram*

109. The muscle terms for wall or partition are: *diaphragm and septum*

110. Musculoskeletal System (Muscle and Bone: Classification) terms for straight include _____ and _____. They are used by certified Orthot/ist and Prosthet/ist members (A.O.P.A.) who design & fit prescribed appliances. *rectus and orthotic*

111. A procedure of making a record of muscle activity is called: *electro/myo/graph/y*

112. The condition resulting in spasms of the nerves and muscles due to an abnormally low concentration of calcium in the blood is: *tetany*

113. A muscle term for crosswise (slanting) is: *oblique*

114. A muscle term that means little table is: *trapezius*

115. The term ortho/ped/ic surgeon (ortho/paed/ic) actually means: *refers to straightening bones of children : by - working by hand*

116. The muscle term that means cheek is: *buccinator*

117. The muscle term that actually means smallest or least is: *minimus*

118. The muscle term peroneus means: *pin*

119. The diagnostic term Anterior Polio/myel/itis means an: *inflammation of the front gray horn of the spinal cord*

120. The diagnostic term My/asthenia Gravis actually means: *heavy because of muscle weakness*

121. The muscle term profundus means: *deep*

122. Epi/leptic Seizures that cause major involuntary muscle contractions are: *Grand Mal Seizures*

123. The diagnostic term Ex/ost/osis means: *condition of bone growing outward through muscles and other tissues*

124. The muscle or bone term radialis (radial) refers to the: *Wrist/spoke*

125. The muscle or bone term olecranon means elbow tip and the term ulnaris (ulna) simply refers to the: *elbow "area"*

126. The muscle or bone term tibial literally means: *refers to the shin*

127. The muscle term soleus means: *sole*

128. The muscle term psoas means: *loin*

129. The diagnostic term Syn/dactylia means: *fingers connected together*

130. The diagnostic term Muscular Dys/trophy means: *muscles that have faulty development; and wasting away of the muscles that did develop properly*

131. The muscle term anterior means: *foremost or front*

132. The muscle term brevis means: *short*

133. The muscle or body term trauma means: *wound*

134. The term gastrocnemius means: *calf of leg or shaped like a stomach*

135. The term brachialis actually means: *arm*

136. The muscle term tri/ceps literally means: *3 heads*

137. The muscle term pronat/or literally means: *turns down/one who*

138. The muscle term flexor means: *one who bends*

139. The muscle term indicis means: *finger*

140. The muscle term iliacus (ilium area) means: *flank*

141. The muscle term tens/or literally means: *to tense or contract/one who*

142. The muscle term femoris literally means: *thigh*

143. The term pollux means: *thumb*

144. The muscle term ad/duct/or literally means: *one who/draws/toward "medially"*

145. The muscle term vastus means: *great or immense*

146. The diagnostic term tendon/itis means: *the inflammation of the sinew or leader connecting muscles to bone*

147. The diagnostic term Pes Planus means: *flat foot*

148. The muscle term supinator means: *turns upward - one who*

149. The muscle term sphincter means: *that which bind together*

150. The muscle term fascia means: *band that separates*

151. The muscle flexor hallucis brevis means: *one who bends or flexes the big toe by shortening (shorter of 2 muscles flexing the great toe)*

152. The machine that records muscle activity is called the: *electromyo/graph*

153. The "actual meaning" of the diagnostic term cardio/myo/path/y is: *a condition that causes poor blood circulation to the heart muscle*

1. The largest region of the brain is the: _____

2. The term "psychology" literally means: _____

3. The spaces within the cerebrum that contain the cerebrospinal fluid are called the: _____

4. The region of the brain that is sometimes referred to as the hindbrain or small brain is the: _____

5. The area of the brain responsible for respiration, heart rate, and smooth muscle control of our blood vessels is the: _____

6. The structure that conducts nerve impulses to and from the brain and serves as a reflex center for some sensory information without input from the brain is the: _____

7. The three layered membrane that covers the brain and spinal cord and literally means membrane is called the: _____

8. The thin layer of meninges that actually means gentle mother is the: _____

9. The delicate middle layer of the meninges is the: _____

10. The cord-like (string-like) structures that carry bio-electrical impulses from one part of the body to another are called: _____

11. A group of nerve cell bodies that are found outside of the spinal cord and brain are referred to as: _____

12. The combining form that means "hard" is: _____

13. The term that means spinal cord inflammation is: _____

14. The combining form en/cephal/o- actually means: _____

15. The combining form phren/o- means: _____

16. The combining form that means "physical sensation, sensitivity, or feeling" is: _____

17. The combining form that means "gray (matter)" is: _____

18. The combining form phas/o- means: _____

19. The combining forms that mean "one" are: _____

20. The combining form ment/o- means: _____

21. The prefixes hemi- and semi- mean: _____

22. The prefixes quadri- and tetra- means _____ and terato- means_____.

23. The word part -iatro- in iatro/genic or ger/iatric/ means: _____-

24. The suffix -paresis means: _____

25. The diagnostic term for inflammation of the brain, spinal cord, and nerve roots is: _____

26. The diagnostic term for inflammation of the gray matter of the spinal cord is: _____

27. The diagnostic term that means blood tumor below the dura mater is: _____

28. The endocrine system and the nervous systems are referred to as: _____

29. The diagnostic terms Neur/itis and Neur/algia mean: _____

30. The diagnostic term Meningo/myelo/cele means: _____

31. The diagnostic term En/cephal/itis actually means: _____

32. The diagnostic term that means tumor made up of nerve cells is: _____

33. The diagnostic term that means disease of nerves within the joints: _____

34. The diagnostic term that means softening of the brain is: _____

35. The diagnostic term Poly/neur/itis means: _____

36. The diagnostic term Cerebr/al Thromb/o/sis means: _____

37. The diagnostic term Neur/asthenia means: _____

38. The diagnostic term for a disease characterized by early senility, confusion, loss of recognition of persons or familiar surroundings, and restlessness is: _____

39. The diagnostic term for a viral disease that affects the peripheral nerves and causes the skin to blister along the course of the nerve is: _____

40. The interruption of blood supply to the brain caused by a cerebral thrombosis, cerebral embolism, or cerebral hemorrhage is called: _____

41. The diagnostic term that means deficient supply of blood to the brain for a short time is called a(n): _____

42. The diagnostic term for an emotional disorder characterized by the use of ineffective skills for coping with anxiety or inner conflict is: _____

43. Signs of brain concussion are unequal pupil size, deafness, restlessness and: _____

44. The diagnostic term for a condition caused by an increased amount of cerebral spinal fluid in the ventricles of the brain is: _____

45. The diagnostic term for a condition characterized by brain damage and lack of muscle control and partial paralysis is: _____

46. The surgical term Neuro/lysis means: _____

47. The surgical term that means excision of a nerve is: _____

48. The surgical term for surgical repair of a nerve is: _____

49. The surgical term that means incision into the nerves is: _____

50. The procedural term Echo/encephalo/graphy actually means: _____

51. The procedural term for X-ray of the brain using air as the contrast medium is: _____

52. The term for X-ray filming of the cerebral ventricles using a contrast medium injected directly through the skull is: _____

53. An instrument used to record the electrical impulses of the brain is called an: _____

54. The diagnostic term for a process that includes the use of a computer to produce a

series of images of the tissues of the brain at any desired depth is:

_____

55. The diagnostic term for a process that X-rays the blood vessels in the brain is:

_____

56. The medical term Encephalo/angio/scler/o/sis means: _____

57. The medical term that means without feeling or without sensation is: _____

58. The medical term that means the same as Quadri/plegia is: _____

59. The medical term Dys/phasia means: _____

60. The medical term that means any disease of the mind is: _____

61. The medical term that refers to originating within the mind is: _____

62. The medical term Neur/oid means: _____

63. The medical term Psych/o/log/ist means: _____

64. The medical term that means mental disease is: _____

65. The medical term hyperesthesia (increase/feeling) means: _____

66. The medical term that pertains to the paralysis of the right or left half of the body is:_____

67. The medical term cephalo/dynia means: _____

68. The term that means para/lysis (near breakdown "to disable") of one limb:

_____

69. The medical term that means softening of the spinal cord is: _____

70. The medical term that means occurring between a seizure or attack is: _____

71. The medical term that means total paralysis is: _____

72. The medical term quadri/plegia means: _____

73. The medical term coma means: _____

74. The medical term shunt means: _____

75. The medical term ataxia means: _____

76. The medical term that means feeling "faint" is: _____

77. The medical abbreviations CNS, PNS, and ANS refer to divisions of the: _____

78. The Cranial Nerves are string-like groups of nerves coming off of the: _____

79. The medical term Psych/iatr/y literally means: _____

80. The term Psycholog/ist literally means: _____

81. The medical term Alzheimer's or Pick's disease refers to: _____

82. The medical term that means Lou Gehrig's disease is also known as: _____

83. The medical term Glioma means: _____

84. The medical term Cerebral Contusion means: _____

85. The medical term Concussion means: _____

86. The diagnostic medical term Down Syndrome refers to: _____

87. The medical term Hemat/oma means: _____

88. The medical term Encephal/o/cele means: _____

89. The medical term Epi/lepsy means: _____

90. The medical term Mening/itis means: _____

91. The medical term Opistho/tonos (backward bending tone) means:

_____

92. The medical term Septic/emia means: _____

93. The anatomical term _____refers to the terminal end of the spinal cord and the roots of the spinal nerves below the 1st Lumbar nerve.

94. The medical term Neuro/fibromat/osis is characterized by: _____

95. The medical term Huntington's disease is characterized
by: _____

96. The medical term Chalazion Cyst (AKA: meibomian cyst) is referred to as a cyst of
the eyelids. It is the extension of the meibomian gland with its oily secretions. The term
literally means: _____

97. The medical term Dacryo/cyst/itis or Lacrimo/cyst/itis means: _____

98. The medical term Herpes literally means _____ in Greek:

99. The medical condition of Hypo/pyon shows pus in the anterior chamber of the eyes:
_____

100. The medical term Hyph/ema means: _____

101. The term Colob/oma is usually a fissure of the iris (& eyelid), ciliary body, or
choroids that is congenital, pathologic, or surgical. The term means: _____

102. The medical term Glauc/oma actually means: _____

103. The medical term Kerat/itis actually means: _____

104. The medical term Opto/metr/ist literally means: _____

105. Miotic Eye Drops cause the eyes pupil to: _____

106. Mydriatic Eye Drops cause the eyes pupil to: _____

107. The E Eye Chart is used to measure: _____

108. The medical term Hyper/opia (excess/sight) actually means: _____

109. The medical term Myoptic (adj.) means: _____

110. The medical term Tetanus (24 different types) usually refers to: _____

111. The medical term Palsy means: _____

112. The Optic (sight), Oculomotor (eye movement), Trochlear (pulley-like), and

Abducens (to draw away) nerves all innervate the eye in some way. These are referred to as Cranial Nerves _____ (OOOTTAFAGVAH).

113. The medical term Bell's Palsy is also known as: _____

114. The medical term Hemi/plegia (Semi/plegia) means:_____

115. The medical term Para/plegia means: _____

116. The suffix -plegi means: _____

117. The medical term Cerebral Palsy (CP) is characterized by: _____

118. The medical term Para/noia literally means "mind/beyond or beside" or refers to a behavior that is out of touch with reality or: _____

119. The term Schizo/phrenia (split/mind - with delusions, persecution, hallucinations, jealousy, and/or catatonia "stupor") actually refers to a type of Psych/osis (loss of reality) that is also characterized by: _____

120. The diagnostic medical term Multiple Sclerosis (MS) refers to: _____

121. Parkinson's disease causes body tremors (shaking), weak speech, shuffling of feet, and depression. Other patients may experience: _____

122. The body term Cerumen is also known as: _____

123. The medical term Myring/itis (typan/itis: drum/inflamed) actually means: _____

124. Aural Atresia refers to: _____

125. The medical term Oto/scler/osis is also known as: _____

126. The medical terms Palpebr/itis and Blepharo/ptosis refer to: _____

127. The medical term Retin/itis Pigmentosa can be called:

_____

128. The medical term Retino/blast/oma is also known as: _____

129. Tay-Sachs disease is one of many genetic diseases that can cause blindness and

death, typically in young _____ children:

130. The medical term Trach/oma refers to a chlamydial (to cloak) infection causing: _____

131. The outer hard layer of the eye (white of eye) is the: _____

132. The transparent anterior part of the sclera is the: _____

133. The eye structure that lies directly behind the pupil and iris is the: _____

134. The highly vascularized middle layer of the eye wall is called the: _____

135. The tear glands that lubricate and protect the eye are called: _____

136. The opening in the center of the iris is called the: _____

137. The muscular membrane that gives the eye its color is the: _____

138. The inner layer of the eye with the vision receptors is the: _____

139. The combining form ocul/o- means: _____

140. The prefix 'bin-' in binocular means: _____

141. The suffix '-opia' means: _____

142. The watery liquid located in the anterior chamber of the eye is the: _____

143. The jellylike liquid located in the posterior chamber of the eye is the: _____

144. The small organs that produce and drain tears from the eye are the: _____

145. The mucous membrane lining the inner eyelids & globe eyeball is the: _____

146. The nerve in the eye that carries visual impulses from the retina to the brain is the: _____

147. The combining forms that mean "eyelid" are: _____

148. The combining form that means "vision" is: _____

149. The combining forms irid/o- or ir/o- literally mean "rainbow" or: _____

150. The combining form that means "tear duct" is: _____

151. The combining form lacrimo/adeno- literally means: _____

152. The combining forms that mean "pupil" are: _____

153. The combining form cry/o- means: _____

154. The word parts that mean two or double are: _____

155. The combining form phot/o- means: _____

156. The word parts that means eye are: _____

157. The combining form ton/o- means: _____

158. The suffix that means abnormal fear of (aversion to) is: _____

159. The suffix -ician in Phys/ician (natural/_____) actually means: _____

160. The diagnostic term Blephar/itis means: _____

161. The diagnostic term Photo/phobia means: _____

162. The diagnostic term Ophthalmorrhagia actually means: _____

163. The term for an abnormal condition of the eye caused by a fungus is: _____

164. The diagnostic term for inflammation of the cornea and iris is: _____

165. The diagnostic term Sclero/malacia means: _____

166. The medical term Dacryo/cyst/itis or Lacrimo/cyst/itis means: _____

167. The diagnostic term Blepharo/ptosis means: _____

168. The diagnostic term Ophthalm/algia means: _____

169. The diagnostic term Dipl/opia actually means: _____

170. The diagnostic term Pan/ophthalm/itis means: _____

171. The diagnostic term Irido/plegia means: _____

172. The condition called _____ (squinting) is a problem of directing the optic eye axes at the same object. It is usually caused by reduced visual acuity, unequal eye muscle tone, or problems with the Cranial Nerves 3, 4, or 6:

173. The term for separation of the retina from the choroid's inner eyeball layer in the back of the eye is: _____

174. The diagnostic term for obstruction of the eyelids sebaceous gland is: _____

175. The diagnostic term for defective curvature of the refractive surface of the eye is:
_____

176. The term for an involuntary rhythmic eye movement (jumping) is:
_____

177. The term that actually means an abnormal membrane fold extending from eye medial conjunctiva to the cornea is a: _____

178. The diagnostic term Cataract actually means: _____

179. The surgical term that means fixation of the retina to the choroid eye layer by extreme cold is: _____

180. The surgical term for the creation of an artificial "mouth-like" opening between the tear sac and the nose is: _____

181. The surgical term for surgical repair of the eyelid is: _____

182. The surgical term dacryo/cyst/otomy means: _____

183. The surgical term Radial Keratotomy actually means: _____

184. The suffix -plegia means: _____

185. The diagnostic term 'Endophthalmitis' means: _____

186. The diagnostic term "Hyperopia" means: _____

187. The medical term 'mydriatic' means: _____

188. With glaucoma, pressure causes atrophy of the _____ and retina, resulting in blindness. _____

189. The surgical term for a procedure in which a cataract is lifted from the eye with an extremely cold probe is: _____

190. Surgical incision procedure of the eye muscle tendon in order to relieve cross-eyed (inward) or wall-eyed (outward) conditions is called: _____

191. The surgical method that removes cataracts by using an ultrasonic needle probe to break up the lens is called: _____

192. A diagnostic instrument that measures the curvature of the cornea is called a(n): _____

193. An instrument that examines the interior of the eye is called a(n): _____

194. The medical term for any non-inflammatory disease of the retina is: _____

195. The medical term for a physician who specializes in Ophthalmology is: _____

196. The medical term that actually means one who is skilled in filling prescriptions for lenses is: _____

197. The medical term for a specialist who studies the diseases of the eye and is a medical doctor is: _____

198. The medical term intra-ocul/ar means: _____

199. The medical term Opto/metr/ist literally means: _____

200. The medical term ophthalmic means: _____

201. The medical term papill/ary means: _____

202. The diagnostic term ophthalmo/pathy actually means: _____

203. The medical terms and abbreviations that refer to the right eye are: _____

204. The medical terms and abbreviations that refer to the left eye are: _____

205. The medical term visual acuity means: _____

206. The medical term for a specialist who examines, diagnoses, and treats the eyes and has the medical specialty letters O.D. is: _____

207. The combining form ocul/o- means: _____

208. The part of the ear that directs sound waves into the external auditory meatus (opening) is called the: _____

209. The combining form labyrinth/o- means: _____

210. The semi/transparent tissue that separates the external auditory meatus (opening) from the middle ear and is part of the middle ear cavity is the: _____

211. The structure in the inner ear that contains balance receptors and endolymph is called the: _____

212. The structure that connects the middle ear with the pharynx (throat) and equalizes pressure on either side of the eardrum is the: _____

213. The bony spaces within the temporal bone of the skull, which contain the cochlea and the semicircular canals, is the: _____

214. The snail-shaped structure in the inner ear that contains the organs of hearing is the: _____

215. The short tube that leads from the outside world to the tympanic membrane of the middle ear is called the: _____

216. The bones of the middle ear that carry sound vibrations to the inner ear are called the: _____

217. The malleus, incus, and stapes make up the bones of the middle ear called the: _____

218. The combining forms acoust/o- and audi/o- both mean: _____

219. The combining form that means "pertaining to the eardrum" is: _____

220. The combining form that means "eardrum" is: _____

221. The combining form auri- and oto- means: _____

222. The combining form ot/o- means: _____

223. The combining form that means "hearing" is: _____

224. The Olfactory (smell), Trigeminal (3/parts), Vagus (wanderer), and the Hypoglossal (under/tongue) Nerves innervate the nose, face and teeth, organs, and tongue muscles. They are referred to as Cranial Nerves (OOOTTAFAGVAH): _____

225. The combining form staped/o- means: _____

226. The diagnostic term ot/itis interna can also be called: _____

227. The medical term for a fungal infection of the ear is: _____

228. The diagnostic term ot/algia means: _____

229. The diagnostic term that means hardening of the ear is: _____

230. The diagnostic term that actually means inflammation spreading from the ear to the mastoid bone behind the ear is: _____

231. The diagnostic term that means inflammation of the mastoid bone and cells is: _____

232. The diagnostic term for a chronic disease of the inner ear characterized by dizziness (Vertigo) and ringing (Tinnitus) in the ear is: _____

233. The diagnostic term that means tumor of the gland that excretes earwax is: _____

234. The diagnostic term that means inflammation of the outer ear is: _____

235. The medical term Myring/itis (typan/itis: drum/inflamed) actually means: _____

236. The diagnostic term for ringing in the ears is: _____

237. The diagnostic term for dizziness (turning round) is: _____

238. The surgical term labyrinth/ectomy means: _____

239. Surgical term for a procedure of repairing an incision into the eardrum: _____

240. The bones of the middle ear that carry sound vibrations from the eardrum are called the: _____

241. The combining form labyrinth/o- means: _____

242. The medical term Myring/itis (typan/itis: drum/inflamed) actually means: _____

243. A delicate instrument used to test hearing acuteness is called a(n): _____

244. An instrument used for the visual examination of the ear is called a(n): _____

245. The procedural term that means the measurement of the movement of the tympanic membrane is: _____

246. The procedural term audio/gram actually means: _____

247. An instrument used to measure middle ear function is: _____

248. The procedural term oto/scop/y means: _____

249. The procedural term audio/metr/y means: _____

250. The term audio/meter means: _____

251. The term aur/al means: _____

252. The medical term that means a specialist who studies and treats the diseases and disorders of the ear, nose, and throat is: _____

253. The term that means one who studies and treats disease of the ear is: _____

254. A specialist who specializes in the study of hearing is an: _____

255. The medical term that means the study of the ear is: _____

256. A Chiropractor specializes in the repositioning of bones with adjustments in order

to relieve nerve and tissue pressure caused by bone : _____

257. The term Psycho/pharmac/o/log/y actually refers to: _____

1. The largest region of the brain is the: *cerebrum*

2. The term "psychology" literally means: *the process or procedure of the science or study of the mind*

3. The spaces within the cerebrum that contain the cerebrospinal fluid are called the: *ventricles or little bellies*

4. The region of the brain that is sometimes referred to as the hindbrain or small brain is the: *cerebellum*

5. The area of the brain responsible for respiration, heart rate, and smooth muscle control of our blood vessels is the: *medulla oblongata*

6. The structure that conducts nerve impulses to and from the brain and serves as a reflex center for some sensory information without input from the brain is the: *spinal cord*

7. The three layered membrane that covers the brain and spinal cord and literally means membrane is called the: *meninges*

8. The thin layer of meninges that actually means gentle mother is the: *pia mater*

9. The delicate middle layer of the meninges is the: *arachnoid*

10. The cord-like (string-like) structures that carry bio-electrical impulses from one part of the body to another are called _____. *nerves*

11. A group of nerve cell bodies that are found outside of the spinal cord and brain are referred to as: *ganglions or ganglia (pl.) "literal meaning knot"*

12. The combining form that means "hard" is: *dur/o- "dur/able"*

13. The term that means spinal cord inflammation is: *myel/itis*

14. The combining form en/cephal/o- actually means: *brain "literally means within head"*

15. The combining form phren/o- means: *mind or diaphragm "phren/ology and phrenic nerve"*

16. The combining form that means "physical sensation, sensitivity, or feeling" is: *esthesi/o-*

17. The combining form that means "gray (matter)" is: *poli/o-*

18. The combining form phas/o- means: *speech*

19. The combining forms that mean "one" are: *mon/o- and uno-*

20. The combining form ment/o- means: *mind "ment/al"*

21. The prefixes hemi- and semi- mean: *half*

22. The prefixes quadri- and tetra- means _____ and terato- means _____. *four and monster*

23. The word part -iatro- in iatro/genic or ger/iatric/ means: *referring to a physician or medicine that treats or cures*

24. The suffix -paresis means: *partial paralysis "paraparesis means slight or near paralysis"*

25. The diagnostic term for inflammation of the brain, spinal cord, and nerve roots is: *encephalo/myelo/radicul/itis*

26. The diagnostic term for inflammation of the gray matter of the spinal cord is: *polio/myel/itis "anterior part of spinal cord horn"*

27. The diagnostic term that means blood tumor below the dura mater is: *subdural hematoma*

28. The endocrine system and the nervous systems are referred to as: *master body systems*

29. The diagnostic terms Neur/itis and Neur/algia mean: *inflamed nerves and pain in the nerves*

30. The diagnostic term Meningo/myelo/cele means: *protrusion of the meninges and spinal cord*

31. The diagnostic term En/cephal/itis actually means: *inflammation of the brain*

32. The diagnostic term that means tumor made up of nerve cells is: *neur/oma*

33. The diagnostic term that means disease of nerves within the joints: *neuro/arthro/path/y*

34. The diagnostic term that means softening of the brain is: *en/cephalo/malac/ia*

35. The diagnostic term Poly/neur/itis means: *inflammation of many nerves*

36. The diagnostic term Cerebr/al Thromb/o/sis means: *condition of a blood clot in the brain "cerebrum"*

37. The diagnostic term Neur/asthenia means: *nerve weakness*

38. The diagnostic term for a disease characterized by early senility, confusion, loss of recognition of persons or familiar surroundings, and restlessness is: *Alzheimer's disease*

39. The diagnostic term for a viral disease that affects the peripheral nerves and causes the skin to blister along the course of the nerve is: *shingles - herpes virus that causes chickenpox "Herpes Zoster"*

40. The interruption of blood supply to the brain caused by a cerebral thrombosis, cerebral embolism, or cerebral hemorrhage is called: *Cerebro/vascular Accident, Apoplexy, or Stroke*

41. The diagnostic term that means deficient supply of blood to the brain for a short time is called a(n): *Transient Ischemic Attack "TIA"*

42. The diagnostic term for an emotional disorder characterized by the use of ineffective skills for coping with anxiety or inner conflict is: *Neurosis "no loss of reality"*

43. Signs of brain concussion are unequal pupil size, deafness, restlessness and: *Nausea or vomiting*

44. The diagnostic term for a condition caused by an increased amount of cerebral spinal fluid in the ventricles of the brain is: *hydrocephalus*

45. The diagnostic term for a condition characterized by brain damage and lack of muscle control and partial paralysis is: *Cerebral Palsy "CP"*

46. The surgical term Neuro/lysis means: *separating a nerve (break)*

47. The surgical term that means excision of a nerve is: *neur/ectomy*

48. The surgical term for surgical repair of a nerve is: *neur/o/plasty*

49. The surgical term that means incision into the nerves is: *neur/o/tomy*

50. The procedural term Echo/encephalo/graphy actually means: *procedure of recording brain structures by use of sound*

51. The procedural term for X-ray of the brain using air as the contrast medium is: *pneumo/encephalo/graphy*

52. The term for X-ray filming of the cerebral ventricles using a contrast medium injected directly through the skull is: *ventricul/o/gram*

53. An instrument used to record the electrical impulses of the brain is called an: *electro/encephalo/graph*

54. The diagnostic term for a process that includes the use of a computer to produce a series of images of the tissues of the brain at any desired depth is: *CAT Scan "Computerized Axial Tomography"*

55. The diagnostic term for a process that X-rays the blood vessels in the brain is: *Cerebral Angio/graphy*

56. The medical term Encephalo/angio/scler/o/sis means: *condition of hardening of the brain's blood vessels*

57. The medical term that means without feeling or without sensation is: *an/esthesia*

58. The medical term that means the same as Quadri/plegia is: *tetra/plegia "4 limbs paralyzed"*

59. The medical term Dys/phasia means: *difficulty in speaking*

60. The medical term that means any disease of the mind is: *psychopathy*

61. The medical term that refers to originating within the mind is: *psycho/genic*

62. The medical term Neur/oid means: *resembling a nerve*

63. The medical term Psych/o/log/ist means: *specialist in the science and study of the mind*

64. The medical term that means mental disease is: *phrenopathy*

65. The medical term hyperesthesia (increase/feeling) means: *condition of excessive sensitivity*

66. The medical term that pertains to the paralysis of the right or left half of the body is: *hemiplegia*

67. The medical term cephalo/dynia means: *pain in the head*

68. The term that means para/lysis (near breakdown "to disable") of one limb: *mono/plegia*

69. The medical term that means softening of the spinal cord is: *myelo/malacia "sarcoma cancer"*

70. The medical term that means occurring between a seizure or attack is: *inter/lepsy*

71. The medical term that means total paralysis is: *pan/plegia*

72. The medical term quadri/plegia means: *paralysis of all four limbs*

73. The medical term Coma means: *sleep-like*

74. The medical term shunt means: *tube implanted in the body to redirect the flow of a fluid*

75. The medical term ataxia means: *lack of gross motor balance/coordination*

76. The medical term that means feeling "faint" is: *syncope*

77. The medical abbreviations CNS, PNS, and ANS refer to divisions of the: *nervous system*

78. The Cranial Nerves are string-like groups of nerves coming off of the: *brain and brain stem*

79. The medical term Psych/iatr/y literally means: *the procedure or process of treating or curing the mind*

80. The term Psycholog/ist literally means: *is a specialist in the science and study of the mind*

81. The medical term Alzheimer's or Pick's Disease refers to: *pre-senile dementia*

82. The medical term that means Lou Gehrig's Disease is also known as: *A/myo/trophic Lateral Sclerosis, or "ALS"*

83. The medical term Glioma means: *glue or glue-like tumor "sarc/oma of neuro/glia brain cells"*

84. The medical term Cerebral Contusion means: *the process of bruising the brain*

85. The medical term Concussion means: *to shake violently "causing brain bleeding"*

86. The diagnostic medical term Down Syndrome refers to: *a genetic defect causing multiple defects seen with varying degrees of intellectual disability*

87. The medical term Hemat/oma means: *blood swelling or tumor*

88. The medical term Encephal/o/cele means: *brain protrusion*

89. The medical term Epi/lepsy means: *seizure upon the mind and body*

90. The medical term Mening/itis means: *inflammation of the membrane that covers the brain and spinal cord*

91. The medical term Opistho/tonos (backward bending tone) means: *tension that bends back and head backward "Tetanus"*

92. The medical term Septic/emia means: *poison in the blood, usually bacterial poison or waste*

93. The anatomical term _____ refers to the terminal end of the spinal cord and the roots of the spinal nerves below the 1st Lumbar nerve. *Cauda Equina "tail/of horse - appearance"*

94. The medical term Neuro/fibromat/osis is characterized by: *multiple fiber-like nerve tumors*

95. The medical term Huntington's disease is characterized by: *shaking or bizarre involuntary movement with de/mentia "away/mind"*

96. The medical term Chalazion Cyst (AKA: meibomian cyst) is referred to as a cyst of the eyelids. It is the extension of the meibomian gland with its oily secretions. The term literally means: *hailstone sac of eyelid*

97. The medical term Dacryo/cyst/itis or Lacrimo/cyst/itis means: *inflammation of the tear sac*

98. The medical term Herpes literally means _____ in Greek: *to creep*

99. The medical condition of Hypo/pyon shows pus in the anterior chamber of the eyes: *corneal ulcers "sores"*

100. The medical term Hyph/ema means: *suffused or stuffed with blood "blood in front of iris/anterior eye"*

101. The term Colob/oma is usually a fissure of the iris (& eyelid), ciliary body, or choroids that is congenital, pathologic, or surgical. The term means: *to mutilate*

102. The medical term Glauc/oma actually means: *Waterfall, Cloudy, or Gray Vision ("caused by an increase in intraocular pressure")*.

103. The medical term Kerat/itis actually means: *inflammation of the eye's cornea*

104. The medical term Opto/metr/ist literally means: *specialist in measuring sight*

105. Miotic Eye Drops cause the eyes pupil to: *constrict*

106. Mydriatic Eye Drops cause the eyes pupil to: *dilate*

107. The E Eye Chart is used to measure: *visual acuity*

108. The medical term Hyper/opia (excess/sight) actually means: *far sighted or farsightedness "see clear in distance"*

109. The medical term Myoptic (adj.) means: *nearsightedness or shortsighted "see clear close up"*

110. The medical term Tetanus (24 different types) usually refers to: *muscle spasms of body caused by bacteria Clostridium tetani toxins*

111. The medical term Palsy means: *varying degrees of paralysis (due to abnormal muscle tone & coordination)*

112. The Optic (sight), Oculomotor (eye movement), Trochlear (pulley-like), and Abducens (to draw away) Nerves all innervate the eye in some way. These are referred to as Cranial Nerves _____ (OOOTTAFAGVAH): *2, 3, 4, and 6*

113. The medical term Bell's Palsy is also known as: *facial paralysis or palsy*

114. The medical term Hemi/plegia (Semi/plegia) means: *paralysis on one half "one side" of the body*

115. The medical term Para/plegia means: *Partial or full paralysis of the lower extremities (legs)*

116. The suffix -plegi means: *paralysis*

117. The medical term Cerebral Palsy (CP) is characterized by: *Brain damage around the time of birth; CP is manifested by abnormal muscle tone, movements, and coordination (dyskinesias)*

118. The medical term Para/noia literally means "mind/beyond or beside" or refers to a behavior that is out of touch with reality or: *refers to abnormal thinking or reasoning "Psychosis - Not Real"*

119. The term Schizo/phrenia (split/mind - with delusions, persecution, hallucinations, jealousy, and/or catatonia "stupor") actually refers to a type of Psych/osis (loss of reality) that is also characterized by: *thought deterioration and lack of social functioning before 45 Y/O*

120. The diagnostic medical term Multiple Sclerosis (MS) refers to: *deterioration or loss of the myelin sheath nerve body covering "paralysis"*

121. Parkinson's disease causes body tremors (shaking), weak speech, shuffling of feet, and depression. Other patients may experience: *muscle and body "voice loss, sphincter problems, with falls & paralysis"*

122. The body term Cerumen is also known as: *ear wax "from modified ear sebaceous or oil glands"*

123. The medical term Myring/itis (typan/itis: drum/inflamed) actually means: *inflammation of the eardrum*

124. Aural Atresia refers to: *closure of the outer auditory or hearing canal*

125. The medical term Oto/scler/osis is also known as: *inner ear hardening - hearing loss*

126. The medical terms Palpebr/itis and Blepharo/ptosis refer to: *eyelid inflammation and eyelid drooping*

127. The medical term Retin/itis Pigmentosa can be called: *animal tracks "retina or net is inflamed causing marks - blindness"*

128. The medical term Retino/blast/oma is also known as: *malignant retinal glioma "causing white or yellow cats eye reflex"*

129. Tay-Sachs disease is one of many genetic diseases that can cause blindness and death mainly in young _____ children: *Jewish, French-Canadian and Irish-American*

130. The medical term Trach/oma refers to a chlamydial (to cloak) infection causing: *rough swollen eye lesions*

131. The outer hard layer of the eye (white of eye) is the: *sclera*

132. The transparent anterior part of the sclera is the: *cornea*

133. The eye structure that lies directly behind the pupil and iris is the: *lens*

134. The highly vascularized middle layer of the eye wall is called the: *choroid layer or posterior uvea*

135. The tear glands that lubricate and protect the eye are called: *lacrimal glands "dacyro- or lacrimo- mean tear"*

136. The opening in the center of the iris is called the: *pupil "pupillo-"*

137. The muscular membrane that gives the eye its color is the: *iris "rainbow"*

138. The inner layer of the eye with the vision receptors is the: *retina "net"*

139. The combining form ocul/o- means: *eye*

140. The prefix 'bin-' in binocular means: *two*

141. The suffix '-opia' means: *vision*

142. The watery liquid located in the anterior chamber of the eye is the: *aqueous fluid*

143. The jellylike liquid located in the posterior chamber of the eye is the: *vitreous fluid*

144. The small organs that produce and drain tears from the eye are the: *lacrimal glands and ducts*

145. The mucous membrane lining the inner eyelids & globe eyeball is the: *conjunctiva*

146. The nerve in the eye that carries visual impulses from the retina to the brain is the: *optic nerve*

147. The combining forms that mean "eyelid" are: *blephar/o- and palpebr/o-*

148. The combining form that means "vision" is: *opt/o-*

149. The combining forms irid/o- or ir/o- literally mean "rainbow" or: *iris*

150. The combining form that means "tear duct" is: *dacryo/docto-*

151. The combining form lacrimo/adeno- literally means: *tear/gland*

152. The combining forms that mean "pupil" are: *pupil- and pupill/o-*

153. The combining form cry/o- means: *cold*

154. The word parts that means two or double are: *bin-, bi-, dipl/o, co-, and di-*

155. The combining form phot/o- means: *light*

156. The word parts that means eye are: *opthalm/o- and oculo-*

157. The combining form ton/o- means: *tension, pressure, or tone*

158. The suffix that means abnormal fear of (aversion to) is: *-phobia*

159. The suffix -ician in Phys/ician (natural/_____) actually means: *one who*

160. The diagnostic term Blephar/itis means: *inflammation of the eyelid*

161. The diagnostic term Photo/phobia means: *abnormal aversion to or fear of light*

162. The diagnostic term Ophthalmorrhagia actually means: *fluid bursting from eye*

163. The term for an abnormal condition of the eye caused by a fungus is: *oculo/myc/o/sis*

164. The diagnostic term for inflammation of the cornea and iris is: *irido/kerat/itis*

165. The diagnostic term Sclero/malacia means: *softening of the sclera "white hard outer eye layer"*

166. The medical term Dacryo/cyst/itis or Lacrimo/cyst/itis means: *inflammation of the tear sac*

167. The diagnostic term Blepharo/ptosis means: *drooping of the eyelid "palpebral drooping"*

168. The diagnostic term Ophthalm/algia means: *pain in the eye*

169. The diagnostic term Dipl/opia actually means: *double vision*

170. The diagnostic term Pan/ophthalm/itis means: *inflammation of all of the eye structures*

171. The diagnostic term Irido/plegia means: *paralysis of the iris "prevents contraction or dilation of pupil"*

172. The condition called _____ (squinting) is a problem of directing the optic eye axes at the same object. It is usually caused by reduced visual acuity, unequal eye muscle tone, or problems with the Cranial Nerves 3, 4, or 6: *strabismus "lazy eye"*

173. The term for separation of the retina from the choroid's inner eyeball layer in the back of the eye is: *detached retina*

174. The diagnostic term for obstruction of the eyelids sebaceous gland is: *chalazion "stye"*

175. The diagnostic term for defective curvature of the refractive surface of the eye is: *astigmatism "usually irregular football shaped cornea"*

176. The term for an involuntary rhythmic eye movement (jumping) is: *nystagmus "to nod"*

177. The term that actually means an abnormal membrane fold extending from eye medial conjunctiva to the cornea is a: *pterygium "wing - triangular thickening of conjunctiva"*

178. The diagnostic term Cataract actually means: *clouding of the lens of the eye "looks cloudy, waterfall, opacity"*

179. The surgical term that means fixation of the retina to the choroid eye layer by extreme cold is: *cryo/retin/opexy*

180. The surgical term for the creation of an artificial "mouth-like" opening between the tear sac and the nose is: *dacryo/cysto/rhin/os/tom/y*

181. The surgical term for surgical repair of the eyelid is: *blephar/oplasty*

182. The surgical term dacryo/cyst/otomy means: *incision into the lacrimal sac*

183. The surgical term Radial Keratotomy actually means: *producing spoke-like incisions to flatten the cornea*

184. The suffix -plegia means: *paralysis*

185. The diagnostic term 'Endophthalmitis' means: *inflammation of the contents of the eye*

186. The diagnostic term "Hyperopia" means: *farsightedness*

187. The medical term 'mydriatic' means: *agent that dilates the pupil*

188. With glaucoma, pressure causes atrophy of the _____ and retina, resulting in blindness. *Optic nerve*

189. The surgical term for a procedure in which a cataract is lifted from the eye with an extremely cold probe is: *cryo-extraction of the lens*

190. Surgical incision procedure of the eye muscle tendon in order to relieve cross-eyed (inward) or wall-eyed (outward) conditions is called: *oculo/tend/o/tom/y*

191. The surgical method that removes cataracts by using an ultrasonic needle probe to break up the lens is called: *phaco-emulsification "lens breaking procedure"*

192. A diagnostic instrument that measures the curvature of the cornea is called a(n): *Keratometer*

193. An instrument that examines the interior of the eye is called a(n): *ophthalmo/scop/e*

194. The medical term for any non-inflammatory disease of the retina is: *retinopathy*

195. The medical term for a physician who specializes in Ophthalmology is: *Ophthalmologist*

196. The medical term that actually means one who is skilled in filling prescriptions for lenses is: *Optician*

197. The medical term for a specialist who studies the diseases of the eye and is a medical doctor is: *Ophthalmologist*

198. The medical term intra-ocul/ar means: *pertaining to within the eye*

199. The medical term Opto/metr/ist literally means: *specialist in the measurement of sight*

200. The medical term ophthalmic means: *pertaining to the eye*

201. The medical term papill/ary means: *pertaining to the pupil*

202. The diagnostic term ophthalmo/pathy actually means: *the development of an eye disease*

203. The medical terms and abbreviations that refer to the right eye are: *oculus dexter and O D or R E*

204. The medical terms and abbreviations that refer to the left eye are: *oculus sinister and O S or L E*

205. The medical term visual acuity means: *sharpness of vision*

206. The medical term for a specialist who examines, diagnoses, and treats the eyes and has the medical specialty letters O.D. is: *Optometr/ist*

207. The combining form ocul/o- means: *eye*

208. The part of the ear that directs sound waves into the external auditory meatus (opening) is called the: *auricle or pinna*

209. The combining form labyrinth/o- means: *labyrinth or maze "part of inner ear"*

210. The semi/transparent tissue that separates the external auditory meatus (opening) from the middle ear and is part of the middle ear cavity is the: *tympanic membrane*

211. The structure in the inner ear that contains balance receptors and endolymph is called the: *semicircular canals*

212. The structure that connects the middle ear with the pharynx (throat) and equalizes pressure on either side of the eardrum is the: *Eustachian tube "anatomist"*

213. The bony spaces within the temporal bone of the skull, which contain the cochlea and the semicircular canals, is the: *inner ear*

214. The snail-shaped structure in the inner ear that contains the organs of hearing is the: *cochlea*

215. The short tube that leads from the outside world to the tympanic membrane of the middle ear is called the: *external auditory meatus "opening" and canal*

216. The bones of the middle ear that carry sound vibrations to the inner ear are called the: *ossicles*

217. The malleus, incus, and stapes make up the bones of the middle ear called the: *ossicles "bones/little"*

218. The combining forms acoust/o- and audi/o- both mean: *hearing "acoustics and audio"*

219. The combining form that means "pertaining to the eardrum" is: *tympan/o-*

220. The combining form that means "eardrum" is: *myring/o-*

221. The combining form auri- and oto- means: *ear "auricle and otology"*

222. The combining form ot/o- means: *ear*

223. The combining form that means "hearing" is: *audi/o- "Auditorium"*

224. The Olfactory (smell), Trigeminal (3/parts), Vagus (wanderer), and the Hypoglossal (under/tongue) Nerves innervate the nose, face and teeth, organs, and tongue muscles. They are referred to as Cranial Nerves (OOOTTAFAGVAH): *1, 5, 10, and 12*

225. The combining form staped/o- means: *stapes or stirrup "middle ear bone"*

226. The diagnostic term ot/itis interna can also be called: *labyrinthitis or inflamed inner ear*

227. The medical term for a fungal infection of the ear is: *otomycosis*

228. The diagnostic term ot/algia means: *pain in the ear*

229. The diagnostic term that means hardening of the ear is: *otosclerosis*

230. The diagnostic term that actually means inflammation spreading from the ear to the mastoid bone behind the ear is: *otomastoiditis*

231. The diagnostic term that means inflammation of the mastoid bone and cells is: *mastoiditis*

232. The diagnostic term for a chronic disease of the inner ear characterized by dizziness (Vertigo) and ringing (Tinnitus) in the ear is: *Meniere's disease*

233. The diagnostic term that means tumor of the gland that excretes earwax is:

ceruminoma

234. The diagnostic term that means inflammation of the outer ear is: *otitis externa*

235. The medical term Myring/itis (typan/itis: drum/inflamed) actually means: *inflammation of the eardrum*

236. The diagnostic term for ringing in the ears is: *tinnitus*

237. The diagnostic term for dizziness (turning round) is: *vertigo*

238. The surgical term labyrinth/ectomy means: *surgical excision of the labyrinth or maze of the inner ear*

239. Surgical term for a procedure of repairing an incision into the eardrum: *myring/o/plast/y*

240. The bones of the middle ear that carry sound vibrations from the eardrum are called the : *ossicles*

241. The combining form labyrinth/o- means: *labyrinth or maze "part of inner ear"*

242. The medical term Myring/itis (typan/itis: drum/inflamed) actually means: *inflammation of the eardrum*

243. A delicate instrument used to test hearing acuteness is called a(n): *audio/meter*

244. An instrument used for the visual examination of the ear is called a(n): *otoscop/e*

245. The procedural term that means the measurement of the movement of the tympanic membrane is: *tympano/metr/y*

246. The procedural term audio/gram actually means: *graphic recording of decibel frequencies of hearing*

247. An instrument used to measure middle ear function is: *tympano/meter*

248. The procedural term oto/scop/y means: *the procedure of visually examining the ear*

249. The procedural term audio/metr/y means: *process of the measurement of hearing*

250. The term audio/meter means: *instrument used to measure hearing*

251. The term aur/al means: *pertaining to the ear*

252. The medical term that means a specialist who studies and treats the diseases and disorders of the ear, nose, and throat is: *Otorhinolaryngologist*

253. The term that means one who studies and treats disease of the ear is: *Otologist*

254. A specialist who specializes in the study of hearing is an: *Audiologist*

255. The medical term that means the study of the ear is: *otology*

256. A Chiropractor specializes in the repositioning of bones with adjustments in order to relieve nerve and tissue pressure caused by bone _____: *subluxations*

257. The term Psycho/pharmac/o/log/y actually refers to: *the science of how drugs work on the mind*

1. The upper chambers of the heart are called the: _____

2. The lower chambers of the heart are called the: _____

3. The valve located between the right atrium and ventricle is the: _____

4. The valve located between the left atrium and ventricle is the: _____

5. The wall that separates the right side of the heart from the left is the: _____

6. The two-layer sac that covers the heart is called the: _____

7. The inner lining of the heart is called the: _____

8. The Pace-Maker is found in the right atria and is also called the: _____

9. The blood vessel that carries blood containing oxygen and nutrients away from the heart to the body tissues (except the lungs) is the: _____

10. The two (2) blood vessels that carry blood cells containing high amounts of carbon dioxide back to the heart are the: _____

11. The liquid portion of the blood in which cells float is the: _____

12. Red Blood Cells (RBCs) are called: _____

13. White Blood Cells (WBCs) are called: _____

14. The organ that breaks down old RBC's in adults is the: _____

15. The transparent and colorless body tissue fluid is called: _____

16. The master gland of the "Immune System" is the: _____

17. The combining forms angi/o- and vaso- all mean: _____

18. The combining form that means "crown or crowning (on top)" is: _____

19. The combining form valvul/o- means: _____

20. The combining forms that mean "vein" are: _____

21. The combining form isch/o- (as in "ischemia") means: _____

22. The combining form sphygm/o- means: _____

23. The combining forms that mean "chest" are: _____

24. The combining form that means "hot, heat, or warm" is: _____

25. The combining forms that mean "sound" are: _____

26. The combining form thromb/o- means: _____

27. The prefix that means slow is: _____

28. The prefix that means fast or rapid is: _____

29. The suffix -poiesis means: _____

30. The suffix that means pertaining to (refers to) in the term card/i/ac is: _____

31. The suffix -graph in the term cardio/graph means: _____

32. The diagnosis of Angina Pectoris literally means _____. The actual meaning is lack of blood flow to the large heart vessels in the chest.

33. The suffix that means condition of hardening is: _____

34. The suffix that means abnormal reduction in number (decrease) is: _____

35. The term that means separation or removal is: _____

36. The diagnostic term that means inflammation of the outer heart is: _____

37. The term that means enlargement of the heart (due to disease) is: _____

38. The diagnostic term Cardio/valvul/itis is defined as inflammation of the: _____

39. The diagnostic term that means abnormal state of a slow heart rate is: _____

40. The diagnostic term Aortic Stenosis means: _____

41. The diagnostic term Coronary Isch/emia actually means: _____

42. The diagnostic term Angio/stenosis means: _____

43. The diagnostic term that means hardening of the arteries is: _____

44. The diagnostic term that means deficiency of blood cells is: _____

45. The diagnostic term that means a tumor composed of blood vessel(s) is: _____

46. The diagnostic term Lymph/aden/itis means: _____

47. The diagnostic term Arteri/o/rrhexis means: _____

48. The "actual meaning" of the diagnostic term cardio/myo/path/y is: _____

49. The inability of the heart to pump enough blood through the body to supply the tissues and organs is called: _____

50. The diagnostic term for chest pain that occurs when there is an insufficient supply of blood to the heart muscle is: _____

51. The diagnostic term Ar/rhythmia means: _____

52. The diagnostic term used to refer to a dilated or varicose (twisted) internal and/or external vein in the rectum is: _____

53. The diagnostic term for the ballooning of a weakened portion of an arterial wall is: _____

54. The diagnostic term that means rapid, quivering, non-coordinated contractions of the atria and/or ventricles is: _____

55. The diagnostic term for distended or tortuous veins usually found in the lower extremities is: _____

56. The diagnostic term Cardiac Arrest is defined as a(n): _____

57. The diagnostic term for a type of cancer characterized by an abnormal increase in white blood cells is: _____

58. The diagnostic term for an inherited bleeding disease caused by a deficiency of the coagulation factor is: _____

59. The diagnostic term An/emia means: _____

60. The surgical term that means surgical excision of the thickened interior (plaque) of an artery is: _____

61. The surgical term for the incision into a vein to remove blood, to give blood, or to give intravenous fluids is: _____

62. The surgical term Angi/o/rrhaphy means: _____

63. The surgical term Thym/ectomy means: _____

64. The surgical term that means creation of an artificial opening (mouth-like) in the muscular layer of the heart is: _____

65. The surgical term Angioplasty means: _____

66. The surgical term for a surgical procedure to repair a stenotic (narrowed) bicuspid valve by breaking apart its 2 leaves (cusps) is: _____

67. The surgical term for a procedure in which a balloon is passed through a blood vessel to the area in which plaque is formed is: _____

68. The surgical technique that brings a new blood supply to heart muscles by detouring around blocked athro/sclerotic coronary arteries is called a(n): _____

69. The use of a medication to dissolve blood clots in a blocked coronary vessel is called: _____

70. The term Phono/cardio/gram means: _____

71. The procedural term for X-ray of the lymph nodes, and glands, after an injection of contrast medium dye is: _____

72. The procedural phrase "Complete Blood Count - CBC" is defined as:

_____

73. The procedural term Lymph/angio/graph/y means: _____

74. The procedural term for X-ray of the blood vessels after an injection of contrast medium dye is: _____

75. The procedural term for X-ray of the veins after an injection of contrast medium dye is: _____

76. The procedural term for X-ray of the lymphatic vessels after an injection of contrast medium is: _____

77. The procedure for making a record of the structure and motion of the heart using sound waves is called: _____

78. A procedural term that means to measure pulse waves and heart beats is: _____

79. A procedural bone marrow biopsy is referred to as: _____

80. The Test that determines the time it takes for blood to form a clot is: _____

81. The Test that determines coagulation activity defects is called: _____

82. The device or instrument that is used to measure arterial blood pressure (pulse pressure) by hand is a: _____

83. The study that uses ultrasound to determine the velocity of the flow of blood within a vessel is: _____

84. A two-dimensional photo/graphic representation of the heart taken after the introduction of radioactive material into the body is: _____

85. The medical term Cardiology means: _____

86. The medical term that means body temperature below normal, 98.6 F., is: (Note: hypo-, sub-, and infra all can refer to less, below, or under) _____

87. The medical term that means removal of liquid from withdrawn blood is : _____

88. The term that means one who studies and treats diseases of the blood is: _____

89. The medical term Hemo/stasis (hemo/stat) literally means: _____

90. The term Anti/coagulant (an aspirin breaks plat/let membranes) means: _____

91. The medical term which means to puncture a vein in order to remove blood, instill medication, or start an intravenous infusion is: _____

92. The medical term for the hearing of sounds within the body through a stethoscope is: _____

93. Application of an electric shock to the myocardium through the chest wall to restore normal cardiac rhythm is called: _____

94. The medical term Sy/stole (together/contract) actually means: _____

95. The medical term Mano/meter is actually defined as: _____

96. The medical term Dys/crasia (faulty or bad/mingling) is actually body symptoms that are defined as: _____

97. The phase in the cardiac cycle in which chambers relax between contractions is called: _____

98. The medical term for referring to the blood vessels is: _____

99. The medical term that means liquid portion of the blood without the clotting factor is: _____

100. Tapping of a body surface with the fingers to determine the density of the body part beneath is: _____

101. The medical term for the phase in the cardiac cycle in which the ventricles contract is: _____

102. The suffixes that mean 'pain' are: _____

103. Cardiomyopathy is referred to as having a problem with _____.
_____

104. The Cardio/vascular Sy/stem is also referred to as the: _____

105. The medical term Hyper/tension means: _____

106. The medical term Lumen means: _____

107. The term "em/bol/ism" literally means "state of a lump within," and actually refers to: _____

108. Poly/cyth/emia Vera (many/cells/blood: true) is the term for: _____

314

109. A Pulmonary Infarction (lung: to stuff into) actually means: _____

110. The term _____ refers to the lack of development of normal numbers of RBC's (Erythrocytes) in the blood.

111. A Macro/phage is referred to as a: _____

112. Hodgkin's disease is a type of: _____

113. The Cardio/vascular Sy/stem is also referred to as the: _____

114. Iso/tonic cells (equal/tension: chamber) have the same tension on both sides of the cells: _____

115. Athero/sclerosis is a type of: _____

116. Mitral Valve Prolapse (MVP) or Mitral Valve Incompetence (MVI) (valve between chambers on left side of the heart) is usually seen in: _____

117. The term Angioplasty literally means: _____

118. An Aortic Abdominal Aneurysm is the _____ of the big blood vessel in the posterior belly that often ruptures and causes death by hem/orrhag/ing.

119. A Varico/cele is the _____ of the veins in the scrotum (male pouch)

120. Tel/angi/ect/asis actually means: _____

121. The parasitic Protozoan Disease Trypano/som/iasis (carried by insects) is called Snail Fever, Chagas' Disease, Tsetse Fly Disease, America Fever or: _____

122. Schisto/som/iasis in man is a type of a _____ infestation. _____

123. A Phlebo/tom/ist is a person who specializes in cutting or puncturing _____ to take blood samples.

124. Coronary Thrombosis is also known as: _____

125. The most important longitudinal heart study in the world is being conducted in what American city since 1946: _____

126. The leading Cardiac Risk Factors are: _____

127. The Framingham study began in: _____

128. Tiny blood vessels in the back of the _____ are viewed with an ophthalmo/scop/e to help diagnose arterio/sclerosis, diabetes, kidney disease, and many other diseases.

129. Ather/oma plaques are fatty thickening or degeneration of large artery walls occurring in a type of arterio/sclerosis called: _____

130. A Stethoscope is placed over the heart valves to listen to the: _____

131. Sickle Cell Anemia (Sickle Cell Trait "Gene") includes the: _____

132. The terms Crenation, Poikilocytosis, and Anisocytosis all refer to: _____

133. The condition of Hodgkin's disease could also be known as: _____

1. The upper chambers of the heart are called the: *atria "means chamber"*

2. The lower chambers of the heart are called the: *ventricles "little belly"*

3. The valve located between the right atrium and ventricle is the: *tricuspid*

4. The valve located between the left atrium and ventricle is the: *bicuspid "mitral"*

5. The wall that separates the right side of the heart from the left is the: *cardiac septum*

6. The two-layer sac that covers the heart is called the: *pericardium*

7. The inner lining of the heart is called the: *endocardium*

8. The Pace-Maker is found in the right atria and is also called the: *S-A Node*

9. The blood vessel that carries blood containing oxygen and nutrients away from the heart to the body tissues (except the lungs) is the: *aorta*

10. The two (2) blood vessels that carry blood cells containing high amounts of carbon dioxide back to the heart are the: *vena cavas "superior and inferior"*

11. The liquid portion of the blood in which cells float is the: *plasma*

12. Red Blood Cells (RBCs) are called: *erthro/cytes*

13. White Blood Cells (WBCs) are called: *leuko/cytes or leuco/cytes*

14. The organ that breaks down old RBC's in adults is the: *spleen*

15. The transparent and colorless body tissue fluid is called: *lymph - watery*

16. The master gland of the "Immune System" is the: *thymus - flowery or spirit*

17. The combining forms angi/o- and vaso- all mean: *vessel*

18. The combining form that means "crown or crowning (on top)" is: *coron/o-*

19. The combining form valvul/o- means: *valve*

20. The combining forms that mean "vein" are: *ven/o- and phleb/o-*

21. The combining form isch/o- (as in "ischemia") means: *deficiency of flow "partial blockage"*

22. The combining form sphygm/o- means: *pulse*

23. The combining forms that mean "chest" are: *steth/o-, pectero-, and thoraco-*

24. The combining form that means "hot, heat, or warm" is: *therm/o-*

25. The combining forms that mean "sound" are: *ech/o- and sono-*

26. The combining form thromb/o- means: *clot "to clump together at one location"*

27. The prefix that means slow is: *brady-*

28. The prefix that means fast or rapid is: *tachy-*

29. The suffix -poiesis means: *formation or development "hemato/poiesis"*

30. The suffix that means pertaining to (refers to) in the term card/i/ac is: *-ac or -iac*

31. The suffix -graph in the term cardio/graph means: *instrument used to record*

32. The diagnosis of Angina Pectoris literally means _____. The actual meaning is lack of blood flow to the large heart vessels in the chest. *vessel : "in" chest*

33. The suffix that means condition of hardening is: *-sclerosis*

34. The suffix that means abnormal reduction in number (decrease) is: *-penia*

35. The term that means separation or removal is: *apheresis*

36. The diagnostic term that means inflammation of the outer heart is: *pericarditis*

37. The term that means enlargement of the heart (due to disease) is: *cardiomegaly*

38. The diagnostic term Cardio/valvul/itis is defined as inflammation of the: *valves of the heart*

39. The diagnostic term that means abnormal state of a slow heart rate is: *bradycardia*

40. The diagnostic term Aortic Stenosis means: *narrowing of the aorta*

41. The diagnostic term Coronary Isch/emia actually means: *deficient supply of blood to the crowning blood vessels of the heart*

42. The diagnostic term Angio/stenosis means: *condition of a narrowed blood vessel*

43. The diagnostic term that means hardening of the arteries is: *arterio/sclera/o/sis*

44. The diagnostic term that means deficiency of blood cells is: *hematocytopenia*

45. The diagnostic term that means a tumor composed of blood vessel(s) is: *angioma*

46. The diagnostic term Lymph/aden/itis means: *inflammation of the lymph glands*

47. The diagnostic term Arteri/o/rrhexis means: *rupture of an artery*

48. The "actual meaning" of the diagnostic term Cardio/myo/path/y is: *a condition that causes poor blood circulation to the heart muscle*

49. The inability of the heart to pump enough blood through the body to supply the tissues and organs is called: *congestive heart failure*

50. The diagnostic term for chest pain that occurs when there is an insufficient supply of blood to the heart muscle is: *angina pectoris "Angina"*

51. The diagnostic term Ar/rhythmia means: *any variation from a normal heart rhythm or contraction*

52. The diagnostic term used to refer to a dilated or varicose (twisted) internal and/or external vein in the rectum is: *hemorrh/oid "blood/resembles"*

53. The diagnostic term for the ballooning of a weakened portion of an arterial wall is: *aneurysm*

54. The diagnostic term that means rapid, quivering, non-coordinated contractions of the atria and/or ventricles is: *fibrillation*

55. The diagnostic term for distended or tortuous veins usually found in the lower extremities is: *varicose veins "twisted appearance"*

56. The diagnostic term Cardiac Arrest is defined as a(n): *sudden cessation of cardiac output and effective circulation*

57. The diagnostic term for a type of cancer characterized by an abnormal increase in white blood cells is: *leuk/emia*

58. The diagnostic term for an inherited bleeding disease caused by a deficiency of the coagulation factor is: *Hemo/philia "blood/love of"*

59. The diagnostic term An/emia means: *decrease in normal RBC numbers, iron, or hemoglobin levels*

60. The surgical term that means surgical excision of the thickened interior (plaque) of an artery is: *end/art/ectomy*

61. The surgical term for the incision into a vein to remove blood, to give blood, or to give intravenous fluids is: *phleb/otomy*

62. The surgical term Angi/o/rrhaphy means: *suturing of a vessel or to repair a vessel*

63. The surgical term Thym/ectomy means: *surgical excision or removal of the thymus gland*

64. The surgical term that means creation of an artificial opening (mouth-like) in the muscular layer of the heart is: *myo/cardi/ostomy*

65. The surgical term Angioplasty means: *surgical repair of a blood vessel*

66. The surgical term for a surgical procedure to repair a stenotic (narrowed) bicuspid valve by breaking apart its 2 leaves (cusps) is: *commissur/otomy*

67. The surgical term for a procedure in which a balloon is passed through a blood vessel to the area in which plaque is formed is: *percutaneous transluminal coronary angioplasty*

68. The surgical technique that brings a new blood supply to heart muscles by detouring around blocked athro/sclerotic coronary arteries is called a(n): *coronary artery bypass*

69. The use of a medication to dissolve blood clots in a blocked coronary vessel is called: *intra/coronary thrombo/lytic therapy*

70. The term Phono/cardio/gram means: *graphic record of heart sound*

71. The procedural term for X-ray of the lymph nodes, and glands, after an injection of contrast medium dye is: *lymphadenography*

72. The procedural phrase "Complete Blood Count - CBC" is defined as: *counting RBC, WBC, and Thrombocytes or Platelets*

73. The procedural term Lymph/angio/graph/y means: *X-ray filming of lymph vessels after injecting contrast medium dye*

74. The procedural term for X-ray of the blood vessels after an injection of contrast medium dye is: *angiograph/y*

75. The procedural term for X-ray of the veins after an injection of contrast medium dye is: *venograph/y*

76. The procedural term for X-ray of the lymphatic vessels after an injection of contrast medium is: *lympangiography*

77. The procedure for making a record of the structure and motion of the heart using sound waves is called: *echocardiography*

78. A procedural term that means to measure pulse waves and heart beats is. *sphygmocardiograph/y*

79. A procedural bone marrow biopsy is referred to as: *stern/al puncture*

80. The Test that determines the time it takes for blood to form a clot is: *coagulation time*

81. The Test that determines coagulation activity defects is called: *"prothrombin time" thrombo/plastin and calcium are added to decalcified plasma to measure the effect of anti/coagulant drugs*

82. The device or instrument that is used to measure arterial blood pressure (pulse pressure) by hand is a: *sphygmo/mano/meter*

83. The study that uses ultrasound to determine the velocity of the flow of blood within a vessel is: *Doppler Flow Studies*

84. A two-dimensional photo/graphic representation of the heart taken after the introduction of radioactive material into the body is: *Cardiac Scan*

85. The medical term Cardiology means: *the science and study of the heart*

86. The medical term that means body temperature below normal, 98.6 F., is: (Note: hypo-, sub-, and infra all can refer to less, below, or under) *hypo/thermia "usually 78 to 90 degrees F."*

87. The medical term that means removal of liquid from withdrawn blood is: *plasm/apheresis "liquid blood/separation"*

88. The term that means one who studies and treats diseases of the blood is: *Hematolog/ist*

89. The medical term Hemo/stasis (hemo/stat) literally means: *stoppage of bleeding or diminished blood flow "circulation"*

90. The term Anti/coagulant (an aspirin breaks plat/let membranes) means: *agent that slows down the clotting process*

91. The medical term which means to puncture a vein in order to remove blood, instill medication, or start an intravenous infusion is: *veni/pucture*

92. The medical term for the hearing of sounds within the body through a stethoscope is: *auscultation*

93. Application of an electric shock to the myocardium through the chest wall to restore normal cardiac rhythm is called: *de/fibrill/ation "process of quivering going away"*

94. The medical term Sy/stole (together/contract) actually means: *cardiac cycle phase where chambers contract raising blood pressure*

95. The medical term Mano/meter is actually defined as: *instrument used to measure the pressure of fluids*

96. The medical term Dys/crasia (faulty or bad/mingling) is actually body symptoms that are defined as: *abnormal or pathological condition of the blood or bone marrow "usually seen with leukemia, anemia, and the RH +/- Factor"*

97. The phase in the cardiac cycle in which chambers relax between contractions is called: *dia/stole "relaxation of heart muscle"*

98. The medical term for referring to the blood vessels is: *peripheral vascular*

99. The medical term that means liquid portion of the blood without the clotting factor is: *serum*

100. Tapping of a body surface with the fingers to determine the density of the body part beneath is: *percussion*

101. The medical term for the phase in the cardiac cycle in which the ventricles contract is: *systole*

102. The suffixes that mean 'pain' are: *-dynia and -algia*

103. Cardiomyopathy is referred to as having a problem with _____. *the heart muscle pumping blood*

104. The Cardio/vascular Sy/stem is also referred to as the: *Circulatory System "circle/refers: classifies together"*

105. The medical term Hyper/tension means: *blood pressure that is above normal - "140/90 mm/Hg or higher above atmospheric pressure"*

106. The medical term Lumen means: *space within a tubular body part or organ*

107. The term "em/bol/ism" literally means "state of a lump within," and actually refers to: *a moving clot*

108. Poly/cyth/emia Vera (many/cells/blood: true) is the term for: *Erythrocytosis "RBC increases cause strokes, heart attaches, & clots"*

109. A Pulmonary Infarction (lung: to stuff into) actually means: *lung blood flow blockage "ischemia is decreased flow"*

110. The term _____ refers to the lack of development of normal numbers of RBC's (Erythrocytes) in the blood. *A/plastic An/emia "bone marrow not producing cells"*

111. A Macro/phage is referred to as a: *large eaters of foreign cells and materials*

112. Hodgkin's disease is a type of: *Lymph/oma*

113. The Cardio/vascular Sy/stem is also referred to as the: *Circulatory System "circle/refers: classifies together"*

114. Iso/tonic cells (equal/tension: chamber) have the same tension on both sides of the cells: *outer cell membrane*

115. Athero/sclerosis is a type of: *Arteriosclerosis*

116. Mitral Valve Prolapse (MVP) or Mitral Valve Incompetence (MVI) (valve between

chambers on left side of the heart) is usually seen in: *women or females*

117. The term Angioplasty literally means: *the surgical repair procedure of a body vessel "usually arteries"*

118. An Aortic Abdominal Aneurysm is the _____ of the big blood vessel in the posterior belly that often ruptures and causes death by hem/orrhag/ing. *ballooning "a widening"*

119. A Varico/cele is the _____ of the veins in the scrotum (male pouch). *twisting "feels like worms in sac"*

120. Tel/angi/ect/asis actually means: *angi/oma "condition of blood vessel/outward swelling/at the end"*

121. The parasitic Protozoan Disease Trypano/som/iasis (carried by insects) is called Snail Fever, Chagas' Disease, Tsetse Fly Disease, America Fever or: *Sleeping Sickness*

122. Schisto/som/iasis in man is a type of a _____ infestation. *Split Bodied Blood Fluke Worm*

123. A Phlebo/tom/ist is a person who specializes in cutting or puncturing _____ to take blood samples. *veins*

124. Coronary Thrombosis is also known as: *Acute Myocardial Infarction or Myocardial Infarction*

125. The most important longitudinal heart study in the world is being conducted in what American City since 1946: *Framingham, Massachusetts*

126. The leading Cardiac Risk Factors are: *smoking, obesity, lack of exercise, and hyper/cholesterol/emia*

127. The Framingham study began in: *1946*

128. Tiny blood vessels in the back of the _____ are viewed with an Ophthalmo/scop/e to help diagnose arterio/sclerosis, diabetes, kidney disease, and many other diseases. *eye*

129. Ather/oma Plaques are fatty thickening or degeneration of large artery walls occurring in a type of arterio/sclerosis called: *athero/sclerosis*

130. A Stethoscope is placed over the heart valves to listen to the: *Aortic Valve, Bicuspid*

and Tricuspid Valves, and Pulmonary Valve

131. The Sickle Cell Anemia (Sickle Cell Trait "Gene") includes the: *Clumping of blood in vessels causing ischemia, infarction, and tissue necrosis.*

132. The terms Crenation, Poikilocytosis, and Anisocytosis all refer to: *cell shapes*

133. The condition of Hodgkin's disease could also be known as: *Lymph Node Hyper/trophy Disease*

1. The lymphoid tissues located behind the nasal cavity are called: _____

2. The partition or wall separating the right and left cavities of the nose is called the: _____

3. Both food and air travel through the: _____

4. The double-sac membrane that covers each lung and lines the thoracic cavity is the: _____

5. The surgical term that means "excision of a lobe of the lung" is: _____

6. The surgical term for the puncture of the chest cavity in order to aspirate fluid is called: _____

7. The medical term 'hypoxemia' means: _____

8. The area in the lungs where oxygen and carbon dioxide are exchanged is called the: _____

9. The space between the lungs in the chest is referred to as the: _____

10. The muscular partition between the thoracic and abdominal cavities is called the: _____

11. The tube extending from the throat to the bronchi is called the: _____

12. The vocal cords or glottis are located in the: _____

13. Pulmonary Endo/scop/y is best used to _____ diseases of the Respiratory System. _____

14. The combining forms rhino/o- and naso- both mean: _____

15. The combining form(s) that means "chest and lungs" are: _____

16. The combining forms that can mean "lung" are: _____

17. The term Ortho/dont/ist literally means: _____

18. The combining form that means "breathe or breathing" is: _____

19. The term(s) _____ that can literally mean without or lack of/tooth/refers to is (are): _____

20. The term Eu/pnea actually means: _____

21. The suffix that means pain or painful is: _____

22. The suffix -ary in the compound term Pulmon/ary (lung/_____) means: _____

23. The suffix that means instrument used for visual examination is: _____

24. The term Dys/phasia means difficult or faulty: _____

25. The term Trachy/os/tom/y actually means: _____

26. The suffix _____ is added to word part Pneumono-/_____ to refer to the surgical procedure of puncturing the lung and aspirating fluids like blood, pus, & lymph. This procedure promotes easy breathing and cell oxygenation.

27. The term Pneumono/hemo/orrhagia means: _____

28. A patient diagnosed with an acute cough usually has: _____

29. The diagnostic term for pus in the pleural space in the chest is: _____

30. The diagnostic term for narrowing or contraction of the larynx or voice box is:

_____

31. A patient with diagnosis of blood in the chest has a: _____

32. The condition where the bronchi of the lungs are dilated outward is: _____

33. When lung tissue swells as a result of distention and loss of elasticity in the alveoli, the condition is called: _____

34. The diagnostic abbreviation for an infection of the nose, pharynx, larynx, and trachea is: _____

35. The diagnostic term that is also referred to as whooping cough is: _____

36. A diagnostic term for a nosebleed is usually: _____

37. The accumulation of fluid in the alveoli and bronchioles is called: _____

38. The diagnostic term for a chronic respiratory disease characterized by paroxysms of coughing, wheezing, panting with shortness of breath is: _____

39. The term Pulmon/ary Em/py/ema literally means lung: _____

40. The surgical term that means surgical repair of the voice box is: _____

41. The Anatomical Root or Stem Word Parts Thorac/o-, Pectero-, and Stetho- all literally mean: _____

42. Pigeon Breeders Chest is different from Pigeon Chest in that the first condition is inherited or caused by Rickets (lack of Vitamin A and D), but the latter condition is caused by a(n) _____ etiologic agent. _____

43. The surgical term that means incision into the trachea is: _____

44. The procedural term for X-ray filming of the bronchi tubes is: _____

45. A physician doing a visual examination of the voice box uses a(n) _____ which is a type of endo/scop/e:

46. A term that refers to food inhalation that blocks the airway: _____

47. The medical term that means excessive carbon dioxide in the blood: _____

48. The medical term Hyp/o/xia means: _____

49. The medical term that means breathing only in a straight position: _____

50. The medical term that means discharge from the nose is: _____

51. The medical term Broncho/gen/ic actually means: _____

52. The medical term that means absence of carbon dioxide in the blood:_____

53. The medical term Eu/pnea means: _____

54. The term that means difficulty in speaking or making a sound is: _____

55. Lobar Pneumonia refers to a lung infection in: _____

56. The medical term that means excessive breathing is: _____

57. The medical term Hypo/pnea actually means: _____

58. The medical term that means containing both mucus and pus is: _____

59. The medical term Nebuliz/er is defined as: _____

60. The medical term that actually means periodic or sudden attack is: _____

61. The medical term Broncho/dilator actually means: _____.

62. The medical term A/sphyxia actually means: _____

63. The medical term that actually means to draw foreign material into the respiratory tract blocking breathing is: _____

64. The diagnostic term Silic/osis is also known as: _____

65. The medical term Chord/itis or Cord/itis actually means: _____

66. The medical term Emphysema literally means: _____

67. The medical term Asthma literally means: _____

68. The medical term Pneumon/ia literally means: _____

69. Cystic Fibrosis (CF) is an inherited exocrine gland disorder that causes thick secretions of _____ to accumulation in the lungs.

70. The medical term Dipther/ia literally means: _____

71. The medical term Pertussis actually refers to: _____

72. The disease of Histoplasmosis or Darlings disease is a _____ infection caused by Histoplasma capsulatum. Bird or cat feces is the source and the disease is characterized by fever, malaise, coughing, respiratory failure, and lymph/adeno/path/y. A major problem for pregnant women and their fetuses.

73. Tuberculosis is caused by a bacterium, Mycobacterium tuberculosis, and causes bacteria colony swellings (tubers) in the lungs and other body parts. TB infects approximately _____ people.

74. The combining form cutane/o- means: _____

75. The Schick Skin Test is used to detect _____, which is caused by the bacteria Corynebacterium diphtheriae.

76. The Mantoux Skin Test is used to diagnose: _____

77. Anthrax infections (Bacillus anthracis bacteria) are classified as infecting the:

_____

78. Bronchitis often progresses to a more severe lung condition called _____, which was the leading world killer around 1900 A.D.

79. The Etiologic Agent (E.A.) or causative agent that is responsible for Anthrax is:

80. An Upper Respiratory Infection is referred to with the Abbreviation:

81. Spiro/metry means to measure the breath and is used to evaluate: _____

82. Bronch/ioles literally means: _____

83. The term Dys/lexia literally means difficult or faulty: _____

84. Pneumono/coni/osis is diagnosed daily in the form of different lung conditions or diseases including: _____

85. The disease of Crypto/cocc/o/sis is a _____that can infect the lungs, skin, brain (CNS), bones, and urinary tract causing death.

86. The disease of Aspergill/osis (to sprinkle/condition) is a soil or dust fungus that causes granular lesion on or in any body organ. Prognosis is poor like most systemic fungal infections. It is treated with: _____

87. The pleura is the covering of the _____. If Pleur/isy develops, the outer two (2) serous membrane layers of this body structure, called the visceral and parietal layers, have become inflamed.

88. Glott/itis is often referred to as Chord/itis or Cord/itis and is an inflamed: _____

89. The condition referred to as _____ is an acute viral infection that is usually seen in infants before 3 years of age (Y/O: years old). It occurs after an URI and causes vocal cord swelling, voice loss, hypoxia, & possible choking:

90. Pneumonia can be caused by: _____

91. Emphysema causes shortness of breath and a(n): _____

92. The incubation period of Influenza is from ____ to ____ days.

93. Kerat/o/sis, leuk/o/plakia, tartar, caries, purpura, fibr/oma, ulcers, gingiv/itis, tonsill/itis, adenoid/itis, squamous cell carcin/oma, catarrh (coryza), cleft palate, thrush, and candid/i/asis are all conditions that are usually diagnosed with a(n) _____ exam by a dentist or medical doctor.

1. The lymphoid tissues located behind the nasal cavity are called: *adenoids*

2. The partition or wall separating the right and left cavities of the nose is called the: *nasal septum*

3. Both food and air travel through the: *mouth and pharynx or throat*

4. The double-sac membrane that covers each lung and lines the thoracic cavity is the: *pleura*

5. The surgical term that means "excision of a lobe of the lung" is: *lobectomy*

6. The surgical term for the puncture of the chest cavity in order to aspirate fluid is called: *thoracocentesis*

7. The medical term 'hypoxemia' means: *deficient oxygen in the blood*

8. The area in the lungs where oxygen and carbon dioxide are exchanged is called the: *alveolus or cavity (alveolar sacs)*

9. The space between the lungs in the chest is referred to as the: *media/stinum*

10. The muscular partition between the thoracic and abdominal cavities is called the: *diaphragm "across/wall"*

11. The tube extending from the throat to the bronchi is called the: *trachea "which means rough"*

12. The vocal cords or glottis are located in the: *larynx - "voice box"*

13. Pulmonary Endo/scop/y is best used to _____ diseases of the Respiratory System. *view and diagnose*

14. The combining forms rhino/o- and naso- both mean: *nose*

15. The combining form(s) that means "chest and lungs" are: *thoraco/pulmono-*

16. The combining forms that can mean "lung" are: *pneumon/o- and pulmono-*

17. The term Ortho/dont/ist literally means: *straight/teeth/specialist*

18. The combining form that means "breathe or breathing" is: *spir/o-*

19. The term(s) _____ that can literally mean without or lack of/tooth/refers to is (are): *an/odont/ia, ar/odont/ia, ir/odont/ia*

20. The term Eu/pnea actually means: *well, easy, true, normal, or good breathing*

21. The suffix that means pain or painful is: *-dynia and algia*

22. The suffix -ary in the compound term Pulmon/ary (lung/_____) means: *pertaining to or state of*

23. The suffix that means instrument used for visual examination is: *-scope*

24. The term Dys/phasia means difficult or faulty: *speech or utterance*

25. The term Trachy/os/tom/y actually means: *creation of an artificial mouth-like opening in the throat and neck*

26. The suffix _____ is added to word part Pneumono-/_____ to refer to the surgical procedure of puncturing the lung and aspirating fluids like blood, pus, & lymph. This procedure promotes easy breathing and cell oxygenation. *-centesis*

27. The term Pneumono/hemo/orrhagia means: *bursting forth of blood from the lung*

28. A patient diagnosed with an acute cough usually has: *rhino/laryngo/tracheo/bronch/itis*

29. The diagnostic term for pus in the pleural space in the chest is: *pyo/thorax*

30. The diagnostic term for narrowing or contraction of the larynx or voice box is: *laryngospasm or laryngo/stenosis*

31. A patient with diagnosis of blood in the chest has a: *hemo/thorax*

32. The condition where the bronchi of the lungs are dilated outward is: *bronchi/ect/asis*

33. When lung tissue swells as a result of distention and loss of elasticity in the alveoli, the condition is called: *emphysema "puffed up"*

34. The diagnostic abbreviation for an infection of the nose, pharynx, larynx, and trachea is: *upper respiratory infection "URI"*

35. The diagnostic term that is also referred to as whooping cough is: *per/tussis "through/cough"*

36. A diagnostic term for a nosebleed is usually: *epistaxis*

37. The accumulation of fluid in the alveoli and bronchioles is called: *pulmon/ary edema*

38. The diagnostic term for a chronic respiratory disease characterized by paroxysms of coughing, wheezing, panting with shortness of breath is: *asthma "to pant"*

39. The term Pulmon/ary Em/py/ema literally means lung: *inward/pus/refers to*

40. The surgical term that means surgical repair of the voice box is: *laryngo/plasty*

41. The Anatomical Root or Stem Word Parts Thorac/o-, Pectero-, and Stetho- all literally mean: *chest*

42. Pigeon Breeders Chest is different from Pigeon Chest in that the first condition is inherited or caused by Rickets (lack of Vitamin A and D), but the latter condition is caused by a(n) _____ etiologic agent. *fungal*

43. The surgical term that means incision into the trachea is: *trache/otomy*

44. The procedural term for X-ray filming of the bronchi tubes is: *broncho/graph/y*

45. A physician doing a visual examination of the voice box uses a(n) _____ which is a type of endo/scop/e: *laryngo/scop/e*

46. A term that refers to food inhalation that blocks the airway: *aspiration "process of/without/breath"*

47. The medical term that means excessive carbon dioxide in the blood: *hyper/capnia*

48. The medical term Hyp/o/xia means: *deficient oxygen to tissue*

49. The medical term that means breathing only in a straight position: *ortho/pnea*

50. The medical term that means discharge from the nose is: *rhinorrhea*

51. The medical term Broncho/gen/ic actually means: *refers to origination in the bronchi*

52. The medical term that means absence of carbon dioxide in the blood is: *a/capnia "causing hyperventilation"*

53. The medical term Eu/pnea means: *normal or good breathing*

54. The term that means difficulty in speaking or making a sound is: *dys/phasic or dys/phonic*

55. Lobar Pneumonia refers to a lung infection in: *one or more of the 5 lobes in the 2 lungs*

56. The medical term that means excessive breathing is: *hyper/pnea*

57. The medical term Hypo/pnea actually means: *deficient rate and depth of breathing*

58. The medical term that means containing both mucus and pus is: *muco/purulent*

59. The medical term Nebuliz/er is defined as: *a device "one who" creates a fine spray or mist*

60. The medical term that actually means periodic or sudden attack is: *paroxysm*

61. The medical term Broncho/dilator actually means: *any agent that causes the bronchi to widen*

62. The medical term A/sphyxia actually means: *suffocation or without pulse "no heart beat- caused by not breathing"*

63. The medical term that actually means to draw foreign material into the respiratory tract blocking breathing is: *a/spiration*

64. The diagnostic term Silic/osis is also known as: *Grinder's disease "stone or metal grinders disease"*

65. The medical term Chord/itis or Cord/itis actually means: *inflammation of the vocal cords*

66. The medical term Emphysema literally means: *puffed up*

67. The medical term Asthma literally means: *panting*

68. The medical term Pneumon/ia literally means: *referring to the lungs*

69. Cystic Fibrosis (CF) is an inherited exocrine gland disorder that causes thick secretions of _____ to accumulation in the lungs. *mucus and pus from respiratory infections*

70. The medical term Diphther/ia literally means: *membrane/refers*

71. The medical term Pertussis actually refers to: *whooping cough and the bacteria Bordetella pertussis*

72. The disease of Histoplasmosis or Darling's disease is a _____ infection caused by Histoplasma capsulatum. Bird or cat feces is the source and the disease is characterized by fever, malaise, coughing, respiratory failure, and lymph/adeno/path/y. A major problem for pregnant women and their fetuses. *fungus or fungus spore*

73. Tuberculosis is caused by a bacterium Mycobacterium tuberculosis and causes bacteria colony swellings (tubers) in the lungs and other body parts. TB infects approximately _____ people. *2 billion*

74. The combining form cutane/o- means: *skin*

75. The Schick Skin Test is used to detect _____, which is caused by the bacteria Corynebacterium diphtheriae. *Diphtheria*

76. The Mantoux Skin Test is used to diagnose: *Tuberculosis "Mycobacterium tuberculosis rod-shaped bacteria"*

77. Anthrax infections (Bacillus anthracis bacteria) are classified as infecting the: *Pulmonary System "lungs", Digestive System "intestines", Cutaneous System "skin"*

78. Bronchitis often progresses to a more severe lung condition called _____, which was the leading world killer around 1900 A.D. *Pneumonia*

79. The Etiologic Agent (E.A.) or causative agent that is responsible for Anthrax is: *Bacillus anthracis*

80. An Upper Respiratory Infection is referred to with the Abbreviation: *URI*

81. Spiro/metry means to measure the breath and is used to evaluate: *Lung Capacity*

82. Bronch/ioles literally means: *small bronchi "small trachea (windpipe) like structures"*

83. The term Dys/lexia literally means difficult or faulty: *words "reading and writing"*

84. Pneumono/coni/osis is diagnosed daily in the form of different lung conditions or diseases including: *Arc welder's disease*

85. The disease of Crypto/cocc/o/sis is a _____that can infect the lungs, skin, brain (CNS), bones, and urinary tract causing death. *yeast-like budding fungus "no spores"*

86. The disease of Aspergill/osis (to sprinkle/condition) is a soil or dust fungus that causes granular lesion on or in any body organ. Prognosis is poor like most systemic fungal infections. It is treated with: *fungi/cidal drugs*

87. The pleura is the covering of the _____. If Pleur/isy develops, the outer two (2) serous membrane layers of this body structure, called the visceral and parietal layers, have become inflamed. *lungs*

88. Glott/itis is often referred to as Chord/itis or Cord/itis and is an inflamed: *phonation apparatus of the larynx "true vocal cords & their opening"*

89. The condition referred to as _____ is an acute viral infection that is usually seen in infants before 3 years of age (Y/O: years old). It occurs after an URI and causes vocal cord swelling, voice loss, hypoxia, & possible choking: *Croup*

90. Pneumonia can be caused by: *Virus, Fungus, and Bacteria*

91. Emphysema causes shortness of breath and a(n): *Barreled Chest Look "Advanced Stages"*

92. The incubation period of Influenza is from ____ to ____ days. *1 to 3 days*

93. Kerat/o/sis, leuk/o/plakia, tartar, caries, purpura, fibr/oma, ulcers, gingiv/itis, tonsill/itis, adenoid/itis, squamous cell carcin/oma, catarrh (coryza), cleft palate, thrush, and candid/i/asis are all conditions that are usually diagnosed with a(n) _____ exam by a dentist or medical doctor. *oral or oro/pharyngeal*

1. The coiled tubular structures arising from the dermis that excrete sweat are the: _____

2. The outer layer of skin is called the: _____

3. The white area at the base of the nail that is half-moon shaped is the: _____

4. Melan/o/cytes in the stratum basale layer of the epidermis produce melanin, which is responsible for: _____

5. The layer of skin that is sometimes referred to as true skin is the: _____

6. The combining forms that mean "nail" are: _____

7. The combining forms cutane/o- (cutaneous), pel/o- (pellagra), -derm- (ep/iderm/is and dermat/itis) , and cut/i- (cut/icle) all mean: _____

8. The term Nettles, Hives, or _____ refers to a rash that may be characterized by wheals. _____

9. The term that means self-producing or self-forming is: _____

10. The compound diagnostic term "Dermato/myc/osis" actually means: _____

11. The compound term "Sebo/aden/itis" literally means: _____

12. The combining forms Hidr/o- and Sudero- both mean: _____

13. The surgical term Rhytid/ec/tom/y literally means: _____

14. The combining form that means "death" is: _____

15. The prefix that means on, upon, or over is: _____

16. The suffix Malac/ia means: _____

17. The suffix "-orrhea" means: _____

18. The diagnostic term Pemphig/us means: _____

19. The suffix that means to view is: _____

20. The suffix that means berry shaped is: _____

21. Pediculosis Corpus is often spread by: _____

22. The prefix that means beside, beyond, or around is: _____

23. The combining form that means "grape or grape-like clusters" is: _____

24. The diagnostic term that means localization of pus is: _____

25. The diagnostic term that means fibrous tumor of the skin is: _____

26. The diagnostic term Hyper-seb/o/rrhea means: _____

27. The diagnostic term Hidr/aden/itis means: _____

28. The diagnostic term that means skin or tissue bruise is: _____

29. The term that means invasion into the skin and body hair by lice is: _____

30. The pre/cancerous skin condition that is characterized by horny and hard skin that was caused by excessive exposure to sunlight is: _____

31. The diagnostic term _____ actually means tissue death or literally "an eating sore." This condition is usually caused by Clostridium perfringens and/or poor blood supply.

32. The diagnostic term fissure actually means cleft, _____, sulcus, and groove.

33. The diagnostic term that actually means the process of scraping away the skin by a mechanical process or injury is: _____

34. A malignant neoplasmic skin condition that spreads to organs & lymph nodes, which is commonly associated with AIDS, diabetes, and lymphoma is: _____

35. The surgical term Rhytid/ectomy means: _____

36. The surgical term that actually means a plastic repair procedure that uses skin from others for a skin graft is: _____

37. The anatomical term Epidermal literally means: _____

38. The anatomical term that means pertaining to within the skin is: _____

39. The medical term that means berry-shaped bacteria in twisted chains is: _____

40. The medical term Cicatrix literally means: _____

41. The medical term that means profuse sweating is: _____

42. The medical term for an agent that softens or soothes the skin is: _____

43. The medical term Nevus means: _____

44. If a patient has a decubitus ulcer, he or she has a(n): _____

45. The medical term that means to scatter over a considerable area is:
_____

46. The medical term that refers to pinpoint or tiny skin hemorrhages is: _____

47. The medical term that means Wart is: _____

48. The medical term Pruritus means: _____

49. The medical term that means small, solid skin elevation is: _____

50. The medical term for a procedure that removes skin blemishes or scars using blister formation is: _____

51. The diagnostic term Derm/abrasion is a skin plastic surgery procedure that literally means _____ surface skin. _____

52. The diagnostic term Contusion literally means: _____

53. The diagnostic term Acne Vulgaris literally means: _____

54. The procedural term Dermatoplasty includes _____ surgery. _____

55. The diagnostic term Seb/orrhea Dermat/itis is also known as: _____

56. The diagnostic term Geriatric Alopecia actually means: _____

57. The disease term Anthrax literally means: _____

58. The diagnostic term Cheil/itis literally means: _____

59. The diagnostic term Curettage of a skin lesion literally means: _____

60. The diagnostic term Furuncle actually means _____ and is a staphylococcus inflection of a hair follicle or hair gland:

61. The diagnostic term Rubella (red) is also known as: _____

62. The diagnostic term Herpes literally means: _____

63. The diagnostic term Rubeola (AKA: German or 9 Day Measles) literally means: _____

64. A diagnostic characteristic of oral Koplik Spots (next to the back Molars "grinders") is associated with: _____

65. The diagnostic term Plantar Verruca actually means: _____

66. The skin condition of Shingles is caused by the Herpes Zoster Virus. This virus also causes: _____

67. The diagnostic term Contracture actually means: _____

68. The disease Smallpox (AKA: Variola Major or Minor) is caused by a highly contagious _____ and is characterized by prostration, a vesicular-pustular rash, and fever.

69. The diagnostic term Carbuncul/osis means the presence of multiple skin _____, which are several lesions placed close together.

70. The diagnostic term Malignant Melanoma actually means: _____

71. The diagnostic term Ichthy/osis actually means: _____

72. The diagnostic term Hirsut/ism literally means: _____

73. The diagnostic term Squamous Cell Carcinoma actually means: _____

74. The diagnostic term Fifth Disease causes a slight red skin flush similar to: _____

75. The diagnostic term Erysi/pelas literally means: _____

76. The diagnostic term Dehiscence actually means: _____

77. The skin diagnostic term Eczema literally means: _____

78. The diagnostic term Helminth/iasis, Ascar/iasis and Vermicul/osis can refer to _____ infections of the skin or the digestive system.

79. The diagnostic term Onycho/myc/o/sis literally means: _____

80. The bacterial infection of the face that is referred to as _____ is characterized by vesicles or sacs that rupture and form a golden crust.

81. The diagnostic term Dys/hidr/osis literally means: _____

82. The diagnostic term Lentigo literally means: _____

83. The diagnostic term Scabies actually means: _____

84. The diagnostic term Tinea Cruris (or crusis) actually means: _____

85. The term Tinea literally means worm, but actually applies to any _____ infection of the body.

86. The diagnostic term for the fungal infection Candid/iasis literally means:

_____

87. The diagnostic term _____refers to red skin caused by an increase in RBCs near the surface of the skin. This proliferative bone marrow condition can cause clots, strokes, heart attacks, vertigo, weakness, tinnitus, extremity pain, and an enlarged spleen cause by excess RBC breakdown.

88. The skin condition of Ringworm is actually caused by a: _____

89. The diagnostic term Cutaneous Ulcer literally means: _____

90. The diagnostic term Thrush is usually a fungus infection of the: _____

91. The diagnostic term Yaws is caused by the spirochete bacteria similar to the one that causes: _____

92. The diagnostic term Sclero/derma is actually an auto-immune reactionary dis/ease like: _____

93. The diagnostic term Urticaria is also known as the allergic condition: _____

94. The diagnostic term Wheal is a ring-like skin lesion associated with: _____

95. The term Tularemia is associated with the town of Tulare, in _____.

96. The diagnostic term Lyme is associated with a town in _____ where this deer tick-borne spirochete bacteria first appeared to man.

97. The diagnostic term Xero/derm literally means: _____

98. The diagnostic term Rocky Mountain Spotted Fever is caused by a rickettsial (small bacteria) organism that is carried by a: _____

99. The diagnostic term _____ literally means "to itch" and this chronic skin condition causes red patches with dry, thick, silvery scales.

100. A skin Lacer/ation literally means: _____

101. Tinea Cruris is more commonly called: _____

102. The term Ascariasis refers to parasitic worms that migrate through the lungs in the larval stage to the _____. The eggs are passed on to the next individual through contact with the feces (hands, water, or food).

103. A Vermicular Pulse feels like writhing _____ when finger monitored.

104. Helminth/ic diseases can attack multiple body systems including the integumentary, digestive, and nervous systems. They are caused by meta/zoa parasitic worms called: _____

105. The term Ascites refers to an abnormal intra/peritoneal accumulation of _____ ml or more of fluid leaking from veins or lymph vessels into a body space. Ascites contains large amounts of albumin protein, glucose, & electrolytes.

106. The term De/fec/ation literally means: _____

107. Cimex lectularius is also known as: _____

108. Celiac disease, causing malnutrition, actually means _____ and causes dia/rrhea, intestinal bleeding, and hypo/calcemia. It is treated with a gluten-free diet (avoid wheat, rye, oats, and barley).

109. The physiologic (function) term De/glutition literally means: _____

110. The terms Masticat/ion and Mand/ible actually mean: _____

111. The multi/foci neo/plasmic (new/growth) condition that causes soft brown/purple papular (pimple) lesion that metastasizes (spreads) to the lymph nodes and viscera (organs) is: _____

112. The term Tinea Pedis actually means: _____

113. Melan/o/cytes (black/cells that give our skin color) are produced in the 5th epidermis skin layer called the _____. It contains cylindric cells and other mitotic cells that migrate upward forming the 4 upper epidermis layers.

114. A bluish _____ skin color is seen with venous congestion, foramen ovale, Tetrology of Fallot, transposition of great vessels, patent ductus arteriolus, heart disease, lung disease, and with cold environmental temperatures.

115. Skin blushing, _____, or redness is usually caused by an increase in blood flow, oxy/hemoglobin, fever, inflammation, trauma "wound", and alcohol.

116. The con/genital or auto/immune skin condition called _____, which means 'to corrupt', actually shows patchy white (non-pigmented) skin areas.

117. The skin color variation of Pall/or is actually a _____, which usually accompanies blood loss, various types of anemia, or shock.

118. The skin color variation of _____ represents an increase in tissue bili/rubin from RBC destruction or liver cell destruction (hepat/itis). This color is best seen in the sclera of the eye, body membranes, and skin.

119. The relative speed with which the skin resumes its normal appearance after being stretched or compressed is called_____. It represents the amount of water in the tissues or hydration. This process is slower in seniors.

120. Chloasma or melasma patches appear on the forehead, nose and: _____

121. The skin condition Vitiligo literally means: _____

1. The coiled tubular structures arising from the dermis that excrete sweat are the: *sudoriferous glands*

2. The outer layer of skin is called the: *epidermis*

3. The white area at the base of the nail that is half-moon shaped is the: *lunula - moon shaped*

4. Melan/o/cytes in the stratum basale layer of the epidermis produce melanin, which is responsible for: *skin color*

5. The layer of skin that is sometimes referred to as true skin is the: *dermis or cutis*

6. The combining forms that mean "nail" are: *unguin/o- or onycho-*

7. The combining forms cutane/o- (cutaneous), pel/o- (pellagra), -derm- (ep/iderm/is and dermat/itis), and cut/i- (cut/icle) all mean: *skin*

8. The term Nettles, Hives, or _____ refers to a rash that may be characterized by wheals. *Urticaria "allergic reaction"*

9. The term that means self-producing or self-forming is: *auto/genesis*

10. The compound diagnostic term "Dermato/myc/osis" actually means: *an extensive skin fungus condition, state of, or infection*

11. The compound term "Sebo/aden/itis" literally means: *inflamed oil gland*

12. The combining forms Hidr/o- and Sudero- both mean: *sweat*

13. The surgical term Rhytid/ec/tom/y literally means: *procedure of cutting out wrinkles*

14. The combining form that means "death" is: *necr/o-*

15. The prefix that means on, upon, or over is: *epi- "epidermis"*

16. The suffix Malac/ia means: *to softening/refers*

17. The suffix "-orrhea" means: *flow or discharge*

18. The diagnostic term Pemphig/us means: *blisters/refers*

19. The suffix that means to view is: *-opsy "bi/o/psy"*

20. The suffix that means berry shaped is: *-coccus*

21. Pediculosis Corpus is often spread by: *Sharing fabrics and combs*

22. The prefix that means beside, beyond, or around is: *para- or par- "par/ot/id - near/ear/refers"*

23. The combining form that means "grape or grape-like clusters" is: *staphyl/o-*

24. The diagnostic term that means localization of pus is: *abscess "tissue goes away"*

25. The diagnostic term that means fibrous tumor of the skin is: *dermato/fibr/oma*

26. The diagnostic term Hyper-seb/o/rrhea means: *excessive discharge or flow of oil*

27. The diagnostic term Hidr/aden/itis means: *inflammation of a sweat gland*

28. The diagnostic term that means skin or tissue bruise is: *contusion*

29. The term that means invasion into the skin and body hair by lice is: *pediculosis*

30. The pre/cancerous skin condition that is characterized by horny and hard skin that was caused by excessive exposure to sunlight is: *actinic kerat/osis*

31. The diagnostic term _____ actually means tissue death or literally "an eating sore." This condition is usually caused by Clostridium perfringens and/or poor blood supply. *gangrene*

32. The diagnostic term fissure actually means cleft, _____, sulcus, and groove. *slit or crack-like sore in the skin*

33. The diagnostic term that actually means the process of scraping away the skin by a mechanical process or injury is: *ab/ras/ion*

34. A malignant neoplasmic skin condition that spreads to organs & lymph nodes, which is commonly associated with AIDS, diabetes, and lymphoma is: *Kaposi's sarcoma*

35. The surgical term Rhytid/ectomy means: *excision of wrinkles*

36. The surgical term that actually means a plastic repair procedure that uses skin from others for a skin graft is: *dermato/hetero/plast/y*

37. The anatomical term Epidermal literally means: *pertaining to upon the skin*

38. The anatomical term that means pertaining to within the skin is: *intradermal*

39. The medical term that means berry-shaped bacteria in twisted chains is: *strepto/coccus*

40. The medical term Cicatrix literally means: *scar*

41. The medical term that means profuse sweating is: *Hyper-Hidrosis*

42. The medical term for an agent that softens or soothes the skin is: *emollient*

43. The medical term Nevus means: *mole or birthmark*

44. If a patient has a decubitus ulcer, he or she has a(n): *pressure bedsore*

45. The medical term that means to scatter over a considerable area is: *dis/seminate "apart or away/sow"*

46. The medical term that refers to pinpoint or tiny skin hemorrhages is: *petechia*

47. The medical term that means Wart is: *verruca*

48. The medical term Pruritus means: *severe itching*

49. The medical term that means small, solid skin elevation is: *papule*

50. The medical term for a procedure that removes skin blemishes or scars using blister formation is: *vesic/ation*

51. The diagnostic term Derm/abrasion is a skin plastic surgery procedure that literally means _____ surface skin. *to scrape away*

52. The diagnostic term Contusion literally means: *to bruise*

53. The diagnostic term Acne Vulgaris literally means: *pointed and common*

54. The procedural term Dermatoplasty includes _____ surgery. *face lifts, eyelid drooping, and belly tucks*

55. The diagnostic term Seb/orrhea Dermat/itis is also known as: *dandruff*

56. The diagnostic term Geriatric Alopecia actually means: *"old age" baldness "fox mange"*

57. The disease term Anthrax literally means: *coal or carbuncle "lesion"*

58. The diagnostic term Cheil/itis literally means: *inflammation of the lip*

59. The diagnostic term Curettage of a skin lesion literally means: *scooping*

60. The diagnostic term Furuncle actually means _____ and is a staphylococcus inflection of a hair follicle or hair gland: *boil*

61. The diagnostic term Rubella (red) is also known as: *3 day measles*

62. The diagnostic term Herpes literally means: *to creep*

63. The diagnostic term Rubeola (AKA: German or 9 Day Measles) literally means: *red or redness*

64. A diagnostic characteristic of oral Koplik Spots (next to the back Molars "grinders") is associated with: *Rubeola - 9 day measles*

65. The diagnostic term Plantar Verruca actually means: *warts on the soles of the feet*

66. The skin condition of Shingles is caused by the Herpes Zoster Virus. This virus also causes: *Chickenpox*

67. The diagnostic term Contracture actually means: *severe contraction of tissues like skin and muscle*

68. The disease Smallpox (AKA: Variola Major or Minor) is caused by a highly contagious _____ and is characterized by prostration, a vesicular-pustular rash, and fever. *poxvirus*

69. The diagnostic term Carbuncul/osis means the presence of multiple skin _____, which are several lesions placed close together. *boils*

70. The diagnostic term Malignant Melanoma actually means: *a black tumor that is bad or cancerous*

71. The diagnostic term Ichthy/osis actually means: *fish-like skin condition with scale-like tissue*

72. The diagnostic term Hirsut/ism literally means: *the state of being hairy*

73. The diagnostic term Squamous Cell Carcinoma actually means: *scaly crab-like cell tumors of the surface tissue "lungs and skin"*

74. The diagnostic term Fifth Disease causes a slight red skin flush similar to: *3 day measles - rubella*

75. The diagnostic term Erysi/pelas literally means: *red/skin*

76. The diagnostic term Dehiscence actually means: *to gape open*

77. The skin diagnostic term Eczema literally means: *to boil out or over*

78. The diagnostic term Helminth/iasis, Ascar/iasis and Vermicul/osis can refer to _____ infections of the skin or the digestive system. *worm*

79. The diagnostic term Onycho/myc/o/sis literally means: *nail/fungus/condition "infection"*

80. The bacterial infection of the face that is referred to as _____ is characterized by vesicles or sacs that rupture and form a golden crust. *Impetigo "means to attack"*

81. The diagnostic term Dys/hidr/osis literally means: *condition of faulty sweating "skin sweat blisters"*

82. The diagnostic term Lentigo literally means: *freckle*

83. The diagnostic term Scabies actually means: *itch mite saliva that causes severe itching*

84. The diagnostic term Tinea Cruris (or crusis) actually means: *Jock Itch "scrotal, crural, anal, or genital fungus itch"*

85. The term Tinea literally means worm, but actually applies to any _____ infection of the body. *fungus*

86. The diagnostic term for the fungal infection Candid/iasis literally means: *glowing white/condition*

87. The diagnostic term _____refers to red skin caused by an increase in RBCs near the surface of the skin. This proliferative bone marrow condition can cause clots, strokes, heart attacks, vertigo, weakness, tinnitus, extremity pain, and an enlarged spleen cause by excess RBC breakdown. *Poly/cyth/emia Vera*

88. The skin condition of Ringworm is actually caused by a: *fungus*

89. The diagnostic term Cutaneous Ulcer literally means: *skin sore*

90. The diagnostic term Thrush is usually a fungus infection of the: *throat or vagina*

91. The diagnostic term Yaws is caused by the spirochete bacteria similar to the one that causes: *syphilis*

92. The diagnostic term Sclero/derma is actually an auto-immune reactionary dis/ease like: *Rheumatoid Arthritis*

93. The diagnostic term Urticaria is also known as the allergic condition: *hives*

94. The diagnostic term Wheal is a ring-like skin lesion associated with: *hives or urticaria - allergic reaction*

95. The term Tularemia is associated with the town of Tulare, in _____. *California*

96. The diagnostic term Lyme is associated with a town in _____ where this deer tick-borne spirochete bacteria first appeared to man. *Connecticut*

97. The diagnostic term Xero/derm literally means: *dry/skin*

98. The diagnostic term Rocky Mountain Spotted Fever is caused by a rickettsial (small bacteria) organism that is carried by a: *tick*

99. The diagnostic term _____ literally means "to itch" and this chronic skin condition causes red patches with dry, thick, silvery scales. *Psoriasis*

100. A skin lacer/ation literally means: *the process of tearing*

101. Tinea Cruris is more commonly called: *Jock itch*

102. The term Ascariasis refers to parasitic worms that migrate through the lungs in the larval stage to the _____. The eggs are passed on to the next individual through contact with the feces (hands, water, or food). *intestines*

103. A Vermicular Pulse feels like writhing _____ when finger monitored. *worms*

104. Helminth/ic diseases can attack multiple body systems including the integumentary, digestive, and nervous systems. They are caused by meta/zoa parasitic worms called: *Tapeworms, Roundworms and flukeworms*

105. The term Ascites refers to an abnormal intra/peritoneal accumulation of _____ ml or more of fluid leaking from veins or lymph vessels into a body space. Ascites contains large amounts of albumin protein, glucose, & electrolytes. *500 - 1/2 Liter or Litre*

106. The term De/fec/ation literally means: *process of feces or stool away*

107. Cimex lectularius is also known as: *bed bugs*

108. Celiac disease, causing malnutrition, actually means _____ and causes dia/rrhea, intestinal bleeding, and hypo/calcemia. It is treated with a gluten-free diet (avoid wheat, rye, oats, and barley). *belly mal/absorption*

109. The physiologic (function) term De/glutition literally means: *to swallow away or down*

110. The terms Masticat/ion and Mand/ible actually mean: *process of chewing and chewer*

111. The multi/foci neo/plasmic (new/growth) condition that causes soft brown/purple papular (pimple) lesion that metastasizes (spreads) to the lymph nodes and viscera (organs) is: *Kaposi's sarc/oma "fleshy tumors"*

112. The term Tinea Pedis actually means: *Athletes Foot*

113. Melan/o/cytes (black/cells that give our skin color) are produced in the 5th epidermis skin layer called the _____. It contains cylindric cells and other mitotic cells that migrate upward forming the 4 upper epidermis layers. *stratum basal "layer/base" - AKA Stratum Germinativum*

114. A bluish _____ skin color is seen with venous congestion, foramen ovale, Tetrology of Fallot, transposition of great vessels, patent ductus arteriolus, heart disease, lung disease, and with cold environmental temperatures. *cyanotic or livid*

115. Skin blushing, _____, or redness is usually caused by an increase in blood flow, oxy/hemoglobin, fever, inflammation, trauma "wound", and alcohol. *erythema*

116. The con/genital or auto/immune skin condition called _____, which means 'to corrupt', actually shows patchy white (non-pigmented) skin areas. *vitiligo*

117. The skin color variation of Pall/or is actually a _____, which usually accompanies blood loss, various types of anemia, or shock. *decrease in skin color*

118. The skin color variation of _____ represents an increase in tissue bili/rubin from RBC destruction or liver cell destruction (hepat/itis). This color is best seen in the sclera of the eye, body membranes, and skin. *yellow-orange "jaundiced"*

119. The relative speed with which the skin resumes its normal appearance after being stretched or compressed is called_____. It represents the amount of water in the tissues or hydration. This process is slower in seniors. *turgor*

120. Chloasma or melasma patches appear on the forehead, nose and: *cheeks*

121. The skin condition Vitiligo literally means: *to corrupt - skin appearance of multiple colors*

1. The lower bulge in the pyloric part of the stomach along the greater stomach curvature is: _____

2. The opening through which food passes into the alimentary (to nourish) canal is the: _____

3. The 2nd portion (5' long) of small intestine that means to empty is the: _____

4. The organ that produces bile is the: _____

5. The small pouch attached to the cecum (blind pouch) is the: _____

6. The sphincter (that which binds together) muscle at the end of the digestive tract is the: _____

7. The small saclike structure that stores bile is the: _____

8. The lining of the structures in the abdominal and pelvic cavities is the: _____

9. The ring of muscles found in opening between stomach and duodenum is the: _____

10. A soft v-shaped mass that hangs from the back mouth roof is the: _____

11. The first section of the large intestine is the: _____

12. The colon is divided into _____ parts, including the cecum, rectum, and anus:

13. The tube that extends from the pharynx (throat) to the stomach and means gullet is the: _____

14. The combining form gastr/o- means: _____

15. The combining forms os-, or/o-, and stomato- all mean: _____

16. The combining form an/o- means: _____

17. "The combining form that means "small intestines" is: _____

18. The combining form that means "rectum (straight) and anus (ring)" is: _____

19. The combining form cec/o- means: _____

20. The combining form that means "gall or bile" is: _____

21. The combining form lapar/o- means: _____

22. "The combining form that means "liver" is: _____

23. In the term "Sial/oma" sial/o- means: _____

24. In the term "Cheil/oma" cheil/o- means: _____

25. The combining form choledoch/o- actually means: _____

26. The combining forms that mean "tongue" are: _____

27. The combining form for small growth is: _____

28. The suffix -pepsia means: _____

29. The diagnostic term that means inflammation of the stomach, intestines, and colon is: _____

30. The diagnostic term that means condition of stones in the common bile duct is:

_____

31. The diagnostic term that means abnormal condition of having diverticula (out-pouchings) in the colon is: _____

32. The diagnostic term gingivitis means: _____

33. The diagnostic term chole/lith/iasis means: _____

34. The diagnostic term that means prolapse of the rectum is: _____

35. The diagnostic term that means salivary stone is: _____

36. The diagnostic term hepat/oma means: _____

37. The diagnostic term recto/cele means: _____

38. The diagnostic term gastro/enter/itis means: _____

39. The diagnostic term that means inflammation of the gallbladder is: _____

40. The diagnostic term for chronic inflammation of the small and/or large intestines, characterized by cobblestone ulcerations along the intestinal wall and the formation of scar tissue, is: _____

41. The diagnostic term for the twisting or kinking of the intestine causing intestinal obstruction is: _____

42. The diagnostic term for the abnormal growing together of two surfaces normally separated is: _____

43. The diagnostic term ulcerative colitis means: _____

44. The diagnostic term for a psychoneurotic disorder characterized by prolonged refusal to eat is: _____

45. The diagnostic term for a chronic disease of the liver characterized by the gradual destruction of liver cells is: _____

46. The surgical term that means crushing a stone in the common bile duct is:

_____

47. The surgical term cheil/orrhapy means: _____

48. The surgical term that means incision in to the abdominal wall is: _____

49. The surgical term that means artificial opening through the abdominal wall into the colon is: _____

50. The surgical term pyloroplasty means: _____

51. The surgical term eso/phago/gastr/oplasty means: _____

52. The surgical term that means removal of gum tissue is: _____

53. The surgical term that means excision of the stomach is: _____

54. The surgical term that means creation of an artificial opening between the stomach and jejunum is: _____

55. The surgical term diverticulectomy means: _____

56. The surgical term that means suture of the tongue is: _____

57. The surgical term for the joining of two normally distinct structures is: _____

58. The surgical term for cutting of certain branches of the vagus nerve is: _____

59. The procedural term for X-ray filming of the gallbladder is: _____

60. The procedural term that means visual examination of the rectum is: _____

61. The term Endoscopic Gastroscop/e is defined as a(n): _____

62. The procedural term meaning visual examination within a hollow organ is: _____

63. The procedural term that means visual examination of the esophagus is: _____

64. The term Proctoscope means: _____

65. The procedural phrase for a barium enema with X-rays is: _____

66. The procedural term for a series of X-ray films taken of the stomach & duodenum after barium has been swallowed is: _____

67. The medical term that means surgical puncture to remove fluid from the abdominal cavity is: _____

68. The medical term Brady/pepsia means: _____

69. The medical term Glosso/pathy means: _____

70. The medical term Stomato/gastric means: _____

71. The medical term Dysphagia means: _____

72. The medical term that means branch of medicine concerned with disorders of the rectum and anus is: _____

73. The medical term gastromalacia means: _____

74. The medical term oral means: _____

75. The medical term a/pepsia means: _____

76. The medical term that means physician who specializes in proctology is: _____

77. The medical term gastro/dynia means: _____

78. The medical term Peritoneal literally means: _____

79. The medical term Abdomin/al means: _____

80. The term for abnormal collection of fluid in the peritoneal cavity is: _____

81. The medical term that means washing out the stomach is: _____

82. Digestive tract waste, expelled through the rectum is called: _____

83. The medical term that means urge to vomit is: _____

84. The diagnostic term for a psychoneurotic disorder characterized by prolonged refusal to eat is: _____

85. The term Di/gest/ion literally means: _____

86. The physi/ology (science of function or nature) term Peristalsis literally means: _____

87. The physiology term Mastic/ation literally means: _____

88. The physiology term De/glutit/ion literally means _____

89. The anatomical term Molar literally means: _____

90. The anatomical term Cuspid literally means: _____

91. The anatomical term Gingiva literally means: _____

92. The combining form Sailo- literally means: _____

93. The anatomical term Incis/or literally means: _____

94. The anatomical term Eso/phagus literally means: _____

95. The diagnostic term Stomat/itis means: _____

96. The diagnostic term Pyloric Stenosis actually means: _____

97. The anatomical term Gastric Rugae literally means: _____

98. The diagnostic term Peptic Ulcer literally means: _____

99. The diagnostic term Duodenal Ulcer literally means: _____

100. The diagnostic term Cholang/itis literally means: _____

101. The diagnostic term Cholecyst/itis literally means: _____

102. The diagnostic term Choledoch/itis literally means: _____

103. The diagnostic term Hepat/oma literally means: _____

104. Hepatitis A, B, and C are caused by a: _____

105. Hepatitis A is also known as: _____

106. Hepatitis B is also known as: _____

107. Hepatitis "_____" may be dormant in the body for years before the Signs and Symptoms appear.

108. The diagnostic term Cholelith/iasis refers to a gall bladder: _____

109. The diagnostic term An/odont/ia literally means: _____

110. The diagnostic term Dental Caries literally means: _____

111. The word parts dento- and donto- both mean: _____

112. The diagnostic term Gastroesophageal Reflux Disease can also refer to: _____

113. The diagnostic term Reflux literally means: _____

114. The diagnostic term Ascar/iasis refers to: _____

115. The diagnostic term Tartar refers to dental: _____

116. The diagnostic term Coloscopy refers to viewing and examining the: _____

117. The diagnostic term Colo/scop/e literally means: _____

118. The diagnostic term Colo/scop/y literally means: _____

119. The diagnostic term Diverticulosis actually means: _____

120. The anatomical term Cecum literally means: _____

121. The diagnostic term Procto/scopy actually means: _____

122. The nutritional physiology term Bolus literally means: _____

123. The nutritional physiology term Chyme literally means: _____

124. The inflammatory characteristics seen during an Upper GI Examination include: _____

125. The medical abbreviation for the Gastrointestinal System (mouth to anus): _____

126. The anatomical term Villi literally means: _____

127. The medical term Enema literally means: _____

128. The diagnostic term Dys/phag/ia literally means: _____

129. The diagnostic term Dys/phonia actually means: _____

130. The diagnostic term "A/phasia" literally means: _____

131. Schisto/som/iasis and Bilharz/iasis are often colloquially referred to as: _____

132. The anatomical term Jejunum literally means _____ and is the 5 foot long section of the small intestine that follows the 10" duodenum. _____

133. The diagnostic term Bulim/ia literally means _____.

134. The diagnostic term Anorexia Nervosa literally means:

135. The diagnostic term Hyper/cholesterol/emia is a blood condition with a cholesterol level above ____ mg per dcl (milligrams per deciliter) in a 20 Y/O.

136. The diagnostic term Crohn's Disease is also known as: _____

137. The diagnostic term Acute Appendicitis actually means: _____

138. The diagnostic term Ile/ostomy actually means: _____

139. The diagnostic term Enter/itis literally means: _____

140. The diagnostic term Dys/entery literally means: _____

141. The anatomical word part colo- or colono- refers to the big intestine. The word part _____ can refer to the small intestine or both intestines.

142. The diagnostic term Gingivoglossitis literally means: _____

143. The alimentary (to nourish) canal is approximately _____ feet long in adults.

144. The diagnostic term Pneumat/osis Intestinal refers to: _____

145. The diagnostic term Abdominal Hernia refers to: _____

146. The suffix '-phagia' means: _____

147. The diagnostic term "Cholecystectomy" means: _____

148. The term _____ refers to the excessive gas in the stomach and intestines.

149. The diagnostic term Eructation refers to: _____

150. The anatomical term Alimentary literally means: _____

151. The diagnostic term Shigellosis refers to: _____

152. The diagnostic term Amebic (Amoeba) Dysentery refers to:
_____

153. The physiological (function) importance of the digestive system is to:
_____

154. The diagnostic term Gastritis refers to multiple small: _____

155. The diagnostic term Beri/beri refers to _____ and is caused by the lack of thiamine (part of B Complex: B-1) in the diet.

156. The diagnostic term Pell/agra refers to _____ and is caused by the lack of niacin or niacinamide in the diet.

157. The diagnostic term Scurvy literally means _____ and is the lack of Vitamin C in the diet.

158. The diagnostic term Fistula refers to a: _____

159. The diagnostic term Atresia refers to: _____

160. The diagnostic term Irritable Bowel Syndrome (IBS) refers to: _____

161. The diagnostic reference of Differential Diagnosis (D.D.) refers to:
_____

162. The diagnostic term Feca/lith refers to: _____

163. The diagnostic term Hiatal Hernia refers to: _____

164. The anatomical term Sphincter literally means: _____

165. The diagnostic term Pyloric Stenosis refers to the narrowing of the lower end of the _____ and can lead to regular vomiting in infants.

166. The diagnostic term Volvulus usually refers to _____of the ileum or the colon.

167. The combining form _____ refers to the tube or canal that starts in at the stomach and moves up to the throat and is called the human gullet.

168. The anatomical term Eso/phag/itis literally means _____ and is often seen in smokers and alcohol drinkers:

169. Typhus literally means: _____

170. A cysto/scopic exam refers to 'looking at' the _____:

171. Cholera can lead to dehydration, vomiting, muscle cramps, and death. It is caused by the bacteria _____.

1. The lower bulge in the pyloric part of the stomach along the greater stomach curvature is: *"antrum" "a walled, nearly closed, cavity or chamber, at the stomach's lower end"*

2. The opening through which food passes into the alimentary (to nourish) canal is the: *mouth*

3. The 2nd portion (5' long) of small intestine that means to empty is the: *jejunum*

4. The organ that produces bile is the: *liver*

5. The small pouch attached to the cecum (blind pouch) is the: *appendix*

6. The sphincter (that which binds together) muscle at the end of the digestive tract is the: *anus "ring"*

7. The small saclike structure that stores bile is the: *gallbladder*

8. The lining of the structures in the abdominal and pelvic cavities is the: *peritoneum "that which holds the lower organs"*

9. The ring of muscles found in opening between stomach and duodenum is the: *pyloric sphincter "gate keeper: that which binds together"*

10. A soft v-shaped mass that hangs from the back mouth roof is the: *uvula "grape"*

11. The first section of the large intestine is the: *cecum*

12. The colon is divided into _____ parts, including the cecum, rectum, and anus: 7

13. The tube that extends from the pharynx (throat) to the stomach and means gullet is the: *eso/phagus "toward/eater"*

14. The combining form gastr/o- means: *stomach*

15. The combining forms os-, or/o-, and stomato- all mean: *mouth*

16. The combining form an/o- means: *pore or ring*

17. "The combining form that means "small intestines" is:" *enter/o- "usually refers to small intestine: Colo- big intestine"*

18. The combining form that means "rectum (straight) and anus (ring)" is: *proct/o-*

19. The combining form cec/o- means: *"blind pouch "cecum"*

20. The combining form that means "gall or bile" is: *chol/e-*

21. The combining form lapar/o- means: *abdominal wall*

22. "The combining form that means "liver" is:" *hepat/o-*

23. In the term "Sial/oma" sial/o- means: *saliva*

24. In the term "Cheil/oma" cheil/o- means: *lip*

25. The combining form choledoch/o- actually means: *common bile duct*

26. The combining forms that mean "tongue" are: *gloss/o- and lingo-*

27. The combining form for small growth is: *polyp/o- "footed growth"*

28. The suffix -pepsia means: *digestion*

29. The diagnostic term that means inflammation of the stomach, intestines, and colon is: *gastroenterocolitis*

30. The diagnostic term that means condition of stones in the common bile duct is: *chole/docho/lith/iasis*

31. The diagnostic term that means abnormal condition of having diverticula (out-pouchings) in the colon is: *diverticul/o/sis*

32. The diagnostic term gingivitis means: *inflammation of the gums*

33. The diagnostic term chole/lith/iasis means: *condition of gallstones*

34. The diagnostic term that means prolapse of the rectum is: *procto/ptosis*

35. The diagnostic term that means salivary stone is: *sialo/lith*

36. The diagnostic term hepat/oma means: *tumor of the liver*

37. The diagnostic term recto/cele means: *protrusion of rectum "into the vagina"*

38. The diagnostic term gastro/enter/itis means: *inflammation of the stomach and intestinal track. Also, the surgical opening is referred to as an iliostomy; and the incision is referred to as an iliotomy.*

39. The diagnostic term that means inflammation of the gallbladder is: *chole/cyst/itis*

40. The diagnostic term for chronic inflammation of the small and/or large intestines, characterized by cobblestone ulcerations along the intestinal wall and the formation of scar tissue, is: *Crohn's Disease*

41. The diagnostic term for the twisting or kinking of the intestine causing intestinal obstruction is: *volvulus*

42. The diagnostic term for the abnormal growing together of two surfaces normally separated is: *adhesion*

43. The diagnostic term ulcerative colitis means: *inflammation of the colon with sores*

44. The diagnostic term for a psychoneurotic disorder characterized by prolonged refusal to eat is: *anorexia nervosa*

45. The diagnostic term for a chronic disease of the liver characterized by the gradual destruction of liver cells is: *cirrhosis "yellow orange color produced"*

46. The surgical term that means crushing a stone in the common bile duct is: *choledocholith/otripsy*

47. The surgical term cheil/orrhapy means: *suture of the lips*

48. The surgical term that means incision in to the abdominal wall is: *lapar/otomy*

49. The surgical term that means artificial opening through the abdominal wall into the colon is: *col/ostomy*

50. The surgical term pyloroplasty means: *surgical repair of the pyloric sphimeter*

51. The surgical term eso/phago/gastr/oplasty means: *surgical repair of the esophagus and the stomach*

52. The surgical term that means removal of gum tissue is: *gingivectomy*

53. The surgical term that means excision of the stomach is: *gastrectomy*

54. The surgical term that means creation of an artificial opening between the stomach and jejunum is: *gastrojejun/ostomy*

55. The surgical term diverticulectomy means: *excision of a diverticulum "outpouching in intestines"*

56. The surgical term that means suture of the tongue is: *glossorrhaphy*

57. The surgical term for the joining of two normally distinct structures is: *anastomosis*

58. The surgical term for cutting of certain branches of the vagus nerve is: *vagotomy*

59. The procedural term for X-ray filming of the gallbladder is: *chole/cysto/graphy*

60. The procedural term that means visual examination of the rectum is: *proctoscopy*

61. The term Endoscopic Gastroscop/e is defined as a(n): *instrument used for visual examination of the stomach*

62. The procedural term meaning visual examination within a hollow organ is: *endoscopy*

63. The procedural term that means visual examination of the esophagus is: *esophagoscopy*

64. The term Proctoscope means: *instrument used for visual examination of the rectum*

65. The procedural phrase for a barium enema with X-rays is: *lower GI Series*

66. The procedural term for a series of X-ray films taken of the stomach & duodenum after barium has been swallowed is: *Upper GI Series*

67. The medical term that means surgical puncture to remove fluid from the abdominal cavity is: *abdominocentesis*

68. The medical term Brady/pepsia means: *slow digestion*

69. The medical term Glosso/pathy means: *disease of the tongue*

70. The medical term Stomato/gastric means: *pertaining to the mouth and stomach*

71. The medical term Dysphagia means: *difficult swallowing or eating*

72. The medical term that means branch of medicine concerned with disorders of the rectum and anus is: *proctology*

73. The medical term gastromalacia means: *softening of the stomach "cancer"*

74. The medical term oral means: *pertaining to the mouth*

75. The medical term a/pepsia means: *without digestion*

76. The medical term that means physician who specializes in proctology is: *proctologist*

77. The medical term gastro/dynia means: *pain in the stomach*

78. The medical term Peritoneal literally means: *one who holds lower viscera "largest serous membrane in the body"*

79. The medical term Abdomin/al means: *pertaining to the abdominal or belly area*

80. The term for abnormal collection of fluid in the peritoneal cavity is: *ascites*

81. The medical term that means washing out the stomach is: *gastric lavage*

82. Digestive tract waste, expelled through the rectum is called: *feces "stool"*

83. The medical term that means urge to vomit is: *nausea*

84. The diagnostic term for a psychoneurotic disorder characterized by prolonged refusal to eat is: *anorexia nervosa*

85. The term Di/gest/ion literally means: *the process of/two/separations*

86. The physi/ology (science of function or nature) term Peristalsis literally means: *to contract/around*

87. The physiology term Mastic/ation literally means: *process of/chewing*

88. The physiology term De/glutit/ion literally means _____. *process of/swallowing/away or down*

89. The anatomical term Molar literally means: *to mill or grind*

90. The anatomical term Cuspid literally means: *one that is pointed*

91. The anatomical term Gingiva literally means: *gums*

92. The combining form Sailo- literally means: *spit or saliva*

93. The anatomical term Incis/or literally means: *one who cuts in*

94. The anatomical term Eso/phagus literally means: *toward/the eater*

95. The diagnostic term Stomat/itis means: *inflammation of the mouth*

96. The diagnostic term Pyloric Stenosis actually means: *condition of narrowing the gate keeper*

97. The anatomical term Gastric Rugae literally means: *stomach folds*

98. The diagnostic term Peptic Ulcer literally means: *digestive : sore*

99. The diagnostic term Duodenal Ulcer literally means: *refers to 12 : sore "the duodenum means 12 fingers and is 10 inches long"*

100. The diagnostic term Cholang/itis literally means: *bile duct inflamed*

101. The diagnostic term Cholecyst/itis literally means: *gall bladder "sac" inflamed*

102. The diagnostic term Choledoch/itis literally means: *gall bladder or bile sac duct inflamed*

103. The diagnostic term Hepat/oma literally means: *liver tumor or swelling*

104. Hepatitis A, B, and C are caused by a: *virus*

105. Hepatitis A is also known as: *Infectious Hepatitis*

106. Hepatitis B is also known as: *Serum Hepatitis*

107. Hepatitis "___" may be dormant in the body for years before the Signs and Symptoms appear. *"C"*

108. The diagnostic term Cholelith/iasis refers to a gall bladder: *stone condition*

109. The diagnostic term An/odont/ia literally means: *refers to without one or more teeth*

110. The diagnostic term Dental Caries literally means: *refers to tooth cavities*

111. The word parts dento- and donto- both mean: *tooth*

112. The diagnostic term Gastroesophageal Reflux Disease can also refer to: *heart burn "GERD"*

113. The diagnostic term Reflux literally means: *to flow again "usually backward"*

114. The diagnostic term Ascar/iasis refers to: *worms in the intestines "usually"*

115. The diagnostic term Tartar refers to dental: *plaque "hardened carbonates, phosphates, and organic matter"*

116. The diagnostic term Coloscopy refers to viewing and examining the: *large intestine*

117. The diagnostic term Colo/scop/e literally means: *instrument to view the big or large intestine*

118. The diagnostic term Colo/scop/y literally means: *procedure of viewing and examining the large intestine*

119. The diagnostic term Diverticulosis actually means: *condition of out pouching in the colons rugae or fold*

120. The anatomical term Cecum literally means: *blind pouch*

121. The diagnostic term Procto/scopy actually means: *viewing the anus, rectum, & sigmoid colon to determine its condition*

122. The nutritional physiology term Bolus literally means: *ball or lump*

123. The nutritional physiology term Chyme literally means: *juice*

124. The inflammatory characteristics seen during a Upper GI Examination include: *rubor, tumor, calor, and dolor "red, swelling, heat, pain"*

125. The medical abbreviation for the Gastrointestinal System (mouth to anus): *GI*

126. The anatomical term Villi literally means: *shaggy hair*

127. The medical term Enema literally means: *to inject*

128. The diagnostic term Dys/phag/ia literally means: *refers to difficult or faulty swallowing*

129. The diagnostic term Dys/phonia actually means: *refers to faulty speaking or speech - hoarseness*

130. The diagnostic term "A/phasia" literally means: *without speech*

131. Schisto/som/iasis and Bilharz/iasis are often colloquially referred to as: *Snail Fever*

132. The anatomical term Jejunum literally means _____ and is the 5 foot long section of the small intestine that follows the 10" duodenum. *to empty*

133. The diagnostic term Bulim/ia literally means _____. *refers to/hungry*

134. The diagnostic term Anorexia Nervosa literally means: *without appetite: caused by a "nervous" condition*

135. The diagnostic term Hyper/cholesterol/emia is a blood condition with a cholesterol level above ____ mg per dcl (milligrams per deciliter) in a 20 Y/O. *230*

136. The diagnostic term Crohn's Disease is also known as: *chronic regional ileitis*

137. The diagnostic term Acute Appendicitis actually means: *sudden inflammation of the appendage attached to the cecum*

138. The diagnostic term Ile/ostomy actually means: *procedure of forming a mouth opening in 3rd part of small intestine*

139. The diagnostic term Enter/itis literally means: *inflamed intestines "bowel"*

140. The diagnostic term Dys/entery literally means: *faulty, difficult, and painful intestines*

141. The anatomical word part colo- or colono- refers to the big intestine. The word part _____ can refer to the small intestine or both intestines. *entero-*

142. The diagnostic term Gingivoglossitis literally means: *inflamed tongue and gums*

143. The alimentary (to nourish) canal is approximately _____ feet long in adults. *30*

144. The diagnostic term Pneumat/osis Intestinal refers to: *condition of air in the intestines*

145. The diagnostic term Abdominal Hernia refers to: *a rupture or protrusion through the abdominal wall*

146. The suffix '-phagia' means: *eating or swallowing*

147. The diagnostic term "Cholecystectomy" means: *removal of gall bladder*

148. The term _____ refers to the excessive gas in the stomach and intestines. *Flatulation*

149. The diagnostic term Eructation refers to: *releasing air from the stomach with a characteristic belch*

150. The anatomical term Alimentary literally means: *to nourish*

151. The diagnostic term Shigellosis refers to: *bacillary dysentery of the bowel*

152. The diagnostic term Amebic (Amoeba) Dysentery refers to: *diarrhea and dehydration caused by the amebic one-celled organism*

153. The physiological (function) importance of the digestive system is to: *break foods down into small ingredients to nourish the body cells*

154. The diagnostic term Gastritis refers to multiple small: *stomach sores or ulcers*

155. The diagnostic term Beri/beri refers to _____ and is caused by the lack of thiamine (part of B Complex: B-1) in the diet. *body weakness "weakness/weakness"*

156. The diagnostic term Pell/agra refers to _____ and is caused by the lack of niacin or niacinamide in the diet. *skin/rough*

157. The diagnostic term Scurvy literally means _____ and is the lack of Vitamin C in the diet. *to scratch*

158. The diagnostic term Fistula refers to a: *pipe stem like tube or passageway*

159. The diagnostic term Atresia refers to: *closure of an opening - "anus, ear, vagina, eye, urethra, +"*

160. The diagnostic term Irritable Bowel Syndrome (IBS) refers to: *painful intestines*

161. The diagnostic reference of Differential Diagnosis (D.D.) refers to: *determining the difference between 2 or more similar health problems*

162. The diagnostic term Feca/lith refers to: *stone like feces or digestive system waste*

163. The diagnostic term Hiatal Hernia refers to: *rupturing or protrusion of the stomach up*

through the diaphragm

164. The anatomical term Sphincter literally means: *to bind together (Tighten)*

165. The diagnostic term Pyloric Stenosis refers to the narrowing of the lower end of the _____ and can lead to regular vomiting in infants. *stomach*

166. The diagnostic term Volvulus usually refers to _____ of the ileum or the colon. *twisting*

167. The combining form _____ refers to the tube or canal that starts in at the stomach and moves up to the throat and is called the human gullet. *esophag/o-*

168. The anatomical term Eso/phag/itis literally means _____ and is often seen in smokers and alcohol drinkers: *toward/the eater/inflamed*

169. Typhus literally means: *stupor "near coma or deep sleep"*

170. A cysto/scopic exam refers to 'looking at' the _____: *urinary bladder inspection*

171. Cholera can lead to dehydration, vomiting, muscle cramps, and death. It is caused by the bacteria _____. *Vibrio cholerae*

1. The process of forming urine begins in the: _____

2. The tubes that carry urine from the kidneys to the bladder are the: _____

3. The muscular, hollow organ that temporarily holds the urine is the: _____

4. The reservoir in the kidney that collects the urine is the: _____

5. The urine producing functional unit within the kidney is called the: _____

6. The opening through which urine passes to the outside of the body is: _____

7. The organ whose functions are to remove waste products from the blood and aid in maintaining water and acid base balance in the body is the: _____

8. The word roots or word parts that means bladder or sac are: _____

9. The root word nephr/o- in its combining form means: _____

10. The root word vesic/o- in its combining form means: _____

11. The root word pyel/o- in its combining form means: _____

12. The root word _____in its combining form means urea or nitrogen.

13. The word roots that means stone or calculi are: _____

14. The word part -/tom/- means: _____

15. The word part glyc/o- means: _____

16. The word part that means rough (semi-circular cartilages in windpipe) is: _____

17. The word part that means water or water-like is: _____

18. The prefix dia- literally and actually means: _____

19. The prefixes poly- and multi- mean: _____

20. The suffix that means abnormal condition or disease is: _____

21. The suffix that means nourishment or development is: _____

22. The suffix -megaly means: _____

23. The suffix -uria means: _____

24. The suffix that means drooping, sagging or prolapsed (kidney) is: _____

25. The suffix that means the loosening, dissolution, breakdown, or separation of (fluids or tissue) is: _____

26. The suffix that means suturing or repairing (kidney) is: _____

27. The diagnostic term Cyst/o/cele means: _____

28. The diagnostic term Uretero/stenosis means: _____

29. The diagnostic term that means inflammation of the bladder is: _____

30. The term that means abnormal condition of water (urine) congesting the kidney is: _____

31. The diagnostic term Uretero/lithiasis means: _____

32. The diagnostic term Nephro/dexto/ptosis actually means: _____

33. The diagnostic term that means excessive development of the kidney is: _____

34. The diagnostic term Ur/emia means: _____

35. The diagnostic term for the condition of kidney stones or Reno/calculi: _____

36. The diagnostic term that means inflamed kidney and renal pelvis: _____

37. The diagnostic term that means kidney tumor or swelling: _____

38. A diagnostic term for multiple renal polyps is: _____

39. The diagnostic term for a congenital defect in which the urinary meatus is located on the upper surface of the penis is: _____

40. The surgical term for the creation of an artificial opening into the kidney is: _____

41. The surgical term Lithotripsy means: _____

42. The surgical term Cystorrhaphy means: _____

43. The surgical term that means surgical fixation or repositioning of the kidney is: _____

44. A ureterostomy (or urostomy for short): _____.

45. The diagnostic term 'Cytoscopy' literally means: _____

46. The functional unit of the nervous system is the neuron and the functional unit of the urinary system is the _____.

47. The diagnostic term "Polycystic Kidney Disease - PKD" refers to the kidney having multiple _____ causing renal (refers to kidney) failure.

48. The diagnostic term "Stag Horn Calculus" refers to _____.

49. The kidney treatment term "lithotripsy" refers to crushing _____.

50. The diagnostic term "Incontinence" literally means _____ and is seen with the lack of control of the bladder or the rectum.

51. The surgical term Nephro/lysis means: _____

52. The surgical term that means incision into the bladder is: _____

53. The test that measures the amount of urea in the blood is called the: _____

54. The anatomical abdomino/pelvic division that contains the kidneys is: _____

55. Immediately after the filtrate passes through the Bowman's capsule it enters the: _____

56. The name for an enzyme that affects round bacteria arranged in clusters is: _____

57. A Fulguration means the same as: _____

58. A person with Hyper/dipsia is suffering from: _____

59. The procedural technique in which X-rays are taken to show an organ or tissue at a particular depth is called: _____

60. Azot/emia is an increase in: _____

61. A Pyelo/gram is an X-ray of: _____

62. An Auto/pathic condition is a disease that: _____

63. A wide surgical incision of the abdomen to detect disease is called a(n): _____

64. The term for an X-ray of the urinary bladder and renal pelvis is:

_____

65. The procedural term Nephro/graph/y actually means: _____

66. The instrument used to view the urethra is called a(n): _____

67. The instrument used for visual examination of the bladder is: _____

68. The procedural term Cysto/urethr/o/gram means: _____

69. The procedure or process of taking an X-ray of the renal pelvis with contrast media injected through the urethra to determine kidney collection area obstructions is:

_____

70. The term Cysto/scop/y means: _____

71. The medical term that means Scanty or Slight Urination is: _____

72. The medical term Py/uria means: _____

73. The medical term that means absence of urine is: ____

74. The term for the study of the male and female urinary system and usually parts of the reproductive system is: _____

75. The medical term hemat/uria means: _____

76. The medical term glycos/uria means: _____

77. The medical term that means destruction of living tissue with an electric spark is also known as (AKA): _____

78. The medical term for a procedure (literally means-to let down into) that uses a flexible tube-like device to withdraw or instill fluids is: _____

79. The term Di/uretic literally means double urine and actually means: _____

80. The term Enuresis actually means: _____

81. The medical term Mictur/ition actually and literally means: _____

82. The instrument used to crush a urinary bladder stone is a: _____

83. _____ and _____ can result in a temporary or permanent change in urination (micturition "making H2O"):

84. The term that means pertaining to the flow force of urine within the urinary tract is: _____

85. The diagnostic term Uro/litho/trips/y literally means: _____

86. The diagnostic term Hydro/nephr/o/sis actually means: _____

87. The diagnostic term Pyelo/nephr/itis literally means: _____

1. The process of forming urine begins in the: *glomeruli capsule "part of nephron"*

2. The tubes that carry urine from the kidneys to the bladder are the: *ureters "small canals"*

3. The muscular, hollow organ that temporarily holds the urine is the: *urinary bladder "vesic/o- or cysto-"*

4. The reservoir in the kidney that collects the urine is the: *renal pelvis*

5. The urine producing functional unit within the kidney is called the: *nephron*

6. The opening through which urine passes to the outside of the body is: *urinary meatus*

7. The organ whose functions are to remove waste products from the blood and aid in maintaining water and acid base balance in the body is the: *kidney*

8. The word roots or word parts that means bladder or sac are: *cyst/o- and vesic/o-*

9. The root word nephr/o- in its combining form means: *kidney*

10. The root word vesic/o- in its combining form means: *bladder*

11. The root word pyel/o- in its combining form means: *renal pelvis*

12. The root word _____ in its combining form means urea or nitrogen. *azot/o-*

13. The word roots that means stone or calculi are: *petro- and lith/o-*

14. The word part -/tom/- means: *to cut or section*

15. The word part glyc/o- means: *sugar*

16. The word part that means rough (semi-circular cartilages in windpipe) is: *trache/o-*

17. The word part that means water or water-like is: *hydr/o-*

18. The prefix dia- literally and actually means: *across, through, complete, or total*

19. The prefixes poly- and multi- mean: *many*

20. The suffix that means abnormal condition or disease is: *-osis*

21. The suffix that means nourishment or development is: *-trophy*

22. The suffix -megaly means: *enlargement*

23. The suffix -uria means: *urine "hemat/uria"*

24. The suffix that means drooping, sagging or prolapsed (kidney) is: *-ptosis "nephro/ptosis"*

25. The suffix that means the loosening, dissolution, breakdown, or separation of (fluids or tissue) is: *-lysis "hemo/lysis"*

26. The suffix that means suturing or repairing (kidney) is: *-orrhaphy "ren/o/rrhaphy or nephr/o/rrhaphy"*

27. The diagnostic term Cyst/o/cele means: *protrusion of the urinary bladder*

28. The diagnostic term Uretero/stenosis means: *narrowing of the ureter*

29. The diagnostic term that means inflammation of the bladder is: *cyst/itis*

30. The term that means abnormal condition of water (urine) congesting the kidney is: *hydro/nephrosis*

31. The diagnostic term Uretero/lithiasis means: *condition of stones in the ureter "small canal"*

32. The diagnostic term Nephro/dexto/ptosis actually means: *drooping kidney to the right*

33. The diagnostic term that means excessive development of the kidney is: *nephrohypertrophy*

34. The diagnostic term Ur/emia means: *condition of urine in the blood*

35. The diagnostic term for the condition of kidney stones or Reno/calculi: *nephrolithiasis*

36. The diagnostic term that means inflamed kidney and renal pelvis: *pyelonephritis*

37. The diagnostic term that means kidney tumor or swelling: *nephroma*

38. A diagnostic term for multiple renal polyps is: *poly/nephro/polpy/o/sis*

39. The diagnostic term for a congenital defect in which the urinary meatus is located on the upper surface of the penis is: *epispadias*

40. The surgical term for the creation of an artificial opening into the kidney is: *nephr/ostomy*

41. The surgical term Lithotripsy means: *surgical crushing of a stone*

42. The surgical term Cystorrhaphy means: *suturing of the bladder*

43. The surgical term that means surgical fixation or repositioning of the kidney is: *nephr/o/pexy*

44. A ureterostomy (or urostomy for short): _____. *Is a surgically created opening in the ureter, redirects the ureter to the outside of the body, and bypasses the bladder*

45. The diagnostic term 'Cytoscopy' literally means: *procedure to view and examine the bladder "urine sac"*

46. The functional unit of the nervous system is the neuron and the functional unit of the urinary system is the _____. *nephron*

47. The diagnostic term "Polycystic Kidney Disease - PKD" refers to the kidney having multiple _____ causing renal (refers to kidney) failure. *sacs or blister appearing in and on the kidney*

48. The diagnostic term "Stag Horn Calculus" refers to _____. *deer antler shape - kidney stone*

49. The kidney treatment term "lithotripsy" refers to crushing _____. *kidney stones*

50. The diagnostic term "Incontinence" literally means _____ and is seen with the lack of control of the bladder or the rectum. *not contained*

51. The surgical term Nephro/lysis means: *separating the kidney from other structures*

52. The surgical term that means incision into the bladder is: *Vesicotomy or cystotomy*

53. The test that measures the amount of urea in the blood is called the: *BUN Test "Blood Urea Nitrogen Test"*

54. The anatomical abdomino/pelvic division that contains the kidneys is: *Lumbar Region*

55. Immediately after the filtrate passes through the Bowman's capsule it enters the: *renal collecting tubule*

56. The name for an enzyme that affects round bacteria arranged in clusters is: *staphylo/lysin*

57. A Fulguration means the same as: *Electrodesiccation*

58. A person with Hyper/dipsia is suffering from: *excessive thirst*

59. The procedural technique in which X-rays are taken to show an organ or tissue at a particular depth is called: *Tomo/graphy*

60. Azot/emia is an increase in: *blood nitrogen*

61. A Pyelo/gram is an X-ray of: *the renal pelvis*

62. An Auto/pathic condition is a disease that: *starts automatically with no apparent cause "within patient"*

63. A wide surgical incision of the abdomen to detect disease is called a(n): *staging laparotomy*

64. The term for an X-ray of the urinary bladder and renal pelvis is: *cysto/pyel/o/gram*

65. The procedural term Nephro/graph/y actually means: *process of X-ray filming the kidney*

66. The instrument used to view the urethra is called a(n): *urethro/scop/e*

67. The instrument used for visual examination of the bladder is: *cysto/scop/e*

68. The procedural term Cysto/urethr/o/gram means: *X-ray film of the urinary bladder and urethra*

69. The procedure or process of taking a X-ray of the renal pelvis with contrast media injected through the urethra to determine kidney collection area obstructions is: *retro/grade pyelo/graphy*

70. The term Cysto/scop/y means: *procedural visual examination of the bladder "procedure-exact steps"*

71. The medical term that means Scanty or Slight Urination is: *olig/uria*

72. The medical term Py/uria means: *pus in the urine*

73. The medical term that means absence of urine is: *anuria*

74. The term for the study of the male and female urinary system and usually parts of the reproductive system is: *urology*

75. The medical term hemat/uria means: *blood in the urine - inflection or hemorrhaging*

76. The medical term glycos/uria means: *sugar in the urine - diabetes*

77. The medical term that means destruction of living tissue with an electric spark is also known as (AKA): *fulguration*

78. The medical term for a procedure (literally means-to let down into) that uses a flexible tube-like device to withdraw or instill fluids is: *catheterization*

79. The term Di/uretic literally means double urine and actually means: *agent that increases the amount of urine*

80. The term Enuresis actually means: *bedwetting or involuntary urination*

81. The medical term Mictur/ition actually and literally means: *the process of urinating or voiding urine*

82. The instrument used to crush a urinary bladder stone is a: *litho/trit/e or "litho/tript/or"*

83. _____and_____ can result in a temporary or permanent change in urination (micturition "making H2O"): *stricture, "to tighten", and stenosis "narrowing condition"*

84. The term that means pertaining to the flow force of urine within the urinary tract is: *uro/dynamics "urine/work"*

85. The diagnostic term Uro/litho/trips/y literally means: *the procedure of crushing a stone in the urinary system*

86. The diagnostic term Hydro/nephr/o/sis actually means: *condition of water "actually urine 95% H2O" backing up into kidney*

87. The diagnostic term Pyelo/nephr/itis literally means: *an inflammation of the kidney and kidney pelvis*

1. The oval or almond shaped male sex organs are the: _____

2. Another term for the male foreskin is: _____

3. The sac in which the testes are contained is the: _____

4. The tube that carries sperm up to the ejaculatory duct is the: _____

5. The coiled tubes in the testes, where sperm are produced, are called: _____

6. The name of the structure that contains arteries, veins, lymphatics, nerves, ductus deferens, and suspends the testes in the scrotum is the: _____

7. The male secretory structures that produce a fluid necessary for adequate sperm motility after ejaculation are called the: _____

8. The sacs located at the base of the bladder (contain alkaline fluids), and open into the vas deferens just before the male ejaculatory duct are the: _____

9. The structure that encircles the upper end of the urethra, below the urinary bladder, and literally means "that which lies before" is the: _____

10. The coiled tube on top of the testes that houses and carries the mature sperm into the vas deferens (ductus deferens) is the: _____

11. The diagnostic term Epididymitis literally means: _____

12. The combining forms that mean "testis or testicle" are: _____

13. The diagnostic term Gonad literally means: _____

14. The combining form that means "glans penis or glans clitoris" is: _____

15. The combining form that means "vessel" is: _____

16. The combining form salpingo- usually refers to the: _____

17. The diagnostic term Orchid/itis or Orchitis actually means: _____

18. The physiologic term Andro/gen/ic literally means: _____

19. The combining forms that mean "Abdomen or Belly" are: _____

20. The term Trans/urethral actually means: _____

21. The diagnostic term "_____" is the protrusion of the ureter (small canal leading from the kidney to bladder) into the kidney or bladder.

22. The diagnostic term "_____" is the backward movement of urine from the bladder into the ureter or from the ureter into the kidney.

23. The term "Glomerulonephritis" is an inflamed function unit of the kidney (Bowman's capsule structures) and is classified as _____.

24. The term Herm/aphrodit/ism (Hermes and Aphrodite/state of) actually refers to the state of having: _____

25. The diagnostic term that means State of Undescended Testes is: _____

26. The diagnostic term that means inflammation of the prostate gland and seminal vesicles is: _____

27. The diagnostic term Balano/preputial means: _____

28. The diagnostic term Orchid/epididym/itis means: _____

29. The diagnostic term Balano/malacia means: _____

30. The accumulation of serous fluid in a sac-like cavity like the tunica vaginalis testis of spermatic cord (contains ducts and vessels) or a serous swelling in a teste is called a(n): _____

31. The diagnostic term that actually means "lack of a male erection or the ability to copulate (diminished blood flow into penile caverns)" is: _____

32. Constriction of the opening in the foreskin of the glans penis is also known as _____.

33. The term that means twisted (enlarged & distorted) spermatic cord veins (in scrotum) is diagnosed by palpating (feeling) worm-like veins is called: _____

34. The surgical term that means incision into the prostate gland to remove a stone is called: _____

35. The surgical term Orchido/pex/y literally means: _____

36. The surgical term that means excision of the prostate gland is: _____

37. The surgical term that actually means male sterilization is: _____

38. The surgical excision of the prostate gland through an incision in the floor of the pelvis (between anus and scrotum) is called a(n): _____

39. The surgical term that usually refers to a male prostatectomy that can be performed by a Supra/pubic (above/private parts) Procedure. _____

40. The surgical term for Circum/cis/ion is actually defined as: _____

41. The medical term that refers to either male (testes) or female sex organs (ovaries) is: _____

42. The period when secondary sex characteristics develop is called: _____

43. An infectious sexually transmitted infection (STI) characterized by gum-like body lesions (gummas) appearing in the tertiary (3rd) stage of the disease (these Lues appear on multiple body parts and organs) is called: _____

44. The surgical sterilization procedure that is regularly used to render an individual unable to produce offspring is called: _____

45. Female and Male Sex Cells are called the _____ and _____:

46. The ovum moves from the ovary to the uterus via a passageway known as the _____ and the term Salpingitis means the tube is inflamed.

47. The muscular middle layer of the uterus is the: _____

48. The large central upper portion of the uterus is called the: _____

49. The microscopic sacs that compose the majority of the space within an ovary are the: _____

50. The vagina connects the uterus to the outside of the body and it literally means _____. Colp/itis is the inflammation of the vagina.

51. The term that means finger-like end of the fallopian tube is the: _____

52. The dark area around the nipple is called the: _____

389

53. The pelvic floor (anus to vagina or scrotum) in both males and females is called the: _____

54. The two pairs of lips surrounding the vagina are referred to as the: _____

55. The pair of mucus producing glands located on each side and superior to the vaginal opening are the: _____

56. The pear-shaped organ whose functions are to discharge the endometrium each month and house a developed zygote, morula, blastocyst, embryo, and fetus: _____

57. The surface of the uterus is covered by a thin outer layer called the: _____

58. The combining form that means "woman" is: _____

59. The combining form that means "female" is: _____

60. The combining form that means "vulva (covering)" is: _____

61. The medical term Oophor/itis literally means: _____

62. The diagnostic term Mastectomy literally means: _____

63. The combining form that means "first or beginning" is: _____

64. The combining forms that mean "uterus" are: _____

65. The combining form colp/o- means: _____

66. The term salping/ocele means: _____

67. The word men/orrhagia means: _____

68. The prefix peri- means: _____

69. The suffix -ial or -al means: _____

70. The suffix that means closure is: _____

71. The suffix -salpinx in the term hemato/salpinx (blood in uterine tube) also means: _____

390

72. The diagnostic term that means painful menstrual discharge is: _____

73. The diagnostic term "A/men/o/rrhea" actually means: _____

74. The medical term that means bloody & pus filled tumor in the vagina is:

_____

75. The diagnostic term that means inflammation of the breast is: _____

76. The diagnostic (total/knowledge) term Metr/o/rrhea actually means: _____

77. The diagnostic term that means a sudden inflammation of the vagina is: _____

78. The diagnostic term that means inflammation of the uterine muscle is: _____

79. The diagnostic medical term Hydro/salpinx actually means: _____

80. The term that means inflamed female pelvic structures and organs is:

_____

81. The diagnostic term that literally means a pipe-like stem opening between the bladder and vagina is: _____

82. The diagnostic term that actually means the growth of the endometrium in or into a portion of the abdomen is: _____

83. The diagnostic description that actually means "my/oma of the uterus" is:

_____

84. The surgical term Episi/o/rrhaphy means: _____

85. The surgical term that means excision of an ovary is: _____

86. The surgical term that means excision of the uterus is: _____

87. The surgical term that means plastic surgery repair of the vagina is: _____

88. The surgical term Complete Mast/ectomy means: _____

89. The surgical term Hyster/o/pexy actually means: _____

90. The surgical term that means excision of the ovary and fallopian tube is: _____

91. The surgical term Perineorrhaphy means: _____

92. The surgical term Cervic/ectomy means: _____

93. The surgical term that actually means the incision of the hymen membrane (procedure of cutting into) is: _____

94. The surgical term that actually means the excise of the hymen membrane (procedure of cutting out)" is: _____

95. The surgical procedure that corrects a weakened vaginal wall, a cyst/o/cele (bladder rupture or protrusion), and a rect/o/cele (rectal "straight tube" protrusion) is called a(n): _____

96. The visual examination of the abdominal cavity through the belly wall is called: _____

97. The surgical procedure for female sterilization is called: _____

98. The surgical procedure for male sterilization is called: _____

99. The instrument used for visual examination of the Fallopian Tube is the: _____

100. The procedural term for the visual examination of the uterus is: _____

101. The term that means the absence of menstruation (monthly flow) is: _____

102. The medical terms Colp/algia and Vagino/dynia literally mean: _____

103. The medical terms Oligo/men/o/rrhea literally mean: _____

104. The physician who specializes in the science and study of diseases and disorders of the female (women) reproductive system is called a: _____

105. The diagnostic medical term that actually means "a white discharge from the vagina" is: _____

106. The diagnostic medical term that actually means a luteo/leuco/gon/o/rrh/eal discharge literally means: _____

107. The white fungus growth that often appears in the vagina and means condition of glowing white is referred to as: _____

108. The medical term that means pain in the breast is: _____

109. The abnormal passageway (pipe-stem canal) between two organs or between an internal organ and the body surface is called a(n): _____

110. The medical term that actually means difficult or painful intercourse is: _____

111. A mature sex cell (Egg "ovum"; Sperm "spermato/zoon or seed/animal") _____

112. Fertilization of the egg normally takes place in the upper 1/3 of the: _____

113. The ex/pulsion of an ovum from an ovary is called: _____

114. The new cell formed by the union of the spermatozoon and the ovum is the: _____

115. The development of an individual from conception through pregnancy is: _____

116. This fetal organ called the placenta absorbs nutrients and oxygen for the unborn child. It also excretes wastes and carbon dioxide for this unborn child. The term placenta literally means _____ because of its appearance.

117. An unborn child from approximately the third month of pregnancy to birth is referred to as a: _____

118. The fet/al (fetus/refers to) membrane is called the: _____

119. The term gravida usually means _____, but literally means_____:

120. The medical term Multi/gravid or Poly/gravid actually refers to: _____

121. The combining word part form for "Umbilicus (navel)" is: _____

122. The diagnostic medical term Omphal/o/cele actually means: _____

123. The term Multi/cyesis literally means: _____

124. The combining form Puerper/o- literally means: _____

125. The term Dys/puerper/al actually refers to a difficult or painful period

393

following: _____

126. The combining word part forms "nat/o- and toci-" literally means: _____

127. The combining forms that mean "milk" are: _____

128. The combining form parto- that is used in the term partur/ition literally means:
_____

129. The combining form fet/o- actually means: _____

130. The word part in its combining form that means "first" is: _____

131. Gestation literally means: _____

132. The combining form that means "head" is: _____

133. The medical term Pseudo/gyneco/mast/ia literally means: _____

134. Molluscum contagiosum, lymphogranuloma inguinale, and trichomoniasis are all transmitted via: _____

135. Urethr/itis (inflamed canal) may be caused by sexually transmitted infections and usually leads next to _____ if early treatment is not started quickly. _____

136. The pregnancy term Ante/partum literally means: _____

137. The compound term "Nulli/parous" actually applies to a women that has: _____

138. The prefixes poly- and multi- mean: _____

139. The prefix that means after is: _____

140. The suffix -orrhexis means: _____

141. The suffix -tocia means: _____

142. Syphilis was a: _____

143. The diagnostic term that literally means difficult or painful labor is: _____

144. A possible term for natural abort/ion or mis/carriage (away/carry) is:

_____

145. Another term for Ec/top/ic Pregnancy is: _____

146. The diagnostic term that means premature separation of the placenta from the uterine wall is: _____

147. The diagnostic term that means abnormally low implantation of the placenta on the uterine wall is: _____

148. The diagnostic term that means congenital herniation at the umbilicus is: _____

149. The diagnostic term that means fetus with a very small head is: _____

150. In a newborn child, a condition caused by the narrowing of the pyloric (gatekeeper) sphincter is: _____

151. The diagnostic term for a congenital condition characterized by varying degrees of intellectual disability and multiple physical defects is: _____

152. The term for a congenital defect of the vertebral column caused by the failure of the vertebral arch to fuse is: _____-

153. The term for a respiratory alveoli membrane collapse in premature babies: _____

154. What is used to examine the cervix and vaginal walls?

155. The procedural term Amni/o/tomy actually means: _____

156. The procedural term for the incision into the perineum at the end of the 2nd stage of labor to avoid laceration (tearing) is ____.

157. The instrument used for examining fetal heart tones is called a(n): _____

158. The procedural term for X-ray of the fetus in the uterus is: _____

159. The procedural term Fet/o/metry means: _____

160. The instrument used for visual examination of the fetus and amniotic fluid is called a(n): _____

161. The procedural term for X-ray of the uterus after the injection of contrast media into the amniotic fluid is: _____

162. The procedural term Pelvi/metry actually means: _____

163. The procedural terms Intro/partubation & Intra/partubation actually mean:

_____

164. The medical term that actually means a woman who has given birth to one viable offspring is: _____

165. A form of depression often seen immediately after childbirth is: _____

166. The medical term that means before childbirth is: _____

167. The term Hystero/salpingo/graphy (HSG) refers to a procedure used to diagnose certain problems of the _____ and _____. HSG is most often used to determine the possibility of a female becoming pregnant.

168. The medical term Lact/o/rrhea or Galact/o/rrhea actually means: _____

169. The medical term Primi/gravida literally means: _____

170. The branch of medicine that deals with diagnosis and treatment of disorders in newborn infants is: _____

171. The medical term that means discharge of amnionic fluid from the uterus during pregnancy is: _____

172. The medical term Cyesis means: _____

173. The term that means woman who has been pregnant two or more times is:

_____

174. The medical term Nat/al means: _____

175. The medical term Amni/o/rrhexis actually means: _____

176. The medical term that means study of pregnancy is: _____

177. The medical term that means woman who has not given birth to a viable offspring is: _____

178. The medical term dys/men/o/rrhea actually means: _____

179. The medical compound term that actually refers to the abnormal heavy flow of milk is: _____

180. The medical term that refers to the first stool of the newborn and means poppy juice is: _____

181. The medical specialty that deals with pregnancy, childbirth, and puerper/ium (after childbirth/refers) is called: _____

182. The normal vaginal blood, mucus, and tissue discharge following childbirth is referred to as: _____

183. The medical term that means "scant menstrual flow" is: _____

184. Parturition in which the feet, arms, or buttock emerge first is called: _____

185. The diagnostic term Epididym/itis actually means: _____

186. The surgical procedure for a Tubal Ligation in women is similar to a _____ in men.

187. Testicular Cancer can be diagnosed in men with an early and simple self-diagnostic procedure called: _____

188. The diagnostic term Phim/o/sis literally means: _____

189. The diagnostic term Epi/spadias literally means: _____

190. The diagnostic term Colp/o/cele actually means: _____

191. The diagnostic term Ectopic Pregnancy actually means: _____

192. The diagnostic term Hydro/cele in males literally means: _____

193. The diagnostic term Balan/itis actually means: _____

194. The diagnostic term Salping/itis actually means: _____

195. The diagnostic term Hystero/salpino/gram can be read by a/an _____ or _____ to determine female body health for reproduction and viability.

196. The Zygote literally means: _____

197. The Morula actually means: _____

198. "Fetus" actually means: _____

199. The colloquial term "clap" refers to what reproductive system infection? _____

200. Signs of AIDs include weight loss, oral lesions and:_____

201. The foreskin secretion Smegma literally means _____. It can cause an irritation and inflammation of the glans penis or glans clitoris (Balan/itis).

202. Trichomon/iasis (trich) is caused by a _____ that causes a mal/odorous frothy yellow to green discharge, itching (pruritus), and burning:

203. Non-Specific Urethr/itis actually means an inflammation of the urethral canal that is caused by: _____

204. Scabies rashes are found between fingers, wrists, and: _____

205. Genital warts can include: _____

206. Treatments for warts (verruca) include salicylic acid and _____.

207. The term Herpes literally means to creep and it can cause diseases like Chickenpox, Shingles, Herpes Simplex I (Oral Herpes), and Herpes Simplex II (_____).

208. The Condylomata acuminata (common genital warts) are contagious STI lesions usually on the anus, vulva, penis, thighs, and/or perineum. The lesions usually are moist, soft, red or pink, and can be: _____

209. A Speculum is used in female pelvic exams to expand the walls of the: _____

210. The diagnostic term that actually means a human with a very large head is _____. The etiology is usually the retention of CSF in the brain ventricles, causing outward skull plate pressure and an enlarged skull.

211. The prefix Cervico- refers to: _____

212. The prefix Feto- refers to: _____

213. The diagnostic term _____ is characterized by hardening of fibrous tissue of the penis corpora cavernosa (stick: body: blood caverns Gk.) causing penal distortion & deflection.

214. The diagnostic term placenta previa (cake: first or early) actually means: _____

215. The diagnostic term abruptio placentae literally means: _____

1. The oval or almond shaped male sex organs are the: *testes*

2. Another term for the male foreskin is: *prepuce*

3. The sac in which the testes are contained is the: *scrotum - which means pouch*

4. The tube that carries sperm up to the ejaculatory duct is the: *vas de/ferens - which means vessel that carries away*

5. The coiled tubes in the testes, where sperm are produced, are called: *seminiferous tubules*

6. The name of the structure that contains arteries, veins, lymphatics, nerves, ductus deferens, and suspends the testes in the scrotum is the: *spermatic cord*

7. The male secretory structures that produce a fluid necessary for adequate sperm motility after ejaculation are called the: *seminal vesicles and prostate gland*

8. The sacs located at the base of the bladder (contain alkaline fluids), and open into the vas deferens just before the male ejaculatory duct are the: *seminal vesicles*

9. The structure that encircles the upper end of the urethra, below the urinary bladder, and literally means "that which lies before" is the: *prostate gland*

10. The coiled tube on top of the testes that houses and carries the mature sperm into the vas deferens (ductus deferens) is the: *epididymis*

11. The diagnostic term Epididymitis literally means: *upon the teste/inflamed*

12. The combining forms that mean "testis or testicle" are: *orchi/o- and orchido-*

13. The diagnostic term Gonad literally means: *seed producer*

14. The combining form that means "glans penis or glans clitoris" is: *balan/o-*

15. The combining form that means "vessel" is: *vas/o- or angio-*

16. The combining form salpingo- usually refers to the: *fallopian or uterine tubes "ducts"*

17. The diagnostic term Orchid/itis or Orchitis actually means: *the inflammation of the testes*

18. The physiologic term Andro/gen/ic literally means: *male/development/refers*

19. The combining forms that mean "Abdomen or Belly" are: *celi/o-, lapar/o-, and abdomen/o-*

20. The term Trans/urethral actually means: *an operation performed through the urethra*

21. The diagnostic term "_____" is the protrusion of the ureter (small canal leading from the kidney to bladder) into the kidney or bladder. *Ureterocele*

22. The diagnostic term "_____" is the backward movement of urine from the bladder into the ureter or from the ureter into the kidney. *urinary reflux*

23. The term "Glomerulonephritis" is an inflamed function unit of the kidney (Bowman's capsule structures) and is classified as _____. *acute, chronic or subacute*

24. The term Herm/aphrodit/ism (Hermes and Aphrodite/state of) actually refers to the state of having: *both female and male reproductive parts*

25. The diagnostic term that means State of Undescended Testes is: *cryptorchidism*

26. The diagnostic term that means inflammation of the prostate gland and seminal vesicles is: *prostatovesiculitis*

27. The diagnostic term Balano/preputial means: *pertains to the glans penis and the prepuce or foreskin*

28. The diagnostic term Orchid/epididym/itis means: *inflammation of the testes and epididymis*

29. The diagnostic term Balano/malacia means: *refers to glans penis or clitoris softening*

30. The accumulation of serous fluid in a sac-like cavity like the tunica vaginalis testis of spermatic cord (contains ducts and vessels) or a serous swelling in a teste is called a(n): *hydrocele*

31. The diagnostic term that actually means "lack of a male erection or the ability to copulate (diminished blood flow into penile caverns)" is: *im/potence - no power*

32. Constriction of the opening in the foreskin of the glans penis is also known as _____. *phimosis*

33. The term that means twisted (enlarged & distorted) spermatic cord veins (in scrotum) is diagnosed by palpating (feeling) worm-like veins is called: *varicocele*

34. The surgical term that means incision into the prostate gland to remove a stone is called: *prostatolithotomy*

35. The surgical term Orchido/pex/y literally means: *procedure of surgically fixating or positioning a testicle*

36. The surgical term that means excision of the prostate gland is: *prostat/ectomy*

37. The surgical term that actually means male sterilization is: *vasectomy*

38. The surgical excision of the prostate gland through an incision in the floor of the pelvis (between anus and scrotum) is called a(n): *perineal prostatectomy*

39. The surgical term that usually refers to a male prostatectomy that can be performed by a Supra/pubic (above/private parts) Procedure. *Transurethral Resection "TUR"*

40. The surgical term for Circum/cis/ion is actually defined as: *surgical procedure of removing the prepuce or foreskin*

41. The medical term that refers to either male (testes) or female sex organs (ovaries) is: *gonads*

42. The period when secondary sex characteristics develop is called: *pubert/y "which literally means private parts/process of forming"*

43. An infectious sexually transmitted infection (STI) characterized by gum-like body lesions (gummas) appearing in the tertiary (3rd) stage of the disease (these Lues appear on multiple body parts and organs) is called: *syphilis*

44. The surgical sterilization procedure that is regularly used to render an individual unable to produce offspring is called: *vasectomy in males and tubal ligation in women*

45. Female and Male Sex Cells are called the _____ and _____: *ova and sperm*

46. The ovum moves from the ovary to the uterus via a passageway known as the _____ and the term Salpingitis means the tube is inflamed. *fallopian tube or uterine tube*

47. The muscular middle layer of the uterus is the: *myometrium*

48. The large central upper portion of the uterus is called the: *fundus*

49. The microscopic sacs that compose the majority of the space within an ovary are the: *graafian follicles*

50. The vagina connects the uterus to the outside of the body and it literally means _____. Colp/itis is the inflammation of the vagina. *sheath*

51. The term that means finger-like end of the fallopian tube is the: *fimbria*

52. The dark area around the nipple is called the: *areola*

53. The pelvic floor (anus to vagina or scrotum) in both males and females is called the: *perineum*

54. The two pairs of lips surrounding the vagina are referred to as the: *vulva - covering or labia "lips"*

55. The pair of mucus producing glands located on each side and superior to the vaginal opening are the: *Bartholin's Glands*

56. The pear-shaped organ whose functions is to discharge the endometrium each month and house a developed zygote, morula, blastocyst, embryo, and fetus: *uterus or womb: metro-, hystero-, and utero-*

57. The surface of the uterus is covered by a thin outer layer called the: *perimetrium*

58. The combining form that means "woman" is: *gynec/o- "gynec/o/logy"*

59. The combining form that means "female" is: *estro- "estr/o/gen"*

60. The combining form that means "vulva (covering)" is: *episi/o-: episiotomy - cut into lower part to ease birth*

61. The medical term Oophor/itis literally means: *ovary/inflamed*

62. The diagnostic term Mastectomy literally means: *breast/out/cut/procedure*

63. The combining form that means "first or beginning" is: *arche/o-: menarche*

64. The combining forms that mean "uterus" are: *metr/o-, hystero-, and utero-*

65. The combining form colp/o- means: *vagina*

66. The term salping/ocele means: *fallopian tube protrusion*

67. The word men/orrhagia means: *monthly/bursting forth - heavy monthly flow*

68. The prefix peri- means: *surrounding or around*

69. The suffix -ial or -al means: *pertaining to or refers to*

70. The suffix that means closure is: *atresia*

71. The suffix -salpinx in the term hemato/salpinx (blood in uterine tube) also means: *fallopian tube or tube*

72. The diagnostic term that means painful menstrual discharge is: *dys/men/o/rrhea*

73. The diagnostic term "A/men/o/rrhea" actually means: *absence of or a lack of a monthly menstrual flow*

74. The medical term that means bloody & pus filled tumor in the vagina is: *hemato/pyo/colp/oma*

75. The diagnostic term that means inflammation of the breast is: *mastitis*

76. The diagnostic (total/knowledge) term Metr/o/rrhea actually means: *abnormal uterine discharge*

77. The diagnostic term that means a sudden inflammation of the vagina is: *acute colpitis*

78. The diagnostic term that means inflammation of the uterine muscle is: *myometritis*

79. The diagnostic medical term Hydro/salpinx actually means: *water in the fallopian tube*

80. The term that means inflamed female pelvic structures and organs is: *Pelvic Inflammatory Disease - P.I.D.*

81. The diagnostic term that literally means a pipe-like stem opening between the bladder and vagina is: *vesicovaginal fistula*

82. The diagnostic term that actually means the growth of the endometrium in or into a portion of the abdomen is: *endometriosis*

83. The diagnostic description that actually means "my/oma of the uterus" is: *uterine fibroid tumor or hystero/my/oma*

84. The surgical term Episi/o/rrhaphy means: *suturing or sewing of a lacerated perineum - vulva to anus*

85. The surgical term that means excision of an ovary is: *oophor/ectomy*

86. The surgical term that means excision of the uterus is: *hyster/ectomy*

87. The surgical term that means plastic surgery repair of the vagina is: *colp/o/plasty*

88. The surgical term Complete Mast/ectomy means: *surgical removal of a breast and other structures in the area*

89. The surgical term Hyster/o/pexy actually means: *surgical fixation, reattachment, or repositioning of the uterus*

90. The surgical term that means excision of the ovary and fallopian tube is: *oophoro/salping/ectomy*

91. The surgical term Perineorrhaphy means: *suture of a tear in the perineum or pelvic floor*

92. The surgical term Cervic/ectomy means: *excision of the cervix of uterus*

93. The surgical term that actually means the incision of the hymen membrane (procedure of cutting into) is: *hymen/otomy*

94. The surgical term that actually means the excision of the hymen membrane (procedure of cutting out)" is: *hymen/ectomy*

95. The surgical procedure that corrects a weakened vaginal wall, a cyst/o/cele (bladder rupture or protrusion), and a rect/o/cele (rectal "straight tube" protrusion) is called a(n): *anterior and posterior colp/o/rrhaphy*

96. The visual examination of the abdominal cavity through the belly wall is called: *lapar/o/scopy*

97. The surgical procedure for female sterilization is called: *tubal ligation*

98. The surgical procedure for male sterilization is called: *vas/ectomy "vessel excised"*

99. The instrument used for visual examination of the Fallopian Tube is the:

salpingoscope

100. The procedural term for the visual examination of the uterus is: *hysteroscop/y*

101. The term that means the absence of menstruation (monthly flow) is: *a/men/o/rrhea*

102. The medical terms Colp/algia or Vagino/dynia literally mean: *pain in the vagina*

103. The medical terms Oligo/men/o/rrhea literally mean: *scanty or slight menstrual flow*

104. The physician who specializes in the science and study of diseases and disorders of the female (women) reproductive system is called a: *Gynec/o/log/ist*

105. The diagnostic medical term that actually means "a white discharge from the vagina" is: *leukorrhea*

106. The diagnostic medical term that actually means a luteo/leuco/gon/o/rrh/eal discharge literally means: *refers to a yellow white seed producer flow*

107. The white fungus growth that often appears in the vagina and means condition of glowing white is referred to as: *candid/iasis*

108. The medical term that means pain in the breast is: *mast/algia*

109. The abnormal passageway (pipe-stem canal) between two organs or between an internal organ and the body surface is called a(n): *fistula*

110. The medical term that actually means difficult or painful intercourse is: *dys/pare/un/ia "unhappily mated as bedfellows"*

111. A mature sex cell (Egg "ovum"; Sperm "spermato/zoon or seed/animal") *gamete "to marry - Greek"*

112. Fertilization of the egg normally takes place in the upper 1/3 of the: *fallopian tube*

113. The ex/pulsion of an ovum from an ovary is called: *ov/ulation*

114. The new cell formed by the union of the spermatozoon and the ovum is the: *zygote "to join - Greek"*

115. The development of an individual from conception through pregnancy is: *gestation "to bear"*

116. This fetal organ called the placenta absorbs nutrients and oxygen for the unborn child. It also excretes wastes and carbon dioxide for this unborn child. The term placenta literally means _____ because of its appearance. *cake*

117. An unborn child from approximately the third month of pregnancy to birth is referred to as a: *fetus "young"*

118. The fet/al (fetus/refers to) membrane is called the: *amniotic sac "lambs Caul appearance"*

119. The term gravida usually means _____, but literally means_____: *pregnant and heavy*

120. The medical term Multi/gravid or Poly/gravid actually refers to: *many/pregnancy*

121. The combining word part form for "Umbilicus (navel)" is: *omphal/o-*

122. The diagnostic medical term Omphal/o/cele actually means: *congenital hernia of the navel*

123. The term Multi/cyesis literally means: *many or multiple/pregnancy*

124. The combining form Puerper/o- literally means: *to bear or childbirth*

125. The term Dys/puerper/al actually refers to difficult or painful period following: *childbirth*

126. The combining word part forms "nat/o- and toci-" literally means: *birth*

127. The combining forms that mean "milk" are: *lact/o- and galacto-*

128. The combining form parto- that is used in the term partur/ition literally means: *to give birth/process of*

129. The combining form fet/o- actually means: *unborn child "months 3-9" - literally "young child" in Greek*

130. The word part in its combining form that means "first" is: *prim/o-*

131. Gest/ation literally means: *to bear or separate/process*

132. The combining form that means "head" is: *cephal/o-*

133. The medical term Pseudo/gyneco/mast/ia literally means: *false/woman/breast/refers to "just adipose tissue in males"*

134. Molluscum contagiosum, lymphogranuloma inguinale, and trichomoniasis are all transmitted via: *Sexual contact*

135. Urethr/itis (inflamed canal) is often caused by venereal disease and usually leads next to _____ if early treatment is not started quickly. *cystitis*

136. The pregnancy term Ante/partum literally means: *before/birth*

137. The compound term "Nulli/parous" actually applies to a women that has: *none/births "no births"*

138. The prefixes poly- and multi- mean: *many*

139. The prefix that means after is: *post-*

140. The suffix -orrhexis means: *rupture*

141. The suffix -tocia means: *birth*

142. Syphilis was a: *fictional shepherd boy.*

143. The diagnostic term that literally means difficult or painful labor is: *dys/tocia*

144. A possible term for natural abort/ion or mis/carriage (away/carry) is: *embryo/tocia or feto/tocia*

145. Another term for Ec/top/ic Pregnancy is: *salping/o/cyesis "tube/pregnancy"*

146. The diagnostic term that means premature separation of the placenta from the uterine wall is: *abruptio placentae*

147. The diagnostic term that means abnormally low implantation of the placenta on the uterine wall is: *placenta previa*

148. The diagnostic term that means congenital herniation at the umbilicus is: *omphal/o/cele*

149. The diagnostic term that means fetus with a very small head is: *microcephalus*

150. In a newborn child, a condition caused by the narrowing of the pyloric (gatekeeper)

sphincter is: *pyloric stenosis*

151. The diagnostic term for a congenital condition characterized by varying degrees of intellectual disability and multiple physical defects is: *Down syndrome*

152. The term for a congenital defect of the vertebral column caused by the failure of the vertebral arch to fuse is: *spina bifida*

153. The term for a respiratory alveoli membrane collapse in premature babies: *Respiratory Distress Syndrome (premature) "RDS or hyaline membrane disease"*

154. What is used to examine the cervix and vaginal walls? *Speculum*

155. The procedural term Amni/o/tomy actually means: *incision into fetal covering membrane to stimulate labor - painless*

156. The procedural term for the incision into the perineum at the end of the 2nd stage of labor to avoid laceration (tearing) is ____. *Episi/o/tom/y*

157. The instrument used for examining fetal heart tones is called a(n): *feto/scop/e*

158. The procedural term for X-ray of the fetus in the uterus is: *fetography*

159. The procedural term Fet/o/metry means: *measurement of the size of the fetus "before birthing"*

160. The instrument used for visual examination of the fetus and amniotic fluid is called a(n): *amnioscope*

161. The procedural term for X-ray of the uterus after the injection of contrast media into the amniotic fluid is: *amniography*

162. The procedural term Pelvi/metry actually means: *measurement of the mother's pelvic size before birth "C Section"*

163. The procedural terms Intro/partubation & Intra/partubation actually mean: *occurring during labor "within/childbirth"*

164. The medical term that actually means a woman who has given birth to one viable offspring is: *mono/para - one/birth*

165. A form of depression often seen immediately after childbirth is: *post/partum*

166. The medical term that means before childbirth is: *ante/partum*

167. The term Hystero/salpingo/graphy (HSG) refers to a procedure used to diagnose certain problems of the _____ and _____. HSG is most often used to determine the possibility of a female becoming pregnant. *uterus and uterine tubes "fallopian tubes"*

168. The medical term Lact/o/rrhea or Galact/o/rrhea actually means: *spontaneous discharge of milk from the breast*

169. The medical term Primi/gravida literally means: *first/heavy "woman in her first pregnancy"*

170. The branch of medicine that deals with diagnosis and treatment of disorders in newborn infants is: *Neo/nat/o/logy*

171. The medical term that means discharge of amnionic fluid from the uterus during pregnancy is: *amniorrhea*

172. The medical term Cyesis means: *pregnancy*

173. The term that means woman who has been pregnant two or more times is: *multigravida "many/heavy"*

174. The medical term Nat/al means: *pertaining to birth*

175. The medical term Amni/o/rrhexis actually means: *rupture of the amniotic membrane at labor or birth*

176. The medical term that means study of pregnancy is: *Cyesiology*

177. The medical term that means woman who has not given birth to a viable offspring is: *nulli/para*

178. The medical term dys/men/o/rrhea actually means: *difficult and painful monthly flow*

179. The medical compound term that actually refers to the abnormal heavy flow of milk is: *lactorrhagia*

180. The medical term that refers to the first stool of the newborn and means poppy juice is:, *meconium*

181. The medical specialty that deals with pregnancy, childbirth, and puerper/ium (after childbirth/refers) is called: *obstetrics "mid-wifery"*

182. The normal vaginal blood, mucus, and tissue discharge following childbirth is referred to as: *lochia - "day 1-6 red, 6-10 brown, followed by yellow and white*

183. The medical term that means "scanty menstrual flow" is: *oligomenorrhea*

184. Parturition in which the feet, arms, or buttock emerge first is called: *breech birth*

185. The diagnostic term Epididym/itis actually means: *inflammation in the curved and coiled structure above the teste*

186. The surgical procedure for a Tubal Ligation in women is similar to a _____ in men. *vasectomy*

187. Testicular Cancer can be diagnosed in men with an early and simple self-diagnostic procedure called: *palpa/tion*

188. The diagnostic term Phim/o/sis literally means: *muzzl/ing*

189. The diagnostic term Epi/spadias literally means: *upon/tear "urethra opening above normal location*

190. The diagnostic term Colp/o/cele actually means: *protrusion or descending vagina to the outside of the body*

191. The diagnostic term Ectopic Pregnancy actually means: *embryo is attached to the female usually outside of uterus - tubes*

192. The diagnostic term Hydro/cele in males literally means: *water like fluid build-up in the scrotal sac "tubes leak"*

193. The diagnostic term Balan/itis actually means: *inflamed glans penis or glans clitoris*

194. The diagnostic term Salping/itis actually means: *inflamed fallopian tubes*

195. The diagnostic term Hystero/salpino/gram can be read by a /an _____ or _____ to determine female body health for reproduction and viability. *Obstetrician mid-wife/refers; Gynecologist women/science/specialist*

196. The Zygote literally means: *union or uniting*

197. The Morula actually means: *mulberry "stage after Zygote" - early stage of stem cells*

198. The Fetus actually means: *young "early human form" - comprises the last 6 months of pregnancy*

199. The colloquial term "clap" refers to what reproductive system infection? *gonorrhea*

200. Signs of AIDS include weight loss, oral lesions and: *lymphadenopathy*

201. The foreskin secretion Smegma literally means _____. It can cause an irritation & inflammation of the glans penis or glans clitoris (Balan/itis). *soap "white-soap"*

202. Trichomon/iasis (trich) is caused by a _____ that causes a mal/odorous frothy yellow to green discharge, itching (pruritus), and burning: *protozoan parasite with a tail*

203. Non-Specific Urethr/itis actually means an inflammation of the urethral canal that is caused by: *multiple possible etiologic agents*

204. Scabies rashes are found between fingers, wrists, and: *thighs*

205. Genital warts can include: *Papilloma "nipple-like raised warts," Molluscum contagiosum "soft flat warts," Verruca acuminata "rough, vulgar or common, warts"*

206. Treatment for warts (verruca) includes salicylic acid and: *Cryosurgery "liquid nitrogen," curettage "scooping," and electrosurgery.*

207. The term Herpes literally means to creep and it can cause diseases like Chickenpox, Shingles, Herpes Simplex I (Oral Herpes), and Herpes Simplex II (_____). *Genital Herpes*

208. The Condylomata acuminata (common genital warts) are contagious STI lesions usually on the anus, vulva, penis, thighs, and/or perineum. The lesions usually are moist, soft, red or pink, and can be: *knuckle-like or nipple-like*

209. A Speculum is used in female pelvic exams to expand the walls of the: *vagina*

210. The diagnostic term that actually means a human with a very large head is _____. The etiology is usually the retention of CSF in the brain ventricles, causing outward skull plate pressure and an enlarged skull. *macro/cephalus or hydro/cephalus*

211. The prefix Cervico- refers to: *"neck"*

212. The prefix Feto- refers to: *"young"*

213. The diagnostic term _____ is characterized by hardening of fibrous tissue of the penis corpora cavernosa (stick: body: blood caverns Gk.) causing penal distortion & deflection. Treatment is limited for this deformity. *Peyronie's disease*

214. The diagnostic term placenta previa (cake: first or early) actually means: *low implantation & possible miscarriage - usually after the 7th month*

215. The diagnostic term abruptio placentae actually means: *premature separation of cake*

1. The _____ Endocrine Gland is referred to as the Master Gland (of the body) because it secretes multiple hormones that influence multiple body function.

2. The name of the Pituitary Hormone that is essential to the growth, development and continue function of the adrenal cortex is: _____

3. The Pituitary Hormone that stimulates uterine contractions during female labor is: _____

4. The pituitary lobe that secretes Adrenocorticotrophic Hormone (ACTH), Growth Hormone (GH), and Follicle Stimulating Hormone (FSH) is called the: _____

5. The _____ pituitary lobe stores and releases Anti/di/uret/ic Hormone (ADH) and Oxy/tocin.

6. The Thyroid Hormone that regulates carbohydrate metabolism is: _____

7. Located in front of the lower voice box and the upper trachea (rough), the _____ Gland is the largest endocrine gland and is shaped like a shield.

8. The four small dime size glands that lie directly upon and behind the Thyroid Gland are the _____ Glands. They secrete para/thormone that is responsible for regulating body calcium usage.

9. The endocrine glands located above each kidney (divided into 2 portions called the medulla "marrow-like" and the cortex "bark-like") are the: _____

10. The name of the hormone that helps to maintain the level of calcium in the blood and is produced by the four Parathyroid Glands is: _____

11. The hormone that plays an important role in the control of blood sugar levels and controls hyperglycemic and hypoglycemic body responses is: _____

12. The hormone that helps the body deal with stress is: _____

13. The compound term "Poly/dips/ia" literally means: _____

14. The combining forms that mean "poison" are: _____

15. The term Hypo/glyc/emia literally means: _____

16. The prefixes e-, ec-, ect-, ecto-, ex-, and exo- all mean: _____

17. The diagnostic term for the state of excessive thyroxin production, which causes high sugar use levels and hyperactivity is: _____

18. The medical term Endo/crin/olog/ist actually means: _____

19. The diagnostic term for a chronic disease caused by under-activity of the Islets of Langerhans (Beta Cells) in the pancreas is: _____

20. Addison's disease (AKA _____) is usually idio/pathic (unique to self/disease) and shows a progressive destruction of the ad/renal cortex. In time the tissue is infected by organisms that cause TB, histoplasmosis, and cryptococcosis. _____

21. The condition resulting in muscle spasms (poor nerve communications) due to an abnormally low concentration of calcium in the blood is: _____

22. The medical diagnostic term Syn/drome actually means: _____

23. The medical term for the sum total of all the chemical processes that take place in a living organism is _____. It literally and actually means - the state of/changing/a lump (of food).

24. The term given to substances secreted by Endo/crine (within blood/secret) Glands that means to urge on is: _____

25. The lack of _____ can cause premature aging.

26. Dia/betes literally means: _____

27. Graves' disease is also known as: _____

28. Dwarf/ism (irregular proportioned and "shortness/state") is often seen with Pro/geria (before/old or aged). The probable cause is heredity factors or the lack of Pituitary _____ production that leads to complete premature aging.

29. The inability to sleep is often caused by the lack of the Pineal Gland to secrete: _____

30. The Parathyroid Gland produces Para/thormone, which regulate body calcium blood levels and prevents: _____

31. How many hormones does the pituitary gland secrete in men? _____

32. The anterior part of the pituitary gland secretes which hormones? _____

33. Birth control pills start releasing _____ early in the female cycle (+/- day 9) which stops the release of LH from the Anterior Pituitary. The inhibition of LH around day 15 stops ovulation. _____

34. The hormone _____ increases in the blood to a level that causes LH to be released from the anterior pituitary. This hormone is the third of the four female cycle hormones (FSH, estrogen, LH and Progesterone)

35. The hormone _____ increases quickly in the female blood from the corpus luteum of the egg to a level that inhibits further Luteinizing Hormone (LH) production from the Anterior Pituitary, which stops ovulation.

1. The _____ Endocrine Gland is referred to as the Master Gland (of the body) because it secretes multiple hormones that influence multiple body function. *Pituitary*

2. The name of the Pituitary Hormone that is essential to the growth, development and continue function of the adrenal cortex is: *adreno/cortico/trophic hormone - ACTH SYN: Corticotropin*

3. The Pituitary Hormone that stimulates uterine contractions during female labor is: *oxytocin*

4. The pituitary lobe that secretes Adrenocorticotrophic Hormone (ACTH), Growth Hormone (GH), and Follicle Stimulating Hormone (FSH) is called the: *anterior lobe*

5. The _____ pituitary lobe stores and releases Anti/di/uret/ic Hormone (ADH) and Oxy/tocin. *posterior*

6. The Thyroid Hormone that regulates carbohydrate metabolism is: *thyroxin or thyroxine*

7. Located in front of the lower voice box and the upper trachea (rough), the _____ Gland is the largest endocrine gland and is shaped like a shield. *Thyroid*

8. The four small dime size glands that lie directly upon and behind the Thyroid Gland are the _____ Glands. They secrete para/thormone that is responsible for regulating body calcium usage. *Parathyroid*

9. The endocrine glands located above each kidney (divided into 2 portions called the medulla "marrow-like" and the cortex "bark-like") are the: *adrenal glands*

10. The name of the hormone that helps to maintain the level of calcium in the blood and is produced by the four Parathyroid Glands is: *parathormone*

11. The hormone that plays an important role in the control of blood sugar levels and controls hyperglycemic and hypoglycemic body responses is: *insulin from the beta cells of the Isles of Langerhans in the pancreas "all/fleshy"*

12. The hormone that helps the body deal with stress is: *epinephrine - alarm stage of the General Adaptation Syndrome "GAS"*

13. The compound term "Poly/dips/ia" literally means: *much/thirst/refers to*

14. The combining forms that mean "poison" are: *toxic/o- "toxic", viro- "virus", or septo- "septic"*

15. The term Hypo/glyc/emia literally means: *low or below/sugar levels/blood - tired and fatigued*

16. The prefixes e-, ec-, ect-, ecto-, ex-, and exo- all mean: *out or outside*

17. The diagnostic term for the state of excessive thyroxin production, which causes high sugar use levels and hyperactivity is: *hyperthyroidism*

18. The medical term Endo/crin/olog/ist actually means: *specialist in the science and study of glands of internal secretion (into the blood stream)*

19. The diagnostic term for a chronic disease caused by under activity of the Islets of Langerhans (Beta Cells) in the pancreas is: *Diabetes Mellitus - sweet or sugar excess - Types I and II*

20. Addison's Disease (AKA _____) is usually idio/pathic (unique to self/disease) and shows a progressive destruction of the ad/renal cortex. In time the tissue is infected by organisms that cause TB, histoplasmosis, and cryptococcosis. *hypo/adreno/cortic/ism - weakness, vitiligo, nausea, and hypotension*

21. The condition resulting in muscle spasms (poor nerve communications) due to an abnormally low concentration of calcium in the blood is: *tetany - tension/of muscle*

22. The medical diagnostic term Syn/drome actually means: *a set of signs and symptoms that run together - together/run*

23. The medical term for the sum total of all the chemical processes that take place in a living organism is _____. It literally and actually means - the state of/changing/a lump (of food). *meta/bol/ism*

24. The term given to substances secreted by Endo/crine (within blood/secret) Glands that means to urge on is: *hormone*

25. The lack of _____ can cause premature aging. *Human Growth Hormone "HGH"*

26. Dia/betes literally means: *through/passing*

27. Graves' Disease is also known as: *Hyperthyroidism*

28. Dwarf/ism (irregular proportioned and "shortness/state") is often seen with Pro/geria (before/old or aged). The probable cause is heredity factors or the lack of Pituitary

_____ production that leads to complete premature aging. *HGH*

29. The inability to sleep is often caused by the lack of the Pineal Gland to secrete: *melatonin*

30. The Parathyroid Gland produces Para/thormone, which regulate body calcium blood levels and prevents: *tetany or muscle spasms*

31. How many hormones does the pituitary gland secrete in men? *6 (six)*

32. The anterior part of the pituitary gland secretes which hormones? *Luteiniz/ing, Growth, Thyroid Stimulating and Adrenocorticotrophic*

33. Birth Control pills start releasing _____ early in the female cycle (+/- day 9) which stops the release of LH from the Anterior Pituitary. The inhibition of LH around day 15 stops ovulation. *Pro/gesterone hormone "before/separation: urge on"*

34. The hormone _____ increases in the blood to a level that causes LH to be released from the anterior pituitary. This hormone is the third of the four female cycle hormones (FSH, estrogen, LH and Progesterone) *Estrogen*

35. The hormone _____ increases quickly in the female blood from the corpus luteum of the egg to a level that inhibits further Luteinizing Hormone (LH) production from the Anterior Pituitary, which stops ovulation. *Progesterone*